WISDOM IN LEADERSHIP

THE HOW AND WHY OF LEADING THE PEOPLE YOU SERVE

CRAIG HAMILTON

SYDNEY • YOUNGSTOWN

Wisdom in Leadership

Matthias Media
(St Matthias Press Ltd ACN 067 558 365)
Email: info@matthiasmedia.com.au
Internet: www.matthiasmedia.com.au
Please visit our website for current postal and telephone contact information.

Matthias Media (USA)
Email: sales@matthiasmedia.com
Internet: www.matthiasmedia.com
Please visit our website for current postal and telephone contact information.

ISBN 978 1 922206 71 8

Cover design and typesetting by Lankshear Design.

For Stu and Tim,
the two men God used to bring me to Jesus,
build me up in him,
and send me out for him.

Acknowledgements

I can't remember doing anything of any value or worth completely on my own. Anything I've ever done—that was anywhere close to important—I've always done with and through a team. I think that's just the way it works; I wouldn't have it any other way and this book is no different.

Thanks first of all to Jesus of Nazareth, who wrote my name in his book way before I ever had the thought to write his name in mine. He gave me everything I am and everything I have. He's the leader I most admire and I aspire to be like him.

Thanks to my wife and best friend, Nicole, who has been a constant source of encouragement and inspiration during the whole writing process, and who has taught me more about leadership than she'll ever know. Nicole, partnering with you in Act Two is going to make Act Three so much more beautiful and powerful.

Thanks to Avalon, Willow and Ezekiel—the team I'm most privileged to lead. A lot of people call me a lot of things, but I only get to be called Dad by these three.

Thanks to Tim Hawkins who taught me first the gospel and second the absolute necessity of being strategic. Even now I often think, "What would Tim do?"

Thanks to Stu Larkin—when I think of what real, personal and biblical leadership over the long term should look like, I think of him and am forever grateful that I am one of the blessed few who can.

Thanks to Bill Hybels, Lyle Schaller, Patrick Lencioni, Jim Collins, Jack Welch, Andy Stanley, Henry Cloud and Marcus Buckingham—leadership mentors from whom I have learned enormous amounts. While none of them has ever spoken to me or knows that I exist, their books and talks have influenced me in more ways than I could even begin to describe.

Thanks to all those who have led me over the years—I have learned many things from observing you all. Lots of those things were good and to be imitated, and others not so much. But either way I'm thankful that you took up the challenge to lead in the first place.

Thanks to John Lavender, who hired me when a dozen others had said I was too young and inexperienced. Your willingness to take risks with young leaders and your deeply pastoral leadership style are qualities many would do well to learn from.

Thanks to all of those who have let me lead them over the years. To paraphrase Darwin Smith, former CEO of Kimberly-Clark, I was always just trying to be qualified for the job. Thanks for letting me make mistakes.

Thanks to Tony Payne and the team at Matthias Media for their surprised, and then enthusiastic, support for this book.

Thanks to Tara Smith, editor extraordinaire, who turned my barely coherent manuscript into something so much better than it ever had any right to be.

Thanks to the many people who read parts of this book in its various stages of development. Thanks in particular to Archie Poulos, David Moore, David Ould, John Gray, Mark McKeown, Peter Orr and Sam Low. Your additions, challenges and clarifications were all extremely valuable and the book is so much better now because of your help. Of course that still means that each and every mistake is mine, and each mistake was probably pointed out to me by one of the above people whose counsel, at that moment, I chose to ignore.

After reading so many books, attending so many conferences, and having so many conversations about leadership, there's a very good chance that some insights I think are mine I actually picked up from somewhere else and have woven them into the fabric of my own thought. I have tried as best I can to follow the breadcrumbs back to the origins, but it is possible I have inadvertently included material that I have failed to acknowledge. If this is the case please contact the publisher and we'll see that it is fixed in subsequent editions.

Contents

NB Key words are included below for the chapters in all but the first section, so that you can see at a glance what each chapter is about. Chapters with a grey background will be of particular interest and benefit to those responsible for leading a team of leaders.

Introduction: How we got here 11

Section one: Leading foundations

1. The biblical model of leadership 25
2. Trust the Bible 31
3. The gospel is God's power 35
4. Prayer is mandatory 43
5. Character is king 47
6. Servanthood is greatness 51
7. God uses means 55
8. Focus on doing your job 61
9. Pragmatism doesn't work in practice 65
10. Don't let what God wants you to do get in the way of who God wants you to be 71
11. Everything must be genuine 77

Section two: Leading yourself

12. Lead yourself // self-leadership 85
13. Your family matters // priorities, planning 91
14. Play to your strengths // strengths-based leadership 99
15. Change your default style // situational leadership 105
16. Time management won't help you // energy, planning 111

17. Arriving on time isn't what you think it is // faithfulness, reliability 115
18. If you're not a good follower then you're not a good leader // submission, modelling, culture 119
19. Leaders have to give up to go up // freedom, responsibility 125
20. People who praise you are probably just as mistaken as those who criticize you // dealing with criticism 127
21. If you're planning on not being hurt then you're planning on not being a leader // pain, people-pleasing 133
22. Develop your forgettory // memory 143
23. Stop listening to yourself // negative self-talk 149
24. The way you view a problem often is the problem // mindset, problems vs opportunities 153
25. Hopetimism // rational optimism 159

Section three: Leading other people

26. Leading is loving // love 171
27. You're just the leader // empowerment, delegation 175
28. Anything worth doing is worth doing badly // training, development 179
29. Praise publicly // praise, encouragement 183
30. Faithfulness buys responsibility // recruitment, selection criteria 187
31. Energy is more efficient than efficiency // efficiency vs effectiveness 191
32. Ideas are born ugly // innovation, culture 197
33. Communicate from the inside out // communication, motivation 205
34. Fail forwards // failure, development, culture, mediocrity 209
35. Everyone already knows // honesty, vulnerability 219
36. Let people say no // recruitment 221
37. Phrases to learn // humility, vulnerability 225
38. Shut up and listen // listening, the power of questions 229
39. Public fans and private critics // feedback, criticism, culture 235
40. Team communication is exponential // team size and communication 239

41. Two foundations of team-building // team-building, trust, vulnerability, care, relationships 245
42. Humble and hungry // recruitment, team-building 253
43. The five C's // recruitment, team-building, evaluation 261
44. Choose your lieutenants // team-building, inner circle, recruitment 269
45. Understand the life cycle of a team // team dynamics 277
46. People deserve to know the truth // feedback, meetings, trust 281
47. Find the awesome // training, development, failure 295
48. Treat them like children // training, development, praise 303
49. You can only drive as fast as the car in front // development, culture, recruitment 307
50. There's no point having a dog and then barking yourself // empowerment, delegation 311
51. Get out of the way of good people // empowerment, delegation 317
52. Give credit and take blame // humility, responsibility 321
53. Free volunteers aren't cheap // volunteers, development 325
54. Don't be afraid of off-ramps // letting people go 331

Section four: Leading the ministry

55. The point is clarity, not labels // vision, mission, strategy, tactics 337
56. What are you trying to achieve? // goals, evaluation, purpose 345
57. Where is here? // planning, evaluation, clarity 349
58. Think in steps // goals, programs, purpose 355
59. Hold hands with your programs // mission, programs, planning, purpose 359
60. Creativity is a lost art // creativity, innovation, culture 365
61. Why systems matter // systems, processes, structures 375
62. Know the reason for the season // organizational rhythm 383
63. Meetings are where real work is done // meetings 387
64. Learn relaxed concern // emotional climate 395
65. Everything has an upside and a downside // strengths, weaknesses 399

66. Numbers don't matter... except when they do // success, metrics, size dynamics 403
67. Never waste a crisis // opportunity, creativity, mindset 409
68. Opportunity does not equal obligation // opportunity, decision-making 413

69. Your people should be able to do a good impression of you // vision-casting 421
70. Ignore the org-chart // development, meetings 429
71. Decide how decisions are made // decision-making, problem-solving 435
72. Hellos and goodbyes matter // meetings 443
73. Red Queen syndrome: a nine-step process for implementing change // change management, power dynamics 447
74. Be an agent of disorganization // complacency, quality, mediocrity 473
75. Waiting is doing something // planning, timing 477
76. Seek raw beauty // excellence, quality 483
77. Bad news is good news // problem-solving, communication 487
78. Celebrate // morale, rest, motivation 493

Introduction
How we got here

And so my conclusion is: it should be both/and

It often seems like there are two ways to live when it comes to being in Christian ministry. You're either a Bible person or a leadership person. You read theology books or you read leadership books. You read books by Don Carson and John Stott or you read books by Bill Hybels and John Maxwell.

And that's a problem.

It's always felt like a problem to me because I'm a Bible guy. I've always been a doctrine guy. Let's talk about models of the atonement and *perichoresis* and *enhypostasis* and *anhypostasis* and the *ordo salutis* and all kinds of other Latin words. Let's talk about preaching and texts and contexts and subtexts. That's who I've always been, and I'm still that guy.

And yet, as a leader in different settings over the years, I observed that when groups of people get together they function in certain predictable ways. I knew it was true that I could lead a group well or I could lead a group badly. And even if I had all kinds of amazing and life-changing things to teach, and even if I explained them as clearly and persuasively as I could, I still had to help groups of people organize and achieve things.

I realized the either/or was a false choice—that all this talk about leading people well wasn't necessarily godless, faithless pragmatism. Rather, it was about living with wisdom and loving my neighbour. And both of those things are in the Bible and God seems to think they're good ideas. So I came to see that if I really wanted to be a Bible guy I probably also needed to be a leadership guy, because it's both/and.

So I set about seeing how I could be both a Bible guy *and* a leadership guy. And through that process I became convinced that it wasn't even biblical to have two separate groups that have nothing to do with each other—leadership people versus theology people—throwing rocks at each other and taking no prisoners. We need leaders who are well trained in theology and in leadership principles. To think otherwise is like asking which blade of the scissors you need the most. To do ministry well requires both.

I'm not the best theology guy in the world. And I'm not the best leadership guy in the world either. But because I am a theology guy, I know that theology people should be, and need to be, leadership people.

And that conviction is what led me to write this book.

What I noticed—both in my own church ministry and as I talked with friends from other churches—was that lots of people are frustrated by how difficult ministry is. Those who are paid full-time by churches, as well as those who are tentmakers working to support themselves and using what time they have for formal and informal ministry, find ministry hard and sometimes frustrating. Lots of people are overwhelmed by the complexity and demands of ministry and many of them struggle with the same problems I had been facing.

And those problems were actually ones that I'd brought on myself because I hadn't learned and observed how people work—individually and in groups.

Every person I spoke with was facing problems that could be solved. Their ministry responsibilities were much more difficult than they needed to be, because they themselves had made them harder. As I read, researched and reflected, I discovered that there are ways to relieve a lot of the frustrations we experience. (A lot of them, but not all of them! This book doesn't claim to unveil the 11 secret herbs and spices for ministry. There is no silver bullet and this book isn't pretending to be one.) Reading this book won't make Christian leadership easy. But it will make it easier. The strategies and principles here won't remove all frustration from Christian leadership. But they will make it less frustrating. The chapters that follow won't solve every problem. But they will help to prevent a whole bunch of unnecessary problems from arising. And what you learn might even provide some solutions to a few of the problems that will inevitably arise in Christian leadership and which you actually do need to confront.

Christian ministry and leadership will always be hard. Sorry about that. We follow a crucified Messiah and we're to take up our cross daily as we follow him. But it can be easier.

And that conviction also led me to write this book.

I've always been a theology guy and I still am. But as I began to explore this concept of leadership I discovered what was going on theologically. I found that it all fit within a robust doctrine of creation.

God brought order out of chaos, creating a structured and predictable universe. Even after the Fall, where sin marred the once-perfect order and chaos re-entered the world, creation was still largely ordered and predictable—not perfectly ordered or predictable, but largely so.

Which meant we could look at the world and observe what was happening and figure things out. We figured out when to plant crops and when to reap them. We figured out there were bones inside us, and organs too, and we figured out how a lot of it worked. We figured out how to build things. We figured out how to do all kinds of things and how a lot of stuff worked.

And by 'we' I don't mean Christians, or even theists. I mean humans. Human beings know a lot of things, and not all of it is specially revealed in the Bible. Lots of it we discovered through observation and experiment and lots of it we discovered by accident.

We call that common grace. God gives humans talents and gifts and brains. We don't earn them; they're given to us by God and we're born with them. And when we use them we come up with things like science and art and music.

The great church father Augustine puts it like this:

> Is it not true that God spoke to Moses, and yet Moses accepted advice about guiding and governing such a great people from his father-in-law, a man actually of another race, with an abundance of foresight and an absence of pride?

> He was well aware that true counsel, from whatever mind it might come, should be ascribed not to man but to the unchangeable God who is the truth.[1]

Mark Thompson is the Principal of Moore Theological College in Sydney, and his insight here is particularly clarifying:

> The undoubted priority [Augustine] gives to Scripture does not result in a refusal to listen to other voices, even the voices of the pagans, when it is clear that they have helpfully observed truth in the world... all truth is God's truth.[2]

This is where we can learn from all those leadership observations. It's where we see common grace leadership at work.

By calling them 'common' I don't mean to say that they're bad. I just mean that they're not exclusively Christian ideas. They're true, but they don't carry the weight of a command from the Lord. They're not special revelations. But people have observed the mostly ordered yet still warped-by-sin creation, and they've recognized patterns and principles in how things usually work, all things being equal.

We might call this wisdom.

The world generally works a certain way. Any given group of people usually behaves in certain predictable ways. Those who have noticed and even studied these patterns have often applied them to running businesses and making money.

These principles make sense and minimize angst and frustration, and the businesses that apply them run better and more smoothly. If these leadership principles are true, then Augustine says they should be ascribed to God. All truth is God's truth.

And that conviction also led me to write this book.

---

1 Augustine, *De Doctrina Christiana,* ed. and trans. RPH Green, Clarendon, Oxford, 1995, Preface 15.

2 Michael P Jensen (ed.), *Church of the Triune God: Understanding God's work in his people today,* Aquila Press, Sydney, 2013, pp. 34-5.

I began my quest to learn more about leadership by gathering data through two means:

1. I started reading all the books I could find that I thought might help me.
2. I started consciously observing what was happening around me during meetings and when large groups gathered. Specifically, I tried to identify all of the factors that determined whether a gathering went well or whether it went badly.

The books on leadership I read by Christian authors seemed to make sensible claims. But they often made them from passages of Scripture that I was pretty sure weren't talking at all about the points these authors were making. Their observations and assertions about leadership seemed to be true, but there was a lot of proof-texting—taking Scripture verses out of context to prove the points they wanted to make.

The other books I read were from the world of business, and so most of them didn't exactly line up with how I viewed the world or what I thought I should be doing as a Christian minister. I don't think the church should be run like a business, so why would I try to make the church more like a business, or incorporate business principles into church life? Surely that would be both naïve and silly, if not dangerous and destructive. In addition, I knew from years of observation that most businesses—including those I'd worked in—are horribly mediocre. So why would I want the church to become like them? The church should, and must be, better. Leading a business well is good, and important, but how much more important is it to lead the church well? Businesses are about making money, but the church is about the glory of God and eternal destinies. Worldly wealth is fine, but it's impossible to compare it with the riches of the gospel.

And yet these books from the world of business had a lot of sensible things to say, and I could see that if I applied their common grace wisdom to the things I'd been doing—tweaking some ideas and applying others just as the authors suggested—they would solve a lot of the problems I'd been experiencing. I also saw that I'd been causing many of these problems, through either my poor people skills or my poor organizational skills. Since I was fairly good at organizing myself, for example, I'd assumed that organizing others meant doing the same thing with more people. As we'll see later in this book, I couldn't have been more wrong.

While I knew that the church isn't a business, I also noticed that most business leadership books aren't really about business either. They're about people: how they work; how they work as individuals and in large groups; how to organize them and how to help them do their work well and better.

I also noticed that these business book-writing gurus had a lot of smart people doing a lot of observing. And they were observing as many of the factors as possible that contributed to whether something went well or went badly—which was exactly what I was trying to do. But these guys were much smarter than I am and had been doing it for so much longer than I had and were able to observe so many more people than I could.

I then realized that, since people are pretty much the same everywhere you go, these observations about how people behave should pretty much reflect how people at my church behave. The major differences I found were the explanations for *why* people behave in certain ways. While business books often assume that people are basically good, I knew that deep inside we're basically bad, cracked and broken by sin. And business authors almost always assume that the universe is a closed system, whereas I knew that the God who created it also actively sustains it.

While these books obviously have their own agendas, and the authors' world views are probably different than mine, what the books contain are in large part simply observations of reality—of how the world works and what happens in this world (whether we like it or not). Can I learn from an atheist whose book is all about how to make money and crush the competition? Well, if his observations are true then they're true—regardless of how he chooses to apply those truths, I can still learn from them and apply them to what I'm doing in the church context.

So even though I saw that some of their conclusions weren't quite right because of what I knew to be true from the gospel,[3] their observations fit within the doctrine of creation and under the category of wisdom.

3 Some older business books, for example, give advice like 'Do not let them see you sweat' and 'Make sure you show them who's boss'. This kind of leadership advice doesn't work and doesn't fit with Jesus' model of servant-leadership.

And that conviction also led me to write this book.

I left Moore College with my theological degree ready to preach, to listen pastorally, to perform baptisms, weddings and funerals, to help people through crises, and to run some small groups along the way.

And I did all of those things with varying degrees of success and poise. But what struck me were all the other bits and pieces I was doing that, during college, it hadn't really occurred to me I would be doing. I was sitting in meetings. I was running meetings. I was working out budgets. I was recruiting people and creating teams. I was running teams. I was putting together rosters. I was being criticized, and since some of the criticisms were true I was trying to address and correct those issues as well. I was trying to change things that existed and trying to create things that had never existed.

Of course I'd been aware that these things needed to be done and I'd had a vague awareness that I'd probably need to do some of them. What surprised me was the amount of time and energy these tasks consumed. The more I did, the more I had to do. Every new relationship added additional relational needs and complexities. I'd had no idea how much of this kind of stuff I'd have to do and I didn't really know how to do any of it. And that was a problem.

I saw the people on my teams struggling with the same problems—I was expecting them to do things for which they had no training either. I needed to help them with skills I didn't have. They were creating and running teams, too, and they needed help to put it all together but I didn't have much help to offer.

And that conviction also led me to write this book.

I don't have a BA degree, much less an MBA. Now that I think about it, I don't even have a first aid certificate. (Note to self: I should probably get on to that.) What I do have is a degree in theology from Moore College in Sydney. And curiosity.

I like to know how things work—but only certain kinds of things. For example, I don't have the foggiest idea how to braid my daughter's hair.

Sometimes I watch my wife do it and I'm pretty sure it involves some kind of magic or alchemy. There are lots of things I don't know. I'm not even sure if you're supposed to take the tea bag out before you add the milk. But I'm especially curious about people and how they relate and interact.

Did you know, for example, that 25% of people believe they're in the top 1% in terms of how well they get along with others? Or that 94% of college professors in the United States believe they're doing above-average work? Ninety-four per cent! Psychologists call it 'positive illusion', and it basically means that we're absolutely horrible at self-evaluation but quite brilliant at self-delusion. That's a curious thing about people.

I'm interested in how people work, both individually and in groups. Big groups and small groups. Small groups work differently than big groups. You probably already know that, but you might never have thought about what makes them different—except that for one of them you need to put out more chairs. But that's the kind of thing that I'm curious about: how do people really work? I'm interested in people because people matter. They matter to God and they matter in a way that's different to how everything else matters. How people work and work together matters, because effective ministry hinges on people working well together.

And all of these convictions—about how much people matter, to me and to God, and about the importance of equipping ministry leaders with good theological principles *and* good leadership practices (based on principles embedded within a robust doctrine of creation)—led me to write this book.

What this book isn't

There are lots of things this book isn't. In many ways this is an obvious thing to say because this book, purely by existing as a specific entity in time and space, quite literally is not most things.

But also, as a subset of the most things that it's not, this book is not a lot of things that you might be assuming it is. For example, this book is not a theology of church and ministry and leadership—although that would be a great and useful book. (Note to self: I should probably get on to that.) This book is definitely a theological book; it's just not a theology book.

Neither is it a book detailing the seven specific steps you need to take to grow your church, or how you should structure your ministries, or what programs you should and shouldn't run at your church so you can be guaranteed explosive growth and get an agent to set you up on a speaking tour.

Neither is it a book about how you should structure your staff team, or about whether each minister should be the shepherd of a specific congregation and act more like a generalist or whether each minister should focus on one area across all congregations and act more like a specialist. That's an important question with lots of implications, and it probably has more than one answer. But that's not what this book is about.

This book is full of things that you probably know already or have heard before, as well as a few things that are so obvious you didn't think they were worth saying out loud. But I hope it also has a whole lot of things that you've never considered or noticed or that you've been vaguely aware of but haven't been able to focus on or crystallize into words. This book will help you to bring all of these concepts into focus so that you can think through them clearly and use them effectively in your ministry.

There might also be things in this book that you'd like everyone involved in ministry at your church to know and understand so you can all be on the same page. This book will help you to have conversations about things that were previously only assumed—if they were known at all. The chapters that follow will help you to train people at your church so that everyone in ministry, whether paid or unpaid, can improve and develop. This is the kind of book you could use in a staff meeting, or with a parish council, or with key leaders, or even with very new leaders.

Who is this book for?

My conviction is that everyone can get better at what they do, as long as they're willing to put in time and effort. This book is for everyone who wants to get better at leading people and is willing to put in that time and effort.

While I do think this book will be useful for anyone who leads anything, I envision two groups of people in particular for whom this material will be helpful.

The first group includes those of you who hold secular jobs but devote much of your remaining time and energy to involvement in ministry at your church. The church doesn't pay you, but you're involved in ministry. You might lead a small group, or lead in the children's or youth ministry; you might lead as part of a team, or you might be responsible for leading a team. This book will help you to be more effective and also to understand at a deeper level the hows, and more importantly the whys, of what's happening around you and in your team. The material here will be of benefit as you lead in various ways at work and in your own family as well as in ministry.

The second group consists of those who are paid by the church to work in full-time ministry. You might be the senior minister of a church, an assistant minister, or a youth minister. You might lead a team of paid staff or a team of volunteers. All of the leadership principles in this book apply equally to leaders in big churches and leaders in small churches, to those leading paid staff and to those leading teams of enthusiastic volunteers. You don't need to wait until your team is all paid staff with business cards and corner offices to begin leading them well. In fact, you shouldn't wait. Leading well in a smaller context is just as important for the love of people and the glory of God as it is in a bigger context. Regardless of the size or location of your church or ministry, this book will help you lead people better and will also show you how to develop them as leaders.

How to make the most of this book

One way to read this book is to start at the beginning and read all the way through to the end. That wouldn't be a bad way to read it—we've been reading most books that way for a while now and it seems like it's worked out fairly well so far. The book is divided into four major sections, and there's some logic to how they unfold. Section one considers some foundational principles and boundary-markers in terms of our own convictions about what leadership is and how it fits into a broader framework. Section two looks at how we are to go about leading ourselves. Section three presses out a little more to examine how we lead people for the sake of ministry, and then section four widens the lens still further to look at how we lead ministry for the sake of people. This final section is about systems and structures and processes and planning—all important facets of ministry that we don't always see clearly or think about intentionally because, while they're an important part of how we serve people, we work through them and usually don't notice them unless they're broken. It's the difference between being hands-on, physically caring for someone, and working out the who, what, when and how so that people are cared for. You could say it's the difference between working *in* the ministry and working *on* the ministry. Another way to make the distinction is to contrast 'vine work' and 'trellis work'.[4] If you read the book straight through from front to back, you'll follow this trajectory from leading yourself through to leading people as part of a ministry.

But you could read the book in other ways as well. For example, you could pick out the section that seems most appealing to you at the moment and read it. You might have noticed that you need to do more work in terms of 'Leading the ministry' (section four)—strategy and structures and that sort of thing—so you could start by reading that section. Or maybe you're pretty good at those things but you realize you need some help with leading people and building teams. In that case you might turn first to the third section, on 'Leading other people'. You could also begin by reading a particular chapter that deals with a specific issue you're facing or that has a title you find intriguing. Just jump in. That works too. The 'See also' part at the end of many chapters directs you to other chapters that will deepen your knowledge and understanding in related areas.

Having said that, I highly recommend that you start with section one on 'Leading foundations'. The problem with foundations is that you don't normally see them and you often forget they're there. This first section makes some of those foundational principles and assumptions explicit so that we're all on the same page. Even if you passionately want to jump into section four about 'Leading the ministry', I suggest you still start with section one because those first chapters establish the framework for everything that follows. Section one is like a lens through which to view and understand the rest of the book.

4 See the excellent book *The Trellis and the Vine: The ministry mind-shift that changes everything* by Colin Marshall and Tony Payne (Matthias Media, Sydney, 2009).

You'll notice as you read through the book that, while every chapter contains material that will be helpful to people in all sorts of leadership positions, some chapters will be of particular interest and benefit for people who are responsible for leading a team of leaders. Those 'frontline leaders' with that type of authority and responsibility need to cultivate certain skills and take care to avoid certain traps. These chapters, marked clearly, are grouped together at the ends of the third and fourth sections (chapters 41-54 and 69-78). If you're not currently a team leader these chapters will still be beneficial for you to read and process—not only might you end up leading a team, but these chapters will also help you to understand what your leaders are seeking to do and the issues with which they're grappling. Being aware of these things will help you to serve them better and make their lives easier.

You might simply read this book yourself and implement what you think is valuable in your ministry. You might decide to buy a copy for the people you lead or for the staff you oversee. You could get a group together to read and meet up periodically to discuss what material from the book you think should be implemented and how you might go about it. You might give sections or chapters to people you want to see develop as leaders, or you might use the book as a framework for ongoing training of a parish council or a leadership team.

There are many options, but the goal is always the same: to help faithful people grow in their competence and effectiveness as they seek to love and serve the people around them to the glory of the Lord Jesus.

Section one

Leading foundations

1

The biblical model of leadership

'The biblical model of leadership' really is a stupid name for a chapter.

Almost everything about that title is unhelpful. It's the kind of heading you might have read in other Christian leadership books or heard at a leadership conference. It's the kind of description that might possibly have fuelled your scepticism about all things leadership or that might even have led you to write off this whole leadership thing entirely.

And I can absolutely understand.

I have met and spoken to countless people who are sceptical about and disillusioned by 'the leadership movement'. They feel as though it's overly pragmatic, too secular, too focused on human effort, and too mechanical and industrial. After all, we're not dealing with machines—we're dealing with people. You can't just turn some dials, set some levels, and pull some levers to get the outcomes you want. It's far more complicated than that.

And when we're dealing with people in terms of spiritual matters—faith and conversion and growth in Christlikeness—it becomes even more complex. Surely we shouldn't think about Christian ministry in terms of systems and principles from the business world. As we've already noted, the church is not a business and should not be run like a business. The fact that most businesses are run very poorly should further fuel our desire not to be like them.

Most of us are smart enough to know when purely secular, pragmatic principles have been baptized with spiritual language and had a Bible verse tacked on to add that extra bit of credibility. You know—the verse that seems plausible at first but then, when you look more carefully, has nothing at all to do with the point being made. It can drive you mental. It drives *me* mental! 'The biblical model of leadership' smacks of exactly this kind of proof-texting, doesn't it?

I can't remember how many times I've heard Proverbs 29:18 used during leadership talks about the importance of vision and vision-casting: "Where there is no vision, the people perish" (KJV). But is the Bible really talking about a well-crafted vision statement here? No. No, it's not. The rest of the verse says: "but he that keepeth the law, happy is he". You might be aware that the Jews loved a bit of what the scholars call Hebrew parallelism. It means that the two halves of a poetic line either say the same thing or contrast with each other so that the second half helps you understand the point of the first half.

The second half of this verse clearly has to do with hearing and obeying the law. Hearing and obeying the revealed word of God. When a person hears and obeys the word of God, life is good. The first half of the verse is in deliberate contrast. When a person doesn't have the word of God, or ignores it, life doesn't go well. So what's the point? Well, it isn't that an organization will perish without a clearly articulated statement of why they exist and what they're seeking to achieve. That may or may not be true, but the Bible isn't giving any input on that discussion with this verse. The verse is about how vitally important the word of God is, and it's ironic—and a bit sad—that this is the verse that's so often twisted to say something far less important. It's no wonder people are disillusioned with talk about leadership in the church when the Bible is used and abused in order to give leadership principles extra 'value'. If people twist the Bible to try to make it say what it's not saying, then it follows that maybe the idea they're trying to promote is in fact wrong, and perhaps even dangerous.

And I can understand that kind of suspicion.

So, in the interest of clarity, let's break down 'The biblical model of leadership', word by word, to see why exactly it's such a stupid title.

'Leadership'

The Bible doesn't use this word very often. The English word, as far as I can tell, only came into use in the 1800s, when it described the position of the leader in the sense of 'you have leadership of this vessel'. It was like an on/off switch. Either you had leadership of the vessel or you didn't. You were the leader or you weren't. By the late 1800s the word had begun to be used more as we often use it today: to refer to the characteristics necessary to be a leader. We often use it in the sense of 'developing in leadership', indicating the skills and knowledge you need to be a good leader. So we think of it more like a dimmer switch—your leadership abilities can improve and brighten.

But the Bible doesn't use the word much at all.[5] The Bible talks about authority. The Bible talks about responsibility. The Bible talks about ruling over people or a country. The Bible talks about being wise or foolish. The Bible talks about godliness and walking in obedience. All of these are components of what we mean when we use the word leadership. But the Bible doesn't talk that much about leadership in the sense of the package of skills and knowledge needed to lead effectively.

'Model'

When we read the Bible it's important to try to work out what the passage we're looking at is seeking to teach us. What's the point that's being made? For example, Psalm 75:3 says, "When the earth totters, and all its inhabitants, it is I who keep steady its pillars". Is the Bible trying to teach us something about God's cosmological support structures? Probably not. This is a psalm, which means it's poetry. The pillars are an image to help us understand God's character as opposed to being a description of the engineering mysteries of the universe. The point is more to do with the fact that when the world begins to appear chaotic and out of control, when life begins to crumble around us, we are to take heart and know that God is still sovereign. The key question isn't whether or not we can use something in the Bible as a model to understand something else. Instead the key question is: What is the Bible trying to teach us?

The problem with finding 'models' in the Bible is that the model is

5 Leaders and leading are mentioned, for example, in verses such as Romans 12:8 and Hebrews 13:17, and in both cases the Greek words are about ruling or governing.

almost never what the passage is trying to teach us. So in Exodus 18 we read about Jethro advising Moses to delegate his authority. Moses takes the advice, and as a result more people are helped and Moses doesn't collapse under a mountain of tasks. Similarly, in Acts 6, the apostles delegate the responsibility of providing food for the widows so that they can focus on the Word and prayer. Two instances of delegation in the Bible. But are those passages actually seeking to teach us about the wisdom of delegation? Or is delegation a principle we already think is true that we have then found an example of in the Bible?

In order to have a model you first need some explicit teaching of a truth or principle. Then you can see that principle at work in a model. But you need to know what the teaching is before you can see the model. That's how a model works.

So, for example, if we talk about a model student we're saying that this person exemplifies everything we want a student to be. But we can say this because we already know what we want our students to be. This model student isn't showing us for the first time what a great student should be like. We already have ideas about what a student should be like and the model student is exemplifying and embodying and modeling those things that we already think and know to be true.

Or take, for example, the biblical teaching "You shall not murder". We have a collection of historical examples and models of how this works in real life and how things go badly when people ignore the command. But we can only understand the models *as models* because we already have the explicit command. That's how models work.

So while it's true that the Bible is full of examples of this or that leadership idea, what's important to understand is that they're examples of things we must already think are true. They're not models that the Bible is trying to teach us. They may be good and they may be helpful. Don't get me wrong—I'm not against delegation. I think it's a great idea! It's just that I'm not sure that's what Exodus 18 and Acts 6 are trying to teach us. There are lots of models in the Bible. Some of these models are good examples for us to follow and some are not. But the model itself doesn't necessarily tell you if it's good or bad. It's just a model, an example. We need explicit teaching in order to understand the implications of the model.

'Biblical'

Now, once again, don't get me wrong. I like this word. Biblical is great. I'm a big fan of biblical. Having a biblical view of the world is a good thing to have. I just don't like the word in this context. While we often find examples of leadership principles in the Bible, as we have seen, our concepts of leadership and teaching about it have come from outside the Bible. Delegation, for example, isn't a biblical idea; it's an idea that's in the Bible. Lots of people around the world and in cultures who have never had the Bible still delegate. Jethro teaches Moses to delegate in Exodus 18 and Jethro isn't an Israelite. Delegation isn't special revelation or biblical; it's just a good idea. Now that's not a bad thing, and the teaching can still be true, but it's not biblical in that sense. That doesn't make it wrong or evil. Lots of things that are true aren't in the Bible. Email is a much faster way of sending a letter than using the postal service. That's not in the Bible, but it's still true. It's not contrary to the Bible's teaching, it's just not found in the Bible's teaching. Everything the Bible teaches is true, but not everything that's true is taught in the Bible. And we're okay with that, right?

But here's our problem: when we call these leadership ideas biblical we give them an authority that they simply don't deserve. Saying that having a vision statement is biblical loads the idea up with all kinds of weight that it shouldn't carry. It's not true that if you don't have a vision you're sinning against the Lord and storing up wrath against yourself for the day of God's judgement. Not delegating isn't something Jesus died for. Having a vision statement isn't a 'Thus sayeth the Lord' kind of thing. People have simply observed the wisdom and benefits of doing so, and therefore they think it's a good idea. You can agree. You can disagree. But it's not a biblical imperative and so we shouldn't put it on that shelf. Having a vision just might be a helpful and wise thing to do. And it looks as though Nehemiah had a clear vision of what he wanted to achieve when he sought to rebuild the wall of Jerusalem. The *example* is biblical. The *teaching* that's being exemplified isn't. And that's okay as long as we're clear on which part is biblical and which part is not.

And, lastly, I don't like the word 'the'

The Bible has a lot of things to say about authority and responsibility and ruling and wisdom and godliness. And the Bible contains lots of models and examples of those things in practice. But to say that there is one, ultimate, *the* model or way of leadership in the Bible is simply not accurate.

Some of the leadership principles in this book are biblical, in the sense that they're expressions of direct teaching from the Bible—such as the centrality of being a servant or the importance of faithfulness—but not every principle in this book is an expression of direct teaching from the Bible and, in fact, most of them are not. But all of them are shaped by a biblical world view and by biblical priorities. And all of them have been forged and refined in the heat of Christian ministry. They're reflections on leading and thoughts I've harvested from people who have led well. But they don't belong on the shelf of authoritative God-speak. They belong on the wisdom shelf. And it's important to be clear which shelf you should put them on.

'The biblical model of leadership' is a stupid title because of the words leadership, model, biblical, and the.

I do want to make it clear, though, that I quite like the word 'of'.

2
Trust the Bible

This almost feels like a silly chapter to write. It feels like saying, "A foundational leadership principle that will ensure that you succeed as a leader is to make sure you breathe and keep breathing for as long as you can. Your improved and consistent breathing will ensure your longevity as a leader and you will also notice a direct correlation between consistent breathing and an increase in the sheer number of things you will be able to achieve." It feels patronizing and maybe a tad condescending.

Of course we know that the Bible has always been, and should always be, our number-one authority and the grid through which we view and evaluate everything else. The Bible is the cornerstone and touchstone of everything that we do. We want to line ourselves up with God's word and we never want to get too far away from it. It's God's revealed word about who he is, where we are, what's wrong with the world, what he's done to fix it, what time it is, what we're waiting for, what we should be doing, and what the point of the whole thing is. It's full of stunning poetry, profound rhetoric, complex narratives, memorable sayings and mind-stretching imagery; and, above and beyond all that, it is the very word of God to us. What the Bible says, God says. Why would we not trust it and build upon it and hold to it? It's a simple choice, really.

But it's not that simple, is it? In the midst of life it's a constant battle to trust the Bible and build on it and hold to it. Worldly wisdom often contradicts the Bible and pushes us to not trust Scripture. Advice from wise friends and family can sometimes contradict the Bible and push us to not trust Scripture. Books from 'great ones' who 'know their stuff'—particularly in the leadership arena—can sometimes contradict the Bible and push us to not trust Scripture. Even our own experience can—for a season, and when Scripture isn't allowed to interpret that experience—contradict the Bible and push us to not trust Scripture.

More than foundational

But at the core of Christian leadership—as an extension of Christian life and faithfulness—is your constant commitment to trust the Bible. Will God's word shape your life and your leadership? Will it shape how you view everything else you encounter and how you evaluate every new insight or development or movement? Or will it be but one vitally important component amongst many? Where will the authority lie?

The degree to which your leadership is built on, shaped by, conforms to, and is accountable to God's word is the degree to which your leadership will be Christ-honouring and kingdom-building—regardless of how successful it looks at the time. Having Scripture as the basis and foundation of your leadership isn't enough. Everything you build on that foundation must also be informed by Scripture and line up with it. We cut out and ignore any secular wisdom that contradicts the Bible. It's a process that requires us to be discerning and gospel-focused.

Bible alone, not Bible only

Trusting the Bible doesn't mean it's the only authority you can trust, or that you cannot learn or benefit from any other source. Far from it. So much of what we know to be true doesn't come from the Bible. Gravity and quantum physics and sausages and the internet are all real and true and part of genuine knowledge about the world, but the Bible (to my knowledge) mentions none of them. It would be hopelessly naïve to suggest that the Bible should be the only source of knowledge or the only authority when it comes to life and leadership. Everything that the Bible says is true, but not everything that is true is in the Bible. So while the Bible, the word of God, is the primary authority, it's not the only authority. We do need to examine every other source and piece of knowledge in the light of the Bible. When there's a contradiction we should carefully re-examine our understanding of Scripture to make sure it really does say what we think it says. And if it does and the contradiction remains, then we should hold to the Bible as our number-one authority. When there's no contradiction, we're free to pursue the truth wherever we find it.

In Peter Jensen's lecture introducing the thought and ministry philosophy of Broughton Knox—one Moore College principal reflecting on another—he summarizes Knox's view of Scripture this way: "Broughton argued that as long as the central theological foundation, that the Bible is God's very word, is secure, all else can minister to the discerning mind".[6] As long as our trust in the Bible as God's very word is secure and unassailed, we should seek to learn from as many sources as we can. "Unless the LORD builds the house, those who build it labour in vain" (Ps 127:1). Trusting the Bible is the number-one leadership lesson and very little else matters if we get this one wrong. And we need to commit to an ongoing process of reflection and repentance to keep on course.

The number-one question for any Christian leader in any circumstance should be this: What does the Bible say? From there we proceed with prayer and discernment.

6 D Broughton Knox, *Selected Works*, vol. 1, *The Doctrine of God*, ed. T Payne, Matthias Media, Sydney, 2000, p. 29.

3
The gospel is God's power

Proclaim the gospel—that seems like a good and straightforward thing to say. Speaking the gospel to each other is a fundamental part of Christian life and, therefore, of Christian leadership and ministry. But if you've ever stopped to really think about what the gospel means, and what it is, proclaiming the gospel quickly becomes more complicated than it first appears.

What is the gospel?

As you probably know, the word gospel means good news. But what's the good news about? Well, it's good news about what God has done in Jesus in history. For example, in 1 Corinthians 15 Paul writes:

> Now I would remind you, brothers, of the gospel I preached to you, which you received, in which you stand, and by which you are being saved, if you hold fast to the word I preached to you—unless you believed in vain.
>
> For I delivered to you as of first importance what I also received: that Christ died for our sins in accordance with the Scriptures, that he was buried, that he was raised on the third day in accordance with the Scriptures, and that he appeared to Cephas, then to the twelve. Then he appeared to more than five hundred brothers at one time, most of whom are still alive, though some have fallen asleep. Then he appeared to James, then to all the apostles. Last of all, as to one untimely born, he appeared also to me. (vv. 1-8)

And in Romans 1 Paul says:

> Paul, a servant of Christ Jesus, called to be an apostle, set apart for the gospel of God, which he promised beforehand through his prophets in the holy Scriptures, concerning his Son, who was descended from David according to the flesh and was declared to be the Son of God in power according to the Spirit of holiness by his resurrection from the dead, Jesus Christ our Lord, through whom we have received grace and apostleship to bring about the obedience of faith for the sake of his name among all the nations, including you who are called to belong to Jesus Christ. (vv. 1-6)

And, perhaps most succinctly, Paul says in 2 Timothy 2:

> Remember Jesus Christ, risen from the dead, the offspring of David, as preached in my gospel... (v. 8)

One thing to notice in all of these passages is how historical the gospel is. The gospel is about what God has done in Jesus *in history*. It's about how Jesus came, lived, died, and rose again. The gospel is not abstract ideas. It's not a philosophy. It's not just truths that have been revealed. It's news about events that really happened in history. Christ died and was raised on the third day.

The gospel isn't the same thing as our testimony. A testimony is one Christian's story about how he or she became a Christian or grew up in a Christian family following Jesus. A person's testimony may *contain* the gospel, depending on how it's told, but the testimony is not the gospel. A testimony is a story about how someone heard and responded to the gospel, and it's a story worth remembering and telling, but it's not the gospel.

The gospel isn't a world view. There is a world view that comes from the gospel, but the gospel itself isn't a world view. The gospel is news. It's news about something that happened.

And what do you do with news? You announce it. You proclaim it. You need to tell people—which is why the old slogan "proclaim the gospel, and if you have to, use words" is saying something helpful but is also saying so much that is unhelpful.[7]

This old saying is helpful in that it points out that our actions matter. If we talk about the gospel and our lives don't match up with what we're saying, our actions will undermine the message—and will probably generate scepticism and cynicism as well. That's a helpful reminder.

But the problem with the saying is that the gospel is news, and news is meant to be spoken. News is mainly to do with words. Yes, how we live as we tell the gospel matters, but the words are central. The words contain the core message, and our actions reinforce or undermine those words, but the actions aren't the substance.

"Tell people your surgery was successful, and if you have to, use words."

"Tell people your new baby has been born, you called him Bill, and if you have to, use words."

"Tell people the war has been won, and if you have to, use words."

It doesn't make sense. When you tell people news you're telling them about something that has already happened, and you're primarily using words. The gospel is news and we announce it with words.

The gospel centres on what God has done for us in Jesus' death and resurrection. It's what *God* has done, not what we do. And it's what God has *done*. The gospel is news about something in the past. Something that has already happened but that has lasting and far-reaching consequences.

Don Carson puts it this way:

> The heart of the gospel is what God has done in Jesus, supremely in his death and resurrection. Period. It is not our personal testimony about our repentance; it is not a few words about our faith response; it is not obedience... Repentance, faith, and obedience are of course essential, and must be rightly related in the light of Scripture, but they are not the good news. The gospel is the good news about what God has done.[8]

7 People often claim that Francis of Assisi said this, but he didn't. Like how Sherlock Holmes never said, "Elementary, my dear Watson". But everyone thinks he did.

8 DA Carson, 'What is the gospel?—revisited', in Sam Storms and Justin Taylor (eds), *For the Fame of God's Name: Essays in honor of John Piper*, Crossway, Wheaton, 2010, p. 162.

What about 'gospel outlines'?

But if the gospel is the good news of what God has done in Jesus in history to rescue and redeem rebellious humanity and clean up the mess we've made, then what about all the other elements in our 'gospel outlines'? Where do they fit?

Well, someone needs to know all kinds of information in order to understand why the gospel is good news. There are things we need to explain so that the gospel makes sense and is understandable. So we often explain creation, that the God of Jesus is the creator God. He owns creation and he judges it. We explain sin—that we have rebelled against God. We explain faith and repentance, the intrinsic demands of the gospel. And all of that is right. We need to help people understand the gospel. We need to help them understand what they have been saved *from* and what they have been saved *for*. But, strictly speaking, the gospel is that God has come in Jesus, in history, as the climax to the history of Israel, and that he lived and died and rose again to rescue us.

The power of God

What do you envision when you think about a display of God's power? Is it some ecstatic display of the Spirit's presence? Or maybe a great miracle, like walking on water or healing a paralytic? Or do you think of the vastness of creation and the crushing strength of, say, a lightning storm?

All of those might in fact be true, biblical, displays of God's power, but I wonder how many of us would immediately think of the gospel as the ultimate display of God's power. Because that's what Paul thinks of in Romans 1, where he says:

> For I am not ashamed of the gospel, for it is the power of God for salvation to everyone who believes, to the Jew first and also to the Greek. (v. 16)

When it comes to leadership and trusting the Bible, the gospel—the demonstration of God's power to save—is the focal point. So I have to ask myself: Do I trust what the Bible says about God saving people through the gospel? Or do I think that God saves people through my programs? Or through my clever advertising? Or through my advanced strategic planning and organizational skills? I'm not against programs or clever advertising or strategic planning and organization. And we'll talk a lot about those things in this book. But the power for salvation does not come from any of those things. God saves people through the gospel.

One of the difficulties is that it doesn't sound all that powerful on paper. There aren't any bells and whistles. It seems a bit mundane, even un-powerful, to describe our calling as people telling people some news about what's already happened. But that's exactly what God asks us to do. It seems like weakness to Jews and foolishness to Greeks. But it's actually the power of God.

Trusting the gospel in action

But you trust the gospel—of course you do. I'm not trying to be patronizing. And you proclaim, persuade, plead, and preach that others should do the same. There's a difference, however, between believing and proclaiming the gospel and allowing the gospel to shape the what and the how of our ministry.

I'm not talking about the question of whether we do relational evangelism or event-based evangelism. Both can be effective, depending on your context. How much you focus on one over the other is, in my opinion, a matter of wisdom and context and freedom.

But when I talk about the gospel shaping our ministry I'm asking a different question. If people were to look at your programs, or your events, or your one-to-one ministry, would they be able to tell that you trust the gospel as God's power to save? Or would they conclude that you're trusting in something else?

Because sometimes something gets lost between what we believe and how we plan. Perhaps you run big events at which 'the gospel bit' is very soft and very short. A five-minute 'spot'. Now that's not necessarily bad, sometimes it's appropriate, but if that's all you do then would I be able to tell it's the gospel that you're trusting in to save people?

It has nothing to do with how high- or low-tech you are. You can have lights and smoke and screens and a high-energy atmosphere, and still clearly preach and trust in the gospel to save. Or you can meet in a dingy hall with flickering fluorescent lights, handing out photocopied paper in a we're-doing-it-last-minute atmosphere and looking every bit as if you're trusting only in the gospel to save (because there's definitely nothing else going on that could possibly save anyone from anything), and yet not be trusting in the gospel at all. Stage lights and good atmosphere don't save anyone. But neither do fluorescent lights and bad atmosphere. Whether the ambience is dazzling or dismal doesn't matter—it's all down to whether or not you trust the gospel.

In Tim Hawkins' amazingly helpful book *Disciples Who Will Last*, he asks this penetrating question:

> If the gospel has not been preached, and people respond, can we say that they responded to the gospel?[9]

Getting the gospel right at your events and in your ministries and programs and whatever it is you do to make disciples is absolutely crucial. If your gospel presentations are vague and quick and designed to be minimally offensive or intrusive and to maximize the chance of responses, then Tim Hawkins' question is blisteringly helpful. Can we say that they're responding to the gospel?

If I were to look at your strategy, your programs, your ministries—all the things you do—would I be able to tell that you've placed your trust in the gospel as God's power to save? Or would I see something else? Have you aligned how you function with the foundations of what you believe?

Paul writes this in 1 Corinthians 2:

> And I, when I came to you, brothers, did not come proclaiming to you the testimony of God with lofty speech or wisdom. For I decided to know nothing among you except Jesus Christ and him crucified. (vv. 1-2)

I don't think he meant that literally the only thing he said was, "Christ was crucified" or that he refused to talk about any other topic. I think he meant, rather, that he ensured that everything he said and every topic he

9 Tim Hawkins, *Disciples Who Will Last: How to transform new believers into world-changing believers*, The Good Book Company, New Malden, 2009, p. 36.

discussed flowed from, was tied to, centred around, or was explained in the light of the cross of Jesus.

Programs don't save anyone. Events don't save anyone. Strategies don't save anyone. Décor doesn't save anyone. Atmosphere doesn't save anyone. Preachers don't save anyone. God saves people. And he does it through the message of the gospel.

Knowing and trusting that the gospel is God's power for salvation means more than having the gospel as the foundation—though that's a good start. It's more than personally believing it for salvation and believing it's how God saves others—though that's also good. Knowing and trusting that the gospel is God's power for salvation means that your trust in the gospel filters down into how you do your ministry. It means making sure that the gospel is the foundation, the shape, the method, the means, the content, and the very centre of your ministry and leadership.

The gospel is God's power to save. Trust it in everything you do.

4

Prayer is mandatory

So much of leadership is about the things you do. The things you control. How you act. How you respond. How you plan. How you implement. Strategy and tactics.

All of that control and all of that activity, however, exists in the context of a God who controls and acts. Your control is real but limited. Your activity is real but contingent. Strategy and tactics are good, essential even—you have strategy and tactics whether you're conscious of them or not—but they are limited.

First things first

There are some battles that you cannot win on your feet. The only way to win them is on your knees. In the end it's God who makes things grow. It's God who brings the rain. Which is why prayer is mandatory. Of all the things you do, prayer is the most important.

Unfortunately, even though I know and have experienced the power of prayer over and over again, prayer is often the first thing I give up and the last thing I try. You may be in a similar situation. This is a big problem because it should be the reverse. It should be the first thing I try and the last thing I give up.

The local church exists to accomplish things that aren't possible. The church exists to see people transferred from the kingdom of darkness into the kingdom of light and to see them transformed into the likeness of the Son of God—all of which is impossible. But with God all things are possible, which is why we need to pray. Unless God is in it, nothing we do will be of any eternal significance. And God may still come and help us and be at work through us even if we don't ask him because he's more concerned about his own glory and about saving people than he is about waiting for our invitation. But it only makes sense to ask for his help.

James tells us that we do not have because we do not ask (Jas 4:2). Unless the Lord builds the house the builders labour in vain, and unless the Lord watches over the city the guards stand watch in vain (Ps 127:1). I don't want to build or guard in vain. And I don't want to not have some brilliant solution to a problem I'm facing, or an opportunity that only my heavenly Father could provide, just because I was too lazy, stubborn, or self-reliant to ask.

For what should I pray?

What should we be praying for? It's one thing to say we should all pray more. Of course we should—we already know that. You're not reading this and thinking to yourself, "Oh, wow. It never occurred to me I should pray. Thanks." If that *is* what you're thinking, then I guess you're welcome.

But I assume you know this. I certainly did. I just didn't do it that often. And even now, on more occasions than I'd like to admit, prayer isn't always my first response. Sometimes in my busyness I forget. But I've been turning to God more often and more quickly. Here's what I've been doing—maybe one or more of these ideas will help you grow in prayer as well.

1. *I changed what I prayed for.* In the past, when I had some big leadership decision to make—like who I should ask to run this team or take on that responsibility—I used to pray that God would help me make the right decision. But I wasn't particularly clear on what I was expecting or asking him to do. And this lack of clarity led to me praying these prayers less and less. I wasn't necessarily expecting God to miraculously implant knowledge in my head or give me a sense of peace about a decision. And those things never happened anyway. Often I made the right decision but felt no peace about it. Even though I knew it was right and it turned out to be right, there was still no peace. And God never once spoke to me in an audible voice telling me what to do.

So I changed what I prayed for. I started praying things like:

> Dear God, help me to not be a coward. Help me to make the decision that is best, not the one that is easiest. Keep me from making a decision out of fear or laziness. Help me to get all the information I need to make this decision. Get me talking to the right person, reading the right book or blog, understanding the right Bible passage. Help me to see the implications of the decision clearly. Help me to articulate the reasons why I feel this is right.

As I prayed like that it became clearer in my own mind what I was actually asking God to do. I also found it easier to notice how God helped me—which then made it easier to thank and praise him and helped me pray more prayers.

In the ideal world I would have prayed more just because I knew it was right and good. But I'm not yet the ideal me, and so there was no use expecting that I would act in the ideal way just because. Praying this way got me a step closer to the ideal. And if you're not yet the ideal you, then there's no point acting like you live in the ideal world. Having said that, if you actually are the ideal you, then please accept my apologies and feel free to just get on with praying and skip this advice. But, if you're not, this might help. It helped me. Pray clearer, less ambiguous prayers.

2. *I specifically planned prayer into the centre of every team gathering and meeting*. Prayer in meetings wasn't new—we'd always prayed at the beginning and again at the end. What was new was praying in the middle of the meeting so we'd be sure to have enough time to pray. And if it meant that we didn't have time to discuss other things, then so be it. That was new. It signalled both to me and to everyone else that prayer was important and that we recognized its importance.

> Running out of time and squeezing prayer in by asking one person to quickly pray for us before we leave communicates that prayer is of minimal value and importance. We began to place a high value on prayer not just by the act of praying, but also by being willing to make prayer more important than other things we missed out on or skipped over so we could spend that time praying.

What I came to realize was that it was more useful to talk to God about people than it was to talk to people about people. I knew that I needed to do both, but prayer was obviously more important and had more of an impact. So I began thanking God for people I was thankful for and I prayed to God about people who weren't working out like I'd hoped. I didn't pray about those who weren't working out to complain to God about them or to accuse them before him. I prayed and asked that he would work in them and grow them, change them, remove whatever the blockage was. But I also prayed that if I was the problem—if *I* was actually the blockage—I'd have the discernment to see that, the humility to acknowledge it, and the courage to repent and apologize. And I only ever spoke to the person about how they were doing after I had spoken to God about that person.

Being a leader means doing a lot of things and being involved in a lot of things and making decisions about a lot of things. And in all of that activity the temptation is to think that, because I'm doing so much and in control of so much, God isn't involved. But that's simply not true. The more things in your life that you're involved in, the more things in your life God is involved in.

In all the doing that we do as leaders, the main thing we should be doing is praying. We should turn first to God to ask him to be at work and to help us. Of all the things we do, prayer is mandatory and should be the first thing we do.

5

Character is king

One of the areas this book focuses on is leadership practices—the skills necessary to lead yourself, to lead others, and to create and evaluate systems and structures. Skills are a very important component of Christian leadership. But they're not the most important component.

The most important and foundational component of leadership is the character of the person. If leadership skills are the *what* of leadership, then character is the *why* and *how* behind that *what*. Character includes qualities like humility, patience, and faithfulness.

Character colours everything

Character is king because it's like the filter through which all of your skills pass on the way out into the world. Your character colours everything you do.

For example, you may technically understand all the things you need to do to run a great meeting. You might even do all the right things—you start on time, you finish on time, you say hi to people, you remind them of why you're meeting and what the stakes are and what the point is, and so on. You tick all the boxes. But if you're a proud, rude, selfish, negative, and aggressive person that meeting will be a horrible ordeal that your people will endure and hate being at—even though you did everything you were supposed to do.

Character colours everything you do.

Build on character

The other reason character is king is because skills are much easier to teach and learn than character is. People can pick up skills relatively quickly, but character isn't something you just pick up. Character is often forged over a long period of time and over multiple experiences, and it only changes with great and sustained effort. It can and does change, but it's much harder to change your character than it is to learn skills.

It's always tempting to be impressed by skills and ability. When a highly competent person comes along, even those of us who know and are convinced that character is king can be tempted to invite them to join the team and give them responsibility—even when we see that they have one or more serious character deficiencies.

But when someone does not have a godly character to match their abilities, any upside or advantage that comes from their skills is almost always undercut by character issues. An arrogant person might not take direction and might insist not just on doing things their own way but also on doing their own things. A person with issues of pride won't take feedback well but will turn everything into a conflict. A negative person will bring a toxic attitude to the team and turn a relaxed and cheerful environment into a tense and defensive one. They might even steal or make false accusations. I've been on teams where highly skilled yet character-deficient 'leadership stars' have caused all of these things to happen. And some of them were, embarrassingly, in teams where I was in charge and responsible for recruitment.

One of the many harmful consequences that can result is that the real stars, those who are truly great—the humble, servant-hearted, genuinely caring leaders—feel out of place and uncomfortable and may even get trodden down. If the circumstances are difficult enough, these truly great leaders might even come to feel that their only choice is to leave and join a different ministry or church. And then you lose the people you really want to keep because of the person you wish you never said yes to in the first place. You end up killing your workhorses to feed the show pony, and that's always a bad idea.

When Paul was writing to Timothy about how to select overseers—

that is, people who oversee a church, we might call them leaders—he told him that character was king. The letters to Timothy and Titus contain a number of these lists of character traits for the various roles of overseers and deacons and women leaders. Here's one such list, from 1 Timothy 3, that is fairly representative of all of them:

> The saying is trustworthy: If anyone aspires to the office of overseer, he desires a noble task. Therefore an overseer must be above reproach, the husband of one wife, sober-minded, self-controlled, respectable, hospitable, able to teach, not a drunkard, not violent but gentle, not quarrelsome, not a lover of money. He must manage his own household well, with all dignity keeping his children submissive, for if someone does not know how to manage his own household, how will he care for God's church? He must not be a recent convert, or he may become puffed up with conceit and fall into the condemnation of the devil. Moreover, he must be well thought of by outsiders, so that he may not fall into disgrace, into a snare of the devil. (vv. 1-7)

This list is either overwhelmingly or exclusively made up of character traits, depending on how you understand "hospitable" and "able to teach". My own view is that they're both character traits.[10] Even if I'm wrong about that, though, nothing changes. The list shows that character is far more important than skills when it comes to selecting people suitable for ministry.

At the outset, then, I want to make it clear that though this book focuses on the practical skills of leadership at various levels, what you believe, and who you are, are far more important. It's just that this book isn't about theology or character but about helping you develop and sharpen your skills. Even though skills are very important, it's critical to be aware that who you are and what you believe are far more important.

10 Paul doesn't talk about *hospitality*, which would be a skill set, but says that a person must be hospitable—which is about who they are, not what they can do. As for "able to teach", it seems strange that Paul would throw a skill into a list of character traits. It seems to me that he doesn't so much mean "skilled to teach" as he does something more like "able to teach with integrity, able to teach things and live them out in his own life". But nothing hangs on this being the case.

Without Christlike character, none of the leadership skills in this book will matter or work particularly well. When it comes to any leadership role, but especially Christian leadership, character is king.

See also

43. The five C's

6

Servanthood is greatness

Jesus turned a lot of things upside down and inside out. Love your enemies. Go the extra mile. Turn the other cheek. Blessed are the meek. The kingdom that Jesus brought was, and still is, a radical departure from the norm. One of the clearest examples of this 'turning the world on its head' agenda is Jesus' proclamation that the first will be last and the last will be first. You can't get more upside down than that.

Upside down

In Mark 10:35-45, when Jesus talks with his disciples about rulers and leaders and how they rule, he famously highlights a number of differences between the way the Gentile rulers exercise authority and how Jesus wants his disciples to act. We focus less often on the similarities that Jesus affirms. James and John want to be number one and number two in Jesus' leadership team. The other disciples become angry with them for asking Jesus about this—presumably they're upset because they didn't think of it first. Jesus takes this opportunity to teach them all something important not just about how leadership and authority will work for his people, but also about himself. In verses 42-45 he says,

> "You know that those who are considered rulers of the Gentiles lord it over them, and their great ones exercise authority over them. But it shall not be so among you. But whoever would be great among you must be your servant, and whoever would be first among you must be slave of all.

> For even the Son of Man came not to be served but to serve, and to give his life as a ransom for many."

Notice that he doesn't speak against the idea of rulers and ruling. He could have if he wanted to, but he doesn't. There's nothing wrong with rulers and leaders. What's sinful is how they go about it. Neither does Jesus speak against the desire to be great. And he doesn't rebuke his disciples for wanting to be first. But what he does do is to change the definition of greatness. He takes the ambition of being first and fills this concept with new content. And he radically reframes what it means to rule.

Christian leaders are not to rule as the Gentile rulers do, by lording it over others and flaunting their authority. Rather, they're to use their authority to serve and they're to rule by serving those they oversee. Greatness is about serving. It's not about being served. In the world, greatness is often measured by how many people serve you or by how many staff you have. Not so with Jesus. With Jesus, greatness is measured by how many people you serve. The way you end up being the greatest is by serving everyone. It's a radical and complete paradigm shift. Your goal as a leader is to serve your team as best you can.

Over them by being under them

As a leader, your job is to help those you lead to succeed. Those people under you don't exist to serve you or to make your life easier. You exist to serve them. The organizational pyramid is reversed. The pyramid doesn't exist to serve and prop up those at the top. The point leader exists to serve everyone else in the organization. You exist to serve the people you lead. You are over them by being under them and you are great by being the least. You are to be their first assistant, head coach, and chief cheerleader. Leadership means servanthood. Jesus isn't against greatness—he just changes the definition. He shows you what real greatness looks like and what true greatness means. And greatness means sacrifice and servanthood.

The model, of course, is Jesus himself. Jesus is Lord, and he does rule, and he does possess all authority, and he exercises that authority. But he does so as a servant. He does so by laying down his life and by giving up his rights and privileges. The great, exalted King of the universe, mighty Messiah, is also and at the same time the suffering Servant who lays his life down and shoulders iniquity on behalf of his people. These two roles aren't in tension, and he isn't one and then the other. The way he is the conquering and ruling Messiah is by being the Servant. Servanthood is greatness.

This is the core of Christian leadership in practice. You want to be a disciple of Jesus? That's a great thing. You want to be a leader? Good. You want to be a great leader? You want to be the greatest? That's good too. Be a servant. Be the greatest servant. Serve everyone you can. Everyone you meet. Be all about others; be in it for others. Do everything you can to grow and develop others. Servanthood is the mark of the Christian leader.

7
God uses means

The God of the Bible is sovereign. He reigns over all things and all people. He is the Lord and there is no other (Isa 45:5). He forms the light and creates darkness, he brings prosperity and creates disaster—he, the Lord, does all these things (Isa 45:7). He sends the rain on the just and the unjust (Matt 5:45). Even the very hairs on your head are all numbered (Matt 10:30).

How God's sovereignty interacts with human will and responsibility is an interesting theological question that I'm planning on avoiding. But I will say that I'm convinced from the Bible that he is absolutely sovereign and in control of all things—both good and bad. Bad things happen in the world and in my life by both God's permission and design. And my main reason for thinking that's true is seeing how it worked at the cross, which was the worst, most evil event in the history of the universe. When Peter explains it in his first big sermon in Acts 2, he says:

> "Men of Israel, hear these words: Jesus of Nazareth, a man attested to you by God with mighty works and wonders and signs that God did through him in your midst, as you yourselves know—this Jesus, delivered up according to the definite plan and foreknowledge of God, you crucified and killed by the hands of lawless men. God raised him up, loosing the pangs of death, because it was not possible for him to be held by it." (vv. 22-24)

Wicked men did a wicked thing, and yet it was God's deliberate plan.

Now this raises all kinds of important questions, but answering them would turn this into a very different book. So the point for us here is that

God is in control and sovereign, regardless of whether you think that's to a large extent or a very large extent or an absolute extent.

The way it usually works

And yet there is more that needs to be said on this topic, because it's important to understand the subtle distinctions the Bible makes here. God's absolute control over all things does not mean that he is the sole agent for what happens in the world. He often—perhaps almost always—works *through* other processes or people.

Take, for example, evangelism. There's a certain flavour of Christian who believes that we aren't supposed to do anything to share the gospel with people because God is absolutely sovereign and it's God who saves people (I've never actually met anyone who thinks like this, but I'm assured they do exist). People call them hyper-Calvinists. Evangelism for hyper-Calvinists simply means opening the doors of the church.

The thinking goes something like this: God will save those he wants to save, when he wants, and he can do it without us. So far, so good. I would agree with all that. But the next bit is where we part ways. Since all of that is true, those in the hyper-Calvinist camp then say, "Therefore we don't—and maybe even shouldn't—do anything". No inviting. No sharing what Jesus has done with our friends. Sometimes even no preaching. Nothing—because God is absolutely sovereign.

Now, like I said, I've never actually met anyone who thinks like that about evangelism, though I'm pretty sure they exist and you might know or even be one of them.

There's one key theological element that those who think like hyper-Calvinists are missing. And that missing piece is that God uses means. God works through people. God works through processes.

When God sends rain on the just and the unjust he doesn't just miraculously cause water droplets to fall from the clear blue sky. He uses an elaborate system, that he created himself, that involves evaporation and high- and low-pressure systems and a whole pile of things I don't quite understand. The result is that rain falls where God wants it to fall. God sends the rain. But he does it through a number of means. He doesn't just send rain directly from the throne of heaven.

And this is how God usually works. He certainly *can* work directly in a person outside of anything else or anyone else—he could convert someone by speaking to them in a dream or by having them just wake up trusting in Jesus—but he doesn't always, or even often, work like that. He normally uses means. He uses people—all kinds of people doing all kinds of things. God uses us as we do things like loving people, sharing with people, inviting people. He uses the ads we place in local newspapers, letterbox drops, personal evangelism, sermons, tracts, books, slogans on t-shirts, and probably thousands of other things. God normally uses normal means, even seemingly mundane means, to accomplish amazing things.

And there's nothing unspiritual, or less spiritual, about any of that. The Holy Spirit is at work in and through all of those means while working in people's hearts to bring them to see the light of the knowledge of the glory of God in the face of Christ (2 Cor 4:6). If God were to convert someone directly through a dream instead of through the ongoing love and witness of a Christian neighbour over a number of years, both would be equally miraculous and equally spiritual.

Ministry hyper-Calvinism

None of that will be particularly new for most of you reading this book. But here's the mistake you might be making: when it comes to church leadership and to the way that God grows churches, you might just be a functional hyper-Calvinist.

That might sound like an insult, but it's not supposed to be. Your objections to, or your discomfort with, talking too much about leadership or church growth or processes and systems might stem from a sense that all of this is discounting the fact that God is at work. You might think these things imply that God isn't involved. They might seem too mechanical or unspiritual.

And maybe sometimes these things are, or can be, mechanical. But leadership and church growth are not necessarily mechanical or unspiritual. Because God uses means, or intermediaries—sometimes these intermediaries are people, and other times they're processes or systems.

When the Bible talks about the growth of the church, it's always God who gives the growth. It's God who changes people's hearts. It's God who works in people by the Holy Spirit to treasure Jesus. It's God who transfers people from one kingdom to the other. It's God who builds his church. Church growth is a miraculous event over which I have no control. The Bible is very clear about this in places like 1 Corinthians 3:5-9, where Paul is discussing factions in the church. He says:

> What then is Apollos? What is Paul? Servants through whom you believed, as the Lord assigned to each. I planted, Apollos watered, but God gave the growth. So neither he who plants nor he who waters is anything, but only God who gives the growth. He who plants and he who waters are one, and each will receive his wages according to his labor. For we are God's fellow workers. You are God's field, God's building.

It's God who gives the growth. It's God who grows the church.

But this doesn't mean that Paul and Apollos didn't do anything in Corinth. Paul planted, and his planting was necessary. Apollos watered, and his watering was necessary. And their doing these things in no way undermines the fact that God gave the growth. Their doing isn't some unspiritual pragmatism. It doesn't signal a lack of faith in the sovereignty of God. Planting and watering in and of themselves don't make anything grow. But planting and watering aren't irrelevant either.

Nor does this passage mean to say that Paul and Apollos did their part without God and God did his part without Paul and Apollos. The point in 1 Corinthians 3 isn't that when Paul is present in the process God is absent. God is present in the whole process. Paul and Apollos plant and water with the strength that God provides.

When Paul does his work, it's not because God is absent. The point is that God is at work and Paul is also present. His role is a real role. His part is a real part. He really plants. Apollos really waters. God invites us to join in and have a real role in the work that he's doing. God will be at work before you, through you, in spite of you, and after you.

The importance of planting and watering

How you plant and how you water have an impact on the upcoming harvest. Every farmer knows this. Farmers who are lazy with their planting and disorganized with their watering create circumstances that are far from ideal for growth. A farmer's irresponsibility has an impact on the size and quality of his crops.

And, whether consciously or instinctively, we know this. We know that if we preach in a language that the people don't understand very few will respond. But I know that if I preach in English in Sydney, Australia to native English speakers, that's a more conducive environment to seeing people respond to the gospel than if I were to preach to them in fluent Hungarian. Or if I were to preach in English to native Kazakh speakers in Kazakhstan. There's no guarantee that anyone will respond to my preaching. It's God who gives the growth. But I speak to English speakers in the English language because I know that what I do matters. That's why missionaries learn the native language and culture in countries where they minister. That's why we translate the Bible into local languages. The idea that because God alone causes growth it doesn't matter what I do is unbiblical dualism.

Of course it's God who grows the church. Of course he can do it without us or in spite of us, and sometimes he does. But when you think about things like leadership, systems, processes, and structures, you're not thinking, "God doesn't grow the church so I need to". We need to ask instead, "I wonder how God grows the church? I wonder what means he likes to use? I wonder what means he most often uses? I wonder what means he doesn't normally use?"

And even if we do everything right God might not choose to save anyone. Because he's sovereign and he's the Lord, he will do what is right in his own eyes. But that doesn't mean that you should do a terrible job because God does what he wants anyway. It means that, because you're serving a sovereign God who gave his Son for you, you plan to do the best job you can to bring him honour and glory, knowing and trusting that God will do what he wants.

Leadership, self-leadership, other-person-centred leadership, systems, structures, and strategies don't make churches grow. But they aren't irrelevant either. Just as he did with Paul and Apollos, God has given us the tasks of planting and watering. As we remember that God gives the growth, it's our responsibility to plant and water as best we can and to find better ways to plant and water.

You're probably pretty good at avoiding evangelistic hyper-Calvinism. But beware of ministry hyper-Calvinism as well. Calibrate your theological apparatus to detect and avoid leadership hyper-Calvinism. A good way to do this is to keep remembering that God uses means, including you and your ministry, to grow the church.

Planting and watering matter because God uses means.

8
Focus on doing your job

When everyone knows and understands his or her role and how it relates to the roles of others, everyone is better able to work at their best, to know what is expected of them, and to assess whether or not they're doing a good job. This kind of clarity is particularly important in any ministry team or partnership. Trying to do someone else's job, either knowingly or unknowingly, is nearly always a recipe for angst and disappointment.

There has always been some debate when it comes to ministry as to what is God's job and what is our job. And often the way the discussion is set up isn't particularly helpful and can lead to unfortunate conclusions.

Ministry God-of-the-gaps

Sometimes the discussion sets up a dichotomy between jobs that are completely up to us and those that are completely up to God. The idea is that we do everything up to a certain point and then, after that, it's out of our hands and the rest is up to God. We do a certain amount and God does the rest.

This is an okay way of describing what's going on as far as it goes, but it's not exactly accurate and it can lead to some difficulties. What's good about this description is that it helps us see that there really are some things that we have no control over but God does. It also helps us see that there are some things that we need to do and that we ought to do those things as best as we can. That's helpful because it takes the pressure off in case we begin to think that everything is our responsibility and that if people don't put their trust in Jesus or grow in Christlikeness then it's all our fault. It stops the cycle of worrying that the results might have been different if only we were more persuasive, or better prepared, or knew more, or had more staff, or whatever. There are things over which I have no control, and it's good to be reminded of that every now and then.

The problem with this kind of thinking, however, is that it's not nuanced enough to accurately describe what's going on. To say that we do everything up until this point—whatever that point is exactly—*and then* God takes over implies that God wasn't involved before that point. I take the ball as far as I can, hand it over to God, and he takes it the rest of the way.

This is the ministry version of the God-of-the-gaps and has the same root cause as ministry hyper-Calvinism—it doesn't acknowledge that God uses means. 'God-of-the-gaps' describes a certain way of viewing the world in which everything we currently understand is a natural process and everything we don't understand is an unknowable and mysterious activity of the Lord that is simply a miracle. What happens is that, as we continue to learn more and more about the world and the universe and the human body, the area that was 'God's domain' gets smaller and smaller. And so what the God-of-the-gaps gives us is a God who constantly grows smaller and smaller as human understanding grows bigger and bigger.

And this way of viewing ministry, where we do what we can do and God does whatever we can't, is a God-of-the-gaps-type view.

What about fruitfulness?

Another unhelpful way of viewing this issue of who does what doesn't divide our jobs from God's jobs but instead seeks to determine what success looks like. In this view the different roles for God and for God's people are generally only implied. Some speak of success in terms of faithfulness—so our job is to be faithful and God's job is to make things happen. Others, usually the more entrepreneurial church leaders from larger churches, tend to talk more in terms of results. Success means results. Sometimes these leaders will use the term fruitfulness instead of results. Ministries and ministers that aren't fruitful, that don't produce results—often measured in terms of things that can be counted, usually baptisms as a way of cataloguing conversions—should be shut down so the resources can be reallocated.

While it's very rarely spoken about outright, it's almost impossible to understand this view of ministry without seeing the whole process as my job. If my success is about results, up to and including conversions, that means I'm accountable for everything right up to and including conversions and baptisms. And if I'm completely accountable, then I must also be completely responsible. Changing the vocabulary to fruitfulness isn't any more helpful because that's just another, perhaps more biblical, way of talking about the kind of results we can count and observe.

We do it together

So then how should we think about what is our job and what is God's job in ministry?

God's job, which he does all by himself without us, is to change people's hearts and transfer people into his kingdom. Conversion. Actually changing people's hearts is something between God and the individual. I do not do that and God does not expect me to.

Everything else—loving, preaching, proclaiming, personal witness—God and I do together. It's not that God does his bit by himself and I do my bit by myself. God does his bit by himself and I do my bit *along with* him.

This is Peter's point in 1 Peter 4:10-11. He says:

> As each has received a gift, use it to serve one another, as good stewards of God's varied grace: whoever speaks, as one who speaks oracles of God; whoever serves, as one who serves by the strength that God supplies—in order that in everything God may be glorified through Jesus Christ. To him belong glory and dominion forever and ever. Amen.

When you serve, you do it with the strength that God provides. You and God are working together. You're serving and he is alongside you giving you strength. When you do your bit, he is there with you.

So make sure you focus on doing your job. Don't try to do God's job. It isn't your responsibility to convert people. That's God's job. When you arrive before the throne, when everything is done, God won't say, "Well done, good and successful servant". He won't even say, "Well done, good and fruitful servant". What he'll say is, "Well done, good and faithful servant". Your job is, in the power of God, to faithfully do the right things for the right reasons.

Check your faithfulness

The dark side of talking about ministry in terms of faithfulness is that people can use it as an excuse for lack of accountability and to justify a ministry style that is overly defensive, cautious, fearful, and perhaps even lazy and defeated. This is not always the case, of course, but sometimes Christian leaders hide their incompetence behind a smokescreen of 'faithfulness'. Often what we call faithfulness isn't actually faithfulness.

It's worth double-checking to make sure that our faithfulness really is faithfulness and not self-deception. Faithfully preaching sermons week after week that are boring or unclear without taking steps to improve your preaching isn't actually being faithful. Nor is faithfully doing the same things in the same way over and over again and never reaching anyone in the neighbourhood around your church. Never trying to do anything better or differently is not being faithful.

Our job as Christian leaders is to faithfully do everything we can think of, taking some risks and enduring some pain, to explain the gospel, love people, and preach the whole counsel of God to everyone we can, as best we can. Genuine faithfulness isn't a front for complacency or laziness. Faithfulness in doing everything God's word requires of us is our job. Be faithful and God will help you. Then let him do his job. Let him focus on results.

You focus on doing your job and let God do what only he can do.

9
Pragmatism doesn't work in practice

One of the sins I struggle with most is impatience. I want things done now—in fact, to be honest, now is often too late. "Is there any way we can make it happen sooner?" I'm not, therefore, a big fan of wasting time—and I feel strongly about not wasting your time either. I want to use my time in a way that's effective. I want to achieve something and move forward. I want to do things that work and I don't want to waste my time on things that don't work. I'm not sure anyone wants to waste their time on things that don't work, but perhaps some people have a higher tolerance for it than others.

But the question when it comes to ministry and leadership is this: What does being successful and effective look like? How do you know when you're doing it?

The answer to that question, especially in leadership books, is often pragmatic. What I mean by pragmatic is assessing a plan or a belief in terms of its practical success. Pragmatism is a way of assessing problems and situations based on their immediate practical consequences rather than on abstract or ideological concerns. In other words, what's right is what works.

The good and bad

There's something good and helpful about pragmatism. Of course you want to do what works. Why would your goal be to do things that don't work? That would be crazy. And in one sense, of course, doing what works leads to success.

One of the somewhat ironic problems with a pragmatic approach to Christian ministry, however, is that although it sounds good in theory it doesn't actually work in practice. And the real problem is that pragmatists end up making decisions and choosing a direction based on immediate practical consequences. *Immediate* is the problem word. Often it's very difficult to determine what will work in the future. Sometimes things don't look promising on paper to begin with but they work out well in the long run. Other times programs or ministries start small and slow but then begin to grow bigger and faster and are longer lasting than other things that seemed more promising at the start. But you can't tell that at first.

It's very often difficult, or even impossible, to foresee the long-term effects of a solution or direction. What appears to be effective at first glance may reveal itself to be ineffective once you get up close and look under the hood. What might at first appear successful may not actually be successful in the end.

Mix in factors such as the law of unintended consequences, and this kind of pure pragmatism begins to unravel. The law of unintended consequences is the idea that when you start with a complicated system—one that you don't completely understand—and mess with it and make changes to it, you often end up with some outcomes that you didn't anticipate or intend. Sometimes these can be good, but often they're bad.

Pragmatic results

In the early 1900s, sugar cane was a big deal in Australia—especially in the northern states like Queensland. But some beetles were getting in the way and destroying crops incessantly. Enter the cane toad. The cane toad, native to South America, had been introduced in places like Barbados and French Guiana in the 1840s to try and control rat populations. It was a total failure. But, for some reason, they were introduced in Puerto Rico in the early 20th century to deal with beetles that were out of control in the cane fields. It seemed to work out. So they introduced them in Queensland in Australia in the 1930s to deal with a similar problem. Cane toads were the ideal solution.

It was an absolute disaster. The cane toads hardly made a dent in the beetle population, but when it came to mass breeding, destroying ecosystems, and wiping out native species, they were very successful. Cane toads are now an out-of-control pest. That's the law of unintended consequences.

What works in the short term may not work in the long term and may, in fact, bring unintended and unwanted results. We see this kind of insight in places like Proverbs 14:12 and Proverbs 16:25 (both are identical):

> There is a way that seems right to a man,
> but its end is the way to death.

Pragmatism by itself doesn't work. But, of course, we want to do things that work and the idea of doing things that work is a good one. But what we need is a way of knowing the following:

1. What does success look like in the first place? And how do we know if what we're doing is working?
2. What guideposts can we set up before we start to help us evaluate whether something will work or not?

That is, we need some principles that will help us assess what will work, and work long-term, to achieve exactly what we're seeking to achieve. What we need is principled pragmatism.

Theologically principled pragmatism

Most people know intuitively what principled pragmatism is. Very few people, especially in Christian leadership and ministry, follow the theory of unconstrained and unprincipled pragmatism. But it's worth clarifying these principles so that they become a part of our conscious understanding and planning.

The Christian leader's principles are theological. When we trust the Bible as the supreme authority and the gospel as God's power to bring about lasting salvation and lasting change, then we have access to the guideposts we need. God himself tells us what he wants us to be doing and gives us some broad methods and boundaries.

The point here is not that the Bible is a compendium of leadership insights for every conceivable situation and circumstance. And we've already noted that the Bible is not a collection of verses to be extracted and applied without giving due weight to their context, intention, authorship, and place in the wider biblical narrative.

My point is simply that, as we pursue truth and seek to think God's thoughts after him, biblically and theologically, certain foundational principles for 'what works' will become clear. The Bible gives us a framework but then allows us great freedom in terms of how those principles might play out in our ministry. For example, preaching the gospel as clearly and persuasively as we can will work to produce disciples. God won't do it any other way than through the gospel. Should we proclaim it in ten minutes or an hour? At the beginning of the meeting or at the end? Or not in a gathering at all but one-on-one? The Bible doesn't specify. Do whatever works best. In one sense you can build a church without preaching the gospel—people do it. They offer all kinds of promises and assurances and great advertising and smoke and lights and competitions and their churches can be quite big. But if people aren't responding to the gospel and putting their trust in Jesus, then they're not really building the church. They're just drawing a crowd. It looks successful, but it's not actually successful. What they're doing 'works' but it doesn't actually work.

There's nothing wrong with promises or smoke and lights or screens or advertising or any of those things. But none of those things are what God says actually builds the church. Pragmatism itself isn't bad. We want to do things that work. We want to do things that achieve what we set out to achieve.

Doing things that work isn't the problem. The problem comes when we decide what to do based on what seems to work rather than on what God asks us to do. What works isn't a reliable guide for what's right. Sometimes doing the right thing—doing what God says—doesn't immediately lead to success. Sometimes doing the right thing leads to suffering or pain or more problems—and this is the opposite of pragmatism. But even when the right thing doesn't seem to work, it's still the right thing. Doing what God says does actually work. It just might not seem like it does at first. Often when we do the right thing we discover much later that it was far more successful than we ever could have imagined. Sometimes there's more than one right thing we can choose and still live according to

God's word—so we pick one and go with it. With pragmatism, we make decisions based on what we think will work even though we don't know nearly enough to predict how it will actually turn out. With theological pragmatism, we make decisions guided by the One who does know what works and how it will turn out.

Take, for example, the martyrdoms of Jim Elliot and his team. They died without converting a single Ecuadorian native. Their deaths might seem to the pragmatist like a colossal waste of potential. Their mission didn't work. Or did it? The ministry of Jim's widow, Elisabeth, has been incalculable. Steve Saint, whose father Nate was killed with Jim, has had an extraordinary ministry among the people who killed his father. And Jim Elliot's diary and powerful story have been the catalyst for so much mission work around the world. A pragmatist might look at those martyrdoms in 1956 as a waste. Their mission didn't work. But it's only that it didn't *seem* to work. They weren't intending to be martyred to create a martyr story, but the consequences of their deaths were untold good for people and glory to God.[11]

Pragmatism isn't necessarily wrong—doing what works is a good thing. What we need is a source that tells us what really works and what the right thing to do is—in the short and long term. Unprincipled pragmatism doesn't work. But theological pragmatism, a pragmatism constrained by theological convictions, does work in the real world—even if it doesn't at first appear to be working as we expect or want it to.

11 See *Shadow of the Almighty: The life and testament of Jim Elliot* by Elisabeth Elliot (HarperCollins, New York, 1989).

10

Don't let what God wants you to do get in the way of who God wants you to be

Workers in every industry need different tools—carpenters use saws and hammers, artists use brushes, bricklayers use trowels. If a carpenter's saw breaks, he needs to get a new saw, an artist a new brush, a bricklayer a new trowel.

One of the primary tools we use in Christian ministry is our own hearts. Sometimes our heart is devoted to Jesus and sometimes it's divided. Sometimes our heart finds its joy in Jesus and sometimes it finds its joy elsewhere. Sometimes our heart trusts in the Lord and sometimes it trusts in itself.

But how does our heart relate to our ministry? How are we to think about the relationship between personal godliness and ministry? What is the relationship between who God wants us to be and what God wants us to do?

Separation and overlap

There are two major mistakes we can make when thinking about this relationship between who God wants us to be and what God wants us to do. One is to see the two areas as being so separate that they have little or nothing to do with each other. The other mistake, at the opposite end of the spectrum, is to see who we are and what we do as completely overlapping or even as being the same thing. At either extreme we risk damaging both our ministries and our hearts.

One helpful analogy is to see who we are as like a freshwater spring, and what we do as a stream of water that flows from that spring. The two are inseparable—no spring means no stream. But they're not the same thing; they're two distinct things. In the same way, your heart is the spring of everything you do, including your ministry, which flows from the spring of your heart. Proverbs 4:23 puts it like this:

> Keep your heart with all vigilance,
> for from it flow the springs of life.

Getting the relationship wrong between who God wants you to be and what he wants you to do cashes out in three main dangers.

Danger number one

Trying to separate the two can lead to thinking that who God wants you to be has no impact on what God wants you to do.

We see this sometimes when ministry becomes 'just a job'. Somewhere along the way you have stopped being a shepherd of the sheep because you're willing, and you have become a hired hand because it's what you do—and you're not sure you can do anything else. You know the right things to do and you keep doing them—preaching, listening to people, organizing the rosters. On the outside, everything seems to be just as it always has been.

But when things change at the spring the effects will be felt downstream. Sometimes it will not be perceptible for quite some time, but eventually the stream will change and people will notice. Even if you keep doing exactly the same things as you always did, your ministry will be different because ministry isn't just a mechanical process. It involves your heart. If your heart changes, your ministry changes also.

When you begin to think that moral failings and secret sins don't matter and won't affect what God wants you to do in ministry, you're in serious danger.

All of us have constant moral failings and constant secret sins. We're not perfect and we won't be this side of the new creation. The problem is not so much having secret sins—the problem is being okay with them and so having an increasing lack of repentance. Just because secret sins and moral failures are constant and expected doesn't make them okay and welcome in our lives. We must be just as constantly repenting of them and dealing with them.

What is hidden will always, eventually, come out. Nothing stays hidden forever and sin always finds a way to the surface of your life. Either you own it and confess it and repent of it yourself—or God will see to it that the sin is exposed and he'll force you to own it and you can repent of it then.

God does this not because he's a jerk and loves to see us shamed and embarrassed. He does it because secret sin, like any sin, is horribly bad for us. It will destroy us and it will destroy our relationships.

What's on the inside will always come out. Who God wants you to be will always have an impact on what God wants you to do. Secret sins will choke your heart and erode your ministry. Deal with them tirelessly and repent of them quickly.

Danger number two

Trying to separate the two can also lead to thinking that what God wants you to do is more important than who God wants you to be.

You might understand that who God wants you to be has a real impact on what God wants you to do and you might agree that constant repentance is necessary. But if you're so busy doing what God wants you to do that you don't have the time or the brain space to be who God wants you to be, you've fallen into the trap of this second danger.

You've got to serve these people and write that sermon and prepare this small group study—there's always so much to do. When what God wants you to do becomes more important than who God wants you to be, one of the first things to drop off the radar is your relationship with God. Your time reading the Bible, praying, sitting under his word and listening to a sermon simply to learn and be challenged or comforted.

At times in my life I've gone a week, sometimes two or three, even a whole month without spending time alone with God reading my Bible. The most alarming part of it was that I wouldn't even notice how long it had been. I was still technically reading my Bible because I was preparing all kinds of sermons and writing Bible studies. My Bible was always open—but it was because I was doing the things God wanted me to do and not because I was seeking to be the person God wanted me to be. What I had to do was more important than what God wanted me to be.

There was a long period in my life when I didn't listen to sermons as a disciple sitting under God's word. Instead I mentally critiqued content and style. I thought about how I would preach the same passage. I mentally logged illustrations. Every time I listened to a sermon it was first and foremost, and sadly often exclusively, an exercise in negativity or personal rhetorical development. I was not acting as a child of his heavenly Father, sitting and listening to be challenged and comforted. I was not seeking how I could be obedient. It wasn't that I didn't think all those things mattered, but deep down, subconsciously, I thought that what God wanted me to do was more important.

When you live like this your heart begins to atrophy. You get weary of ministry. Your love for God and people begins to dim. People become obstacles and frustrations. And what you once thought important becomes more and more of a burden.

These are equal but opposite dangers. The result of the first danger, deciding that who you are doesn't matter, is ineffectiveness. And if this goes on for too long your ministry will be taken away from you. Ineffectiveness is also the result of thinking that what you do is more important than who you are. And if this goes on for too long you'll walk away from your ministry yourself.

Danger number three

When you see who you are and what you do as completely overlapping, you can begin to think that what God has called you to do *is* what God has called you to be. This third danger doesn't have as much to do with personal godliness and discipleship as it does with where you find your worth and value.

You begin to equate how you're doing as a person with how things are going with your ministry. When your ministry appears to be successful, your self-esteem rises. When your ministry is tanking, so does your sense of self. This 'who I am is what I do' correspondence is extraordinarily dangerous.

If things are going well in ministry—people are growing in their faith and being converted, the poor are being helped and transformed—and you draw your value as a person from those successes, then pride is just around the corner. Because that success *is* you—not something that God did through you and allowed you to play a part in, but something that displays your worth.

On the other hand, if the ministry is not going well—if leaders are quitting, if people are upset and critical, leaving the church, and walking away from Jesus—and you draw your value as a person from the success of the ministry, then despair is just around the corner.

It's perfectly right to find joy in people growing and joining the kingdom and enduring hardship well—and it would be strange if you didn't share in that joy. It's also perfectly right to feel sadness when people walk away from Jesus, or criticize you (fairly or unfairly), or when people continually reject the call to put their trust in Jesus as their Lord and Saviour. All of that is perfectly legitimate. Joy in the highs and sadness in the lows is totally normal. But that's not the same as finding your worth in those successes or failures. That's a very different thing, though sometimes the line between the two can be very fine.

Your ultimate and deepest joy and sense of worth doesn't come from what you can or can't do or what you do or don't achieve. God assigns you your value and worth completely apart from what you do. Your value as a person has nothing to do with your ministry. God doesn't love you less when your ministry is tanking and he doesn't love you more when all you do is win.

Doing and being

It's not that who you are and what you do are completely unrelated and separate, because they're related. What you do flows out of who you are. What God does through you is based on, and caused by, what God has done and is doing in you.

Jesus' disciples made this same mistake once. They mixed up the relationship between what they were doing and what God had made them to be. In Luke 10, Jesus sends the 72 out on mission. When they return, they say, "Lord, even the demons are subject to us in your name!" (v. 17). Jesus knows they're heading down a dangerous path, and so he immediately helps them understand this relationship. He says to them,

> "Behold, I have given you authority to tread on serpents and scorpions, and over all the power of the enemy, and nothing shall hurt you. Nevertheless, do not rejoice in this, that the spirits are subject to you, but rejoice that your names are written in heaven." (vv. 19-20)

Do not find your ultimate joy and worth in the success of what God has sent you to do, instead rejoice in what God has made you to be, a child of the kingdom.

It's important to understand these dangers and to know yourself. Do you tend towards too much separation or too much overlap? In the end Satan doesn't care which side of the boat you jump out of so long as you jump out. What God has called you to do flows out of what God has called you to be. He has called you to be a disciple, with other disciples, to go and make disciples. What God does through you flows from what God does in you. And what God does in you flows from what God has already done for you.

Don't let what God wants you to do get in the way of who God wants you to be.

11 Everything must be genuine

You can't fake it for very long. Whatever 'it' is, eventually the truth will come out. Whether it's overselling yourself in a job interview, pretending to like a band to impress a girl or a sport to impress a guy, buying a pair of glasses to make you look more grown-up, or insisting that you enjoy your mother-in-law's cooking, what's on the inside will eventually come out. You can't pretend forever.

When it comes to leading a team, whatever you do and say needs to be genuine. Beyond honesty being the best policy and God's requirement, it's important because the pressures of the role will eventually push the reality to the surface whether you like it or not. Generally the cracks will begin to show when you least want them to, when you're under a lot of pressure and stress. It takes a lot of effort and concentration to maintain a façade. And when more effort and concentration is required elsewhere—for example, when you're in a crisis—that's when the mask, if there is one, will begin to crumble.

Being genuine means that if you say something is important to you, it needs to be important to you. If you say that you care, you really do need to care. If you say you want someone's opinion, then you need to take their opinion into account. If you've lost your enthusiasm and passion, then be real about that and don't try to manufacture it. Artificial substitutes, no matter how close to genuine they get, will always taste different. Be who you are.

A genuine risk

Being genuine can be an uncomfortable and risky thing—especially when you're talking about a lack of enthusiasm for the cause or a loss of passion for the vision. As the people you lead see your enthusiasm wane, they might in turn lose their enthusiasm for the cause. They might feel less inclined to follow you. There's no way to avoid the fact that genuineness is a genuine risk. But here are two thoughts to keep in mind:

1. Enthusiasm is not the same as commitment. A lull in enthusiasm is normal and natural. No-one can be enthusiastic all the time. The passion I feel for a project can wax and wane while my commitment remains consistent. It's possible to lose enthusiasm for a season without losing commitment. It's helpful for your team to understand that and for them to see you model rock-solid commitment as emotions ebb and flow. A lack of enthusiasm isn't something to be welcomed, mind you—when this happens you need to work out where it went and how to get it back. And you should be genuine about it precisely *because* you'll need your team's help and prayers to turn the situation around. But remember that, even though enthusiasm and commitment are different, they do overlap.

2. While being genuine is risky—and there's no getting around that risk—it is, without a doubt, far riskier to try to fake it. When people discover you've been faking it in some area of your ministry, your credibility will be damaged across the board. Credibility doesn't come in discreet, hermetically sealed units. And without credibility it's very difficult to lead anyone, anywhere. Imagine that everything you say and do and lead sits on a layer of water like toys in a bathtub. When you take a cup of water out of the bath, the loss of water is spread throughout the bathtub. Every toy sinks slightly lower. It's the same with credibility. When you lose credibility in one area, it affects everything else you say and do and lead. Everything sits slightly lower.

Integrity

When you lead an inauthentic life, not only do you sacrifice your credibility once people find out about it, but you also sacrifice your integrity—and this happens immediately, whether anyone ever finds out or not. Whenever you're not completely genuine, your integrity is compromised. Integrity is about wholeness. The word itself comes from the same word as 'integer', which refers to a whole number. Integrity means you don't have parts. What you believe is the same as how you behave. The you who exists in one setting with one group of people is essentially the same as the you who exists in another setting with another group of people. Obviously you talk about different topics and use different vocabulary in different settings—I'll have different kinds of conversations with my kids, for example, than I do with my friends or with my boss. Though I may dress differently and speak in different ways appropriate to the context, I'm still me and what I think and say is consistent across those different circumstances. Integrity means consistency of substance. It means that you're genuine.

The major difference between sacrificing your credibility and sacrificing your integrity is that a sacrifice of integrity happens whether people know it has happened or not. Integrity isn't dependent on the knowledge of others—you either have it or you don't. Credibility, on the other hand, depends on the perceptions of others. You can lose your integrity without anyone knowing. And then you will lose credibility once people discover your lack of integrity. Integrity is not a dial—it's a switch, and it's either on or it's off. You can't have 'mild integrity'. Cheating on genuineness is a quick way to lose integrity because, as soon as you pretend to be, think, or feel something different to who you really are, you've lost your wholeness.

Genuine doesn't mean extroverted

Being genuine doesn't mean, of course, that you have to wear your heart on your sleeve and tell everyone everything. Although how much you feel comfortable telling people will depend to a large degree on your personality, being genuine isn't the same as over-sharing. In fact, leaders need to be careful what they say, to whom, and when. Being genuine doesn't mean confessing every sin to every person. It's simply about being real with your team. It's about meaning everything you say—from saying that you're excited to saying that you're sorry. It's about being consistent and having all the parts line up so that what you say and believe matches up with how you behave.

Being real with ourselves

Every one of us, at some point in time and probably more often than we'd like, feels like we're being less than genuine—maybe even like a complete fraud. And we all know that we can't just switch the genuine switch to 'on' when we realize it's accidentally switched off or suddenly be completely genuine after reading a chapter in a book that tells you to be genuine.

But the point of this chapter is to remind you to keep being honest with yourself. First, be honest about where your heart is. I don't know anyone who's always enthusiastic about everything that they have to do all the time. Most of us go through patches and seasons where we have to decide to keep doing the right things even when we aren't 'feeling it'. This is normal and there's no benefit in trying to hide it from yourself.

As we said above, however, just because it's normal doesn't mean it's good or something we should accept. The point of being honest and genuine with yourself is so that you can be honest and genuine with God. Constant repentance is the mark of a leader just as it's the mark of every Christian. All of us need to be constantly turning to God to ask for help—anything close to constant genuineness comes from near-constant repentance, which requires that we be ruthlessly honest and genuine with ourselves.

Art and science

Leading people well is both an art and a science. In this book we'll try to unpack and demystify some of the science. The danger is that some people might think mastering the science will mean mastering leadership.

Mastering techniques and skills is good, but these things won't automatically make you a good leader. Leadership is much more than skills and techniques and science. You may master the skills necessary to listen to people well and make them feel loved and cared for, but if you don't actually love and care for them, people will know. You may master the skills of developing people and giving feedback, but if you don't really believe that everyone can get better, people will know.

You can't just pull the levers and go through the steps to produce the right outcome because people aren't machines and leadership isn't a science. The techniques don't just 'work'—they help to crystallize and sharpen what already exists in your heart. If we already love these people and want to serve them, then the skills and techniques help to complete that package.

If the skills and techniques of leadership are like seeds, then who you are deep inside is like the soil. If you love people and want to serve them and believe they can improve, if you believe that mistakes are normal and opportunities to learn and that with hard work you can get to where you want to go, then leadership techniques and skills can grow in the soil of your heart. Without that kind of soil, the techniques themselves will never mask that lack of authenticity and will never produce the fruit of real leadership.

Everything must be genuine.

Section two

Leading yourself

12

Lead yourself

The leadership books sometimes talk about 360-degree leadership. What they mean by this is that leadership isn't only about leading people below us—south. That's the natural and default way most of us think about leadership. We lead and have authority over what happens under us. We often lament that we don't have the position or authority to change things because we're not the boss with the power to lead downwards. But that kind of thinking is too narrow. We also lead east and west—that is, we can lead our peers, or people who are on the same leadership level as we are. This type of leadership is different from the classic idea of southward leadership. But we can influence and lead horizontally—perhaps more than we might think. And we can also lead up, or north—we can lead the people who lead us by supporting them, caring for them, and seeking to influence them. This way of thinking helps us to broaden our leadership horizons and capitalize on a myriad of often unnoticed opportunities. Leading in each direction requires unique skills and presents different challenges.

The hardest person to lead

The one leadership direction that's often overlooked, however, is leading yourself. The hardest person you will ever lead is yourself. And you're the most important person you'll need to learn how to lead—which is very different from saying that you're the most important person in your world, because you're not.

Why is leading yourself the most important leadership? There are multiple reasons, but consider first the scope of this leadership. You don't simply lead yourself for a single project or event. You lead yourself in every project and every event. You speak to yourself more than you speak to anyone else. You have constant access to yourself and you influence everything that you do—every thought, word, and deed. Your leadership of yourself affects your leadership of everyone and everything else.

You're the hardest person to lead because you know yourself better than you know anyone else. You know your inner motivations and fears in a way that no-one else does. And yet, paradoxically, you also know yourself the least. Traits and issues that you see clearly in others you can't see in yourself. You'll diagnose other people's problems and blockages much more quickly than you will your own. Generally speaking you won't be impressed with yourself or your title or position, and so when you tell yourself to do something you'll be less inclined to care. And again, paradoxically, you'll excuse yourself more than you'll excuse any other person. I always have good justification for my character flaws and unreliability and for putting off those things I said I'd do. "I had a busy day; I'm very tired." My excuses are always valid in a way that other people's excuses don't seem to be. And so we can easily avoid hard conversations with ourselves and thus prevent self-transformation and growth because we're quick to believe our own lame excuses.

To be a great leader you must make sure you lead yourself. Self-leadership doesn't just happen. It takes intentional and rigorous discipline. You need to take responsibility for you. It's your responsibility to make sure you're doing okay. It's your responsibility to make sure you're following Jesus. It's your responsibility to make sure you're growing as a leader. There's no guarantee that the leader above you will lead you well or even know how to lead you well and look after you. Maybe they should know, but lots of things don't happen that should. You need to lead you.

In order to do this you'll need to be yourself, motivate yourself, and question yourself.

Be yourself

It's always tempting to be someone else. I'm often impressed by other people and wish I could be more like them. I wish I could be as eloquent as this person and as relationally savvy as that person. I wish I could preach with the same clarity and profundity as this person and wish I had the depth of historical knowledge that person has. And if only I had the ability to exegete culture and make them laugh like that person. I wish I had the courage of this person and the pastoral sensitivity of that person—and on and on.

Some leaders act a certain way because they think they have to. Some ministers act a certain way because they think that's what a minister is supposed to be like. But why should Peter, who was direct and bold, try to be like careful and nuanced Paul or like eloquent Apollos? Peter should be Peter. And I should be me and you should be you. You need to be comfortable in your own skin so that you can say, along with Paul, "But by the grace of God I am what I am" (1 Cor 15:10).

In order to be comfortable being yourself you need to know yourself well—who you are, what you like, what energizes you, what you're good at, what you're not good at, what drains you, and what relaxes and recharges you.

These things aren't always easy to figure out. It took me a long time to find out what recharges me. It took me a long time to work out what places and activities refresh and relax me. It took me some time to understand what I'm especially good at when it comes to dealing with people. I'd always been good at art and design, and I knew that. But I'm also good at some other things of which I wasn't aware. If some of these attributes are still vague for you, then make a decision to be extra conscious and aware of what's happening over the next 12 months when you're doing certain things or spending time in certain places. Does the beach relax you? Or the mountains? Do you prefer rivers or heights? Sand or snow? Inside or outside? Does an active and bustling atmosphere recharge you or do you prefer quiet and solitude? Do the same for what energizes you and what drains you. Spend some time trying to figure yourself out.

When you know who you are, be who you are. Do whatever you can to organize your life so that you can do more of the things that energize and recharge you. See if you can do fewer of those things that drain you. Try and spend a bit more time in places that refresh you. Can you get there once every six months? What about once a month? What about once a week?

Be who you are and who God has made you to be. Wage war against sin, by all means, but don't wage war against neutral distinctives. Do all you can to improve your skills, of course, but don't beat yourself up because you're not someone else. Learn all the leadership and interpersonal skills you can, but don't try and learn to be someone else. Use your time to be you, rather than trying to be whoever it is you think you're supposed to be. Figure out what makes you who you are—the you-ness that God has created. And then don't just happen to do things or go places, but be intentional about going, doing, being, liking and not liking. If you're eloquent, be eloquent. If you're deep, be deep. If you're simple, be simple. Let Peter be Peter, let Paul be Paul, let Apollos be Apollos. By the grace of God you are what you are. The person you're supposed to be is you. Get better at being you, and be the best you that you can be.

Figure out who God has made you to be and then do it on purpose.

Motivate yourself

Finding motivation can be difficult, and often we feel that it's someone else's job—the boss's or the leader's, for instance—to motivate us. While leaders and bosses most definitely have a role to play in motivating us, at the end of the day it's your job to motivate you. No-one can do it for you.

What bosses and leaders can do for you is seek to energize you. They might remind you why you started in the first place, what it is you're trying to achieve, why it's worth it, or what God has to say about it. Leaders and bosses can do their best to make sure the environment and systems aren't frustrating—or that they're at least minimally frustrating. They can do their best to do what they say they'll do. In effect, they can do a lot to try to make sure you're not demotivated. But they can't actually motivate you. (Thoughtful posters on the wall certainly won't do it.)

Some of us lose enthusiasm and motivation more quickly than others. Some of us experience a powerful draw to downward-spiral thinking, and so we look first and often to things that aren't working and that are going badly. We think in black-and-white terms—things are either perfectly awesome or woefully bad (and when things are not perfect, the only other option is that they're dreadful). In this downward spiral we find it difficult to think of creative ways forward. Some of us need to learn a whole new way of thinking, a whole new thought pattern. And no-one can do it for you. People can describe it, articulate it, and model that kind of hopetimism for you. But no-one can actually do it for you. That part is up to you.

Others of us need to overcome the inertia of unhelpful patterns that we have learned from family. Or the inertia of constant failure. We need to put that inertia aside and consciously look for ways to keep ourselves motivated. People who are always motivated and enthusiastic make it look like it's innate, but motivation doesn't work like that. Everyone needs to motivate him or herself. Some people do it without thinking. Others need to be more deliberate about it. People who seem naturally motivated aren't just gifted—it's not that you either have motivation or you don't. The people whose motivation seems constant and effortless are always doing things that keep them motivated, whereas others need to do those same things more consciously.

What can you do to motivate yourself? It's simple, really. It involves all the things you expect your boss to do for you. It's a matter of reminding yourself, or preaching to yourself, about why you started in the first place. Remind yourself what you're trying to achieve. Preach to yourself about why it's worth it and what God has to say about it. Discipline yourself to call to mind specific examples of why what you're doing is valuable and important. And then? Discipline yourself to actually do these things.

Question yourself

Following are the self-leadership questions I've accumulated and modified from a few different sources over the years. I ask myself these questions at least once every six months, just to make sure I'm doing okay and heading in the right direction.

1. Is my character submitted to Christ?
2. Is my commitment solid?
3. Is my vision clear?
4. Is my passion hot?
5. Is my pride subdued?
6. Are my fears in their place?

7. Is my own personal baggage in check?
8. Is my pace sustainable?
9. Is my zeal to serve developing?
10. Is my heart for God increasing?
11. Is my capacity for loving people deepening?
12. Am I playing to my strengths?
13. Am I still learning?
14. Does my family recognize me?

Bill Hybels, quoting some advice given to him, puts it this way: "The best gift you can give the people you lead... is a healthy, energized, fully surrendered, and focused self. And no-one can make that happen in your life except you."[12] More than vision and more than goals and more than plans, what they need from you is you.

It's always more about people than it is about products, and the same holds true for you. What your people need is you firing on all cylinders. They don't just need the golden eggs; they need the goose that lays them. The stronger and healthier you are, the more eggs there will be and the better quality they will be. And no-one can make that happen under God except you. The first person you need to make sure you lead is you.

See also

14. Play to your strengths

12 Bill Hybels, *Courageous Leadership: Field-tested strategy for the 360° leader*, Zondervan, Grand Rapids, 2009, p. 185.

13 Your family matters

One of the easiest ways to get a group of ministers to shift uncomfortably with guilt is to ask them how their families are coping with ministry. They will speak about the tension in their homes, the arguments, the feelings of neglect. They will speak about not being around in the evenings or on weekends.

There's no way around it: ministry is hard. And doing it full-time doesn't make it any easier. There's very little anyone can do to make it easy or to make it low-pressure or no-pressure. Ministry, like any job, has upsides and downsides and, like any job, it puts unique pressures on a family.

We all know this, but it's worth being reminded every now and then: your family matters.

Leadership and the family

Your family is one of the most important groups of people that God has given you the authority and responsibility to lead. God has given that role to you and your spouse and, if you're the husband, then God has given you the role of leader among equals.

God has given this extraordinarily important leadership role to everyone who has a family—which is a lot of people. Every husband or wife is in a God-given, God-appointed leadership position—whether or not they realize it and regardless of whether they have any leadership qualities. Some people fulfil this role better than others, but the point is that in one sense leadership isn't that special—it's an ordinary part of every family. And because it's an ordinary and very familiar part of family life we can tend to overlook our responsibilities to lead our families, especially when there are other, larger, more demanding and public groups and activities to lead. But as leaders of ourselves and our families we need to remember the central importance of this God-given leadership role.

Your family

Having said all that, here's a truth I'm just going to dump on you: Your family isn't the most important thing in the world.

I know that's a bit controversial and sounds wrong when you first hear it, but now that you've read it once and you're more prepared for it, read it again: Your family isn't the most important thing in the world. Jesus is. God's glory is. There might be a few other things that are also more important.

But the fact that something isn't the most important thing in the world doesn't make it unimportant. Some things can be extremely important without being the most important things. It's critical to be able to say that our families aren't the most important things in the world because it's critical that we see and understand the world as it really is.

What makes this whole family versus ministry issue so difficult to navigate is that the other stuff we do is so eternally important. We're trying to save people from eternal destruction. We're trying to see people grow in Christlikeness. We're trying to see the fame of God's name extend across the nations. It's all very big, very weighty stuff. And when it's all that versus family, it can be difficult to compare them.

But the problem is that we're thinking about it all wrong.

They're more important than you might think

When we conceptualize this tension in terms of ministry versus family, or even ministry on the one hand and family on the other, we're doing it wrong. Whether we mean to or not, and I suspect we don't mean to—when we put the question this way we're saying that whatever else our family is, it's not part of our ministry. The implication then is that you won't do any ministry among your family because ministry is in that other category. I don't think anyone actually thinks this, and everyone I speak to thinks that they most definitely have a ministry to their own family. They're called to love and serve and be there for them. They're called to lead them. They're called to help them understand and trust and obey the Bible's teaching. So it doesn't make sense to frame the tension in a way that puts family and ministry in separate categories when we know they don't belong in separate categories.

My suggestion is that it's more accurate, and more helpful, to think of the whole thing as ministry. The tension we feel, then, is a tension between different ministries and responsibilities that God has given us rather than between the ministry God has given us and the family God has given us. All of it, though, is ministry.

People sometimes push back on this idea of thinking of the whole thing as ministry because they think it devalues family, treating them as just another job to do. While I understand this criticism, I wonder if it says more about the critic than it does about the idea. Because I'm not sure I think about my ministry as just a job to do. Nor do I see it as some kind of burden. There are definitely parts of the job that I like more than others and things I prefer to do over others, but my job is an extension of who I am, and so when I say that my family is part of my ministry I'm thinking of them as one of the things I love most about my job?

One great thing about conceptualizing your family as a part of your ministry is that it helps you to see them as they really are: people God has given you to love, to serve, and to help grow as disciples. And so as you think about all the people you long to see converted and passionately trusting in Jesus and walking by faith in obedience and standing up boldly for Jesus to their friends you'll include your family in that group. Your family isn't in a separate category because they're a part of all that. The whole thing is ministry.

When you finish your ministry, what will you walk into?

It's likely that you won't serve in a church forever. At some point you'll probably officially retire and the church that you've worked for, and in, and with for so long will say goodbye. The church will get a new minister and you'll go home.

Imagine for a moment that you've fast-forwarded to the end of your official ministry career. You're saying goodbye to all those people you love. You're reminiscing and hugging people. Maybe you have something in your eye and maybe you're walking around each room of the building, struggling to let go. But eventually you wave goodbye and walk out the doors of your church for the last time and you leave them behind—still in God's care, but no longer in yours. And it's over. You'll probably still be active in ministry in some way, but that time of formal leadership of a church is over and you're walking into the rest of your life.

The questions to ponder are these: What will you be walking into? Who will be there? Will you walk into the rubble and collateral damage of what was your family—after years of neglect and faithfully, like clockwork, disappointing them time after time? Will you walk into the ruins of what should have been? Or will you walk into relationships that are strong and full of love and trust and security? Once your leadership role in the church is over, your leadership role in your family will continue.

This might sound like a selfish way of thinking about it, but it's not supposed to be. Rather, it's some of the fruit and God-given reward of being faithful to your leadership role in your family.

And if this is the future you'd like, a future where you say goodbye to the church you've led and walk into the arms of the family you still lead, then you need to start leading now in a way that moves you towards that future. And no matter where you are and how close that future is, no matter how you've led your family up until now, it's not too late to make a course correction—the sooner you make it the better. Lead now in a way that will take you where you want to end up.

A new way to think about priorities: situational priorities

When you're considering how to lead your life and shoulder your responsibilities in a way that honours your family but doesn't overstate their place in the universe it's helpful to think about priorities—and even to think about how we think about priorities. Most people conceptualize their priorities as a list. Number-one priority followed by number-two priority and so on. Sometimes we even write them down to help us clarify how we'll live. A priority list might look something like this:

1. God
2. Hobbies
3. Falling over
4. Family
5. Friends
6. Ministry

You may have seen a similar list before. And this one might, shockingly, be exactly what yours would look like (if that's the case for you, the reason it's so uncannily accurate isn't particularly amazing—it's just that I asked all your friends about you). But the problem is that the list isn't very realistic. Do you really only ever see your friends when there's absolutely no possibility you could spend time investing in your family? Do you really only go to work when there's no way for you to spend time with either your family or your friends?

Or is it just that whenever there's a clash you choose your family or friends over the work you do at church? But is that really the case? Or are you sometimes away at a conference while some of your friends are seeing a movie?

But even if you were to flip friends and ministry it wouldn't be realistic—there will still be times when you won't answer a phone call or reply to an email because you're sitting around the table having dinner with friends.

The problem isn't the order of the priorities; the problem is forcing them into a list. The list format isn't helpful because it doesn't reflect how your life actually works. My suggestion is that you reframe how you think about priorities. Instead of conceptualizing them as a list, static and immovable, think of them instead like lily pads on a pond. I call this idea 'situational priorities'.

Picture a big circular pond with lily pads floating on the surface. The lily pads that are closer to the centre of the pond are more important than those nearer the edge. The centre of the pond is high priority and the edge of the pond is low priority. Now picture a big rock in the middle of the pond that cannot be moved. That rock is God. He is the centre of your life and will always be your number-one priority. Everything you do is in relation to him—what he thinks, what he wants, what he commands.

Everything else in your life is assigned to a lily pad. One lily pad represents your immediate family, another your extended family, and another your hobbies. Maybe there's a lily pad for each different church ministry you lead or are involved in. And so on.

What happens is that, as situations and circumstances change, the lily pads float in toward the centre or out toward the edge. For example, it's Saturday afternoon and you're preaching the next day. Your wife suddenly begins screaming in agony, clutching her back. You call the ambulance and look after her. As you head to the car to follow the ambulance, you remember that you're supposed to be preaching tomorrow. You make a phone call and ask another preacher to step in for you. In this situation, the family lily pad floated in very close to the centre of the pond and the church preaching one drifted out a bit.

Or imagine another weekend where your son or daughter is playing in their football Grand Final on Saturday morning. You carefully plan your week so that the sermon is already done and Saturday morning is free. Yet, even though you've done everything you could, the weather is against you and the game is postponed until the following morning, when there will be a hundred people waiting to hear you preach the word of God. You need to preach and there's no chance of someone else covering for you. So Sunday morning the rest of the family head off to the match with the video camera, and as soon as you finish the sermon you hop in the car to cheer them on in the second half while someone locks up back at church. What just happened? In this situation, preaching floated in slightly closer to the centre than family for a brief period of time and then floated out again.

Situations almost always govern the order of our priorities. There will never be a situation where God is not the number-one priority, so he doesn't move from the centre of the pond. Everything else floats around, depending on the exact and unique circumstances of the moment.

This way of looking at priorities doesn't help you figure out what should, in any given circumstance, be the priority. You'll need the word of God and wisdom to make those determinations. And thinking about situational priorities is a bit more complicated than the simple list. But even with the list, you need to work out what the priority is in each circumstance. While the list is a conceptual tool that makes it simpler to visualize your priorities, it can also cause you to feel guilty for no good reason—simply because you violate the artificial construction that you created. The pond is a way to conceptualize it all that allows for the ebb and flow of real circumstances.

Our families are not in competition with our ministries, neither are they entities separate from everything else. They're an important part of our ministries and it's our job to lead them lovingly and faithfully and responsibly.

Don't neglect them, but don't make them an idol either. Your family matters.

14

Play to your strengths

None of us is good at everything. I'm not and (I'm sorry to be the bearer of bad news) neither are you. Although I've probably never met you, I'm absolutely confident I can say there are some things that you simply aren't good at. I might even go so far as to say that, like the rest of us, you're not good at most things.

Even so-called all-rounders aren't really all-rounders. When we call someone, say a cricketer, an all-rounder what we mean is that, in the very narrow field of skills specifically related to cricket, this person is fairly good at all those skills. But in terms of literally every other possible skill that exists in the universe they're woefully unrounded.

Can you remember back to school and those harrowing times when you'd get your final report card with your final grades for that year? Imagine receiving a report card with the following grades:

English—A+
Maths—A+
History—A+
Chemistry—A+
Biology—D
Food Tech—A+
French—A+
Sport—A+

What would you have focused on? What would your parents have focused on? Wouldn't the conversation probably have started something like, "What happened in biology?"

But why?

Weakness fixation

All of us, whether we're parents or not, are fixated on trying to eliminate weaknesses. Marcus Buckingham, credited as the pioneer of the 'strengths revolution', writes:

> Most organizations take their employees' strengths for granted and focus on minimizing their weaknesses. They become expert in those areas where their employees struggle, delicately rename these 'skill gaps' or 'areas of opportunity,' and then pack them off to training classes so that the weaknesses can be fixed. This approach is occasionally necessary: If an employee always alienates those around him, some sensitivity training can help; likewise, a remedial communication class can benefit an employee who happens to be smart but inarticulate. But this isn't development, it is damage control. And by itself damage control is a poor strategy for elevating either the employee or the organization to world-class performance.
>
> As long as an organization operates under these assumptions, it will never capitalize on the strengths of each employee.[13]

We implicitly believe that we'll grow and make the most impact if we develop our weaknesses—even though we're absolutely certain that we'll never be good at everything, or even most things. While we know that we have strengths, instead of spending our time and energy developing those areas we seek to make our weaknesses not as bad. But the truth is that areas of opportunity are *not* areas of opportunity. You have the most potential for growth in your areas of strength.

Some people are extraordinarily good at administration while others are horrible at it. The time just flies for some people while they're filing and folding and filling in forms. For others, time grinds almost to a halt when they do those things.

Some people are extraordinarily good at speaking in front of groups. They're natural and relaxed and they love it. Others would rather do just

13 Marcus Buckingham and Donald O Clifton, *Now, Discover Your Strengths*, Free Press, New York, 2001, p. 8.

about anything else and either dread or avoid it entirely.

Some people are brilliant when it comes to hosting people in their homes and making guests feel comfortable and welcome and as though they're members of the family. Other people find extending hospitality very draining.

We're all different, and the key is to find your strengths and dive into developing them—while not being concerned that you're not good at everything else.

Strengths redefined

Marcus Buckingham, who has been writing about this subject for years, has redefined strengths and weaknesses in a very helpful way. He says that we usually define strengths as the things we're good at and weaknesses as the things that we don't do as well. This, he says, is close but not close enough. Sometimes it's true, but it's not always true. Instead, he says, we should define strengths as activities that make us stronger. After doing these activities we feel alive, satisfied, energized. The time seems to fly by when we're engaged in these activities—hours feel like minutes. And our weaknesses are those activities that make us feel weaker, drained, and tired. While we're doing these things time turns to molasses—minutes feel like hours.[14]

Here's the interesting part: sometimes our weaknesses, by this definition, can be things we're quite good at. And sometimes strengths—things that we enjoy and that energize us—will be things that we're not good at yet.

I'm quite good at administration. I know what needs to be done and I can design a process to get things done quickly and efficiently. I can set up a system to ensure numbers are tracked and data is input. I can figure out which data we need compared to what other data on what timescale and how we might visualize it. I can do all this easily and competently—I just hate doing it. After a day spent doing administrative tasks I feel weak, drained, and tired. Admin is a weakness of mine, even though I'm good at it.

You probably have skills and tasks like that in your life too—things that you can do well, maybe even very well, but that you hate doing. They

14 Marcus Buckingham, *Go Put Your Strengths to Work: 6 powerful steps to achieve outstanding performance*, Simon & Schuster, New York, 2011, pp. 85-6.

suck your energy so that you feel drained and dread having to do them again. That's because those things are actually some of your weaknesses.

Another way to discover your strengths is to be aware of times of rapid learning. Are there certain subjects you master extraordinarily quickly? Have you encountered new tasks or situations that you were able to grasp rapidly or areas in which you were able to gain expertise much more quickly than usual? Being able to learn something quickly is often a sign that you're encountering a strength.

But what about character weaknesses?

Before we get too carried away, I should note that this doesn't apply to everything in life. When it comes to character issues, like the fruit of the Spirit, we definitely need to continue to work on both strengths and weaknesses. It's not right to say, "Oh well, patience just isn't one of my strengths". We need to work on patience—especially if it's a weakness. It won't do to say, "I'm just not a faithful person. That's just how God made me." It's always important to work on all aspects of who we are, and when it comes to character maybe we need to work especially on our weaknesses.

As you're deciding where to put your time and energy, determine first whether or not a particular weakness is an aspect of your character. If it is, it's important to invest in that area. When it comes to talents and gifts, however, it's unrealistic and a waste of time to try and do that. Ignore your weaknesses as much as possible and focus on your strengths.

We can't ignore every weakness

Sometimes you will have weaknesses in a skill area that must be addressed. Even though you're playing to your strengths and leaning into your gifts, every now and then there will be a task that must be done—and it must be done by you. Sometimes there's no-one who can work with you to be strong where you are weak, no-one who can take the responsibility for that task from you. What do you do?

In that case it's appropriate and necessary to work on that particular weakness. If it's critical that this task be done, and be done by you, then you need to bite the bullet and invest the time to improve your skills so that this task doesn't hinder your ministry. It would be a waste of time to seek to become really great in this area or to try to make it a strength. As Buckingham says, this is damage control, not development. Become okay at it. Get good enough at it so that it doesn't undermine your strengths and wreck other things.

One way of tackling this is to ask yourself this question: Is there a way I can use one of my strengths to help me develop this weakness? That's a creative question. Look for a way that you can leverage one of your strengths in the process. Maybe admin is a weakness but one-on-one relationships are a strength. Is there a way you can have someone over to watch a movie or go out for coffee while you fold letters and stuff them into envelopes and talk about life and ministry as you work? That way you get to use a strength while you endure a weakness. It might take the edge off. Using a strength to develop a weakness will not only make the effort more bearable, it will also help you progress faster.

And, while you're doing that, be praying that God would provide you with someone who could help—someone with a strength in that area who could take that particular responsibility off you. Working in your areas of weakness should always be a temporary solution. Develop them so that they don't undermine you and your ministry, but don't make it your goal to be great at them.

If we were all eyes...

Anyone can get better at anything—that possibility is one of the delightful things about being human. But it's a smarter use of our time to try to improve skills and talents that are strengths instead of working on our weaknesses. The amount of time and energy we put into shoring up our weaknesses may help us improve to some degree, but the improvements will be small and incremental. If we were to spend that same amount of time and energy on our strengths, then the improvements would be far more substantial. We'll cover more ground and make more progress if we focus on areas where we're already strong.

We know this from the Bible. In 1 Corinthians Paul talks about gifts for many chapters. Although each one of us is gifted in some way, we don't all have the same gifts. We're not all ears. We're not all eyes. There are many parts but one body. Ears don't have to be eyes. Ears can be ears. God has made us this way. If you're an ear, instead of increasing your eye-ness focus on being a better ear. Be who you are. Don't feel guilty that you're not someone else.

Better together

Playing to our strengths both requires and helps foster interdependence. This is one of Paul's points in 1 Corinthians 12, where he gives us an image of the church as a body. We need each other. We can't do it without each other. As we identify our weaknesses we are to gather people around us who can complement us—people who are strong in those areas that drain us. This is how the body works together. The eye needs the foot and the foot needs the eye.

If you're an administration and systems person, then find a people person to work with you. If you're a big-picture person, then find a details person to help you implement. If you're a good initiator, find someone who can help you maintain things. If you're a creative ideas person, find a practical person to help you sift and choose between ideas. Gather a team around you so that together you can be as strong as possible.

God has designed all kinds of people with all kinds of strengths, and he has designed us to work together. We need each other. I need what you have and you need what I have. What you don't need to be is an all-rounder. Instead you need to identify your strengths and weaknesses and gather allies who can help you and complement you and cover your weaknesses while you cover theirs.

When it comes to character and Christlikeness, work on your weaknesses as well as your strengths. When it comes to skills and gifts, play to your strengths as much as you possibly can.

See also

47. Find the awesome
65. Everything has an upside and a downside

15

Change your default style

Not all leaders lead the same way. There are many different leadership styles: delegating, visionary, directional, authoritarian, strategic, managing, motivational, coaching, cheerleading, entrepreneurial, reengineering, and many more. Many of these styles overlap and all of them have their strengths and weaknesses. Some people lead with one style and some people can lead with a variety of styles. Everyone has a natural, or default, leadership style—a style that feels most organic and comfortable. You may or may not be conscious of what that style is, but either way there will be a natural groove that you slot into most easily where you don't need to concentrate on 'leading'.

Two mistakes

There are two big mistakes that leaders can make in this area. The first is to assume that a certain leadership style—usually the leader's own default style—is the only or best way to lead. While it's true that certain leadership styles are better suited for particular circumstances or for the individual temperaments of the people being led, it's not the case that any one leadership style is the only or best way to lead in any and all circumstances.

The second big mistake, which often stems from the first mistake, occurs when leaders use their default leadership style at all times without modifying it to suit the particular situation or person at hand. When the only tool you have is a hammer, everything will begin to look like a nail. If the only leadership style you use is an authoritarian, directive style you might function well in a crisis or with people who don't quite yet know what they're supposed to do, but you will frustrate and alienate highly competent and creative people. The wider the range of leadership styles available to you, the more flexible you can be in how you lead and the more effective and helpful you will be. The more you're able to tailor your leadership style to the situation, the better leader you'll be.

So far, so good. Not every person is the same and different people function best under different leadership styles. When we adapt our leadership style to the people and circumstances, we will be more effective. But there are still further advantages to having a range of leadership styles at our disposal—because it's not just different people who require different styles. Depending on their own growth as a leader and their skill and confidence level for each particular role or task they're taking on, a single individual will respond better to different styles of leadership at different times.

Individuals progress through a life cycle in the roles they take on that's similar to the life cycle of a team (see chapter 45, 'Understand the life cycle of a team'). Each of these stages is normal and predictable, and each stage requires a different kind of leadership. We'll talk first about the individual stages of development that people move through, then we'll talk about what the appropriate leadership style for each situation looks like.

Individual development

Each stage of a person's development is marked by a combination of either high or low competence and high or low enthusiasm.

Stage 1: Enthusiastic beginner

People in this stage are new to a role or responsibility. They're pumped up and excited. They don't really know what they're supposed to do or how to do it, but they're keen. They might not have been involved in leading anything before, or they might be very experienced leaders in a new role or responsible for a task they've never done before. Low competence, high enthusiasm.

Stage 2: Disillusioned learner

At this stage people have been doing the role for some time and are still learning what needs to be done. The task is harder than they first thought it was going to be, the learning curve is steep, and they feel like they're falling behind. They know enough to know that they aren't doing very well and have a fair way to go. This is the lowest point and the hardest stage to navigate. At this stage they feel the temptation to quit most strongly. Low competence, low enthusiasm.

Stage 3: Capable but cautious

These people have the basic skills and know-how to get the job done, but they're very conscious and deliberate about each step they take. The skills aren't 'natural' yet, but they can perform the tasks required at a satisfactory level. They're competent enough to handle the tasks on their own but are not yet convinced that they could do it alone. High competence, low enthusiasm.

Stage 4: Self-starting flourisher

These people can perform the task from start to finish. Most of the skill set is second nature. With information about the task and due date they can proceed to achieve it and be trusted to troubleshoot through most roadblocks autonomously. At this stage they might also perform at a high level—not simply doing what's required but fulfilling the role with a high degree of excellence. They might be ready for a new challenge. High competence, high enthusiasm.

Targeting your leadership style

Each person you lead will move through these stages at a different pace and will need to be led with a different style at each stage.

Stage 1 leadership: Directing

Enthusiastic beginners need clear instructions on exactly what is expected—what they need to do, how, and when. They're keen and energetic but will need you to point them in the right direction. The main things they need from you, their leader, are *clarity* and *information*. They'll need a highly directive leadership style and will need you to manage them quite closely.

Stage 2 leadership: Coaching

Disillusioned learners also need a fair amount of direction in terms of what needs to be accomplished because they're still learning exactly what the role requires and how to do it. But they also need a lot of encouragement and positive feedback to bolster their motivation. Because they're beginning to realize how much they don't know and can't do and how much they still have to learn, and because their initial enthusiasm is drying up, you'll need to help them weather the storm. They'll feel like they're failing and will need you to reassure them that this is normal. Keep looking for small wins, facets of things or steps in the process that they did well, and make sure to point them out so that they can see that it's not all bad. They'll need you to be attentive and to observe them closely without making them feel as though you're scrutinizing them. Sometimes it can be difficult to find examples of where they're improving and you'll need an extraordinary level of concentration. Reassurance from you that they're at least improving will be a big help in turning around their lack of motivation. At this stage what they need from you is mainly *feedback* and *encouragement*.

Stage 3 leadership: Supporting

Capable but cautious leaders don't need as much instruction or direction as they did previously, which means you'll need to give them more space and not manage them as closely. They'll also need a lot of time with you to talk through what they're doing and they'll need you to encourage them and assure them they're on the right track. Your job is to give them confidence. They can do the job but don't think they can. So they'll continue to ask you for advice and want to know what you think they should do. The temptation for you will be to keep telling them exactly what to do, as you've been doing in the previous two stages. But at this point you need to begin turning the question back to them and asking what they think the way forward is. At this stage they'll be able to come up with something pretty good, and your role is to encourage them and to help them refine their ideas. This will give them the confidence to make a decision. And, when it goes well, they'll have confidence to make another one. Then another one. And another. What they need most from you at this point is for you to take the time to *listen, reassure* them, and *build their confidence.*

Stage 4 leadership: Delegating

Self-starting flourishers just need you to give them the task and the due date. Give them space and freedom to do it their own way. Although their motivation is already high and it will probably stay high because they're doing a good job, you still need to be their cheerleader and encourager. The temptation for you as their leader at this stage will be to leave the person alone. That would be a mistake because, while they won't need as much of your time and oversight as they once did, they'll still need you to check in with them to see how things are and if there's anything you can do to help. You'll want to give them space without isolating them. At this point you can begin giving them other, related, tasks and more responsibilities. The main things they need from you at this stage are *trust* and *opportunities.*

In some cases the person you're leading will progress through these stages at a steady, even pace. Others will progress through one stage quickly and perhaps linger in another. Sometimes a person who has various different roles and responsibilities will be at a different stage for each role. You might, for example, have a very experienced team leader who's at stage four in that role but who has also been learning to preach for a while and is at stage two in that area of ministry. How you treat this person in their role as a preacher will need to be very different from how you treat them as a team leader.

Your default style will naturally suit one stage better than the other three stages. What you will need to do is develop your skills in those other three styles (directing, coaching, supporting, or delegating) so that you can lead each person individually such that he or she can perform their best, with minimal frustration, at each stage. Using a default style in every circumstance is fine for a novice leader. But as you transition to being an expert practitioner, your leadership will display more subtlety and you'll be able to be more nuanced in how you apply different leadership styles to different people under different circumstances.

Go beyond the default setting.

See also

28. Anything worth doing is worth doing badly

29. Praise publicly

45. Understand the life cycle of a team

16
Time management won't help you

For a long time I worked hard to manage my time well—to plan my schedule, allocate time to various tasks, minimize distractions, and so on. I read a couple of books on time management that were quite helpful and I listened to successful people speak about the importance and value of managing my time well. But there was still something that didn't quite sit right with me about the whole time management enterprise.

I only recently figured out what had been bothering me, but it has revolutionized the way I think about and approach my week. What I realized was that, as helpful as those time management practices are (and they are genuinely helpful), the reality is that time management doesn't actually exist.

It's all just a mirage. You can't actually do it. That's not to say that learning all of those traditional time management skills wasn't helpful or worth the effort. Planning your schedule is a good thing to do. Minimizing distractions is a good thing, and I'm glad I do it. Trying to handle a piece of paper or an email only once is a good thing—cutting down on double handling saves a lot of time. Writing lists of next action steps so I know what I need to do next is useful. An urgent/important matrix has clarified things for me for a long time. I understand why people write and read books about these disciplines and listen to speakers on these topics. But they're not really about time management, are they?

They're about self-management. What I realized was that all these skills and processes I was learning and implementing were very useful, but I wasn't actually managing time itself. I was just managing myself so that I didn't waste as much time.

So what I came to see is that I can't manage time, but I can manage energy. And that has turned the way I conceptualize and plan my work upside down.

You can't manage time

You can manage a lot of things: yourself, others, systems, businesses, your hair. But time is not one of those things. You can't make time go faster or slow it down. You can't make it more efficient. No matter what you do, you cannot increase the amount of time it outputs per minute. Time doesn't respect or care about you. It won't listen to you and it will not be managed by you. As they say, time will march on—with or without you.

As I said above, what we normally refer to as time management is really self-management. What you're doing is managing yourself—what you do within time and how focused you are with the time you have.

But thinking purely in terms of time and minutes and planning and distractions is still only part of the story. If time management is actually self-management, the question remains: What specifically about myself am I managing? What should I be thinking about and what tools should I be utilizing?

You can manage energy

We've all had the experience of blocking out two hours to work on a project and, at the end of that time, realizing that we've hardly achieved anything. Maybe your mind was wandering all over the place or felt like mush. Thoughts just weren't coming. At other times, though, you'll have a short block of time, maybe half an hour, and in that small window you're ultra-productive—thoughts flow, decisions are easy and obvious, and you're laser-focused. And you find that you've achieved a disproportionate amount of work in a quarter of the time. Why? Did you manage your time better in that half hour? Maybe—but maybe not. Time had very little to do with it. If it were purely about 'time spent' then it wouldn't work that way. But it does work that way because it's not really about time. It's also about energy.

One way to conceptualize this idea is found in the book *Leading on*

Empty by Wayne Cordeiro. His suggestion is to think about your day in terms of bursts of energy.[15] Everyone has a certain number of bursts of energy to spend across the day. It takes a bit of trial and error to work it out, but you need to determine how many of these bursts of energy you have each day. Maybe for you it's five. Maybe it's seven. Everyone is different.

Each day you have a finite amount of energy that you need to replenish before you can go again. Once you work out how much you have, you need to think carefully about how you'll assign that energy on a given day. If you have a meeting at night, it doesn't make sense to use up all of your energy before dinner. Do you want to assign all of your energy to work, so that you have nothing left for yourself or for your spouse and family? There used to be times when I'd finish work and come home with nothing left to give to my family. I was with them, but I wasn't present because I'd used up all my energy for work. That was definitely not a good way to manage my energy, and certainly not over the long term. There are still days when I finish work absolutely exhausted because I haven't managed my energy properly. But that's happening less and less because I'm getting better at it. I haven't forfeited the amount I've been able to achieve either. I've been managing my energy better and so I've actually been achieving more.

Your energy is a finite resource, but it's also depleted at different rates by different tasks. And, again, it doesn't have much to do with time. There are some activities I do that don't take up much time but take up a whole truckload of my energy, while other activities consume much more time but use up far less energy.

For me, leading either a wedding or a funeral depletes my energy very quickly. It's an amazing privilege to be a part of them—they just demand a lot of energy and, regardless of the circumstances, I find them equally draining. It's not the emotions or the time involved—these occasions just deplete a big chunk of my energy. So I need to manage my energy use carefully on days when I'm conducting weddings or funerals.

On the other hand, I find high-pressure, intense, combative, high-

15 Wayne Cordeiro, *Leading on Empty: Refilling your tank and renewing your passion,* Bethany House, Bloomington, 2010, pp. 117-21.

stakes three-hour meetings about staffing, strategizing or problem-solving very exciting and these kinds of meetings energize me. In certain cases I'll be more energized when I leave than I was when I arrived. Or put me in a room where we're going to discuss some aspect of theology and debate back and forth to try to figure out what the Bible really has to say about such-and-such and that won't drain my energy very much either.

You might understand what I mean here or you might have no idea why weddings and funerals, or meetings, would affect me this way. It's not about introversion or extroversion, because both involve stress and pressure and a lot of people. Those kinds of meetings drain some people incredibly quickly, and others find that officiating at a wedding or conducting a funeral doesn't drain them much at all. Everyone is different and it's important to think consciously about your own energy level and which tasks deplete and restore your energy.

Figure out how many bursts of energy you generally have each day. And then determine which of your necessary tasks require a large amount of energy and which only require a small amount of energy. With those insights, you can intentionally plan your days and weeks. You'll still need to watch and plan the timing of things, as there's only a certain amount of time in each day. But there's no use planning 26 hours of work per day. There's no use planning ten hours worth of work if you've only got eight hours in which to do it. You'll still need to manage your time in that sense. But, by the same token, you have only a certain amount of energy each day as well. There's no point planning to use eight bursts of energy per day when you only have five to give. That's a recipe for disaster. You'll either find ways to get more energy that will end up destroying you in the long term, or you'll end up doing a lot of important things really poorly.

By all means manage how you use your time to be more effective and efficient in the way you plan and administer certain activities. But remember that's self-management, not time management. It's impossible to manage time—but you can, and should, manage your energy.

See also

31. Energy is more efficient than efficiency

17
Arriving on time isn't what you think it is

Arriving on time isn't the same as driving into the driveway on time. You may have arrived at the venue on time, but you haven't arrived at the meeting or the appointment on time. You still need to park, make sure you have everything you need, get out of the car and lock it, walk to the door, and find the people you're there to see.

Arriving on time is about love

Arriving on time sometimes isn't what you think it is. It isn't about being born a certain type of person or coming from a certain type of family. Some people come from families that were always on time, while others come from families that were never on time. Some who grew up with being late are actually better about being on time as a reaction against that, but everyone needs to work hard to be on time. No-one consistently arrives on time naturally or by accident.

Arriving on time isn't a desirable option—as though there are many equally valid arrival options and, among those options, being on time is the ideal to aim for. For a Christian leader, being late sometimes will be a reality no matter how hard we try because we live in an imperfect world, but we need to do everything in our power to try to be on time. Arriving on time isn't an option.

Arriving on time is about love and respect for other people. It's about what you choose to value and what you want to communicate.

Arriving on time is about choosing what you value because when you show up to a meeting on time—regardless of whether you or someone else has scheduled the meeting—it shows respect to the rest of the team who worked hard and made choices so that they could arrive on time. If someone has come straight from work and didn't have time to go home and get changed or have something to eat but arrives on time to the meeting and then you wander in late, that dishonours their effort, lowers your standing in their eyes, increases their frustration with you—and perhaps with the ministry—and diminishes their loyalty to you. But when you arrive on time, you say with your actions that you recognize the value of other people's time. When you arrive on time, you show that you're serving the others with the way you use your time, considering them more valuable than yourself. When you honour someone's time you honour that person. And when you dishonour someone's time, you dishonour that person.

As the great theologian Karl Barth recognized:

> ...to have time for another, although in the abstract this says little, is in reality to manifest in essence all the benefits which one man can show to another. When I really give anyone my time, I thereby give him the last and most personal thing that I have to give at all, namely myself.[16]

Arriving on time is also important because it communicates to your team that they can rely on you and that you're a person who keeps your word. And if you demonstrate that you keep your word even in small things, like arriving when you say you will, that will give people confidence that you'll keep your word in bigger things. Being on time is a character issue. Can people trust and depend on you? Are you reliable? Will you do what you say you'll do? These are big questions that your team is always asking and that your actions are always answering.

What if you end up being late?

Sometimes, despite your best intentions and regardless of how much you love people and value them, you will be late. The best way forward when

16 Karl Barth, *Church Dogmatics I.2*, Hendrickson Publishers, Peabody, 2010, p. 55.

you're late for a meeting that you're running is to simply walk in and apologize genuinely—no excuses, no minimizing. Simply apologize to the whole team for being late, make sure you give everyone eye contact and thank them for being on time even though you weren't so that everyone knows you value their effort to get there when they said they would, and start the meeting. You might tell them your valid excuse a bit later on, or you might not. Excuses won't honour them, but an apology will.

If you're late to a meeting you're not running, enter the room, apologize briefly, and be as minimally disruptive as possible. Excuses and explanations won't help at that moment, and if your excuses sidetrack the meeting then you increase the impact of your lateness and make it worse. It's best to be genuinely sorry and minimally disruptive. Explain after the meeting; apologize during.

But if you plan ahead—taking into account the likelihood of forgetting your wallet, hitting all the red lights, getting a last-minute phone call, and everything else that could go wrong—and arrive on time, you communicate that this group and this meeting are important and that you will be there for them when they need you. Arriving on time is about showing love and respect and honour to others—and it's one of the most important, yet underrated, things you can do as a leader.

See also

26. Leading is loving
37. Phrases to learn

18

If you're not a good follower then you're not a good leader

In our world, and even in Christian circles, submission is often a four-letter word. For many people it carries connotations of inferiority, subjugation, ill treatment and abuse. And the word has those connotations for so many because that is often exactly how submission plays out in reality. Most people have had some experience with a domineering boss, a demeaning co-worker, or an aggressive spouse.

But those experiences aren't inherent in the concept of submission. Submission doesn't *have* to be that way. Submission has to do with role and context. When I'm driving my car and the policewoman asks me to stop and pull over, I submit to her. I don't do this because she's better than me or superior to me. But, because of her role and the context, I do what she says. But in church on Sunday, when I invite everyone to stand and sing our final song, the same woman (now sitting in the congregation) submits to me and stands when I ask her to. She doesn't submit to me because I'm better than she is but because of my role and the context.

Even beyond that, however, we know that submission isn't an inherently negative posture because it's the posture of our Lord Jesus. Even though he is equal to the Father in power, dignity, and nature, he willingly, joyfully, and enthusiastically submits to the Father in all things. He always has and he always will. And this submission doesn't make Jesus inferior to the Father in any way. Submission is an aspect of Christlikeness. Being a good follower, submitting to others, is essential to being a good leader because character and Christlikeness are essential for being a good leader. Following is about Jesus.

Willing and able

But hang on a second. Leaders aren't followers. That's the whole point, isn't it? Good followers follow good leaders. Don't good leaders need to be different from followers?

Yes, leaders do need to lead, and they are different from those who follow. Yet leaders must also be able to follow and submit. There are some leaders who cannot submit to the direction of others, who refuse to follow anyone else, who feel they must always call the shots and take the lead and run the show. Such leaders feel that they need to be in positions of power and authority and, if they must follow, they do it begrudgingly and with much difficulty. They cannot follow well and happily.

This is a problem—and it isn't about different people being wired differently. It's not about gifts and talents and personalities. It's about character. It's about servanthood and humility. It's about Christlikeness. If you cannot follow, then you cannot lead—not truly, or well, or in a deeply Christian way.

Part of what makes a leader a leader—though we don't often talk about this characteristic—is their desire to lead. It's natural that leaders will want to lead. But leaders must also realize that they don't *have* to lead and they still need to be able to follow. If you're a person who simply cannot submit, cannot align yourself to another, cannot let others make the call, or cannot follow well, then you won't have the necessary skills and characteristics to lead well.

When a leader works under another leader he or she must learn and display a number of key qualities: patience, ability to influence, negotiation, compromise, faithfulness, diligence, perseverance, and so on. Being able to work under a leader you don't respect, admire, or trust or like is a mark of maturity. If God has placed a leader over you, then he expects you to submit to that leader. That is his will for you, even if that person is bad or incompetent. It's important to note, however, that there's a big difference between an incompetent leader and an immoral leader. We'll talk more about this below.

Submitting to authority, being a follower, is a mark of maturity. Those who can't follow, or are unwilling to follow another leader, shouldn't lead. It's a lack of character that needs to be addressed.

Jesus shows us both

People will sometimes say that they simply can't be followers because they're born leaders. God has wired them that way. They need to get out there and run their own shows. These people are incredibly dangerous, because being able to follow is a heart issue. Being an exceptionally strong leader in no way impacts whether or not you can follow. It has nothing to do with it. In fact, we know that leading and following go together—because that's how Jesus does it. Jesus is the greatest leader the world has ever known and he submits to the Father in everything. If you're an exceptional leader then you will also be a great follower. Those who cannot follow are not good leaders—and they never will be until they can learn to submit to and follow others.

If the heart of leadership is servanthood, then the raw material that makes you a good leader will also make you a good follower. Followers serve, submit, obey, take orders, complete tasks, and help the team. Followers never make it all about themselves and always contribute to the larger objective. And if you can't do those things, then you can't lead well.

When it all goes wrong

At some point, however, you'll probably encounter a situation in which you'll find yourself unable to submit to a leader because of his or her bad leadership or incompetence. What then? What do you do when a leader takes you in a direction that you feel is so unwise you simply cannot follow?

First you need to clarify for yourself whether this is a right or wrong decision or a better or worse decision. Right or wrong decisions have to do with moral choices. My leader is asking me to join him in robbing a bank. What should I do? This isn't about preference or opinions. Stealing is wrong and dishonours God and your neighbour. Better or worse decisions, on the other hand, have nothing to do with moral choices. Your leader thinks that singing five songs in the Sunday service is best and you think it would be better to have four. It's important to you, but it's not a moral issue.

The second thing you need to do when you disagree with your leader in a certain area is to articulate what you think is the problem with this decision and why you think it's a problem. You should then—and this is very important—formulate an alternative course of action that you think is better. You can make your case much more persuasively when you can propose an alternate course of action.

After you've thought through the issue in this way, you'll need to communicate with your leader—not with every other person on the team or everyone else you know. Your leader is still your leader at this point, and you need to make sure they understand that you're still seeking to submit to them. They need to know that this is the framework for the conversation before you put your case forward as persuasively as you can. You articulate what you see the problem to be, and you propose your alternative solution, and you do your absolute best to change your leader's mind.

If you persuade this leader to change his or her mind, good job. You get on with it. Sometimes you won't change their mind, but instead the leader will explain a broader context or share more information that will help you better understand the decision that's been made. Your leader might end up persuading you but, whether you end up agreeing or not, part of your submission to this person as your leader is to listen, to seek to understand, and to be willing to be convinced. But what if you've listened carefully but are not convinced and still have serious concerns about the decision?

The answer to this question depends on whether it was a right or wrong issue or a better or worse issue. If the latter, then it's your job as a follower to do everything you can to make that decision work and make the outcome the best it can be. You did what you could to persuade the leader otherwise, but as a member of that team it's now your responsibility to execute the leader's decision with the same energy and enthusiasm you'd pour into implementing your own idea. If you simply can't go along with it, you cannot remain on the team and seek to undermine that initiative, either actively or passively. At that point you need to talk to your leader and respectfully remove yourself from the team. But if it's purely a matter of preference or style or if it's about whose idea is better, a mark of maturity will be your ability to submit and contribute with everything you have.

If, however, the decision involves an issue of right and wrong and you cannot, in good conscience, submit to it, you must step down from the team. If your leader is demanding that you do something you believe is immoral and rebellious towards God, you are under no obligation to submit. In that case you explain to the leader, respectfully and humbly, that while you really wish you could submit to them, your obligation is first to the Lord—and so since you cannot do what they are asking you to do you are removing yourself from the team.

While I hope you never find yourself in this kind of situation, it does happen and it's wise to have a strategy in place to deal with it. In all this, the heart of the matter is a genuine desire to submit to leadership. As a last resort, however, you might sometimes need to say, "I'm sorry. I cannot submit to you in this."

Model what you expect

As a leader you must also be a good follower because the people you lead will, to a certain extent, take their cues from you. The way you treat the person who leads you will show people who are following you how you think they should treat you. You will model how they're to act when they disagree with you by the way that you react when you disagree with those who lead you. Is the way you treat your leaders the way you'd like your team to treat you? You're modelling how to speak about another leader regardless of whether you respect that leader or not, how to work wholeheartedly to accomplish someone else's vision, and so on.

This is especially true if the person who leads you, and under whom you work, is far from perfect and not the best leader in the world. Because the people you lead are also under a person who's far from perfect and who isn't the best leader in the world.

You want your team to act a certain way towards you, and you want them to speak about you in a certain way—especially when they find it difficult to work with you. So you will need to model this for them. Treat your leaders the way you'd want your people to treat you.

Being a good follower is at the core of Christian leadership. If you're a great leader, that means you must also be a great follower.

19
Leaders have to give up to go up

Leadership is servanthood. Your job as a leader is to serve those you lead and to do everything you can to develop them and benefit them. The more people you have to lead, the more people you have to serve.

Sometimes when you first start out as a leader it can be tempting to look at the people higher in leadership over you and think to yourself, "I can't wait to be in that position. I'll be able to do what I want and I'll have lots more flexibility. The more authority and responsibility I have, the more freedom I'll have to do what I want." But that's not how it works—and especially not in Christian leadership.

When you're one of the people, the followers, the organization exists to benefit you. Anyone who's in leadership will be serving you, either directly or indirectly. When you're a new Christian, the whole thing is about helping you to grow and develop. There are official courses and structures and groups designed to help and serve you. There will also be a whole lot of horizontal acts of service taking place—people serving you who aren't a part of any official structure. And that's a good thing. Sooner or later, you're encouraged to begin serving those around you as well.

Service is sacrifice

But as you grow in your faith you begin to lead others, whether in an official capacity with a title or in an unofficial capacity as you reach out to love and serve those around you (meeting with another person over coffee to read the Bible, for example). And as this happens it becomes more about others and less about you. You focus on what's best, most helpful, and most beneficial for the people you're serving.

Leaders and organizations sometimes forget this and think that the higher up you go the more it becomes about you, the more the organization's practices are shaped around you. But leadership is servanthood, and the more you lead the more you serve. And the more you serve, the more you will sacrifice. Leadership is never about getting more perks and titles and positions.

Leadership requires a sacrifice of time and a sacrifice of preferences. Sometimes you'll need to sacrifice what you want to do or what interests you in order to put time into the people you're leading and to deal with their issues and concerns.

As you lead more and more, it will all become less and less about you in countless ways. The more you lead, the more sacrifice is required of you. The more you lead, the more you're required to serve. The more authority and responsibility you have, the less freedom you have to do whatever you want.

When you're a member of a small Bible study group, for example, you have a certain level of commitment to the group and to the other people in the group. But when you feel a bit under the weather, or you have a competing commitment, you can just skip the group. And people do—maybe they shouldn't, but they do. When you're responsible for leading the group, however, that option isn't open to you. It's not particularly relevant whether you feel like it or not. You need to be faithful and you need to be there and so, in this way, when you move from being a member of a group to being a leader you don't gain freedom; you give up freedom.

And the more leadership responsibility you accept, the more you'll need to give up. If you expect it to be different you'll either be bitterly disappointed and frustrated with the people you're supposed to be serving or you'll twist your leadership so as to make it all about you and your comfort and prestige—and in the process the people you're supposed to be serving will become disillusioned by your selfishness.

Christian leadership is about servanthood and so, though it might at first seem counterintuitive, as you gain authority you will lose freedom. Which means that leaders will need to give up as they go up.

20

People who praise you are probably just as mistaken as those who criticize you

We were preaching through the book of Mark a few years ago at our church and the time came for me to preach Mark 13. Mark 13 is a notoriously difficult, and therefore very controversial, chapter. There are about as many views on what Jesus is talking about as there are commentaries.

In brief, the basic point of my sermon, right or wrong, was that I think in Mark 13 Jesus begins by talking about the destruction of the temple and transitions to talking about his own upcoming crucifixion. Where exactly that transition occurs I'm not really sure, and I change my mind every alternating Tuesday.

So I preached the sermon and explained why I think what I think. At the end of the service I stood at the front door of the church and shook hands and said goodbye to people as they left—the ancient and venerable practice in the Anglican church known as 'facing the music'. There happened to be a visiting minister from a local church there that morning as he was on holiday. He's a fellow labourer in the difficult task of building the church and preaching the Word, someone who understands what it's like to struggle over the Scriptures and preach the Word in weakness. He's a brother who I could sow into and who could sow into me and, like iron sharpens iron, we could spur each other on in the honourable yet overwhelming task of proclaiming the gospel to a dying world. On the way out I thanked him for coming, wished him the best for the rest of his holidays, and expressed my wish that the gospel would ring forth from his church with ever greater blessing—or some other appropriate benediction to that effect. He shook my hand and, before letting go, pulled me close and looked right into my eyes and scowled, "It must be nice to get paid to not know things". I didn't know what to say. So I said, "See ya". He left. I didn't feel as sharpened as I was hoping I would.

A constant companion

Criticism is the constant companion of any leader, and certainly of any Christian leader. It's simply the air we breathe—the painful and sometimes crushing air we breathe. One reason for this criticism, which can feel constant, is that we're rarely able to please everybody. There will always be people who thought the other idea was better, and they will let you know. Another reason is that, as a leader, you're not trying to just do what everyone wants. Rather, you're trying to do what's right—whether it's popular or not. It's true that if you're a leader but no-one is following you then you're actually not leading; you're just out for a walk. But it's also true that you're not really a leader unless you go for a walk because you know it's right and you're willing to have no-one come with you. Henry Ford, inventor of the motor car, once said that if he did what people wanted then he would have invented a faster horse. He didn't give them what they knew they wanted; he gave them what he knew they needed. What all this means is that if you're a leader then people will criticize you. They'll criticize you when you do a bad job and they'll criticize you when you do a great job.

You can't tell, therefore, whether you're doing a good job or a bad job based on the level of criticism—because you'll be criticized either way. Criticism is an ever-present reality. (If it's not, that might be because either you're not actually leading anything or you've trained people to not communicate the criticism directly to you, which just means they're telling it to everyone but you).

So if criticism will be an ever-present reality for us as leaders, then the question is this: What do we need to know in order to cope and deal well with it? We need to be aware of three main things when it comes to dealing with criticism.

People who praise you are probably just as mistaken as those who criticize you

CH Spurgeon knew what he was talking about when he wrote about ministry, and in this matter of criticism in particular he has plenty to teach us.

Everyone loves being praised, but criticism is often hurtful. We're usually more than happy to receive praise, and we accept and cherish those compliments. But rarely is this the case with criticism. We're much more discerning about criticism. "Are they right? They're probably not, but is there a kernel of truth in what they said? No, probably not."

When people are happy they're normally content to cruise along and you don't often hear from them. But when something upsets them and they aren't happy, they let you know. This means that, as a leader, you'll normally hear more criticism than you will praise. And that's normal and to be expected.

One of the problems this unbalanced volume of feedback creates is that we correspondingly skew our reception towards receiving praise, because it's relatively so rare, and away from criticism, because it's so constant. This is almost always an unconscious coping mechanism, but it leads to us becoming much less discerning of praise than we are of criticism. We accept all praise as probably true, but we're sceptical of criticism.

In reality, though, we're probably more often than not right when it comes to our critics and wrong when it comes to our supporters. Our critics often don't have all the information. They don't understand all of the factors we face, which means that their criticism often doesn't account for the actual circumstances and the options we had available. But the same is also true of those who praise us—they don't know all the information or understand all the factors and circumstances either.

We need to be able to downgrade both praise and criticism. Both can be very helpful and also very wrong.

Here's how Spurgeon puts it:

> ...it is always best not to know, nor to wish to know, what is being said about you, either by friends or foes. Those who praise us are probably as much mistaken as those who abuse

us, and the one may be regarded as a set off to the other, if indeed it be worth while taking any account at all of man's judgement. If we have the approbation of our God, certified by a placid conscience, we can afford to be indifferent to the opinions of our fellow men, whether they commend or condemn. If we cannot reach this point we are babes and not men...

[Renounce] the love of self. Judge it to be a small matter what men think or say of you, and care only for their treatment of your Lord.[17]

Focus on the gift

Every critic is your friend. They might not realize that, but they are. Whether they give you criticism with love and care or criticize you out of hatred while trying to tear you down, every critic is giving you a gift. How? Every critic is helping you get better. And just because some of them are rude about it doesn't mean they're not right or deeply insightful—or at least partially right. Whether they wrap the gift carefully and lovingly or give it to you in the bag from the place where they bought it, the wrapping doesn't change the value of the gift. You cannot buy openness and honesty; as soon as you pay for it, it becomes compromised. No amount of money can purchase this kind of candour, so whatever you do don't despise it when it is given to you.

It's easy to focus on the manner in which a person delivers criticism. The words they use, the timing, their tone. All of those elements can be unhelpful or hurtful, but if you want to grow as a leader you need to discipline yourself to look past these elements. Let yourself feel the pain, wish that it could have been different, and be upset if you need to be—but it needs to be a short visit; you can't stay there. You need to push past the hurt and get to the substance of the criticism. What was the person actually saying? Is there any truth to it? How could you do it better next time? What can you learn from this? As difficult as it can be, you have

17 CH Spurgeon, *Lectures to My Students*, Christian Focus, Ross-shire, 1998, pp. 368-9, 371.

to overlook the manner and ugliness of the wrapping so that you can carefully examine the gift.

Both praise and criticism should be weighed, not counted

Along with your critics, you will no doubt also have a number of raving fan boys and fan girls who just love and support everything you do no matter what. There's also probably a group or two somewhere in between. Not everyone will like everything or everyone. There will always be both praise and criticism. The temptation is to count—the number of people who praise and the number of people who criticize. If there's more praise than criticism, we conclude, then it was good—and if there's more criticism than praise it wasn't good.

This counting method is a bad idea because not all opinions are created equal. Everybody has an opinion and everyone is entitled to that opinion. But that doesn't mean that every person's opinion is as valuable or accurate or thoughtful as every other person's opinion. Most people who have an opinion on something aren't qualified to form it, even though they're entitled to hold it. But just because they're entitled to form an opinion and hold it and even share it doesn't mean that I'm obligated to venerate it, take it onboard, or even care about it.

If we go ahead with the counting method then the temptation will be, whether it's a conscious or unconscious decision, to either seek out the opinions we're after and avoid the ones we don't want to hear, or else to surround ourselves with a court of fan boys and fan girls so that we always hear more praise than criticism. Creating a court of yes-men and fan boys and fan girls is not a wise way to proceed.

But, rather than counting praise and criticism, we need to weigh it. Some people will have a problem with, and criticize, everything. So their criticism on a particular issue won't usually be that weighty. That doesn't mean you should write them off and ignore them. As they say, even a broken clock is right twice a day. But if the person is generally critical you can treat their criticism as less weighty.

Similarly, praise from the person who always tells you that you're brilliant and the best and that you do everything well—though nice and probably kind-hearted—shouldn't automatically be weighted highly.

But when you find people who are insightful or can be counted on to always tell it like it is, good or bad, you'll want to give more weight to their opinions. Or when someone offers you feedback on a topic that is within her area of expertise, you will probably give more weight to her thoughts than you would to the opinion of someone with no knowledge in that area.

In practice, this counting method normally means that if 50 people criticize you and one person praises you, it will feel like you've done a bad job or made the wrong call. And yet, while we often come to that conclusion, we know that the numbers themselves don't provide enough information for us to be able to make that judgement. What if the 50 people are all fools, or they all hate you for other reasons and so are biased against you on this issue? And what if the one person who praises you is the only person with any expertise in this area? Or what if the other hundred people who wanted to praise you had to go home early and so didn't get the chance to tell you?

Counting is generally a good skill to have, as is being open to criticism. But when it comes to determining the value of that criticism, counting isn't a good idea. Both praise and criticism should be weighed instead of counted.

Those who are in leadership need to expect criticism. Seek out people you can trust and listen to them. And be slow to write off your critics. They just might be saying something useful.

See also

21. If you're planning on not being hurt then you're planning on not being a leader

21

If you're planning on not being hurt then you're planning on not being a leader

One of the fundamental principles that many people seem to build their lives around is the avoidance of pain. As a general rule, that's what I do. If I can do something the hard way or the easy way, I choose the easy way. Why not?

At the shops, if I have to buy more than five items I use a trolley. Most people do—rather than trying to balance everything in a giant, wobbling stack in one arm. We don't create a pile of our purchases at the front of the store and walk back and forth to dump new items on the ground in our pile. Getting a trolley is so automatic you probably don't even think of the more difficult and time-consuming alternatives. Similarly, if I'm undergoing surgery—maybe getting all of my wisdom teeth hacked out and ripped from my skull—I'll take the anaesthetic thanks. Why wouldn't I?

The problem of pain avoidance

We've invented lots of ways to avoid pain in many different areas of life. And most of them are good and wise. The problem comes when we try to avoid pain above all else. That's a problem first of all because it's impossible, and second of all because making pain avoidance our top priority often leads to worse pain.

If you're already experiencing the pain of an inflamed appendix, for example, but try to avoid the pain of surgery, then sooner or later you'll experience excruciating pain, and probably death, from a septic and exploded appendix. In many different instances, trying to avoid pain only leads to worse pain.

Avoiding pain is also impossible because, if you're a Christian, you're promised suffering. You might only suffer a little; you might suffer a lot. As Paul explains to Timothy, "Indeed, all who desire to live a godly life in Christ Jesus will be persecuted" (2 Tim 3:12). Even more than that, however, if you're a Christian you have been called to love—to love God and to love others. And because both you and those you love are broken by sin, your relationships will be the cause of both joy and pain. Sometimes it will be the pain of conflict, sometimes it will be pain caused by misunderstanding, and other times it will be the pain of loss.

Trying to avoid all relational pain will only lead to a deep, isolating pain. CS Lewis describes this powerfully:

> To love at all is to be vulnerable. Love anything, and your heart will certainly be wrung and possibly be broken. If you want to make sure of keeping it intact, you must give your heart to no-one, not even to an animal. Wrap it carefully round with hobbies and little luxuries; avoid all entanglements; lock it up safe in the casket or coffin of your selfishness. But in that casket—safe, dark, motionless, airless—it will change. It will not be broken; it will become unbreakable, impenetrable, irredeemable.[18]

It's a good idea to avoid avoidable pain and stupid pain, like slamming your fingers in the car door or dropping a brick on your foot or falling down the stairs. Definitely avoid that kind of pain if you can. But some pain, as we'll see, is purposeful and necessary. It's a mistake to try and avoid this kind of pain. Instead we need to embrace it.

18 CS Lewis, *The Four Loves: The much beloved exploration of the nature of love*, Harcourt Brace, New York, 1960, p. 121.

Leading is pain

If you're a leader, you will come to know and love people who are suffering deeply. Most people have a story, one they don't recount very often, of deep wounds and profound hurt—and they carry this story everywhere they go. Count it a privilege if they choose to tell you their story. That's one kind of pain—sharing the pain of others.

If you're a leader, you will also encounter people who hurt you. Some will lash out and hurt you intentionally—and perhaps you'll deserve it, perhaps you won't. Some people will hurt you unintentionally, but the pain will be equally real.

A third kind of pain comes from leading itself. Because leading is about authority and responsibility, leaders need to make decisions. Leadership is knowing where we are and where we need to be and doing whatever we need to do, for however long we need to do it, to get there. Sometimes we'll make decisions that are good and right but also painful. Other times we'll make bad decisions that will be very costly to ourselves or to others. As leaders, we're the focal point—often for good things, but also for criticism. And, sooner or later, the criticism will hurt even the most self-assured person with skin as thick as an elephant's. We will receive criticism from others as well from ourselves.

Leading is pain. It's part of the job. And if you're planning on not being hurt then you're planning on not being a leader. If you haven't already, you need to accept this fact, stop being surprised by pain, and start expecting it.

Even as you read this you can probably think of some necessary pain that you should have been walking into that you have, instead, been avoiding. Maybe you've been avoiding a hurting person and secretly hoping that someone else will love them. Maybe you're putting off a painful conversation you know you need to have with someone. Maybe you can't quite bring yourself to pull the trigger on a painful decision that you know you need to make.

All of us will have to face these kinds of decisions and situations from time to time. You might even feel as though these are the only types of situations you ever face. But you can't keep avoiding them. The more you walk away from this kind of necessary pain, the more you abdicate and undermine your own leadership.

If pain is an inevitable and normal part of leadership and we know we need to embrace necessary pain in order to lead people toward the place they need to go, how can we stop avoiding it? How can we increase our pain threshold?

The answer is that, instead of avoiding pain, we start avoiding two other things. First, we avoid procrastination. And second, we avoid being people-pleasers.

Let's call him Chad

Most of the time we know what we should do. When we encounter a difficult circumstance, a difficult person, a difficult conversation, or a difficult decision, most of the time these things are not difficult because we don't know what to do. Usually we know what to do but just don't want to do it because we're afraid of the pain.

I was once at a church with an extraordinarily difficult person on my team. Let's call him Chad. Chad was often negative, mean, and cruel to people, but in the blink of an eye he could be very nice and kind. He was very faithful to the ministry, but at the same time he was also passive aggressive. He could be very rude and snarky. Nothing was ever his fault. He refused to take responsibility and always blamed someone or something else. He was defensive, prickly to deal with, and he was a toxic member of any team or group.

You might know a person like Chad.

Chad's behaviour often brought his immediate leader to tears. But in conversations about these behaviours Chad never acknowledged that anything was his fault and so never apologized. The problem was never in the room. Chad would then get upset, claiming that he was being picked on and intimidated.

Did I mention he was very difficult to deal with?

The whole team wanted to love Chad and so they gave him a lot of grace and endured a lot of hurtful behaviour. We were praying for a change and really wanted him to pull through. We wanted to see the best and think the best and hope for the best. But after two years of Chad being on the team, nothing had changed and the team was hurt and frustrated. We had met with Chad multiple times over those two years to talk through the issues. He met first with his direct leader, then with another team leader, and then, finally, I met with him—several different times.

We wanted to show love and grace even at the end, although many people advised me just to get rid of him and tell him, "Thanks for coming". Maybe they were right and I was wrong—maybe I was too gracious. Perhaps my 'grace' was just a mask for cowardice.

But, although it was the last thing I wanted to do, I knew I had to do something. I wanted to ignore it, write another sermon, meet one-on-one with one of my favourite friends for a vanilla malt thickshake. I would have preferred to do anything else. If the options were between having this conversation with Chad and shaving my legs with a cheese grater, I'd need to flip a coin.

But it was becoming a huge problem—not just for the immediate team but for the wider team as well. So finally we organized a meeting and I sat down with him and was as clear and as explicit as I could be, outlining the issues we had discussed many times over the two years and pointing out how nothing had changed. I tried to be as kind as I could be. I didn't want to be angry or accuse him of anything. I was very conscious of talking about *what* had happened and not speculating about *why* it might have happened. After outlining the issues we'd been talking about for two years I explained that I didn't want to talk about those issues anymore. Instead I wanted to talk about a new problem—the problem that talking about these things wasn't working. And I told him that we really needed to see some improvements soon—by the end of the next term, ten weeks away. We weren't looking for perfection, but we wanted to see progress. And I made it clear that we wanted to work with him and help him to see that happen.

And let me say, it turned out brilliantly.

Well, that's what I'd like to say. But the truth is that it couldn't have gone worse.

Chad was blisteringly angry. I received multiple emails from him after the meeting that were absolutely scathing. Other people on the team received similar emails. I received emails from Chad's parents that tore me apart. People who didn't even go to our church were calling me up, writing me emails, asking how I could have treated him so poorly? "I don't care what you do, you need to make this right. You need to apologize." And on and on it went. It was awful.

Now my point is not that I'm somehow special because I went through this. I'm not telling you this for sympathy or because a counsellor was too expensive. I'm telling you this precisely because I'm not special. I'm telling you this because this is normal—not that it happens every day, but it's certainly not unique. You probably have your own stories like this. Maybe yours are even worse. We should hang out.

But I had to walk towards the pain. Avoiding it was a terrible idea. I've performed an autopsy on this entire saga multiple times, and the only thing I regret is that I moved too slowly. I should have taken this step many months earlier.

Almost as soon as Chad left, the team was a thousand times better. The difference was palpable. The team was so much healthier, so much happier, so much more open, so much more relaxed. The tangible difference was amazing.

And maybe part of waiting so long—almost two years—was wanting to be gracious and to show love and to believe the best of people. But along with that desire there was also probably a whole bunch of wanting to be *seen* to be gracious and to be *seen* to be loving. And mixed in with all of that was the plain old problem of being a coward and being afraid to walk towards the pain.

Which leads to the second danger to avoid.

Being a people-pleaser

Wanting to be a people-pleaser is one of the most dangerous temptations leaders face. Everyone wants to be liked and needed. There's often a fine line between serving people and being a people-pleaser—and sometimes we find ourselves doing things and serving people *so that* people will like us. It can be so subtle that we don't even notice it's happening. But little by little we stop doing what's right and start doing what people want us to do. And because sometimes the right thing is also what people want, it can be hard to spot that we've made the switch. Often it only becomes clear when what's right is diametrically opposed to what someone wants us to do. But as soon as you stop doing what's right you begin forfeiting leadership.

The reason that Paul often warns against people-pleasing is that it's such a strong temptation for the Christian leader. So, for example, in 1 Thessalonians 2:4 he says, "so we speak, not to please man, but to please God who tests our hearts". And in Galatians 1:10 he says, "For am I now seeking the approval of man, or of God? Or am I trying to please man? If I were still trying to please man, I would not be a servant of Christ."

Do you notice the stark contrasts he sets up? You either please people or you please God. You live either for God's approval or for the approval of others. And, most challenging of all: if you try to please people then you're not a servant of Christ. For Paul this is absolutely critical. It's either God or people. Sometimes what God wants will also please the people. But we need to be absolutely vigilant that we don't slide from pleasing God to pleasing people. It wrecks our leadership, it puts us on a trajectory that will wreck our ministries, and in the end it will wreck our lives.

You might be wondering why I say that people-pleasing will wreck not just your ministry but also your life. It's because becoming obsessed with what people think about you is one of the fastest ways to forget what God thinks about you. And once you lose sight of what God thinks about you, it won't be long before you're overwhelmed by the contradictions of the crowd. Once you lose that anchor—that your identity is found in Christ alone—it won't be long before you're swept out to sea.

It's not that simple

People-pleasing is bad. But it's not that simple. While it's true that Paul often speaks very firmly against people-pleasing, that's not the only way he speaks about it. 1 Corinthians 10 is the conclusion of a very long and nuanced argument that begins in 1 Corinthians 8. We can't follow all the brilliant twists and turns of his argument here, but the main point is the importance of love. You may have knowledge, but you must use it in love. You may have freedom and rights, but you must use your freedom in love. This is a sacrificial love, which means inconveniencing yourself for the good of others. Everything you do should be governed and ruled by love.

But in 1 Corinthians 10, Paul says:

> Give no offense to Jews or to Greeks or to the church of God, just as I try to please everyone in everything I do, not seeking my own advantage, but that of many, that they may be saved. (vv. 32-33)

Paul doesn't want to offend anyone; he's trying to please everybody in every way. And he's not just trying to please them by doing things that he likes doing anyway. No, Paul says he's doing everything he can, regardless of his own preferences, to please *everybody* in *every* way.

All this sounds a lot like people-pleasing, which, as we've seen, he issues stern warnings about in other places. So is he contradicting himself? Well, no. And the distinction Paul makes here is very important for those of us who are in Christian leadership.

The important difference

Being a people-pleaser means that you do whatever makes people happy in order to make things easy for yourself. You do what people want so that they will like you more, or love you more, and so that you can avoid pain and hard decisions.

The pleasing people that Paul talks about in 1 Corinthians 10, however, is not for his own good but for their own good. It's about the good of others and doing what's best for them. This kind of people-pleasing isn't about wanting to be loved by others or making life easier for yourself. It's about seeking the good of others—even if that entails inconvenience and pain for you. And what is this good that he wants for them? "That they may be saved." This is very different from people-pleasing, and seeking the good of others is one of the ways that you increase your pain threshold.

The salvation of others was Paul's chief concern. Everything he did, he did for the glory of God and for the salvation of other people. He used his knowledge and his freedom not for himself and for his own sake, to please himself and make life easy for himself, but so that others might be saved.

The more we're able to keep this goal front and centre in our own hearts, the easier it will be to walk towards the pain. We'll endure pain and setbacks and difficult circumstances and difficult conversations—all for the good of others, that they might be saved.

As you increase your pain threshold, you will more readily walk into the mess and pain of the people and circumstances around you. And you'll be able to lead into that pain and then out through it. I hesitate to say that leading through pain will become easier, because I'm not sure that it does. But it will become easier to accept. And often the fear of the hit is worse than the hit itself, and the more you get hit and see that you can absorb it, the less you'll fear it.

Walk towards the pain and accept it. Because if you're planning on not being hurt then you're planning on not being a leader.

See also

20. People who praise you are probably just as mistaken as those who criticize you

22
Develop your forgettory

People with hyperthymesia, an extremely rare condition, retain an enormous amount of information about their life experiences. They can remember every detail of what they did every day going back years and sometimes decades—what the weather was like, what day of the week it was, what they were wearing, what they ate for each meal, and so on.

One such person with hyperthymesia is a woman in California called Jill Price. She has an amazing memory, and at first it sounds like a superpower you'd love to have. It would make tests, for example, so much easier if you could memorize literally everything. But unfortunately it doesn't work that way. The ability doesn't extend to memorizing things like facts for school. It only seems to function for facts and experiences that are directly related to her everyday life.

Jill says she finds this "agonizing" and "completely exhausting". Because, along with all the good memories she has, she also remembers every bad memory with stunning clarity. Every moment of pain, every emotional wound, every angry and hurtful word, every mistake, every disappointment, and every failure are all vividly alive in her mind as though they happened only minutes ago. She became deeply depressed and even believed she was going crazy.[19]

Forgetting is a virtue

Forgetting often gets a bad rap. We're inconvenienced and even hurt by losing the car keys, misplacing the remote, and forgetting important

19 Samiha Shafy, 'The science of memory: an infinite loop in the brain', *Spiegel Online International*, Berlin, 21 November 2008 (viewed 7 February 2015): http://www.spiegel.de/international/world/the-science-of-memory-an-infinite-loop-in-the-brain-a-591972.html

meetings or birthdays or anniversaries. And forgetting can have much more serious implications, like Freud's theory of repression and the pain of Alzheimer's. But forgetting is often not a failing of the mind or a passive process. For decades now psychologists have been saying that forgetting is actually an active, though often subconscious, process. More than that, they say that forgetting is, almost counterintuitively, a vital part of the process of remembering. Your brain is constantly working at an amazing speed to sort, arrange, evaluate and delete information that it doesn't think will be needed again. People often don't realize, however, that forgetting is also a vital part of emotional health.

Neuroscientists know that the inability to forget can hinder or even obstruct emotional recovery in trauma victims. Our brains are designed to forget as well as remember. And remembering can be just as unhealthy as forgetting. Most people are bad at forgetting things—and leaders certainly aren't exempt from this problem.

Now you might say, "Hang on just a second, I don't think that's my problem. I think I'm too good at forgetting things. I forget a lot of things. It's one of the things I do best. What I need is to learn how to remember things like names, dates, and appointments. Forgetting things is probably an overdeveloped strength, if anything."

There may be truth in that. You probably do need to remember things better. And you probably forget a lot of things. If you're anything like me, you've forgotten most of the things you've ever said or done. You forget most of the things you read. You've forgotten the majority of things that have happened to you. When people ask me, trying to start a conversation, "Hey man, what did you get up to today?" My usual answer is, "To be honest I have, quite literally, no idea. But I'm pretty sure it was productive. I may have eaten a sandwich." If you try to remember all the ads you saw yesterday on TV, billboards, or posters you can probably remember a few. Maybe some of you will remember a dozen or so. The industry rule of thumb is that you saw as many as 5000 ads yesterday.[20] But thankfully you've already forgotten most of them. Forgetting is normal and necessary.

20 Louise Story, 'Anywhere the eye can see, it's likely to see an ad', *The New York Times*, 15 January 2007 (viewed 7 February 2015): http://www.nytimes.com/2007/01/15/business/media/15everywhere.html

But just because you do something a lot doesn't mean that you're good at it. So just because you forget a lot of things, the vast majority of things even, that doesn't mean you're good at it. We often forget the wrong things. And we remember the wrong things too. We remember things we shouldn't.

I'm not talking about violent, abusive, traumatic incidents that require genuine professional counselling. Suppressing these experiences without properly dealing with them is not a good idea. I'm talking about fully facing a negative memory, remembering what happened, learning from it, and then letting it slip into non-memory.

Over-remembering

All of us have these negative memories of normal, everyday occurrences that we normally would, and should, forget. But instead we hold on to them and obsess over them. Our anger or embarrassment or hurt inhibits the natural process whereby memories fade, and we remember things that should have been forgotten long ago.

These memories include social situations where you said the wrong thing and made a fool of yourself. You remember with blistering precision times when you tripped or fell and embarrassed yourself in public. And you remember how people laughed. You remember times when you tried something and failed. You might remember things people said in ridicule. You remember how awful and small you felt. You remember times when people spoke harsh criticism to you that still feels like a block of ice in your stomach. These kinds of memories are vivid, often playing on a continuous loop in your mind. They gnaw at you.

Many of these memories involve the opinions of people whom you wouldn't normally be concerned about at all. And you might assume that everyone else remembers these incidents with the same clarity that you do. You might wonder if people think about them often, if these things are what they think about when they think about you and talk to you. You'd probably be shocked to know how little other people actually think about these incidents at all—most of them have probably forgotten what you've chosen to remember.

How to develop your forgettory

So if you're remembering certain things—like embarrassments, failures, disappointments, unduly harsh criticism—that it would be healthier for you to forget, what can you do to develop your forgettory?

1. Make sure you face the memory properly. Remember it, think it through once, and let it play out in your mind.

2. See the memory from a different perspective. Sometimes we remember an incident because we're remembering it in the worst possible light, emphasizing the negatives. Try to think about it in a more balanced way. Can you see something—anything—positive in the incident? Think realistically about how much other people are remembering it. How many people will remember it in a year? Five years? Ten years? And if it's already been that long, or perhaps even longer, you can be fairly certain that others have already forgotten it. Although you've probably witnessed countless moments where someone has fallen or failed publically, it's likely that you can't recall the specifics of very many at all. And it will no doubt be the same for others and their memories of us.

3. Shove the memory away. Force your mind to go blank. Make a conscious effort to stop thinking about it. I personally find this quite difficult to do. I try to shrink the image in my mind. I make it small, desaturate the colour, and turn the sound down. And I keep shrinking it until it's gone. This technique works for me, though it might not work for everyone. Shoving it away sounds kind of simplistic, doesn't it? And it is. And just as some people are better at blocking bad behaviours, so some people are better at blocking bad memories. But you need to find a way that works for you to consciously stop thinking about it.

4. The memory will keep reasserting itself. Every time it does, push the memory away again.

5. Replace the memory with something else—a memory of a time when things went well, a time when you accomplished something

you were trying to do, a place or people you like or, better yet, call to mind your favourite Bible verse. I find Philippians 4:8 particularly helpful when I'm trying to replace a negative memory:

> Whatever is true, whatever is honourable, whatever is just, whatever is pure, whatever is lovely, whatever is commendable, if there is any excellence, if there is anything worthy of praise, think about these things.

6. Whenever the memory threatens to return, do something else. Go for a walk. Send a text message. Draw a picture. Say hello to someone walking by.

We should try to develop our memories so we can keep in mind the things that matter. Forgetting is sometimes a breakdown in the natural and helpful process of memory. But recognize that's only half the problem. Sometimes remembering is a breakdown in the natural and helpful process of forgetting. You're not as good at forgetting as you might think you are.

You also need to develop your forgettory.

23

Stop listening to yourself

Martyn Lloyd-Jones, leader and preacher at Westminster Chapel in London from 1939 to 1968, made this profound observation in a book called *Spiritual Depression:*

> Have you realized that most of your unhappiness in life is due to the fact that you are listening to yourself instead of talking to yourself? Take those thoughts that come to you the moment you wake up in the morning. You have not originated them but they are talking to you, they bring back the problems of yesterday, etc. Somebody is talking. Who is talking to you? Your self is talking to you.[21]

We know that the people we choose to listen to shape who we are and what we do. Whether you listen to your friends, your critics, your circle of yes-men, your spouse or your doctor, who you listen to is critically important. A lot of people run their lives off course because they listen to the wrong people—like kids who get in with the wrong crowd. We run off course when we become consumed with what our critics think and work to make them happy. The same thing happens when we listen exclusively to our fans and ignore genuinely helpful feedback until it's too late. We too often focus on what people say instead of focusing on what God says. And that's always a bad idea. But the one person most people (and not just leaders) listen to too much is themselves.

You need to stop listening to yourself.

21 D Martyn Lloyd-Jones, *Spiritual Depression: Its causes and its cure*, Eerdmans, Grand Rapids, 1965, pp. 20-21.

The still small voice

We all have a small voice in our head that tells us we can't do it. As leaders we're not immune to this. From time to time, and perhaps more often than you'd like to admit, you'll find yourself listening to that voice that tells you things that aren't true. The voice urges you to stop, to quit, to give up, to stop trying, to not try at all, to be afraid, to take the easy path. When you get up to preach your first sermon it says to you, "You can't do this. You failed every oral assessment you ever had in high school. This is the bit coming up that you tripped over every time you practised. It's a hard bit. It's coming up. You're going to mess it up." And when you get up to preach your five hundredth sermon that same voice says, "You're not good enough for this. You're a sinner. You're a hypocrite." Sometimes it's so loud you can't hear yourself talk. And sometimes it's so loud that it drowns out the music you're playing or the sound of the crowd when you're playing sport. Sometimes it's all you can hear. That's the voice.

It's the voice inside your head that tells you that you should probably just give up because God has already given up on you. God has proven himself untrustworthy, the voice tells you, and so there's no point. The voice tries to convince you that everything in your life is bad and it's all your fault and it will always be this way. That's the voice.

And the problem is that you listen to it.

The solution is to start talking to yourself. Instead of listening to yourself, as Lloyd-Jones reminds us, you need to start talking to yourself. Tell yourself about the things in your life that aren't bad, because not everything is. Tell yourself that all the bad things that are happening aren't personal—some might be, but not everything is. Things won't always be this way. The sun always rises, the tide always turns, and this too shall pass.

This quote from Spurgeon captures the thought:

> You never met an old salt, down by the sea, who was in trouble because the tide had been ebbing out for hours. No! He waits confidently for the turn of the tide, and it comes in due time. Yonder rock has been uncovered during the last half-hour, and if the sea continues to ebb out for weeks, there will be no water in the English Channel, and the French will

> walk over from Cherbourg. Nobody talks in that childish way, for such an ebb will never come. Nor will we speak as though the gospel would be routed, and eternal truth driven out of the land. We serve an almighty Master... If our Lord does but stamp His foot, He can win for Himself all the nations of the earth against heathenism, and Mohammedanism, and Agnosticism, and Modern-thought, and every other foul error. Who is he that can harm us if we follow Jesus? How can His cause be defeated? At His will, converts will flock to His truth as numerous as the sands of the sea... Wherefore, be of good courage, and go on your way singing.[22]

You need to start telling yourself that perseverance is a virtue, that God never gives up, that he always finishes what he starts, that he has kept all his promises, and that your labour in the Lord is never in vain.

You need to start talking to yourself about the fact that of course you're not good enough, of course you're a sinner—that was never the criteria. It's not about you. It has never been about how good you are. It's always been about the God who uses and redeems sinners. Of course you're not good enough. The treasure has always been stored in jars of clay.

Self-help and Psalm 42

While this might sound like empty rhetoric and self-help pop psychology, it's not. It's simply telling yourself the truth instead of listening to lies. It's about believing the truth instead of lies. It's about talking to yourself instead of listening to yourself.

In Psalm 42 the psalmist talks about this phenomenon of listening to yourself and talking to yourself. In verse 3 he writes:

> My tears have been my food
> day and night,
> while they say to me all the day long,
> "Where is your God?"

22 CH Spurgeon, *An All-Round Ministry*, Banner of Truth, Edinburgh, 1960, pp. 395-6.

The psalmist is very aware that things aren't going well. It seems as though God has left him and everything looks bad. So what does he do? Instead of listening to himself, he starts talking to himself. Verse 5 says:

> Why are you cast down, O my soul,
> and why are you in turmoil within me?
> Hope in God; for I shall again praise him,
> my salvation and my God.

His soul had been doing the talking, and it had been wearing him down and crushing his hope. And so he starts talking to himself instead, reminding himself of who God is.

Talking to yourself isn't about fooling yourself or lying to yourself or hyping yourself up and tricking yourself to believe in the power of positive thinking. This is about telling yourself the truth.

There's no way that everything in your life is bad. If you're reading this, then it means you can read! I don't know if you've ever stopped to think about how amazing that is. These 26 different English letters can be rearranged into an almost infinite number of combinations. Since you recognize these squiggles, I can send any kind of message I want to you. I can encode any idea into a form that you, whom I probably have never met, are able to decode and understand. That is a miraculous thing! Aren't we brilliant? But it doesn't feel like that sometimes. Reading feels mundane and we take it for granted. Imagine how many other things in your life are just as brilliant, or even more brilliant, that you haven't noticed?

It's also important to remember that things will change. For starters, the resurrection and new creation will happen. And, as Philippians 1:6 reminds us, God is faithful and trustworthy: "And I am sure of this, that he who began a good work in you will bring it to completion at the day of Jesus Christ".

That little voice in your head doesn't know what it's talking about, so you need to learn to stop listening and start talking.

24

The way you view a problem often is the problem

Postmodernism, as a phenomenon, has received mixed reviews. Some say it's all bad while others celebrate its radical relativism as progress for our society. I'm of the personal opinion that's it's been partly good and partly bad. On the positive side, postmodernism has reminded us that the idea of the purely objective observer is a myth. There is no perspective-less viewpoint. Everyone views the world through the lenses of their own upbringing, culture, biases, and blind spots. This does not, as some claim, render all of our observations meaningless and mean that we are unable to encounter the truth. Truth still exists and we still have access to it. But what it does say is that we must be aware of, and seek to compensate for where necessary, our own viewpoints.

Much has been written about this complicated issue and debate continues to rage. But the point for us to remember is that where you stand determines what you end up seeing.

As leaders we know that we'll encounter problems. That's a given and we expect them. But sometimes the way we view a problem is more of a problem than the problem itself.

The problem of shoes

There's a famous story of two shoe salesmen who want to sell shoes on a tropical island. Neither man has been to this island, so they both travel over to ascertain the strength of the market and the potential for future sales success. One of them sends a telegram back home saying: "Situation hopeless STOP they don't wear shoes STOP". The other sends a very different telegram home: “Glorious opportunity STOP they don’t have any shoes yet STOP”.

They encountered the same situation and viewed the same problem, but they viewed it entirely differently. Each viewpoint led to a dramatically different outcome.

The way you view a problem often is the problem.

Where are you standing?

Where you’re standing determines what you see. Life looks different depending on whether you’re standing in a hole in the ground or in the middle of a forest or on a mountain overlooking a forest. This is probably so obvious that it doesn’t need saying, but the problem is that we often don’t translate this insight from physically looking at landscapes to mentally considering problems.

There are three broad categories for viewing problems problematically, and none of them are wise.

No problem

First, you can view the problem as not a problem. This kind of denial is most often a result of pride, because if we admit that the problem actually is a problem we need to admit that it happened on our watch and that we may have contributed to it in some way. And since that can be a very difficult thing to admit, sometimes it seems easier to pretend the problem doesn’t exist.

This kind of denial can also be caused by hubris, which is a specific flavour of pride. Hubris is characterized by the fear of admitting responsibility for a mistake. Success can engender this type of arrogance that believes it cannot fail or make mistakes. The ship is unsinkable. The team is unbeatable. The plan cannot fail. Denial like this, caused by hubris, is extremely dangerous. Jim Collins, in his empirical study of how great companies fail and fall, identifies hubris as the first of five stages in the collapse of an organization:

> Great enterprises can become insulated by success; accumulated momentum can carry an enterprise forward, for a while, even if its leaders make poor decisions or lose discipline. Stage 1 [Hubris Born of Success] kicks in when people become arrogant, regarding success virtually as an entitlement, and they lose sight of the true underlying factors that created success in the first place.[23]

If you ever hear yourself, or anyone else on your team, talking like this you have a serious problem—much more serious than any other problem you're trying to solve.

Sometimes, though, we can view a problem as not a problem because it doesn't look like a problem. Some problems take a long time to germinate, and so when they explode in full bloom as a problem for everyone to see it's too late. And since the seed was sown so long ago it can be difficult to trace the cause.

It's like being out in the sun unprotected. So you get a little sunburned? No big deal. Put some aloe vera on it, endure a couple of days of discomfort, and you're back to normal, right? Wrong. Under the skin's surface, all kinds of cancer formation is going on that perhaps won't show itself for decades. Sunburn is a big problem, but it doesn't seem like a big problem initially—and by the time we see the problem it's too late.

But if someone explains why sunburn is actually a much more serious problem with long-term consequences, then we need to decide whether or not we trust their wisdom and counsel. In the same way, if someone points out a potential problem, or the seed of a problem, to us we need to weigh how much trust we have in that person and whether we should defer to their wisdom or keep our own counsel.

The wrong problem

The second way to view a problem problematically is to identify the wrong problem. Sometimes, for example, what at first seems like a problem with

23 Jim Collins, *How the Mighty Fall: And why some companies never give in*, HarperCollins, New York, 2009, pp. 20-21.

people is actually a problem with a system. At our church we have four services on a Sunday: 8:30 am, 10:15 am, 5 pm, and 7 pm. For a long time, we had a great number of people arriving late for both the 10:15 service and the 7 pm service. It wasn't unusual for people to show up ten or 15 minutes after the service had started. But we didn't see this happening to the same extent at the other two services at 8:30 am and 5 pm and we wondered why. It wasn't a generational thing, because the phenomenon happened across age groups. It wasn't that the majority of our lazy or unreliable people attended these services. The people who arrived late to those services were on time for all sorts of other meetings and gatherings. For a long time, though, this was our basic conclusion—that there was some kind of spiritual issue. It was a heart issue. They weren't committed. Worship wasn't a priority. And for some of them that probably was true, but it wasn't true for all of them. This wasn't a satisfactory explanation because many of these latecomers were committed, reliable people who knew how to be on time. It was even contagious. People who changed from one service to another began arriving late—people who were always on time at 5 pm became latecomers at 10:15. What was it? Could it be a culture problem at those two services that was causing people to turn up late? Were people learning that 'turning up late is how we do it here' and so just blending in with the way the service worked?

As it turns out, it was much simpler than that. It was a parking problem. The 8:30 am people and the 5 pm people were often still around when people arrived for the 10:15 am and 7 pm services, and so there wasn't much parking available. Or the spots that were available were all the way at the back of the car park and all the good spots closer were taken. And so people soon learned that if they arrived right when the service started or just after there would be more good spaces available. We knew it was a complex problem with lots of factors, but we had assumed the main factor was a spiritual problem stemming from a lack of commitment when, in fact, it was mainly a problem with the facilities. We were viewing the problem all wrong.

Or sometimes what looks like a problem with the people in your team is actually a problem with the way you've communicated. I once led a team in which the people were being really unreliable. Sometimes people didn't show up—and they wouldn't tell me beforehand or mention it afterwards.

I was getting really frustrated. Why didn't they have the decency to tell me beforehand? And then it dawned on me that I had never told them that I needed to know beforehand if they weren't coming. I had definitely expected them to tell me, but I had never actually told them that. And so when I asked them to please send me a message if they weren't able to make it, explaining that it would make things a lot easier for me, they said things like, "Oh sorry, I had no idea that it caused an issue". Or, "Oh I didn't realize that you wanted me to. Absolutely I can do that." After that meeting, people let me know beforehand if they couldn't make it. I'd thought it was a problem with them, but it turned out to be a problem with me. Sometimes a problem looks like one thing on the surface, but it's important to make sure that you've identified the problem correctly.

A hopeless problem

The third way to view a problem problematically is to see the problem as being hopeless when it's actually not, or to prematurely declare a problem to be hopeless. Often when a problem arises it can be such a shock or disappointment that it completely knocks the wind out of your sails. The problem seems too big, or too complex, and there seems to be no way forward and nothing you can do. Sometimes problems of that magnitude exist, but not nearly as often as we think they do. We can feel very confident sometimes that a problem is hopeless, and we make this call very early on before we've given it much thought or gained much perspective or asked for any outside advice. When we face big, overwhelming problems, it can be tempting to focus on all the things that we don't control or can't control. And with big problems there often are a lot of things that we don't control. This lack of control can quickly lead us to the conclusion that the problem is hopeless. This way of viewing a problem is a problem. Instead of focusing on all the things we can't control, we need to focus on finding the things that we can control. When we do this, we will often discover a whole boatload of factors over which we do have some control, and areas where we can make an impact. Sometimes declaring a problem to be hopeless too early can lead us to overlook solutions that are available to us but that aren't immediately obvious.

It's also worth saying that not every problem is a glorious opportunity in disguise; often they are, but sometimes they're not. Some problems really are just problems with no upsides—horrible circumstances or potentially threatening positions. But often you don't know that for sure right away, or even until much later. So there's wisdom in at least being open to the possibility that there's more to a problem, and that there still might be hope. You don't want to jump in a hole and view the problem from there when being up high at the top of the mountain might be a better vantage point.

When you discover a problem, or when someone on your team brings a potential problem to your attention, the questions to ask are questions such as: Am I viewing this problem well? Is there another viewpoint from which I can look at this issue? If I thought this problem had an interesting upside, what might it be? If I thought this problem might have a hidden opportunity, how would I find it? What kind of problem is this? Is this circumstance as hopeless as I think it is? What things can I still control? How can I maximize the impact of those things that I do still control?

Your viewpoint, how you look at a problem, really matters. Because the way you view a problem often is the problem.

See also

77. Bad news is good news

25
Hopetimism

There are two teams in this challenge. The challenge is to outsell the other team. The people on these teams all took a sales aptitude test and those who scored the highest were put on one team, while those who scored the lowest (that is, those who failed), were put on the other team.

You, as one of the chosen team leaders, flip a coin to see who gets to pick their team. If you win the coin toss you get to lead the best and brightest. If you lose you have to take the team of dropouts and sales deadbeats.

The coin is tossed. You call heads. The coin hits the ground, bounces from edge to edge a couple of times, and begins to spin on the spot. Slowly it stops.

Heads. You get the smart team. You call yourselves the A Team.

You engage all the leadership skills you've learned. You cast a compelling vision, you train the A Team to the best of your ability, you do some trust falls, you set milestones and BHAGs (big, hairy, audacious goals) and stretch goals and SMART (specific, measurable, achievable, relevant, and time-based) goals and every kind of goal you can think of, you source them the best sales equipment you can, you have glossy brochures printed. It's time to go win.

You know that the team that fields the best players always wins. And the A Team has the best players—the best and brightest.

When the competition is over you open the champagne—just to save time—and then the results are read out. "Congratulations. The winning team, by an absolute landslide, is... the B Team!"

What!?

How could that possibly have happened? You did trust falls! What about the aptitude test? The challenge was to sell and you had the best salespeople. The other team had the people who couldn't sell. What. Just. Happened?

Well, here's the secret. The sales aptitude test wasn't the only test they used to pick the two teams. They also did a mindset test. The best salespeople were also pessimists. The sales deadbeats were optimists. And the optimists won.

A guy called Dr Martin Seligman conducted a very famous study in the 1980s for the Metropolitan Life Insurance Company. Seligman tracked 15,000 new insurance sales recruits. Each recruit had taken two tests—one was the regular sales aptitude test and the other was Seligman's optimism test. In amongst these new recruits was a group of people who had totally flunked the sales aptitude test but had scored in the 'super-optimist' range in Seligman's profiling.

The super-optimists outsold the pessimists in the regular group by 21% in the first year and by a staggering 57% in the second year.

It gets more interesting. Those who scored in the top half of the group for optimism outsold the bottom half by 37% over the two years. And those in the top 10% for optimism outsold the bottom 10% by 88%.

Eighty-eight per cent.

In 1995 Seligman went on to study optimism across a variety of sales industries, including real estate, car sales, and banking. The results were always the same. Optimists outsold pessimists by between 20% and 40%.

Seligman found that optimists tend to treat obstacles as temporary setbacks and often ascribe them to either internal or external factors that can be changed rather than seeing them as inherent, unchangeable roadblocks. Pessimists, on the other hand, tend to take obstacles personally. What optimists see as fleeting and localized, pessimists see as permanent and pervasive.[24]

Peter Schulman conducted similar studies that were published in 1999, again using an insurance sales force as his subjects. His study showed that optimists outperformed pessimists by 35% and that pessimists were

24 Martin EP Seligman, *Learned Optimism: How to change your mind and your life,* Pocket Books, New York, 1998.

twice as likely to quit within the first two years on the job.[25]

In almost every arena in life, from school to sport to business to relationships, optimists are more likely to be successful than pessimists—and by a big margin, too.

But here's the really interesting part: when you zoom in close to look at each individual sale—will they or won't they buy my insurance—it was the pessimists who were right. They predicted accurately that the sale wouldn't happen. The people didn't make the purchase. Zoomed in like this, it was the pessimists who were more in touch with reality. The optimists were more irrational.

But when you zoom out and look at how the two groups processed those individual moments of setback or failure, it was the optimists who were more in touch with reality and the pessimists who were operating irrationally. The pessimists were wrong—it wasn't always going to be like this.

One more story

What's going on here? And what relevance does all this have to church leadership? Well, the relevance is huge. But the take-home point most definitely isn't going to be me telling you to just think irrationally because at least it works. Our God is a God of order and rationality. There's something else that both Seligman and Schulman either didn't know or overlooked. But before we get there, I have one more story that will get us a bit closer to understanding what's going on here.

In Jim Collins' book *Good to Great*, he tells a story about a guy called Admiral Jim Stockdale. Stockdale spent eight years, from 1965 to 1973, as a prisoner of war in the 'Hanoi Hilton' POW camp during the Vietnam War. He was tortured over 20 times during those eight years.

He spent those eight long years never knowing whether or not he would see his family again. He had no rights, no release date, and was not treated with any degree of dignity. It's a depressing story—even when you know it has a happy ending and he makes it out alive and reunites

25 Peter Schulman, 'Applying learned optimism to increase sales productivity', *Journal of Personal Selling and Sales Management*, vol. 19, no. 1, winter, 1999, pp. 31-7.

with his wife! And if it's depressing to read, even when you know the ending, you wonder how on earth Stockdale dealt with it all while he was a prisoner and had no idea how the story would end. Collins asked him.

Stockdale responded, "I never lost faith in the end of the story. I never doubted not only that I would get out, but also that I would prevail in the end and turn the experience into the defining event of my life."

Stirring stuff. A few minutes later, Collins drummed up the courage to ask his next question. "Who didn't make it out?"

"Oh, that's easy", Stockdale replied. "The optimists."

Collins was understandably confused. Wasn't Stockdale an optimist? No he wasn't. Stockdale explained that the optimists were the ones who said they'd be out by Christmas. Then Christmas would come and go. And then come again. And go again. And the optimists died of broken hearts.

Optimists die first.

And then Stockdale turned to Collins and said, "You must never confuse faith that you will prevail in the end—which you can never afford to lose—with the discipline to confront the most brutal facts of your current reality, whatever they might be".[26]

Stockdale was so close. So close to being right. So close to the truth. So close to a rational optimism. At least he confronted the brutal facts of his circumstances. But then he made up his hope and his faith. His faith wasn't based on anything. It was just faith that he would prevail. But he didn't *know*. Our faith, on the other hand, is based on something (or rather, someone); and we *do* know. The resurrection is real. We will prevail. But Stockdale didn't have the resurrection; he didn't have that piece of reality that turns optimism from being irrational to being rational and grounded in reality. He had faith in something he didn't know. He had faith when he didn't have evidence.

So close yet so far

Christian faith is totally different. Our faith is based on evidence. Our faith is in a God who has made promises and who has completely delivered

26 Jim Collins, *Good to Great: Why some companies make the leap... and others don't*, HarperCollins, New York, 2001, pp. 83-5.

on every promise in the past, and so we trust that he will deliver on his promises again.

Optimists have a hope that is no hope at all. It's an irrational hope, disconnected from reality. In the end it's a hopeless hope, which makes it sadly ironic.

Pessimists obviously don't have any hope. That's the whole point of being a pessimist. Things aren't going to turn out well and the pessimist knows it. Things don't go well. Mistakes happen. Not everything is a glorious opportunity. Some circumstances are just awful. You fail things. You get sick. You get hurt.

But the Bible calls us to something quite different from either optimism or pessimism. The Bible doesn't call us to be optimists. We know that sin is real and suffering is real and that we will experience much of both. People, at their core, are not good. We call it total depravity. The world won't slowly get better onward to utopia. And God never calls us to be irrational.

But the Bible also doesn't call us to be pessimists either. In our culture there's something cool about being cynical and pessimistic. And it seems that a lot of Christians have followed the culture without thinking about it, and this may be one of our present cultural blind spots. I suspect that people 50 years from now will look back at this generation and wonder why we acted like this and how we didn't see it as a mindset shaped by our culture rather than a mindset shaped by the Bible. Because the Bible doesn't encourage us to be pessimists.

The Bible calls us to a third way. I call it hopetimism.

A life without Jesus is a life without hope. But a life with Jesus is a life filled with hope.

Two theological foundations

Two fundamental theological factors set the foundation for hopetimism. Seligman and Schulman both leave these factors out, and so their theories eventually unravel into irrationalism. But these two facts stabilize an otherwise volatile and unbalanced outlook on life. The first is the fact that we know the God of the Bible, who is all-powerful and sovereign over all things. The other fact is the resurrection of Jesus Christ from the dead.

Those two facts change the game.

The Bible is full of circumstances that looked hopeless. Abraham was 100 years old, and his wife Sarah was 90. She couldn't have kids and yet God said they'd have a son. Their circumstances appeared hopeless. But, remember, your hope isn't based on the shape of your circumstances.

The Israelites were slaves in Egypt and had been there for 400 years. The circumstances, to all appearances, seemed hopeless. Moses said, "Pharaoh, Pharaoh, ooh baby, let my people go". God sent plague after plague and Pharaoh still said no. Nine plagues, nine times he said no. Circumstances still looked hopeless. In fact, they looked worse than before.

Finally God sent the plague on the firstborn sons and Pharaoh finally let the people go. But then he changed his mind and the Israelites were trapped at the Red Sea! Circumstances looked hopeless again.

But when you're measuring your circumstances you're measuring the wrong thing.

All of a sudden God parted the waters and they walked through on dry ground with a wall of water on either side.

And so the Bible goes, story after story, circumstance after circumstance.

When it comes to how you view the world, the future, and your life, if you're measuring your circumstances then you're measuring the wrong thing. Your hope is not based on the shape of your circumstances but on the size of your God.

Then we arrive at the cross. Jesus promised that he is the Messiah, God's chosen King, and that he will rule and reign and save. And then he's betrayed by the Jews, crucified by the Romans, and dies on a cross.

Imagine that you were there and you had followed him right up until this point. You'd trusted him and believed in him and given up everything to follow him. And then you see him die. You wake up on Saturday and the situation is hopeless. Nothing in your circumstances indicates that there's even one slim chance for hope. The Romans came for him and now they're no doubt coming for you. It's over.

But hope isn't based on the shape of your circumstances, which means that when we use them as a guide for whether we should be optimistic or pessimistic we're using the wrong measure. Hope is based on the size of your God.

The size of your God

Just how big is God? He's infinitely big! He weighs mountains on a scale like they're cherry tomatoes. The nations are like a drop in a bucket and like dust on the scales. You know whom God consults when he needs to be enlightened? No-one! That's who. No-one has ever taught God anything. Whatever you want to teach him he already knows. God knows every star by name and it's like he calls each of them one by one. They only continue to exist because God wants each one of them to keep existing.

At the end of Isaiah 40 the prophet connects all this up and says:

> Even youths shall faint and be weary,
> and young men shall fall exhausted;
> but they who wait for the LORD shall renew their strength;
> they shall mount up with wings like eagles;
> they shall run and not be weary;
> they shall walk and not faint. (vv. 30-31)

They don't renew their strength because their circumstances change or because their situations improve. It's because they wait and hope and trust in the Lord.

We lose our hope when we view our God as small and our circumstances as big. But that's not how things are in reality. When our God seems small and our circumstances appear to be overwhelming it's because we've lost touch with reality. The reality is: our circumstances are small, the nations are a drop in a bucket, and our God is massive. And so if our circumstances are horrible but small and our God is good and huge, then there is every reason for hope and there is a mountain of evidence to keep going. And to keep going with hopetimism—in touch with reality, even the brutal facts of reality at its bleakest, and yet confident and positive about the future.

Sunday has come

But this isn't the whole picture. There's another bedrock on which the house of hopetimism is built. So far we've been talking very Old Testament—not that there's anything wrong with that—but it's just not the whole picture.

If you'd been there on Easter Saturday and everything was bleak and dark and against you and there was no hope on the horizon, you'd be forgiven for being a bit depressed and pessimistic. But what we know now that they didn't know on that Saturday 2000 years ago is that Sunday was coming.

The other part of hopetimism is the resurrection of Jesus Christ from the dead.

We don't live on Easter Saturday. Sunday has already come. The resurrection has happened. Which means that Jesus has been vindicated and enthroned as King. The cross and death and darkness weren't the end of the story. The tomb was empty and Jesus was resurrected—physically resurrected.

This means two things for us. First of all, it means that Jesus really is the Messiah of Israel and therefore the King of the world. And, secondly, his resurrection is the firstfruits of a larger harvest. Just as he was, so shall we be. We will also be resurrected into new, physical bodies built to live in the new, physical creation. What happened to Jesus is the preview trailer for what will happen to us—real, literal, physical resurrection.

And so we have all the more reason for hope and courage. Even in the midst of darkness, no matter how bad our circumstances get, our future is assured. It is a future of glory, even if on the way the journey is full of suffering and disappointment and trouble.

Which means that, unlike Seligman, Schulman, and Stockdale, we have a real reason to be confident that the future will turn out okay and that we will overcome. Where they're irrational in their hope for the future, we are rational because our God is sovereign and our King is alive. Death, for Stockdale, was the destroyer of his hope. His hope was to survive, and so death was the end of hope. But for us death has no sting and cannot destroy our hope. Even death cannot stop hopetimism because our King has conquered death. Our future is sure and certain and we know that it turns out okay because of the resurrection of Jesus.

Circumstances are temporary

Hopetimism doesn't say that everything will always be good or that everything you attempt will always succeed. And hopetimism doesn't say that you're never going to face any problems. That would be irrational.

Hopetimism allows us to confront the most brutal facts of our current circumstances and still have a sure and certain hope for the future, based on evidence, that we will prevail. Hopetimism looks evil and failure and disappointment and problems and pain square in the face and right in the eyes and says:

> You will not win. You do not win. I have seen the future in Jesus and it is resurrection. You will not win. Because my God is bigger and my King is alive. And so I refuse to lose.

Our hope is not based on the shape of our circumstances because if you're measuring your circumstances then you're measuring the wrong thing. Our hope is based on the size of our God and on the heartbeat of our King—and our King is alive.

Hopetimism is in touch with reality, like pessimism often is, but hopetimism avoids the irrationality of optimism. And it can do this because of who God is and what Jesus has done. In other words, it can do it because of theology.

Learned hopetimism

Here's some more good news: you can learn hopetimism. Hopetimism is just theological truths making their way from your head to your heart. It's theology shaping the way you view the world. It's doctrine informing mindset. It's what you know changing how you think.

Hopetimism is a new category that the Bible creates in your mind. Hopetimism is what the secular world is desperately scraping and clawing for and is not quite able to find. It's as though people have an inkling that it exists but they can't find how to get to it. And they can't put the jigsaw puzzle together because they don't have all the pieces. They're trapped between optimism and pessimism and forced to embrace irrationality either way. But in Christianity God gives us all the pieces and puts it together so that we can be optimists who are rational.

Pray that God would change your mindset and create the category in your mind. Actively pursue it. Think and mull it over. Keep the two bedrocks—the size and sovereignty of God along with the resurrection of

Jesus—front and centre in your mind. Think them into each other. And you will grow in hopetimism.

Your God is bigger than any circumstance and he cannot be stopped. And your King is alive forever and he will not be stopped.

And so you engage with life not with pessimism, not with optimism, but with hopetimism.

See also

22. Develop your forgettory
23. Stop listening to yourself
24. The way you view a problem often is the problem

Section three

Leading other people

26
Leading is loving

If you have a clear and powerful vision, but have not love, you are only a resounding gong or a clanging symbol. If you have a huge crowd of people following you, but have not love, you are nothing. If you have all the skills and strategy you can acquire, but have not love, you have nothing.

This is the blazing centre of the entire book. Everything orbits around it and everything flows from it. Leading yourself, leading other individuals, and leading a team are all about love and about seeking the best for others, even at great cost to yourself. Love is considering the needs and wants of others to be more important than your own.

No love = no leadership

Since Christian leadership is driven by love, if you don't have love then you don't have real leadership. Why? God is the original and model leader. He invented leadership and was the first to lead. God is love, and he has been for eternity, which means that his leadership flows from, is driven by, is energized by, and is characterized by love. So if his leadership is the leadership from which all other leadership derives its name, then my leadership is only true leadership to the degree that it is marked by other-person-centred love. Those whose leadership isn't characterized by this other-person-centred love have a counterfeit leadership, a forgery that might mimic the original in a lot of ways but will never be authentic.

To lead a team you need to genuinely love them. If you're going to lead them you need to serve them. If you're going to serve them and want them to succeed, you will need to love them.

Everything in your leadership is about love. Seeking to run your meetings so you don't waste people's time is about love. Telling people the truth, both the positive and the negative, is about love. Admitting mistakes and saying you're sorry is about love. Giving people clarity on *why* you want them to do something, beyond just the what and the how, is about love. Allowing people the space to fail and also celebrating improvement and milestones is about love. Leadership is about love before it's about anything else.

Love made known

But there's more. It's not just that love should drive and energize your leadership. Your leadership should also be marked and characterized by love. That is, your team needs to know that you love them. Each and every person. This is how God leads you. It's not just that his love drives what he does; he also makes sure he shows us and tells us so that we know that we are loved. He demonstrates his love for us in that while we were still sinners Christ died for us.

If God has given you a team to lead, then God has given you a team to love. It's the same thing. Now this doesn't mean that you have to be best friends with everyone on your team, or that you should go on holidays with them and hold hands, share an ice cream cone, and ride a tandem bike. It simply means that you genuinely care about them and about what's happening in their lives and how things are working out for them. It also means that you want what's best for them and are actively seeking to build and grow them.

The people you lead need to know that you aren't simply interested in the job that they can do for you or the results that they can achieve for you, but that you care about them. Do the people on your team know that you love and care for them? Have you ever told them? What have you done to show them?

There is a pragmatic edge to this, because caring about how the people you lead are doing and loving them as individuals will affect how they perform in the job you have for them to do. This is particularly true in a ministry context, where heart and character are so central. But you need to love them above and beyond the fact that it makes good pragmatic sense. If you love them so that they will work harder and better and be more loyal, then you haven't really loved them. You need to love them because God has given them to you to be loved. If you love them genuinely, however, you will have a better team.

Do you remember the story of the golden goose? Once upon a time, a man and his wife owned a unique and precious goose. Every day the goose would lay a single solid gold egg. And the couple quickly became very rich.

The man's wife said to him, "Just imagine how many golden eggs are inside that goose. Why are we waiting every day for her to lay them? We could be richer much faster."

"That's brilliant!" the man said.

So the husband and wife killed the goose and sliced her open, only to find that inside she was just like every other goose. She had no golden eggs inside her, and the couple had no more golden eggs.

The couple didn't care about the goose. They only cared about what the goose could do for them—the eggs the goose could produce. And in the end they had no eggs and no goose.

But if they had loved the goose they would have been able to enjoy both the goose and her eggs. If all you care about is the ministry your people can do, without caring for them as people, then in the end you will lose both them and the ministry that they do.

Leadership is all about love—love for the people you lead as well as love for the people your team is seeking to serve. And so, in a very real sense, this book about leadership is a book about love. Leadership is always pastoral, and without love you may be able to do a convincing impersonation of leadership but you will never be a true leader following the true Leader. As 1 Corinthians 13:13 reminds us:

> So now faith, hope, and love abide, these three; but the greatest of these is love.

See also

41. Two foundations of team-building

27
You're just the leader

Leadership is a high calling. It's demanding and requires a difficult skill set. It's both art and science. Leaders need to commit themselves to learning—constantly and continuously. But let's not overstate it. What makes leadership so important isn't that we need leaders. It's not that leaders are so great and important that we cannot survive and would be lost without them, but thankfully when we have the 'great ones' everything will be okay. Sometimes that might be true, but it's not what makes leadership so important.

Leaders don't need to be great

What makes leaders and leadership so important and necessary is that leaders mobilize and equip others to play their part in growing the kingdom and to do great things in service to God and love for others. Leaders are vital because they enable and draw out the servant-hearted greatness of others around them.

When we think of leaders we often think of great ones. Great preachers, great thinkers, great strategizers, great planners. And some leaders are those things. One leader might be the greatest preacher in the room. Another leader will be the greatest thinker in the room. Some leaders will be the most insightful strategizers in the room. Some leaders will seem to be able to see into the future so they can plan accordingly. But here's the critical thing to grasp: you don't have to be any of those things to be a great leader.

People often find this so hard to grasp that it's worth saying it again: you don't have to be the greatest at any of those things in order to be a great leader. Great preachers can also be great leaders, but mediocre preachers can also be great leaders. Great thinkers can be great leaders, but so can mediocre thinkers. Being a great individual contributor has nothing to do with being a great leader, and often great individual contributors have the hardest time becoming great leaders.

When you lead a team you're not necessarily the greatest person in the room. You're not necessarily the smartest person in the room. Your idea won't necessarily be the best idea. You're just the leader.

Your job

Your job as the leader is to unleash the people God has given you so that they can be who God has saved them to be and to do the good works that God has prepared for them to do. Your job is to multiply what gets done by unleashing the people around you.

You don't need to come up with all the ideas or all the answers. Your job is to lead. Your job is to raise the question, or perhaps to create an environment where there is safety for others to raise the question. It's your job to help the group think through the question, brainstorm possible solutions, discuss those options, then decide on a course of action. Your job is to make sure people understand the problem and how this solution might address that problem. Your job is to make sure people understand their roles and responsibilities in making that solution happen. Your job is to keep people focused on the task and energized. And your job is also to ask the questions to determine whether or not the solution is actually solving the problem.

None of that requires you to be the smartest person in the room or to be the one who thinks up the perfect solution. You're just the leader. Your job is to make sure that underlying and invisible problems do get raised, that solutions are put forward, and that everyone agrees to go after one of those solutions. You don't need to have all the answers. What you need to be able to do is to get the best people for this particular problem in the room, draw the answers out of those people, help them to execute the solution, and then ask the question: Did it work? Your job is to harness the collective brilliance of the room, not to be the sole font of brilliance in the room.

Leadership is vitally important in that it facilitates ministry getting done, but it's not important because the leader is important and can do great things. Leaders are just the leaders. Leadership is important because leaders help the rest of God's people to become great by serving the world.

See also

47. Find the awesome
51. Get out of the way of good people
55. The point is clarity, not labels

28
Anything worth doing is worth doing badly

The things you do and the things you're responsible for are important. If they weren't, you wouldn't waste your time doing them. They matter and they need to be done well. Quality is important. We worship a God of excellence and we strive to do our best—not to earn his favour or salvation but because we already have it in Christ.

The tension of training

So quality is a high value. But as a leader you also need to raise up and train new leaders who can take on important tasks, multiply the ministry, and free you up to focus on other areas or to develop new important tasks.

Doing things well and developing new leaders are both valuable and necessary objectives. The trouble is that these two agendas often clash. Training someone up means, almost by definition, that in the beginning they won't be particularly good at whatever it is they're learning to do. And they almost certainly won't be as good at it as you are. If you're training someone, then there will often be a predictable drop in quality while the new leader learns the skills and makes their mistakes.

How can you remove this tension? One solution is to refuse to pursue quality. Decide to settle instead for mediocrity or even poor quality. If you do this, people who are still in training and who aren't yet very good at what they do will fit in perfectly.

The other way of removing the tension is to stop training people and do everything yourself. Or you could ask only very talented, experienced people to do things for you. The upside is that you know things will continue to be done well and you'll ensure consistent high quality. The downside is that you fail a key task as a leader in not multiplying yourself by releasing others. You stop adding value to the people in your team and you severely restrict the impact you could have by hindering the multiplication of effort. This particular path means you have high quality in the short term but big problems in the long term. The experienced, accomplished people who are here today won't be here forever. And when they leave you'll have no-one to step into their roles.

The reality of quality

The simple truth is that, when you train people and multiply yourself, there will be a dip in quality. But this dip will be temporary, because over time the people you've trained will get a handle on the tasks and the quality will begin to rise and sometimes even surpass your own level of expertise. You'll end up with not just a quantity increase, but with a quality increase as well. But in order to get there you'll have to be able to cope with a dip in overall quality along the way.

So that's why I say that if the task is worth doing then it's worth doing badly in order to train people.

Imagine what would happen if you simply did not have enough time to do everything you wanted to do. Perhaps this is not that hard to imagine. Imagine that the lists of things you wanted to do, wanted to preach, wanted to start, and the people you wanted to care for, was too long for you to do all by yourself. In this completely imaginary world certain tasks either get cut from that list and so don't get done at all, or you hand them on to someone else who you know isn't as competent as you are but who you know will see that they get accomplished. Which do you choose?

Let me ask the question a different way. What if there were ten people who needed to be cared for and discipled. And imagine you only had time to meet with two of them. And imagine also that there was another person who had the potential, with a bit of help and training, to meet up and care for people. That person had enough time to care for five people, but the care they would be able to give would be lower quality than the care you could give. What should you do? You could either care for two people and leave eight uncared for, or you could care for one yourself and use the rest of your time to meet with this other potential caregiver to equip them to care for five people. So in the end six people would be cared for, though not as well as they possibly could have been.

If it's a task worth doing, then it's a task worth doing badly. In the above scenario an extra four people receive care—this care might not be perfect, but at least it will be genuine.

Just because the task won't be done as well when someone else does it shouldn't stop you from enlisting that other person's help. Anything worth doing is worth doing badly.

See also

34. Fail forwards
47. Find the awesome
48. Treat them like children

29 Praise publicly

Words are incredibly powerful. We've all had the experience of being cut to the core when a person has used his or her words against us. Someone might have used words against you to demolish your confidence or destroy a dream. And when people use words to hurt us in front of a group or crowd—maybe in a classroom or in front of a group of co-workers—the hurt, damage, and embarrassment is multiplied.

The power of words is extraordinary, as is the power of a group. And so words spoken in front of a group are very powerful indeed.

The power of praise

But words aren't only powerful when they're used negatively. Praise is one of the most powerful tools you have at your disposal as a leader. Some of us will run for months on the power of one simple word of praise from a person we respect. We're probably all able to vividly remember specific moments when someone special praised us—even though those moments might have happened years or even decades ago. Because words and groups are both enormously powerful, public praise is an incredibly powerful way to inspire people to go where they need to go and achieve what they should be achieving.

All of us as leaders need to make sure that we praise the people we lead. For some of us it might even take planning. You might block into your schedule, for example, an hour in which you write some handwritten notes, send some text messages, or write a quick email or private social media message. Taking the time and effort to praise people is a vital piece in your ongoing plans to develop them. But public praise, which is our focus here, is also very important and slightly different.

Why do we publicly praise people? To acknowledge and encourage them in what they've done. We want to honour them and we want others to honour them as well. The apostle Paul does this over and over again in his letters. In Romans 16, for example, he mentions Phoebe, who "has been a patron of many and of myself as well"; Prisca and Aquila, to whom "not only I give thanks but all the churches of the Gentiles give thanks as well"; Andronicus and Junia, who are "well known to the apostles, and they were in Christ before me", and many others. In 1 Corinthians 16 he praises Stephanas, Fortunatus, and Achaicus: "for they refreshed my spirit as well as yours. Give recognition to such people". Paul's letters are full of such praise for his fellow workers in the Lord.

The clarity of praise

Praising publicly brings clarity. Such praise announces and reinforces the kinds of behaviours and values you're looking for. Let's say, for example, that you want people on your team to 'go outside their comfort zone'. This is a great thing to call people to do, but the problem is that it's a bit vague and ambiguous. What does it actually mean? How would I know if I'm doing it?

You could explain and articulate more carefully what you mean. This would be a good thing to do. But an even better idea is to point to some specific examples of people who are doing it. When someone goes outside their comfort zone, steps up and tries something new that they've never done before, praise them for it. Point it out to the team and explain why that's a great example of what you were talking about. Praising people when they do things that you want them to do gives you a chance to provide a concrete example of what it might look like in real life. And so the people on your team will begin to better understand how you'd like them to grow and develop.

In order to reap the benefits that public praise brings, your praise will need to be specific. Saying, "You're doing great work, Mary. Keep it up!" is good, and it's better than nothing, but it's not great. It's not concrete. It's vague and it doesn't show people specifically what Mary did, what made her work great, or what exactly you want to see more of in her and in others. In addition, praise that is vague won't feel as affirming to Mary. Mary will also probably be somewhat confused as to what it was you thought was good. It will feel to her something like when a person asks you, "How's it going?" It's nice that they ask, but you know that they're being polite and don't actually care. When someone asks this question you don't feel as though the person is interested in your wellbeing. "Good work" has the same kind of vibe about it. It's nice and polite, but it doesn't express any deep appreciation for what the person has done. Powerful praise is specific praise.

Public praise is also beneficial to the wider team because what gets rewarded gets done. This is the case whether you work with volunteers or paid staff. You might have resources, financial or otherwise, with which you can reward your teams for a job well done. But often we don't have the resources to do that. Whether or not you have these resources, public praise is often a powerful reward that doesn't cost you anything. (Though it is worth pointing out that, even among paid staff—and particularly in a church—very few people are motivated by financial bonuses. Praise is still an incredibly powerful motivator for paid staff.) If you publicly honour a person and hold them up as an example to follow, then that person will learn that what they did is what you're after. They'll feel rewarded and affirmed and so they'll do more. And the rest of the team will seek to follow and emulate that person too.

Finally, it's worth emphasizing how important it is that public praise be accompanied by genuine private praise. If you only ever praise people publicly, no matter how genuinely, people will begin to think it's only a motivational tool. They'll begin to suspect that it isn't authentic and that you only ever praise them simply to manipulate them. Just as that would be a horrible thing to do, it would also be a horrible thing to unintentionally communicate. Your public praise needs to be genuine and it needs to be seen to be genuine. Not all praise should be, or needs to be, public.

Public praise allows you the opportunity to deepen the impact of the praise in the life of that person. It also gives you an opportunity to communicate and reinforce the goals and values you're looking for from the team.

Praise genuinely. Praise specifically. Praise frequently. Praise publicly.

See also

37. Phrases to learn
40. Team communication is exponential
47. Find the awesome
52. Give credit and take blame
53. Free volunteers aren't cheap

30

Faithfulness buys responsibility

Jesus once said, "One who is faithful in a very little is also faithful in much, and one who is dishonest in a very little is also dishonest in much" (Luke 16:10). We should not be surprised to learn that, as always, he knew what he was talking about.

Waiting for small things

Before you entrust a person with much—for example, a significant project, oversight of a team, or a smaller group to care for—you need to first see them being faithful with smaller tasks. Being reliable and on time, bringing an item they said they'd bring, organizing a smaller component of a larger event, and so on are all indicators that the person is mindful of the importance of building trust.

If a person can't deliver on those smaller responsibilities then you should not entrust them with larger responsibilities. Although this makes perfect sense and is easy to say, in reality it's hard to do. We often find ourselves with not nearly enough time or people to accomplish everything that needs to be done. Sometimes we don't have a system or a pipeline through which people can show themselves faithful in small tasks before being given more responsibility. When we feel desperate, willingness to do the job becomes the only criterion.

So when someone comes along who seems confident, or acts as though they're confident, the temptation can be to give them authority over much before we've seen them being faithful with a little. This lack of discipline on our part to honour the principle always leads to pain and difficulty later.

It's easy to be overawed by a big personality or captivated by the mirage of someone who can talk a good game. But show ponies don't always deliver, and good intentions don't win prizes. Those who are faithful in the little things, however, can be entrusted with more.

It's important to begin setting in place some systems so that people can show themselves to be faithful in small things. You might then promote them quickly, but there is great wisdom in first seeing a person's faithfulness when given responsibility for only a little.

Shortcuts

But what if you're really stuck? You know you need to have a way to observe and test people, and you usually do, but you have a particular anomalous situation with a significant gap and you also have an untested person who's willing and seems competent for the role. What then?

You need to create some shortcut opportunities to observe the person's faithfulness. You might ask them to bring something for the Sunday service—perhaps even something you could have brought yourself without much effort—but you ask them to see if they do it. You might organize to meet and talk through the role. Then you observe whether or not they turn up on time.

None of this should take the place of proper observation over a period of time and in a variety of situations. Circumstances aren't always ideal, however, and we need to work with what we have. Such shortcuts are a way to honour the principle while acknowledging the reality.

When you give more responsibility to those who have already shown they can faithfully deliver in the small things, it enables you to have more confidence that they'll achieve what they've said they'll do. When you give big responsibility to someone with either no runs on the board or a track record of unreliability, it makes it difficult for everyone to trust and get behind them until that person has proven him or herself.

Be aware of the currency you're using

The currency you're looking for when it comes to handing out responsibility is faithfulness. You're not looking for the person who's the loudest, the most charismatic, the nicest, or the one you 'click' with the best. Those currencies are all valuable in their own way and in certain circumstances, but they're worthless in the market of responsibility.

Some people are highly competent and have the gifts and skills to excel at large tasks but refuse to put in effort on tasks they deem beneath them. That kind of heart attitude is toxic, and you need to overlook such people for leadership until you've had time to work with them and witness a change in how they think and act.

Similarly, there are those who are highly competent but unreliable. Even though they might be very skilled, you cannot entrust them with more responsibility. Highly competent but unreliable people are functionally incompetent. If you're competent at a task only some of the time, you're actually not competent at that task at all.

The heart of a servant is foundational. A servant-hearted person will be faithful even in small, menial, or out-of-the-spotlight tasks. Competence is important, but competence without faithfulness is useless.

Faithfulness in the small things gives you a glimpse into how a person might cope in the future. Faithfulness in other areas shows you something about how that person will respond in new areas of responsibility. Those who can be trusted with little show that they can be trusted with much.

When you're looking to assign new responsibilities to new people, you're looking for a track record of faithfulness. Have they been faithful in small things? It's easy to be dazzled by loud, confident, or nice people. But it's faithfulness that buys responsibility.

See also

42. Humble and hungry
43. The five C's

31

Energy is more efficient than efficiency

Efficiency is a good thing. Getting things done with less waste, in less time, with less redundancy, and requiring fewer people is a goal worth pursuing. If you and your team can accomplish more in less time and with less effort, you can allocate the time and person-hours you save to other tasks. That's a positive thing. We should all look at how we work and ask whether there's a better, faster, more efficient way. There's nothing necessarily wrong with that.

Up to a point.

Because there does come a time when the pursuit of efficiency starts to become a hindrance. You eventually reach a tipping point at which you're spending so much energy to become more efficient that you're not actually getting done the thing you're trying to get done. In other words, the pursuit of efficiency becomes inefficient. This can happen for a variety of reasons.

The wrong road

The pursuit of efficiency can become a hindrance simply because you're trying to achieve the wrong thing. This isn't just an efficiency problem—a bad idea is a bad idea, no matter how well intentioned you are or how efficiently or energetically you pursue it. All efficiency means in this case is that you fail more quickly, with less effort and less redundancy.

Pursuing the wrong thing is a particular issue with efficiency because efficient progress can mask the fact that you're actually going down the wrong road. It will look from the outside like you're moving forward, getting better, being successful. But you're only moving forward and getting better at things that aren't helping and that don't actually matter. As management and leadership pioneer Peter Drucker once said, "Nothing is less productive than to make more efficient what should not be done at all".[27]

If you're travelling in the wrong direction it doesn't matter how good the fuel economy is, how fast the car can go, or how smooth and straight the road is. Going the wrong way faster won't get you to your destination any quicker.

An end in itself

Efficiency can also become inefficient when, in pursuing the good goal of efficiency, you begin to lose focus on the quality of what you're pursuing because you over-streamline the process. If efficiency is the pure goal—or understood to be the pure goal, with no further qualification—then quality will inevitably be sacrificed in exchange for swiftness or lower costs.

While this exchange of quality for efficiency isn't always a problem, it can easily become one. Efficiency is a good thing and we should seek it wherever we can reasonably do so while also maintaining the quality and focus on what we want to achieve.

The point of efficiency isn't efficiency. The point of efficiency is to help you do what you're doing better. You pursue efficiency in order to be more effective. Efficiency works best as a tool and a means to an end. It's not the end itself.

A common mistake

Another common mistake is to confuse efficiency with effectiveness. The way you make a system more effective, provided it's already achieving the right thing, is to make it more efficient. The more efficient a system is, the more work will get done with less effort. The system might be, for example, roster creation, run sheet distribution, or money counting.

But because efficiency and effectiveness are so tightly linked in any system, it's easy to get them confused and even to begin to think that the

27 Peter Drucker, *Managing for the Future,* Routledge, New York, 2013, p. 156.

two are synonymous—that is, to start thinking that efficiency is the *same* as effectiveness. As long as you're focused on the system alone, there's often no problem in confusing efficiency with effectiveness.

The problem comes when we transfer this mental model from working with systems to working with people and we make efficiency the goal of people work—or, if not the goal, then at least the main method for increasing effectiveness. When it comes to working with people, efficiency very rarely helps you to be more effective. Making efficiency your aim in meetings, pastoral care, training courses, preaching, or leading small group Bible studies would end up making these activities less effective. People would feel both used and uncared for because you'd be treating them as if they were equipment. Computers, cars, and dishwashers should be made more efficient in order to be more effective. But it doesn't work that way with people.

When you deal with people, the goal is to be more effective, not more efficient. Efficiency isn't bad—it's just not the goal. If efficiency will help you to be more effective, then great. Figure out how to be more efficient. Just don't confuse efficiency with effectiveness.

The diminished returns

Most commonly, efficiency implodes in the following way. You work to streamline your systems and processes to trim the fat and increase efficiency. It's all going well and the results are encouraging. You realize that it's been worth the effort, and so you keep going. You search for more ways to increase efficiency because you've been able to get more done with less effort and resources. At a certain point, however, the energy expended to make the processes more efficient is no longer worth the effort. The efficiency that you gain isn't worth the energy it took to get there.

There comes a point where just getting stuff done yields better results than trying to do things more efficiently. Sometimes putting your energy into doing the tasks at hand rather than seeking to trim all waste and redundancy down to the second is both more effective and more efficient.

Energy will get more done

People with a certain type of energy will get more things done in less time with more enthusiasm than the person focused on efficiency. This is not an erratic and unfocused energy but a disciplined and focused one. People with this kind of energy will work more and achieve more than purely efficient people. If you have to choose between an efficient person who will help others to be more efficient or an energetic person who has a high capacity and is able to energize others, choose energy over efficiency. More will get done.

As we've seen, the relentless pursuit of efficiency can really get in the way. It might be that instead of expending brainpower on becoming more efficient, it would be better to expend that effort on doing better things or even simply on *being* better, which isn't the same as being more efficient. This is the case particularly if you're working with people.

In some cases efficiency actually stifles creativity and innovation. It can stifle appropriate risk-taking. It can stifle passion and enthusiasm for all things except efficiency itself. At the beginning, new ideas are rarely, if ever, more efficient than old ideas. In a regime where efficiency is king, innovation will be an oppressed minority. Ed Catmull, co-founder of Pixar Animation, puts it this way:

> Making the process better, easier, and cheaper is an important aspiration, something we continually work on—but *it is not the goal*. Making something great is the goal.
>
> I see this over and over again in other companies: a subversion takes place in which streamlining the process or increasing production supplants the ultimate goal, with each person or group thinking they are doing the right thing—when, in fact, they have strayed off course. When efficiency or consistency of workflow are not balanced with other equally strong countervailing forces, the result is that new ideas... aren't afforded the attention and protection they need to shine and mature.[28]

28 Ed Catmull, *Creativity, Inc.: Overcoming the unseen forces that stand in the way of true inspiration*, Random House, New York, 2014, pp. 134-5.

Efficiency can end up working against you so that you actually achieve less *and* take longer to accomplish your goals.

Efficiency is good to a point, but that point comes more quickly than you might think or notice. After this tipping point is reached the law of diminishing returns sets in and pursuing efficiency becomes a hindrance and itself an inefficient use of time and resources. It's better to focus on energy—finding people with energy and finding people who can energize others. Then those energetic people—working within the appropriately efficient systems you've set up—will achieve more results more quickly.

Energy is more efficient than efficiency.

See also

16. Time management won't help you
56. What are you trying to achieve?
59. Hold hands with your programs
75. Waiting is doing something

32
Ideas are born ugly

We've all shared the experience of being in a meeting and seeing an idea born. A person puts forward an idea, something that hasn't been proposed before. But immediately the rest of the group jumps on the idea and rips it apart. It won't work. We've tried it before. It sounds risky. They bombard it with questions about specifics—how and when and for whom and how much—and then move on to more solid discussions that are less experimental. And everyone in the room has learned a valuable lesson: we don't do the new here. So keep it to yourself.

But the irony is that no-one would actually say that. No-one would even think that's what the team believes. "Of course innovation is good. We all want to do new things. Try new things. Be open to new things. We want to hold to the truths that are unchanging but deliver them in new ways to new people. We've gone from candles to electricity. From outdoor toilets to indoor plumbing. From street parking to off-street parking. From song sheets to overhead projectors to data projectors. We have websites and sermons on podcasts. We do these things and we've made changes. We're not against the new."

And yet, in the meeting, when the new is put before us, the immediate instinct is to bombard it into oblivion with questions.

Two phenomena, 'the mere exposure principle' and 'loss aversion', are responsible for new ideas being killed before they have a chance. When combined, mere exposure and loss aversion bias us towards the status quo.

Mere exposure

Psychologists have been studying the mere exposure principle for decades. The psychologist Robert Zajonc coined the term 'mere exposure effect' back in 1968.[29] This principle says that the more familiar a thing is to a person, the more they will prefer it. *Merely* being *exposed* to something makes us more positive towards it.

Let's discuss your face. You may be surprised to learn that you're not as familiar with your face as you think you are. Sure, you've been looking at it daily in the mirror as you brush your teeth or do your hair, but the face you've been looking at isn't actually your face. It's a reverse image of your face reflected in a mirror. Everyone else who looks at you actually sees the reverse image of the face you know.

Researchers once gathered a group of subjects and developed two different photos of those people's faces: one photo showed what their face looked like to everyone else in the world, and the other was the mirror image—the face that person saw in the mirror.

When asked which photo they preferred, as predicted by the mere exposure effect, the subjects preferred the photos that resembled their mirror images and their friends and loved ones preferred the photos that hadn't been reversed.[30] We like our mirror image face more than we like our real face because it's the one we've seen most often.

What this means for new ideas is this: we will prefer the status quo not because it's better or more helpful but merely because it's familiar.

Loss aversion

The second phenomenon that affects our ability to consider new ideas is loss aversion. Daniel Kahneman is the leading psychologist in this area. Loss aversion means that people's tendency to want to avoid loss is stronger than their desire to make gains.

Consider the following question that Kahneman asks (and for the sake of the exercise, imagine you think gambling is okay for the sake of science):

> You are offered a gamble on the toss of a coin.
> If the coin shows tails, you lose $100.

29 Daniel Kahneman, *Thinking, Fast and Slow*, Farrar, Straus and Giroux, New York, 2011, p. 66.
30 Chip Heath and Dan Heath, *Decisive: How to make better choices in life and work,* Crown Business, New York, 2013, p. 164.

If the coin shows heads, you win $150.

Is this gamble attractive? Would you accept it?[31]

Most people don't like this bet and wouldn't take it. To make the choice you need to weigh how you would feel about winning $150 against how you would feel if you lost $100.

Overall the deal is positive, by which I mean there's a good chance that you'll win more money than you'll lose. And yet still the gamble probably isn't that attractive. For most people the fear of losing $100 is greater and more intense than the hope and possibility that you'll win $150. Kahneman concludes that "losses loom larger than gains".[32] We want to not lose more than we want to win. This is loss aversion.

And so when we hear new ideas, no matter how good the idea is we'll be thinking much more about what we'll be losing if we implement it than about what we'll be gaining. Even if we'll gain more than we lose.

Mere exposure + loss aversion = status quo

When you combine the mere exposure effect with loss aversion, the result is an incredibly strong bias towards the status quo. The status quo emits a powerful conserving force. The status quo is so familiar that we know exactly how it works—we know what isn't good about it, what questions it raises, and what we'll lose if we move away from it. If we think about moving away from the status quo and embracing a new idea we can almost touch and taste what we'll lose. Gains from a new idea, on the other hand, are imaginary because they exist only in the future. We distrust the unfamiliar. New ideas aren't as clear as old ideas. Lots of factors and outcomes are unknown.

And so we stick with what we know.

We like to think that we carefully weigh the merits of new ideas and judge them objectively and without bias. But the truth is that when it comes to assessing new ideas we're deeply irrational.

31 Kahneman, *Thinking*, p. 283.
32 Kahneman, *Thinking*, p. 282.

Protect the ugly baby

So how do we overcome the mere exposure effect, loss aversion, and this irrational bias towards the status quo?

There are two ways you can help your team, and yourself, to be more open to new ways of thinking. First, you need to accept that ideas are born ugly. Second, you need to understand that new ideas are fragile and need protection.

The fact that ideas are born ugly is hard to accept. We often have the notion that great ideas are birthed fully formed, glittering in all their glory. But that kind of idea is extremely rare. Most ideas are born disproportionate and lanky. They aren't fully formed and often they're either missing key components or have too much of one thing over another. They need to grow and be refined.

And, like any newborn, new ideas are fragile and need protection. Holding a newborn baby is risky business. You need to get yourself ready, sit down in the chair, make sure you're stable. Carefully place your arms in the baby-holding position in anticipation of the transfer. Be careful to support the neck.

When you drive a baby home from the hospital you don't just throw him or her on the back seat of the car. You don't even just put a seatbelt on them. No, you strap them into a giant reinforced capsule that is itself strapped and bolted into the car.

Why? Because they're fragile and they need protection. New ideas are the same. They're fragile and easily destroyed. They barely exist and can be eroded into nothing with only a few pointed questions or scathing comments.

Ed Catmull, one of the three founders of Pixar and the current president of Walt Disney Animation Studios, lives in the world of new ideas. He was present for the birth of some of the greatest creative ideas in modern cinema, including *Toy Story, Finding Nemo,* and *Wall-E.* He writes this about the birth of new ideas:

> If, while in this vulnerable state, [a new idea] is exposed to naysayers who fail to see its potential or lack the patience to let it evolve, it could be destroyed. Part of our job is to protect the new

from people who don't understand that in order for greatness to emerge, there must be phases of not-so-greatness.[33]

A new idea might be as close to creation *ex nihilo* as we can get. One moment it didn't exist and then suddenly, out of nothing, the idea comes into existence. New ideas are an amazing phenomenon, but they are delicate and need space to exist, solidify, and develop.

You and your team, therefore, need to be patient with new ideas. Don't overwhelm them with questions. Delay judgement. Allow the idea time to percolate in your mind and in the minds of your team members. Don't criticize it too early.

When someone raises a new idea, thank them. Simply say, "Thank you for your idea". Allow the person time to explain it. As the leader, you need to pioneer the way for finding the potential within an idea and highlighting it for the team.

When people begin criticizing the idea or asking too many detail-oriented questions, you need to be the one to jump in to protect the idea—even if you're not yet convinced that the idea is a good one. It's your responsibility to protect new ideas and allow them the space they need to grow and develop. This doesn't mean you need to approve and implement every idea. What it means is that you give your approval for the idea to exist and for the person proposing it to put some of their time—not all, but some—into strengthening and solidifying the idea. It means you lead the way in asking questions that foster rather than hinder the idea's development.

Such questions will enable the person to articulate what's unique about the idea or how it fills a need. They won't be questions about the details of implementation. Good questions might include:

1. Can you tell me some more about where this idea came from?
2. What problem is currently being overlooked that you think this new idea will solve for us?
3. How is this idea different from [this other thing that is similar that we already do]?
4. What do you think are the next steps for exploring and developing this idea?

33 Catmull, *Creativity, Inc.*, p. 132.

Notice how these questions help the person to keep thinking about their idea without overwhelming them with questions about details that don't need to be worked out yet.

New ideas need friends

As the leader it's your responsibility to counteract the forces of mere exposure and loss aversion. Simply allowing the idea to remain on the table will help undermine those forces that pull you towards the status quo. The system is geared to favour the incumbent. Protecting the ugly newborn idea must be a conscious effort and the leader must drive it.

In the Pixar film *Ratatouille,* the jaded and feared food critic Anton Ego reviews the restaurant run by Remy, the movie's hero. Ego declares that Remy's cooking has "challenged my preconceptions about fine cooking... [and has] rocked me to my core". He goes on to give one of the most powerful critiques of criticism and one of the most eloquent defences of the new that I have come across. He says:

> In many ways, the work of a critic is easy. We risk very little yet enjoy a position over those who offer up their work and their selves to our judgment. We thrive on negative criticism, which is fun to write and to read. But the bitter truth we critics must face is that in the grand scheme of things, the average piece of junk is probably more meaningful than our criticism designating it so. But there are times when a critic truly risks something, and that is in the discovery and defence of the *new.* The world is often unkind to new talent, new creations. The new needs friends.[34]

The business-as-usual, established ideas and ways of doing things do not often need protection from new ideas. The message does not change, and novel theology should be suspect. But we do need to constantly challenge and update how we do things and how we communicate the gospel, so we need to combat mere exposure and loss aversion to protect the new—the future.

Be a friend to the new.

34 *Ratatouille,* 2007, motion picture, Pixar, Walt Disney Studios, Buena Vista, CA.

See also

34. Fail forwards
38. Shut up and listen
51. Get out of the way of good people
60. Creativity is a lost art

33
Communicate from the inside out

In 2012 our church began a partnership with a church in Kenya. This church was similar to ours in a lot of ways, but it was also different enough that we knew they would challenge and sharpen us. The partnership would push us from a different perspective—it would expand our horizons and make us better, more effective, and more useful. The relationship would also enable us to serve and sharpen another church and so help them to also be better, more effective, and more useful.

As we began talking about the possibility of this partnership, I knew why we should do it. There were lots of great and persuasive reasons. I talked a lot with all kinds of different people about why we should do it. We had lots of 'why'.

I just had no idea how we would do it. How were we going to afford it? How would we even set it up in the first place? I didn't know. I knew why we should do it and why it needed to happen, but I didn't have the foggiest idea what we were actually going to do or how we were going to do it.

And so we did it. A perfect opportunity arose and we worked out the 'how' and the 'what' as we went along.

What about the 'why'?

When it comes to communicating, however, that's not the way things normally happen. Most of the time we know what we want to do. When we're recruiting people, for example, we usually know what we want them to do. When we're trying to inspire people to action, we know what we want to see happen. We're usually very good at the 'what', which is often clear and concrete.

And we're normally good at the 'how' as well. It's usually a bit harder than the 'what', but we will usually have at least a rough idea of how we'll do the 'what'.

Rarely, however, will we talk about why we're doing something. Sometimes we know exactly why we need to do something, but for some reason we never get around to talking about it; we stick instead to the what and how. Other times we won't even have a clear idea ourselves about why we're doing something. We might have a vague feeling, but when we try to articulate the rationale it comes out jumbled and feels much less persuasive than it did in our head just moments earlier. Or sometimes what we think is the why turns out to be a what or a how in disguise.

For example, we might say something like: "We need two volunteers to help with welcoming at the Sunday morning church service. Two of our welcomers are moving house and have had to take themselves off the roster. Here's what's involved: you would need to arrive half an hour before the service, hand out the church brochure and say 'hi' to each person as they come in. If you'd like to help, jot your name and email down on the communication card and we'll be in touch."

What was the why in that explanation? The closest we came to a why was: "Because two people are moving house so they've taken themselves off the roster". But that's not actually a why. It's a what in disguise. It's actually just a version of the first sentence.

What if we replaced that first sentence with this: "Because there are so many people coming on a Sunday morning, we need more help to hand out the orders of service". That's sounding closer to a why, but this time it's actually just how in disguise. It's actually the third sentence masquerading as a why.

We often find it difficult to recruit or inspire people for this very reason—we either don't know the why or what we think is a why turns out to be a what or how.

Now this isn't to say that whats and hows aren't important, because they are. You need to tell people what and how. But you also need to tell them why it matters. Because the why is the most important part.

Starting with the 'why'

Instead of starting from the outside and talking about the what and the how and never getting to the why, we need to flip it around and communicate from the inside out.[35] We need to start with the why. People don't care as much about the what and how as they do about the why. Tell me why we need to do this. When you tell people why, you begin answering questions like: What's the point of it? Why does it matter? What would happen if we didn't do it and why would that be so bad?

Imagine if, in that announcement about welcomers, you said something like, "We believe first impressions matter and we want to make sure people know straight away that whoever they are, wherever they've come from, and whatever they've done, they're welcome at this church and we're glad that they're here. So we're looking for two people who'd be keen to help us make sure people are welcomed well on Sunday mornings. You'd need to arrive half an hour before the service and hand out the church brochure and say 'hi' to each person as they come in. If you'd like to help, jot your name and email down on the communication card and we'll be in touch."

The first sentence tells you why. The second sentence tells you what. The third sentence tells you how, and the final sentence tells you the action you'd need to take.

Perhaps that's not the best announcement ever, and you could probably work out a better way to say it, but it's at least an improvement on the first attempt and more likely to inspire someone to volunteer. The reason it's better is because you've told people why it matters, and you've told them that first. You've communicated from the inside out.

This inside out communication isn't just for announcements—it's applicable to all communication. Tell people the why. Whether you're leading a meeting, having a one-on-one conversation, preaching a sermon, or talking to your kids, give them a why. Even just a glimpse of why will be better than nothing at all. As you open a meeting, remind everyone why this meeting matters, why it's a good use of their time, and why the decisions you're about to make will be worth the effort. Of course people

35 Simon Sinek in *Start with Why: How great leaders inspire everyone to take action* (Penguin, New York, 2009) first crystallized this insight for me.

should already know this, and maybe they do, but it's also easy to forget. If it's difficult for you to crystallize and articulate the why, it's probably even more difficult for your team to crystallize and remember it. So serve and love them by giving them a glimpse of the why before you start. This focus will make for a better meeting with more engaged participants.

The why is the key because it's the why that matters, that convinces and engages people. So as a leader you have to make sure you know and communicate the why, even if you don't quite know the what or the how. Even before the what and how are clear, people who know and understand the why will come with you.

See also

40. Team communication is exponential
55. The point is clarity, not labels

34

Fail forwards

Failure is always a difficult thing to experience, but when the things you do matter to God and matter eternally, failure seems even more costly—we want to avoid it at all costs.

In addition to this pressure, some of us unhelpfully link our sense of self-worth to how our ministry goes. When the ministry's going well, that means I'm good. When the ministry's going badly that means I, as a person, am not going that great. It's no wonder we're ultra-vigilant to avoid failure.

On the other hand, we often hear people say things like, "Failure isn't an option. It's a necessity." Failure is good, they say, and we need to embrace it and maybe even pursue it in some way. But when you hear that it just doesn't feel right. Something is off. How much failure is acceptable before you say to someone, "You know, maybe this isn't for you"? Sometimes failure causes a lot of damage and people get hurt.

But there is still some truth in the "necessity of failure" idea. Failure is a normal part of learning. Imagine a child sitting down for the first time at a piano or picking up a guitar. You show them a few notes and they try to play a note or strum a chord. Imagine what would happen if you then said, "Wrong! The piano is obviously not for you. Hop down and go watch TV."

We know there's something normal, natural, and necessary about failure. But we also know that it's also not always normal, natural, and necessary. We instinctively feel that there must be some point where we hit a failure saturation level that's dangerously high. But what is that point? How do we navigate this tension?

The first thing to recognize is that failure itself is neutral. This is a tough thought, and at first it seems counterintuitive. We're so prone to thinking that failure is bad and to be avoided at all costs. Success, we're told, is better. And of course it's better. But failure can sometimes be a necessary step on the journey towards success—as in the case of learning a musical instrument, or learning anything new for that matter. Failure is perfectly normal and we should be expecting it. And yet, sometimes failure happens not because we're learning something, trying our best and reaching past our current levels of proficiency. Sometimes failure happens because we get lazy or because we don't try that hard in the first place.

Failure can be a good thing or it can be a bad thing. It depends on the failure. Not all failure is a step forward towards success. Sometimes failure is a step backwards. We need to learn to distinguish between the two types of failure and treat them differently.

Failing backwards

Failing backwards is the type of failure that occurs because of neglect, moral collapse, or sheer stupidity. Failing backwards isn't about failure that takes the project backwards or failure that's costly. The failure may not take the project backwards. It might be costly or it might not be. The 'backwards' isn't referring to the failure itself but to the backwards path that leads to this type of failure.

Sometimes a person fails because he or she is lazy and can't be bothered to do the things they know they should do. This type of failure is not helpful or productive. Sometimes this laziness manifests itself in a person or team making the same mistakes over and over again. This is failing backwards.

Sometimes a person fails because of arrogance. When someone is overconfident they often skip over certain tasks they know should have been done because "Those rules don't apply to me. I've done this so many times before." This arrogance can lead to unchecked assumptions, to key processes being ignored, and to failure. This is also failing backwards.

Sometimes failure results from lack of planning. It's not that someone tried and just wasn't able to foresee every possible option and problem but that they didn't even try in the first place. The person thought they could 'wing it' and 'figure it out when we get there'. And the results of that kind of attitude are inevitable. This is failing backwards as well.

Failing backwards refers to the path that leads to the kind of failure that's caused by laziness, arrogance, overconfidence, lack of planning, or some other form of neglect.

Failing forwards

Failing forwards, on the other hand, is the kind of failure that's perfectly normal and necessary on the road toward success. It's the kind of failure that happens when you're diligent, thoughtful, careful, and accepting of guidance and counsel—and yet you still don't succeed.

You can say you've failed forwards if you've tried something new and done the best you could but it didn't work. What makes failing forwards different from failing backwards is that the person did the best they could.

As a leader, you need to help the people you lead experience more failing forwards and less failing backwards. You also need to help yourself have more failing forwards moments. This is what the pro-failure people are trying to get us to do.

If you never fail at all, ever, that's a problem. Never failing is a sign that you're playing it too safe and thinking too small. If the only times that you, or your team, ever fail is when you fail backwards, then you have a problem and you need to ask some hard questions. Are you failing because of laziness, arrogance, overconfidence, lack of planning, or something else? If you're trying new things and trying as hard as you can to make them work, you'll be failing forwards regularly.

Michael Jordan, perhaps the greatest NBA player of all time, knew the importance of failure and has talked openly about the significant role that failure has played in his life. He attributes his success to a combination of the thousands of shots he missed and the hundreds of games he lost.

Learning

The other piece of the failure puzzle is that, whether you're failing backwards or forwards, the one thing you must be doing is learning from your mistakes. This won't always happen automatically. Sometimes people will learn from their failures without your help, but others simply aren't introspective reflectors and so you will need to help them. If your team fails backwards, you must point it out to them so they can learn from what went wrong. If your team fails forwards you must help them to find the lessons that will help increase their chances of success next time. What could they have done better? Help them learn.

There's a famous story about Tom Watson Jr., the CEO of IBM during the 1950s and 1960s. The story may or may not be true, but it certainly fits with the culture of IBM in those days. A vice president at IBM had overseen a failed development project that had cost the company somewhere in the ballpark of ten million dollars. Ten million dollars in the 1960s was a lot of money. Watson called this vice president into his office and the vice president, expecting to be fired, crafted and brought with him a letter of resignation. When the vice president presented the letter to the CEO, Watson simply shook his head. "Fire you!?! You are certainly not leaving after we just gave you a ten-million-dollar education."

The only thing that would make failing forwards unacceptable would be if no-one learned anything from it.

Every failure requires an autopsy, which requires gathering the people involved and establishing that you're not looking to assign blame or to make people feel badly. Rather, you're all trying to work out what happened, why it died, and what you would do differently next time. In other words, you want to learn. You're cutting the failure open and poking around, looking for contributing causes. "Why did it die?"

In Jim Collins' book *Great by Choice,* he empirically evaluates companies that survive and thrive even during the most uncertain and chaotic circumstances. Collins' research team noticed in these companies this same dynamic of constant learning and a fanatic obsession with avoiding making the same mistake twice. "Even [great companies] make mistakes... but they view mistakes as expensive tuition: better get something out of it, learn everything you can, apply the learning, and don't repeat".[36]

Without an autopsy learning might happen, but equally it might not. Some people might learn, others might not. But if you have an autopsy you're communicating to your team, "We are going to learn from this".

36 Jim Collins and Morten T Hansen, *Great by Choice: Uncertainty, chaos, and luck—why some thrive despite them all,* HarperCollins, New York, 2011, p. 87.

You help everyone on your team to learn from the experience and to share their learning with one another. By doing it together you will all learn more than you would if only some of you reflected individually.

Whether you failed backwards or failed forwards, or perhaps some combination of the two, you must make sure that you and your team learn from the failure—especially if the education was expensive.

Recklessness

Sometimes we hesitate to embrace failure as normal and positive, and even necessary, because what we're doing is important and the idea of embracing failure sounds like we're talking about intentionally failing. We'd never be reckless with the important work we're doing to fail for the sake of failing.

But that's not what failing forwards means. Failing forwards is about doing the absolute best you can *and* embracing failure as necessary. You do this when you stretch to achieve something slightly outside your grasp, to do a little more than what you're confident you can do. Perhaps you invite more people than you've ever invited before. Perhaps you start something you've never tried before. Perhaps you implement something you've never done before.

Maybe you're positive that you could start two new small groups this year at your church. And so you go ahead and start two new groups. That's a great thing. But what if you stretched and said, "We're positive we could start two new groups this year. We're much less sure about whether we'd be able to start three. But we're going to try and see what happens." If you actually succeed in starting three, wow! Praise God. That's great! If you get two off the ground but not the third—well, that's very interesting. There are all kinds of fun conversations that can come out of that attempt. How come it didn't happen? Were there enough people who were keen to join a small group? If there were, how come we couldn't make it happen this time? What could we do differently to find and contact every person who was keen to join a group? If there weren't enough people interested, is there a way we could help more people see the value of being in a group? How hard did we try to see people far from God come to put their trust in him? What could we do this year to contact more people who don't yet know Jesus? What could we do this year to help people understand and feel like they're missing out when they're not in a group? And so on. Those are all really interesting and productive questions for a team to discuss.

There's nothing reckless about thinking about trying to start three groups instead of two. It's not naïve, either. It's stretching and challenging. Maybe you'll get there and maybe you won't, but you will have tried hard and learned from the experience either way.

It's the same with trying something new. If you're trying as hard as you can to reach people, grow people, and help people, then you'll be trying things you've never done before. You'll start things that you think will work and be helpful. You don't know that they'll work or be helpful, but you think they will be. And so you try them. If something works, that's great—and you ask how you can you improve it. If something doesn't work, well, that's very interesting. Then you ask why not. Was it the timing? Was it how you publicized it? Was it the content?

If, in your autopsy, you come to believe that the failure was due to recklessness on your part, or because you overreached what you could reasonably expect to do, or because you were naïve or ignored wise counsel, these would be indicators that maybe you failed backwards. In that case there might be some deficiencies in you or in your team's culture that you need to address. And that's a great thing to learn and then to address.

Just do something

One of the most dangerous cultures you can create is a culture dominated by the desire to avoid mistakes. Avoiding mistakes isn't bad. The problem comes when avoiding mistakes becomes the dominant motivation—when you won't try something because it might not work, or because no-one else has tried it before, or because people might not approve.

The cultural pressure subtly shifts from passionately seeking to spread the message that Jesus is King to avoiding mistakes at all costs. The verbal message, of course, will stay the same: "We exist to make disciples". But the real, underlying message is this: "We exist to avoid mistakes". This kind of culture is guaranteed to produce mediocrity.

You don't need to wait until you have the perfect answer, the perfect plan, or the perfect program. When we won't do something unless it's perfect we have 'perfection paralysis'. But having the perfect plan isn't what matters. What matters is that you have *an* answer and *a* plan. Get the best answer you can and then *do something*. Make a decision—even if you don't have all the information and there's still more research you can do. The ideal situation, with 100% information and 100% chance of success, is a mirage. This is called 'theoretical analysis paralysis'. Knowing everything is overrated. 60% will do, and now is a good time to act. The best time to plant a tree is 20 years ago. The second best time is today.

A culture driven by a passion to avoid mistakes results in people who say, "Well, sure, we never actually did anything. But at least we didn't make any mistakes." As General George Patton once said, "A good plan violently executed now is better than a perfect plan next week".[37] Waiting until you have concrete confirmation that a plan is absolutely guaranteed to succeed, coupled with fear of making a mistake, is a sure-fire formula for ineffectiveness.

Creating a culture

Creating a culture in which trying new things and stretching forward are accepted and encouraged, and not punished, is vitally important. It's also very hard to do. You need to create a space where people know they have permission to fail forwards. People are often punished and criticized for going too far, but rarely are they blamed for not going far enough.

So how do you start creating a culture where failing forwards is accepted and encouraged? Here are four behaviours you can start with:

1. Talk clearly and openly about it with your team. Gather them together and explain the difference between failing backwards and failing forwards. Tell them that you'd like to see the team members trying new things and stretching themselves, and that you want to give them the permission to do that.

37 General George S Patton, Jr., *General George S Patton, Jr. Quotations,* The Official Website of General George S Patton, Jr., CMG Worldwide, Inc., Indianapolis, 2001 (viewed 29 August 2014): http://www.generalpatton.com/quotes/

2. Talking is a good start; it's cheap and easy. The problem with talking is that it's cheap and easy. There needs to be more. And it needs to start with you, the leader. Unless you put yourself out there and stretch in an area for which you're responsible, or try something new or different, your team will still be hesitant to do it themselves. If you stretch and succeed, great. Stretch some more. But if you stretch, fail, and accept that failure as necessary and helpful for learning, then your team will begin to follow suit.

3. When members of your team do follow and start pushing forward and stretching to achieve more than they're confident they can, you'll need to make sure you don't punish them when they fail forwards. You'll probably be tempted to, and you might not even think about it—it might just reflexively happen. So you'll need to be very conscious and deliberate in order to help people find what's interesting about the failure and help them learn.

   You're modelling this kind of response to failing forwards for the rest of the team, too. Others may naturally ridicule the person who failed forwards, perhaps only slightly or even just as a good-natured joke. It's of utmost importance, though, that you maintain a zero-tolerance position against that. Even if it's just a joke. You'll need to firmly but graciously remind people that failing forwards is to be encouraged and celebrated.

   If a person fails backwards, you still mustn't punish the failure itself. You're trying to create a culture where failure is accepted and expected. People may misinterpret your reprimand for failing backwards as a reprimand of failure itself. They may not be able to make the fine grade distinctions between failing forwards and failing backwards. This kind of confusion will seriously cramp the style of your effort to create the space for the permission to fail.

   So you'll need to make sure you're extra clear. Reprimand the characteristics that led to the failing backwards—the laziness, the arrogance, the lack of planning, the undisciplined assumptions—and not the failure itself.

4. Reinforce failing forwards by who you reward and why. Don't reward people who always succeed. This can be very difficult because it seems so wrong and backwards. "But they're always succeeding. Why wouldn't I reward them for success?"

   The reason you wouldn't reward them is because they've set their bar too low. If you can always jump over the bar it's because it's too low. If a person hits 100% of their goals and plans, that's probably a good indicator that they're playing it safe. You don't want to reward playing it safe. People like that need to stretch themselves. They need to push further.

   You need to reward the people who are pushing their boundaries and trying new things—trying to reach new people, innovating new ways and methods. Honour the people who are failing forwards. Mention them to your team; tell their stories. Don't just tell the story of their eventual success. Remind people of the failures that it took to get them there.

Failure itself is neutral. Sometimes it's the result of bad habits and behaviours, and sometimes it's the result of someone trying to go further than they currently think they can. Learn to distinguish between failing backwards and failing forwards. And give your team the space and the permission to keep growing.

See also

28. Anything worth doing is worth doing badly
31. Energy is more efficient than efficiency
41. Two foundations of team-building
46. People deserve to know the truth
48. Treat them like children
64. Learn relaxed concern
77. Bad news is good news

35

Everyone already knows

Weaknesses are embarrassing things. We all want to be good at everything—or, if not good, at least decent. But we're not, and it's not being overly pessimistic to say that we never will be. There will always be things I'm not good at and I will always be flawed—and not just in terms of skills and abilities. I will have weaknesses and flaws in how I relate to other people too.

As we face the reality of our flaws and weaknesses, most of us will employ some common strategies. We will hide our weaknesses, minimize them, or deny them. We pretend they don't exist. We don't talk about them, we don't acknowledge them, and we try our best to ignore them.

The idea seems to be that if I ignore or deny my weaknesses then others won't see them. If I don't point them out they won't notice them.

The assumption behind this flawed thinking is, of course, that my flaws and weaknesses are not very noticeable anyway; they don't make much impact; and they're relatively harmless.

Weaknesses are obvious

But the truth is often the exact opposite. My flaws and weaknesses are some of the most obvious and easily noticed aspects of who I am. They make a huge impact on the people around me and this impact is of the negative variety and can be, and often is, quite harmful and hurtful.

And here's the biggest reality check: everyone already knows.

Whatever the weakness is, the people on your team already know all about it. If you're not that good at planning, people already know. If you're not good at making decisions, people will have noticed. If you're not good at encouraging people, they already feel it. If you're not good at thanking people, they already know. And if you're not good at being on time? Yep, they know that too.

Our weaknesses and flaws aren't small blemishes that we can easily mask with a bit of makeup; they're huge and obvious deformities.

Just admit it

So the point is that if you try and pretend they don't exist, you either make yourself look like a fool or you make your team think you can't be trusted. So, as painful and scary as it might be, it's important to own your weaknesses. Don't try to hide them, make excuses for them, or minimize them. Rather, be upfront in owning them and apologizing for them.

Sometimes you might even be the last one to find out. You may come to a sudden realization that you're not that good, for example, at giving clear direction to your team.

If you've just discovered that this is a weakness, guess what? Everyone else already knows. They've just been patiently waiting for you to figure it out as well. So if you mention it to them their reaction will not be, "Really!?! Well, that is a surprise to me." Their reaction will more likely be, "Finally".

They already know.

So there's no point denying or pretending that a weakness is not obvious. The sooner you can realize it and own it, the better. Everyone already knows what your weaknesses are and they probably know more of them than you do.

So don't hide them. Be brave enough to admit them—not to be proud of them or to make a joke out of them, but to acknowledge their existence and the impact they have on the people you lead. Acknowledge how your flaws make things harder for your team and thank them for putting up with those flaws and working around them. Your team will thank you for it and respect you more because of it, and they might even give you more grace and forgiveness as well.

See also

37. Phrases to learn
41. Two foundations of team-building
46. People deserve to know the truth

36

Let people say no

There are a lot of things to ask people to join, do, and be responsible for. There are lots of things you'd like to see happen—lots of plans and dreams and 'one day whens'. And so we ask people to be involved in this, coordinate that, or take the leadership of this.

There are also lots of reasons to not ask certain people to be involved in things. Maybe someone doesn't quite fit the role, or there's someone else who would be better at it or who would enjoy the role more or who would have more time to devote to it. Some people haven't yet displayed the Christian character and maturity necessary for a given role, or the role is beyond where they could fairly stretch their leadership currently, and so on.

There are many perfectly legitimate reasons, depending on the person and the circumstances, to not ask someone to be involved in a specific ministry role. Not everyone is best suited for everything.

An illegitimate reason

But there's also an illegitimate, though very common, reason for not asking someone. You may be familiar with it and you may have even used it yourself: "I won't ask them because I already know they'll say no".

Not asking because you think they'll say no is a bad reason not to ask. You should always let people say their own no. If they say no, that's fine. Let them say it. No hard feelings, no problems—there are other people who will be great. Saying no isn't the end of the world and we don't need to protect people from saying it.

Besides, without asking you don't really know that someone will say no. You might think they will and you might even be pretty sure they will. But you don't actually know.

What if the role you have in mind is exactly the kind of opportunity this person has been hoping and praying would come their way? What if they've been saying no to everything else to keep themselves available for this? What if they would normally have said no to something like this but God has been working on them and, for no discernable reason that you or even they can understand, they inexplicably say yes?

Maybe that's unlikely. Maybe nine times out of ten you get it right and you can predict a no. That still leaves one out of ten offers where God might surprise you and your 'number-one pick' agrees to be involved. It might be unlikely or a long shot, but crazy things happen sometimes. Let people say no for themselves.

None of us likes to be rejected. And if we're pretty certain we can predict it coming, why would we willingly put ourselves in that kind of position? Or if we're pretty sure someone will say no then we might see asking them as a waste of time, prolonging the recruitment process. And we usually don't have unlimited time to recruit people—the clock is ticking and we need to find someone before Sunday.

These are all compelling arguments for saying no for people. Letting people say their own no is harder than saying it for them. It takes longer and it's more personally taxing. Hearing no isn't fun and it doesn't take long to become jaded by it.

Even though all of that might be the case, it's still worth letting people say their own no. Asking someone honours that person and treats them with respect and dignity. The request may also spark something in them so that, the next time you ask, they're more ready to commit. You just never know what a person is thinking until you ask.

But what about burnout?

As you read this, you might largely agree with asking people even if you're pretty sure they'll say no. But perhaps you still feel slightly uncomfortable. What about the person who already does too much but who loves to serve? In order to love them, and in some ways to protect them from themselves, you might be tempted to say their no for them. You might decide not to ask that overcommitted person not out of laziness or fear of rejection or overconfidence in your ability to predict the future, but out of good old-fashioned love and care for that person. Wouldn't that be the exception to the rule?

I understand this objection and resonate deeply with it. I don't want to overload people and burden them with responsibilities. Seeing people burned out and jaded by ministry is a sad thing, and especially for those of us whose job it is to pastor people. And it's a terrible thought that under my watch someone might become burned out and jaded about serving others because I overloaded them and made them carry a load that they were never designed to carry. It's a mistake I've made before, and one I'll probably make again, but I'm in no hurry to be at that place again any time soon.

So what do you do with a person like that? How do you love them and protect them from themselves? How do you protect them from something great and beautiful, like a heart to serve, being twisted into something negative and harmful, like overloading themselves?

A different kind of ask

You protect them by still asking them. If you think this is the best person for the role, you should pitch it to him or her. Treat them with respect as a decision-making human being and let them say their own no. But the way you ask them, and what you ask them to do, will need to be slightly different in order to love and help them in their weakness.

When you ask, you preface the question with the two facts you both know are true: first, they love serving and being helpful; and, second, they're already serving and being helpful. After you make those two facts clear you can talk with them about the new role or opportunity, and you communicate it from the inside out so that they understand the why.

The next step, though, is the critical difference between this type of ask and a normal ask. Because you then carefully explain that you're *not* asking them to *add* this to their current ministry load. You're wondering, instead, whether they would like to *replace* a current ministry responsibility with this one or whether they'd prefer to continue what they're currently doing.

This is the critical move—you make your discussion about replacement rather than addition. You're asking whether this new opportunity is one the person would like to do *instead* of something they're currently doing. It may be that some of the things this person is currently doing could be done just as well by others, whereas he or she is clearly the best person for this new role. And so you may even point that out if it seems right to do so.

But what you want to do above all is add in those extra boundaries, terms, and conditions in order to help them make a good decision. And you allow them the privilege of making the decision and saying their own yes or no.

A caution

One last caveat: if you're the leader responsible for all the ministries this very busy person is involved in, then there should be no problem asking them to drop one and pick up another because you're 'stealing' your own person. If, however, this person is on multiple teams—each under the authority of a different leader—you'll need to have a different conversation before you head out recruiting.

You'll need to talk with all the leaders of the teams this person belongs to so that you're all in agreement that this person may stay where he or she is currently serving or choose to leave one of the teams to take on this new ministry role. Because these team leaders may be affected by the end result, they should be included and in agreement with the process.

We don't know the future, and people still have the ability to surprise us—and God most certainly has the ability to surprise us. So if you think a person would be great in a certain role but is a long shot, ask them anyway. Who knows what will happen? Let people say no for themselves.

See also

30. Faithfulness buys responsibility
43. The five C's
44. Choose your lieutenants

37

Phrases to learn

Leadership isn't about formulas, step-by-step guides, or easy solutions. Leadership is an art form, and it's a difficult one at that. It's about who you are, being genuine, and careful planning as well as being open to crucial spontaneous moments. Which is why formulas don't always work and are more often than not unhelpful. Leadership is not just about doing the right thing. It's about doing the right thing for the right reasons in the right way at the right time.

Despite this fluidity, however, there are some critical moves that are worth scripting. One of those critical moves is a collection of key phrases that are worth memorizing and drilling over and over again so that they become natural and almost spring-loaded.

There are four phrases that most leaders find very hard to learn and then to use in natural conversation. If you can learn these four phrases, and the genuine heart that's beneath them, then you'll love people better and lead them much more effectively.

Phrase one: "I don't know"

None of us knows everything. That's obvious. But it's easy to feel that, when we're in leader-mode, it's our job to know everything. People are counting on us to know everything. They need clarity and direction. They need someone decisive. Someone they can trust.

There's some truth in all of those things—people are counting on us and they do need clarity and direction. The problem is that pretending to have clarity and direction when you don't have either doesn't provide clarity or direction. It provides the illusion of those things, and in due course that illusion will result in the reality of confusion and mistakes.

One of the most helpful things we can do for the people we lead, in those times where we don't know something, is to tell them that we don't know. Just say it. It's not as bad as you think it is. People might be a bit shocked to start with, but they'll soon get used to it.

Saying "I don't know" will give you a chance to find the answer and get smarter. "I don't know" won't be the sum of everything you say when confronted with your own ignorance. You'll also have to say, "We need to find out the answer". But you can't talk about finding the answer until you first admit that you don't know. The hard part is admitting that you don't know, but once you do that it gets easier because you'll be able to gain knowledge and explore solutions.

Phrase two: "You're better at that than I am"

As we've said, the leader doesn't need to be the most competent person in the room. You might happen to be the most competent person in the room, but it's not necessary that you are.

As soon as you realize that you're not the most competent person in the room, you need to acknowledge it—admit it to yourself and announce it to everyone else. You can still be the leader and not be the best. If someone is better than you at something then you need to unleash them, learn from them, and be careful not to restrict them.

In fact, your goal as a leader is to recruit and develop people who are better than you are. So you need to be secure enough within yourself to be able to do that. If you can only lead people who aren't as good as you are, then by definition you will always have an inferior leadership team. But if you can lead, inspire, and motivate people who are better than you are, you'll achieve far more.

Saying "you're better than me at this" requires both confidence and humility—confidence to both know and be comfortable with who you are, and humility to be able to admit it.

Phrase three: "Do you think..."

As a leader, and especially if you are *the* leader, your voice carries a lot of weight. People will listen to what you say. And they won't just listen; they'll be inclined to agree and do what you say. Or, if they don't agree, they'll at least do what you ask. This is not because what you say is good or right or wise, although it may be. They'll be inclined to agree and do it simply because you said it and you're the leader.

This situation is extremely dangerous.

This behaviour means that your team is devolving into the kind of team that implements ideas based not on their merit but rather on who proposed them. This is one of the dangers of a strong, competent leader. When your team is in danger of implementing bad ideas because the leader proposed them, it's like a car that needs a wheel alignment, constantly in jeopardy of veering off the road and crashing into a ditch. A car in need of such a repair requires constant attention just to keep it going straight, and so your team will be in constant danger of crashing itself into a ditch.

Ideas need to be implemented because they're good and because they're the best you could come up with—not because the powerful people suggested them.

Since you, as the leader, are the most powerful person in the room, your ideas will be given more credit than they deserve. You need to find a way to counterbalance that. This counterbalancing process will require a number of individual strategies that you'll need to implement rigorously. One of those strategies is prefacing your ideas with "Do you think..." By building this kind of less-than-declarative temperature into your statements you vastly increase the amount of permission you give people to disagree or refine your ideas. That simple phrase communicates to them that this isn't a statement of what we're doing but an option for us to consider.

Anything you can do to lighten the freight behind your ideas will help you and your team make better decisions. Sometimes you need to put all the weight you can behind your statements, and there's a time and a place for that. But that won't be all the time and in every place.

You need to help people recognize and distinguish between the kinds of ideas you're putting forward. Is this a declaration of direction or an option to add to the mix?

"Do you think..." will help you do that.

Phrase four: "I'm sorry"

"I'm sorry" might be one of the hardest phrases to learn, and it might also be one of the most important.

Owning up to a mistake is hard. Owning up to a mistake when you're the leader can often be even harder. And being able to say "I'm sorry" on top of that can seem impossible.

But, as a leader, you need to model this kind of repentance. When you make a mistake, when you say or do something hurtful, whether intentionally or by accident, you need to admit it and make it right as quickly as you can. Saying "I'm sorry" is the best way to begin to do that.

You gain nothing by being a leader who refuses to apologize for causing legitimate problems or making real mistakes. You don't gain respect. Relationships aren't strengthened. Trust isn't built. Nothing good comes from refusing to apologize or from pretending nothing happened. Apologizing is the right thing to do. Even though it gets easier with practice, it will always be hard and you'll never want to do it—all the more reason to make sure you learn how to say it. Because, unfortunately, you'll probably need to say "I'm sorry" often.

See also

27. You're just the leader
29. Praise publicly
35. Everyone already knows
41. Two foundations of team-building
42. Humble and hungry
46. People deserve to know the truth
52. Give credit and take blame

38
Shut up and listen

Leaders are often—not always, but often—very good talkers. Or, even if they're not very good at it, they're usually constantly practising. Which I guess is something. The leader is generally the one running the meeting, giving the talk, explaining the vision, persuading the uncertain, calming the angry, answering the question, and giving the advice. And there's nothing wrong with any of those things.

The problem is that sometimes leaders do those things when they shouldn't. There's an entire skill set of leadership that leaders often neglect: the skill of listening.

You can be great at all different parts of leadership, and you need to be, but if you fail as a listener then your leadership effectiveness will plateau far beneath where it could and should be. People won't follow you as wholeheartedly as they might. They won't trust you as much as maybe they could and, over time, your influence will slowly atrophy. Being a poor listener hampers your ability to lead well.

The love of listening

Listening is crucial for leadership because listening to someone is a display and outflow of your love for that person. Just as leadership is about loving those you lead, so listening is about loving those you listen to. When you give another person the space and time to speak to you, and you listen to them attentively, you treat them with honour and dignity.

It's not that easy, though. Listening is more than simply not talking. It's hard work. Listening is about allowing the other person to speak, but it's also about creating a space in which they feel allowed to speak in the first place.

Questions communicate

It's important to make space for people to be heard in lots of different circumstances. In a meeting you're leading it can be tempting to speak quickly and often. You have ideas, and you like those ideas, and there are so many things to get through that the more you speak the faster the meeting seems to go because no-one else is talking and there's no discussion. But 'getting through things' isn't always the point of a meeting or the wisest way to approach a meeting. If you know that you're a finite human, that you're prone to making mistakes, and that the people on your team are smart people, then it's wise to hear what they have to say. Which means you need to listen—which means not talking, and it might also mean learning to ask better questions.

If your team is made up of smart people who are better at things than you are, and it should be, then you'll want to learn from them. And the only way you'll learn is if you stop talking and start listening. You're not learning when you're talking because you can only say things that you already know. You might crystallize and clarify things by speaking them out loud, but the thoughts were already there and they're not new to you even though they might feel new as you give voice to them. To learn something genuinely new you need to stop talking.

Questions and listening are a very powerful combination for communication and for reinforcing vision and values. Statements and declarations are good and useful, but often questions are much more dynamic. What you ask questions about reveals what you really care about. I once heard Andy Stanley give a powerful example of this. Imagine you're at work and you get a call from your spouse, who seems upset. "I've just been in a car accident," your spouse tells you. The question you ask first is very important. The question you ask at this point is going to communicate in a powerful way what it is that you value. If your question is, "Is the car okay?" what are you communicating to your spouse about what you really value? Questions and listening can be powerful tools in communicating vision and values to your team.

Listening is about caring for people

A lot of leaders fall into the trap of becoming very good at speaking and telling people what to do while not practising the skills of listening and actively showing people that they care about them. The ability to listen well and ask questions is often an area that is vastly underdeveloped in the leader's repertoire. There are three skills in particular that are in high demand, but often in low supply, among leaders. They're not complicated skills, but they can be difficult to master.

The first skill, above all, is the ability to not talk. This cannot be overstated. Humans form theories and hypotheses very quickly and we are highly skilled at pattern recognition—but although this is a great skill it doesn't always help us. Often we make diagnoses too hastily, whether it's regarding a personal issue with an individual or a problem with a program or a structure. A swift categorization of an issue or problem yields little benefit, and that little benefit diminishes still further when we speak too quickly. The number-one skill we need when we encounter a problem, whether it's a pastoral situation or any other kind of issue, is the ability to be quiet and to let the other person talk and explain.

An easy and common mistake is to not listen carefully enough, or at all, and then to make a premature diagnosis and suggest the wrong solution. In an exam situation, it's of vital importance to make sure you're answering the question that is being asked. Giving the right answer to the wrong question, no matter how well you argue or how much evidence you give to support your conclusions, gets you no marks in the exam. It's not enough to give the right answer. You need to give the right answer to the right question.

We do need to expose every problem, and particularly pastoral problems, to the Bible's wisdom and the light shed by the gospel. But just because a biblical perspective on a person's problem is of primary importance doesn't mean it should be given first. This is a common mistake.

Yes, advice is good, and the person coming to you with a problem may need it. Yes, biblical reflections are good and the person may need to have those pointed out to them as well. And you might get to one or both of those in due time. But the gift that people need from you first of all is the gift of a space to talk and a listening ear. When you listen to someone, you give them a gift.

At least some of the time, and perhaps most of the time, people already know what they should do and what the Bible says about an issue. What they need is the space to process what they already know and to convince themselves that they should do it.

But even if the person genuinely doesn't know what they should do and isn't quite sure what the Bible says on the matter, there is still wisdom in listening deeply first. You need to make sure the answer that you're giving answers the question that is being asked. Sometimes the initial question is only the presenting issue. The deeper cause may be something else entirely. A lack of listening may lead to a misdiagnosis or to perpetually treating symptoms rather than causes. It's very important to make sure that we're giving a solution that deals with the problem. No matter how biblically sound and eloquently delivered your advice on a leadership issue or pastoral care issue may be, if it's a solution to the wrong problem then it's no solution at all.

Listening is more than not talking

The second skill worth learning is listening itself. Not talking is not the same as listening. Not talking is certainly a prerequisite, but it is not the thing itself. There's a dismissive kind of listening, a pseudo-listening that comes in a number of forms. There's the kind of listening where you're only half paying attention. The kind of listening where, inside your head, a second conversation is taking place between you and yourself. While you're not talking and thinking about some other topic—what you need to do next, who you need to speak to, what you need to remember to buy from the shops on the way home—you're not genuinely listening.

In another type of pseudo-listening, you overhear a nearby conversation that you wish you were a part of instead of being stuck in this other conversation. And so while you're talking (or not talking) to the person in front of you, you're engaged in the conversation next to you. This is not genuine listening.

A third type of pseudo-listening occurs when listening is merely a bothersome, though socially necessary, precursor to your next chance to talk. You're not actually listening to what's being said at all. What you're actually listening for is an extended pause, which will signal the end of that person's talking and your chance to begin. This is another common counterfeit for genuine listening. All of these kinds of pseudo-listening are dismissive and reveal a lack of love for the person talking to us.

Genuine listening is about more than just not talking. It's about actively engaging with what a person is saying. Remembering it. Thinking about it. Whether the context is a discussion in a meeting or speaking with a person one-to-one, it's about listening for what's being said and also for what's not being said. What is the person leaving out? What aspect have they not touched on yet? What are they overlooking or perhaps even potentially hiding?

Asking questions

The third foundational skill for listening, along with not talking and actually listening, is the ability to ask questions. We ask questions to make sure we're hearing the person properly and understanding them rightly. We want to get as accurate a picture as possible of what they're saying. This generally means taking the broad statement that they've made and sharpening it and adding clarity to it. Sometimes when viewed from a distance two objects can appear very similar and yet, when you move in closer for a more detailed look, they suddenly snap into focus as two entirely different things. That's the sort of clarity that you're seeking when you listen to someone. You want to know as best you can what exactly is going on, what it's about, and what might be going on beneath the surface. Assume that there's more than meets the eye.

Asking questions also helps you to avoid dispensing advice and wisdom. It helps you to stop talking and to listen actively. It's a mechanism that assists you in waiting and allowing people to be, and to feel, heard and understood.

If you find yourself prone to making judgements quickly and talking before you've really heard the person, you might try and self-enforce a new rule: no wisdom or advice until you've asked ten questions.

Ten questions might sound like an eternity of questions! You might not think you'd be able to come up with ten. But what if you tried? What you might find is that, before you even get to the end of your ten questions, people will come up with the answer to their problem themselves and even convince themselves why they need to solve it in a particular way—which is a brilliant outcome. If this happens, you will have helped someone figure out the course of action to take and motivated them to go do it while also building their confidence and ability to solve their own problems.

Listening can be a very difficult skill to practise and learn. But it's a skill every leader needs to develop. As Dietrich Bonhoeffer wrote in his book *Life Together*:

> Just as love to God begins with listening to His Word, so the beginning of love for the brethren is learning to listen to them... Christians, especially ministers, so often think they must always contribute something when they are in the company of others, that this is the one service they have to render. They forget that listening can be a greater service than speaking.[38]

If you find yourself unable to listen carefully and patiently, and if the temptation to dispense wisdom and give advice is simply too strong for you to overcome, you will increasingly find yourself talking about the wrong things and giving advice that doesn't help. You will find yourself doing a lot of talking but not actually talking to the right people about the right problems.

See also

26. Leading is loving
32. Ideas are born ugly

38 Dietrich Bonhoeffer, *Life Together: The classic exploration of faith in community*, Harper & Row, New York, 1954, p. 97.

39

Public fans and private critics

A good thing in the wrong place can be a big problem.

In *A Short History of Nearly Everything*, Bill Bryson writes about how bacteria, in the wrong place, can be deadly:

> At least 10 percent of young adults, and perhaps 30 percent of teenagers, carry the deadly meningococcal bacterium, but it lives quite harmlessly in the throat. Just occasionally—in about one young person in a hundred thousand—it goes into the bloodstream and makes them very ill indeed. In the worst cases death can come in twelve hours.[39]

When microbes that normally do no harm, or even perform a helpful task, get into parts of the body where they're not meant to be, serious problems can occur.

Criticism is similar. Careful reflection and thoughtful feedback are good things, in that they help us to improve what we do. Feedback leads to improvement, which leads to more feedback, which leads to more improvement. This iterative process of continuous, incremental improvement is the most common path from mediocrity to excellence. Very few people, skills, or programs go from being not that great to being spectacular in a single leap. Most will make incremental improvements that compound over time.

Feedback and criticism are indeed good things. But, in the wrong place and at the wrong time, they can also be incredibly damaging.

39 Bill Bryson, *A Short History of Nearly Everything*, Random House, New York, 2003, p. 314.

Who and when

Imagine your church begins a new strategy to improve its music in the Sunday service. In order to reach more young families and help people focus on praising God, the team decides to strip back the morning band so that it only includes vocals and the bagpipes.

And you, as a member of that team and as a keen observer of people who also has a discerning ear, have noticed that it sounds horrible. Even though you're an admirer of the noble bagpipes, you feel that the combination of bagpipes and vocals, in the community and culture in which your church exists, is probably not the best combination for this exact moment in time to reach the people you're trying to reach.

This is good and helpful feedback. And so you decide that it would be best for you to communicate this feedback to every person who comes to the morning church service, including every visitor who arrives for the first time. You also make sure you tell every person who serves you at the local supermarket.

What we now have is a good thing in the wrong place.

The criticism was good, but it was expressed to the wrong people. The criticism, of course, should have been brought back to the team that made the decision—to the people with the power to do something and make changes. That's where the criticism belongs. But now this criticism has mutated into gossip and, like the bacteria Bill Bryson mentions, this criticism is in the wrong place and so instead of being helpful and productive it's causing harm to people and undermining the work of the gospel.

Public and private

The people on your teams should be public fans and private critics.

Being a public fan doesn't mean pretending to love things you don't actually love. It's not about being fake or disingenuous. But it does mean that once a decision has been made by the team, each member of the team accepts responsibility for making the decision work and does everything they can to make the plan a success. And slamming the decision in front of everyone who'll listen is probably not the best way to make it work.

Being a private critic doesn't mean keeping your criticism to yourself. It's not about being a silent critic, but it is private. It means offering criticism when the team is back in the room together—or, if it's more appropriate, sharing the criticism only with the person involved and the team leader.

Establishing a critically healthy culture

Sharing criticism in a healthy way isn't just the responsibility of team members. It's also your responsibility as team leader. You need to give people a safe place where they can say what they think without fear of being reprimanded or labelled as a negative whinger, as long as their criticism isn't mean or harsh or cruel. Honest criticism can still be kind and presented with humility. But you need to provide team members an outlet so that they can air their views. You need to make it clear where and when they can articulate their honest criticism, and where and when it is not appropriate.

What is unhealthy is insisting, whether explicitly or implicitly, that people be public fans *and* private fans. Neither is it healthy for people to be public critics *and* private critics. Criticism is a good and necessary thing that you need to hear in order to improve, but it can be toxic and unhealthy when given in the wrong places and at the wrong times.

Establishing this culture of public fans and private critics requires clarity and permission. You'll need to explain and model how to give criticism that's honest and constructive and that comes from a place of love and humility, and when and where it's good and when and where it's unhelpful. You'll also need to work hard to create the space and genuinely give people the permission to give feedback and criticism—even if it's criticism of you or of one of your favourite and most treasured ideas. You need to make sure people aren't penalized for giving honest criticism, so long as that criticism isn't cruel and mean-spirited. And one way of giving this kind of permission is to humbly and gratefully accept such feedback yourself.

This can be a hard culture to create because criticism can be genuinely painful, even when it's not mean or unfair. It can be hard to gauge sometimes when criticism crosses that line into meanness, and you as the leader need to have a consistent internal barometer so that when people do cross that line you're able to call them on it and have them apologize. You'll also need discipline to make sure that the same rules apply to you as they do to others. If people can criticize others they should be able to criticize you as well, and when your own criticism crosses over into meanness you'll need to apologize too.

It's a hard culture to create, but it is a necessary one. Criticism in the right place at the right time is good and healthy. Criticism in the wrong place can be very damaging. But if you can get it right, and do it well, you will constantly improve and grow both healthy programs and healthy teams.

See also

41. Two foundations of team-building
46. People deserve to know the truth
77. Bad news is good news

40

Team communication is exponential

Leadership is deeply about relationships. As a leader you're always leading a group of people, and those people are following you so that together you can strive towards a future that is better than today. You know the people you're leading, they know you, and you're doing this together. And because leadership is so relational, communication is vitally important. You need to communicate with the people you lead and they need to communicate with you and with each other.

And the fact that communication is so difficult complicates leadership. Not only do I need to crystallize in my own head what it is I think or want to see happen, but I also need to extract that from my brain and find the words to articulate those thoughts in a way that communicates what I mean so that others understand and can play their part. But even once I've worked out how to get the vision out of my head, the person I'm communicating with needs to receive and understand those thoughts. And the other person may very well misunderstand or mishear me, either due to my own incompetence or because of some difficulty on their end. They then gather their thoughts on what they've received from me, clarify and articulate them back to me, and the process continues.

Seems simple enough

When it's just you and me, this process isn't overly complicated. After we go back and forth a few times there's a reasonable chance that we'll be fairly close to being on the same page.

It becomes harder when there are more people involved in the communication process. Where there are multiple voices going back and forth there are many more opportunities for misunderstanding or mishearing.

I suspect we're still in the realm of the obvious at this point. But here's the part that we often overlook: the complexity of team communication grows exponentially. When there are more than two of us communicating, the communication doesn't just get gradually more complicated. The complication multiplies with each additional person. The lines of communication compound.

When two people are talking, there's basically one line of communication that both people travel on, back and forth. In a three-person team there are three lines of communication. In both of these situations, any miscommunication would become immediately apparent and you could have everyone up to speed on what's happening relatively quickly. Everyone would feel close to everyone else and know the plan and what's happening. And if you did need to have a follow-up meeting to further clarify anything with anyone who had questions you could simply meet individually with each team member without much trouble. But, obviously, you can't do that with six or 30 people every time you have a meeting.

If there are six people on your team, then you suddenly jump up to 15 lines of communication. You could still meet one-on-one with each of

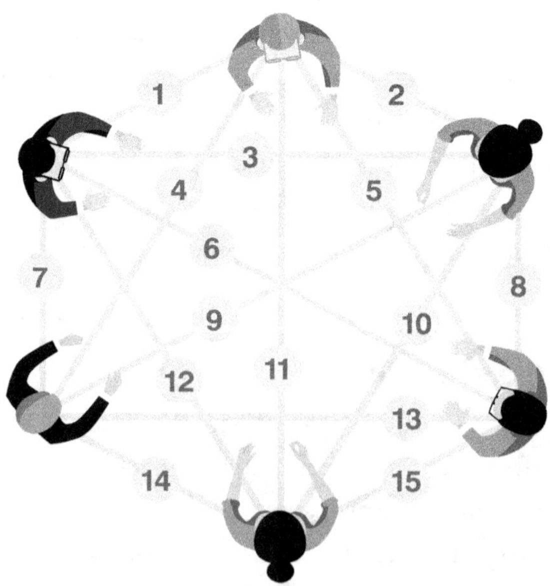

these people, but it would be more unwieldy and the time between team meetings would increase due to the increased volume of meetings you're having. So people will begin to feel less connected to you and to each other. There will be more misunderstandings, people will increasingly need clarification, and confusion will become more common. None of this is because you're communicating less well or because people are not listening as carefully, but simply because the lines of communication have increased exponentially and so the message becomes increasingly distorted.

If the number of people on your team jumps from six to 16, there will be 120 lines of communication. Adding only ten more people adds 105 additional lines of communication. It gets complex very quickly. People increasingly feel left out and like "no-one told me". Holding 16 one-on-one meetings is very difficult to maintain, simply from a time perspective. In addition to the logistical difficulty of that many meetings, it also becomes nearly impossible to communicate exactly the same information across those 16 meetings. The speed of communication slows down considerably, the team becomes noticeably less nimble, and mid-course corrections while keeping everyone informed—which used to be easy—become almost impossible.

If you double the number of team members so there are 32 people on your team, you're not just doubling the number of lines of communication to 240. With a team of 32 people you will have a staggering 496 separate lines of communication. Communication goes exponential.

Multiple, overlapping, and redundant

Since people need information and need to know what's happening, good communication is vital for a team to function well. But the more people you have on your team, the harder this is to accomplish.

When a team has up to about five people communication is fairly straightforward. With one-on-one meetings and summary emails, people will be kept informed and will feel like they're kept informed. Sometimes you'll talk about an upcoming meeting, put it in a calendar of dates at the beginning of the year, post about it to a closed Facebook group, and have different levels of team leaders talk to people and send text messages to remind them. And some people will still say, "Oh, I didn't know that was on! No-one told me." So being kept informed is like the message sent, and feeling like you're kept informed is like the messaged received.

Once your team has more than about five members, this communication strategy begins to become more and more of a hindrance. One-on-one meetings can no longer be the main mode of communication. As the team gets larger, you'll need more than just one or two methods for communicating information—you'll need multiple, overlapping, and redundant forms of communication.

If you've started with one-on-one meetings with a few key leaders within a larger team you'll need to add group meetings. If you've been holding group meetings you might need to start one-on-one meetings with key leaders (or meeting with a smaller group of key leaders). You'll also create Facebook groups and send consistent emails, texts, and Facebook messages. You'll distribute paper copies of what you're doing and who's doing what—in addition to any other modes of communication that work for you and your team. You'll want to find out what methods of communication the people on your team prefer. There's no point sending emails if no-one on your team has an email address or if they only check it once every six months.

Not only will you have multiple modes of communication, but they will also overlap and be redundant. That is, they'll all communicate the same message each time. You'll communicate the same information more often, in various forms and locations. Why? Because the network will have become so complicated that, in order to weave the net as tightly as possible so that nothing drops through and no-one feels as though "they weren't told", you'll have to tell them multiple times. If they skipped that part of the message in one form of communication, or misunderstood it, the idea is that they have a second or third or fourth chance of getting it in one of the other methods of communication.

Communicating efficiently will become less and less of a priority, because that goal of efficiency will begin to increasingly clash with the goal of actually communicating.

Now clearly you'll need to use your wisdom so that you don't end up punishing the members of your team who received and acknowledged the message the first time with an avalanche of identical messages. And you'll need to experiment a bit to find that point where everyone knows what's happening without being oversaturated. You'll want to make sure that your message fits the method of communication as well—a text message won't be the best way to relay a detailed 500-word explanation. The goal is to communicate effectively.

Communication compounds in complexity. And so your communication needs to be multiple and redundant. An increase in the number of people misunderstanding or feeling out of the loop is probably not a sign of a lack of commitment in your team or evidence that people concentrated and cared more back in the good old days. It's probably a sign that you need to upgrade your communication style to better match the complexity of your context.

See also

29. Praise publicly
33. Communicate from the inside out
69. Your people should be able to do a good impression of you

41
Two foundations of team-building

Teams aren't built overnight. It takes a long time to develop a group of individuals into a team. Sometimes we get confused about this because we instinctively label any group of leaders as a team. That's not necessarily wrong or an unhelpful practice, but we need to remember that labelling a group of individuals as a team doesn't make them a team.

Most people know this, at least instinctively. But what's much more difficult is knowing exactly what you need to do to take a group and turn it into a team.

Although there are many factors that play a part in this complex process of team-building, and even though many other chapters in this book will address various aspects of this issue, there are two main foundations that need to be laid down before anything resembling a team can be built.

The first foundation

The first foundation in building a team is stability. Every member of your team is wondering about the answers to three main questions:

1. Can I trust you?
2. Do you care about me?
3. Are you committed to this?

They may not know or be aware that they're asking these questions. In fact, if you were to ask them what questions they had as they joined your team I'd be surprised if anyone asked these questions. But, deep down, these are the things they really want to know. You know that's the case because if you did everything you could to show that the answer to these questions is no, it wouldn't be long before they hated being a part of your team and were looking to leave. No-one wants to be part of a team in which they: can't trust the leader; feel that he or she doesn't care about them; and know the leader isn't committed to the goal. Imagine being on a team like that. Seriously, how long do you think you'd stick around? I know I'd struggle to stay for very long, no matter how committed I was to the vision.

In order to build stability, you need to show your teams that your answer to all three questions is yes. How do you do this? Well, you do it all the time in every decision you make. Every decision either reinforces or undermines one of these yes answers.

Trust

If people like you, they might listen to you. But if they trust you, they'll follow you. You need to show yourself to be a person worth trusting in order for people to trust you. You signal that trustworthiness, or lack thereof, in everything you do and every decision you make.

This probably all seems really obvious and you might even be tempted to skip this bit. You might even be skimming this whole section. Of course we need to trust each other for a team to work. Surely every team already does this. But, as it turns out, the truth is that most teams don't trust each other. Why not? Because they focus on the wrong kind of trust.

If you say you want the team to arrive on time and be prepared, for example, then you also need to arrive on time and be prepared. If the vast majority of the time you arrive when you say you will, the team will know they can trust you. This is called 'predictive trust'. People know you, they know what you do, and they know how you behave. You do what you say you'll do. They can predict your behaviour. And predictive trust is a great help when working with a team. But while this is all very good, predictive trust is simply the entry point for being a productive human being—it's not the kind of trust you need to build the foundations of a great team. Predictive trust is more of a permission to play type of trust. You can't even join the game if you don't have that, but now that you're in the game you need a different, deeper type of trust that's not less than, but is more than, predictive trust.

You need the kind of trust that comes from letting yourself look weak in front of the team. With this kind of trust, you can admit your mistakes and weaknesses and be confident that people won't take advantage of that or think less of you for it. Patrick Lencioni says it like this:

> When everyone on the team knows that everyone else is vulnerable enough... that no-one is going to hide his or her weaknesses or mistakes, they develop a deep and uncommon sense of trust. They speak more freely and fearlessly with one another and don't waste time and energy putting on airs or pretending to be someone they're not.[40]

Predictive trust is certainly necessary for you to work in a group competently. But being able to work in a team is so much more than working in a group. To work in a team you need to develop weakness-based trust, which is a kind of trust that can be built very quickly and is much more powerful. If you're the team leader, this has to start with you. You'll need to go first, be vulnerable, admit you're human, and be courageous enough to be weak in front of your team. If you don't do it they never will. But if you can model it for them and make sure you encourage them when they do it rather than penalize them, this trust will grow rapidly and your group will begin functioning as a team.

Care

People want to know if they can trust you, but they also want to know whether you care about them or whether you're just using them. And it's not enough for you to care about them—they also need to know that you care.

There are lots of ways you can show people that you care. You take the time, for instance, to get to know the people on your team. You check in with them regularly to see how they're going as people, not just as members of your team. You're genuinely thankful for the work your team does and you make sure you tell them so. You say that you're sorry when you make a mistake and you mean it. You listen to their ideas and care about their feedback. You treat them like real contributors and not just as helpers filling

40 Patrick Lencioni, *The Advantage: Why organizational health trumps everything else in business,* Jossey-Bass, San Francisco, 2012, p. 27.

a gap. All of these things will communicate that you care about them.

If you want to build a strong team, people have to know that you care about them and that others on the team care about them as well. The stronger and deeper the relationships are between team members, the better the team will function. They'll make better and quicker decisions, they'll deal with conflicts better, and they'll lead through crises better. Neuroscience tells us that our brains run on three things: oxygen, glucose and relationships. Henry Cloud recounts an experiment that was done with monkeys to measure the effects of relationships on cortisol levels in the brain. Cortisol is a hormone closely associated with high stress levels.

In this experiment, a monkey was put in a cage and exposed to high levels of psychological stress, loud noises, and flashing lights. All of this totally freaked him out. Then they measured the levels of stress hormones in the monkey's brain.

Next, the researchers changed one factor in the experiment. They opened the cage door and put one of the monkey's friends in the cage with him. That was all. Then they exposed them both to the same loud noises and flashing lights. The circumstances remained exactly the same—nothing changed except that his monkey-friend was with him. Then they took another measurement of the first monkey's cortisol levels. The result? The stress hormones in his brain had dropped by 50%. The pair of monkeys was twice as good at handling stress as the lone monkey was. Monkeys' brains, it seems, are designed to function in relationships. And so are ours. Cloud concludes:

> More research findings about the positive effects of supportive connections continue to pour in, and they are equally compelling and conclusive: *our brains need positive relationships to grow and function well.* Whether for monkeys in a cage, financial wizards on Wall Street, or your own... team members, relationship is the key to high performance.[41]

41 Henry Cloud, *Boundaries for Leaders: Results, relationships, and being ridiculously in charge,* HarperCollins, New York, 2013, pp. 82-3 (emphasis mine).

Commitment

Thirdly, people want to know if you're for real, if you're committed to this team and what it's trying to accomplish. Not just committed for now, but actually committed. What will you give up for this? What will you miss for this? How sick do you need to be to skip this? Because if they're going to come with you, they're going to miss things, give up things, and skip things. They want to know if you're willing to do likewise.

There's a difference between being committed for now and being committed. When you're committed for now you're still scanning the horizon for a better opportunity, a bigger platform, or a more prestigious position. You're not satisfied with where you are and so you're not focused on what you're doing. You wouldn't ever be like this, would you? You might say that you're committed, but are you just committed for now? If you're really committed to what you're doing, you'll invest yourself in it. You'll plant yourself, put your head down, and get on with it. People can tell if you're looking around to try and find something better. They want to know if you're committed. In order to build a team, you need to show people that they can trust you to be real and vulnerable, that you care about them, and that you're committed.

If you do or say too many things that communicate that your answer to one of those questions is no, you will never succeed in building a team.

Developing a culture of care, trust, and commitment takes a lot of time, and it starts with the team leader. Everything that you want to see in your team needs first to be seen in you. You need to show yourself trustworthy, you need to show that you trust your team, and you need to be vulnerable with them.

Speak honestly. Share deeply. Admit mistakes freely. Ask forgiveness quickly.

Make sure people know that honest opinions are valued, that they don't need to tiptoe around issues, that they have permission to speak freely. And then defend that freedom at all costs. Verbally reprimand those who ridicule an honest moment or who break group confidence and spread information to people they shouldn't. Control your own emotions and opinions so that people have the space to be honest and vulnerable without fear that they'll have their heads bitten off or their contribution ridiculed.

Set the tone of trust and vulnerability and protect it vigorously. It only takes one lapse to destroy months of work in this area. Teams are built on stability.

The second foundation

The second foundation necessary for building a team is time. It takes time, and lots of it, to build a team. So the more time you can spend together, the better position your group is in to grow into a team. This is more than simply doing the job together, though that's part of it.

Of course team-building requires much more than simply spending time together. If you're doing everything else wrong but spending lots of time together, you won't go very far in building a group of people into a team. You might actually end up pushing people further away from each other. On the other hand, though, if you try to do everything else right but hardly ever spend time together, your team-building will be seriously hindered. Pure time is an important component of team-building that's often overlooked.

So much of what differentiates a group from a great team revolves around things like relationships, trust, mutual commitment, and care. This means that those characteristics are necessary components for building a team. It takes time to develop trust. It takes spending time together to develop relationships. It takes time and prolonged exposure for people to begin to understand each other in terms of how you each react, respond, reflect, and relax. It takes time to collect and cultivate the kinds of shared experiences that bond people together—highs and lows, tragedies, triumphs, and frustrations. It's rare for those things to happen quickly in life in general, let alone amongst groups of individuals achieving a task.

So you need to work out ways to get your team together periodically to simply spend time together. Hang out, have breakfast, watch a movie, go to a restaurant, go to the beach, do things where people can bring their boyfriend, girlfriend, spouse, or kids along.

You might be thinking, "I don't have time for that. Do we really need to? It's not a very efficient use of time. Can't we just turn up and do the job? We're all so busy just trying to find the time to do that. It just seems a bit soft and touchy-feely." And I totally understand the reservation. People are busy. We're busy! But it really isn't a side salad type of thing. It's the main meal. The job is to lead this team of people to best achieve whatever your objective is. Building the team is about maximizing the power of the machine that you're using.

And it's not about doing some lame trust falls and 'team-building exercises'. Teams are built on relationships of trust, openness, and mutual commitment. Without these components, just turning up and doing the job won't be as effective or as enjoyable. When people trust each other and are committed to each other, the work is far easier and happens far more quickly with fewer disruptions and breakdowns. Dealing with, and developing, people often doesn't seem very efficient—and in one sense it isn't—but the investment compounds over time, and a well-built and developed team is exponentially more effective than either a lone individual or even a poorly built group of individuals. It just takes time.

See also

26. Leading is loving
30. Faithfulness buys responsibility
35. Everyone already knows
46. People deserve to know the truth
52. Give credit and take blame

42
Humble and hungry

When you need to find someone to fulfil a role of increased responsibility, what qualities should you be looking for in this potential leader? Although it depends on the role, there are general characteristics that are important for a leader in any role. But because these are hard to define and pin down, sometimes we're more likely to just go with our gut feel about a person. Sometimes that works and sometimes it doesn't.

We need to look, for example, at character over competencies. But we need to go still further. Are there particular character qualities that are more important than others for these more responsible leadership roles? Are there combinations of qualities that are better than other combinations? Obviously skills aren't the most important thing, but they're not unimportant either. How important are they?

In my opinion and experience, there are two qualities that differentiate good leaders from great leaders, and good leaders from great leaders of leaders. When I'm looking for people to lead other leaders, I look for emerging leaders who are humble and hungry.

What about everything else?

I'm not saying that everything else is less important—that it doesn't matter, for example, about honesty or drunkenness so long as a person is humble and hungry. Far from it! But those issues are more 'permission-to-play' qualities. There's a certain baseline that we expect all of our leaders to start from before we even think about giving them responsibility. So the question, from that baseline, is this: How do you identify those with potential to be given more responsibility?

More often than not, I've found this combination of humility and hunger for the cause to be the determining factor. It's the combination of both qualities that's the key, and sometimes it's hard to spot.

Many of us are very conscious of trying to recruit and develop the people around us to grow and lead. Some people have a good eye, an almost intuitive ability to find and develop great leaders. What are they seeing that the rest of us often don't see? I think it's humility and hunger.

The danger of one-size-fits-all

Although having an eye for talent is important, we want to be careful not to treat everyone the same way. Some people need to be nurtured, not recruited. It's essential that we be conscious of nurturing the broken and hurting who won't, in the short term, be leaders. But, even as we love and care for them, we should be thinking about where we'd like to see them serving others at some point.

Another important point to remember is that often the people with this combination of humility and hunger don't seem like obvious choices to be leaders. They aren't always particularly confident. They aren't always extroverted. They aren't always charismatic. And these qualities of humility and hunger are perhaps the most difficult for people who don't already possess them to develop. But they can be developed—with time and the desire to do so. This kind of development is a mysterious process. The Holy Spirit works through the Scriptures and the deep truths of the gospel as well as through the person's desire to change and, often, through difficult and painful circumstances that hone the person's faith and trust in God.

Just because people seem weak or uncharismatic or timid or meek or introverted doesn't mean they're not potentially great leaders. We need to broaden our search beyond the stereotypical Alpha-type person.

Humility

Humility is an often-misunderstood characteristic. We sometimes think that humility means saying we're not good at things when we really are. Of course there are lots of things that we're not good at. In fact, I'm not good at most things. There's a small handful of things that I am actually any good at.

I have no talent or ability in the musical instrument department, and I struggle with most things to do with cooking. It's best to find someone else if you need anything mechanical fixed or anything in a language that's not English. I could go on. I'm not good at the vast majority of things.

But there are some things that I am good at. I might not be the best in the world, but I'm still pretty good. Often we think that, if we're to be humble, we should say we're not good at those things either. But that's not humility—that's just lying.

Humility means that you understand your place before God and before others. It's not about downplaying your skills and abilities and, in fact, it's not about your skills and abilities at all. Rather, it's an internal posture towards God and people. Humility is recognizing that things aren't all about you. It's not thinking less of yourself; it's thinking of yourself less. Humility is considering others as better and more important than yourself.

Humility can manifest itself in a very loud, confident, and extroverted person and it can manifest itself in a very shy, quiet introvert. We often equate pride and arrogance with loud people and humility with quiet, anxious people. But that's not that helpful a distinction. Some of the quiet introverts I've met have been some of the most arrogant people I've encountered. Introverts can sometimes mask their pride because it's a seething disdain for others that rarely expresses itself but lurks constantly just beneath the surface.

But truly humble people lead well because, in their humility, they recognize that their leadership isn't about them. The ministry isn't about them. It's not about the fame of their name. It's not about speaking on better platforms. It's not about having the most friends on social media. It's not about being looked to as the guru. It's not about being the smartest person in the room. It's about the cause. It's about others. It's about the fame of no other name but Jesus' name. It's about seeing people saved and helping them grow.

Humble people are ready to learn. They're okay with being wrong. They're okay with being told bad news—about the ministry or even about themselves. They're okay with feedback. When someone offers them helpful and constructive criticism they don't put up their walls and get defensive. Instead, they lean in and say, "Tell me what I can learn. Help me get better." They accept feedback. They get better. Proud and arrogant people can still get better, of course, but it will happen more slowly because if they insist on rejecting feedback then they'll only be improving those areas that they themselves have noticed need improving. As they screen out external perspectives they'll be ignoring what others are noticing. In addition, they'll still need to climb over the walls they put up and work through their defensiveness. The ceiling on how much the proud person can improve is much lower than it is for humble person, who is willing to learn from others and more willing to accept help.

Hunger

The other major quality I look for in potential leaders is hunger—not in terms of food, but in terms of seeing disciples made and grown. Hunger for the mission. People with this hunger have a drive and desperation to see people loved and served and saved. They're hungry to see whatever setbacks or failures they're currently facing overcome, to see problems solved. That kind of deep, unshakable commitment to the cause and passion for the mission is what I mean by being hungry. These people aren't really compelled or motivated from the outside—rather, their compulsion and motivation come from within.

This kind of hunger is attractive. Others are drawn to it and will want to be led by it. When things are going well, someone who doesn't have this deep hunger can lead adequately. Even a pessimist can lead the way when things are travelling along okay. But when things don't go as planned, when there are setbacks and problems, most people don't want to follow a pessimist. In difficult times people will be drawn to the leader with the determination and inner drive to solve the problem. They will follow the leader who knows that this setback won't last forever and that it *must* be overcome because the stakes are too high and the mission is too important.

People who are hungry for the mission don't feel despondent and defeated by setbacks and problems. They have confidence that the tide will turn, even if it takes some time.

Being hungry means having a passion to see people saved, to see them grow in Christlikeness, and to help them develop their own passion to see disciples made. Hungry people desire these things even if achieving them requires great personal cost and sacrifice—and even if it means toiling in obscurity.

The power of this combination

This combination of humility and hunger can be found in people in any kind of industry. Christianity doesn't have a monopoly on this combination, and it isn't unique to Christian ministry. Christianity does, however, have a critical advantage. And that advantage is the gospel. The gospel itself creates this combination of humility and hunger in people.

The gospel produces this kind of humility in three ways. First, it makes clear that we need to be saved; and second, it forces us to acknowledge that we can't do it for ourselves. Our salvation is given to us and is based on the work of someone else. We never deserved it, we can't earn it, and we don't contribute to it. The gospel also produces this kind of humility because the one it proclaims, whom we follow, is the humble and crucified Messiah—the one who made himself nothing, who didn't come to be served but to serve, and who became poor so that we might become rich. We're called to follow him and imitate his attitude. Lastly, the gospel produces this kind of humility because as Christians our lives no longer centre around ourselves—they centre around Jesus. We exist to glorify him and point others towards him. 'For what we proclaim is not ourselves, but Jesus Christ as Lord, with ourselves as your servants for Jesus' sake' (2 Cor 4:5).

At the same time as it produces this gospel humility, the gospel also produces a hunger—not a hunger for self-promotion, or self-focus, but a hunger for the cause. This hunger is an eagerness to glorify God and to see others find the same life and salvation that we have. The fact that the gospel is good news creates the motivation to see it spread; the news is good and we need to spread it.

So while Christians aren't the only ones who have this unusual combination of humility and hunger, Christians do have an advantage because the gospel pushes us towards this fusion of qualities. Some develop this combination more quickly than others, and it's always a process of growth, but the blueprint is all there in the gospel itself. It requires and increases humility because we don't deserve our salvation, and at the same time the gospel produces in us a passion for good works—not in order to attain salvation but because salvation has already been given to us freely as a gift.

So how do you develop these characteristics in yourself and in others? There's no easy answer or shortcut, but the place to start is the gospel itself. The way to develop humble and hungry people is by proclaiming the gospel. Developing yourself or others all begins with grappling with the gospel, understanding it deeply, and thinking seriously about its implications as it rolls out and into every corner of life. Help people see how the gospel produces humility and at the same time generates a hunger to glorify God and see people loved and served and saved, no matter the cost.

Together, the characteristics of humility and hunger make a powerful combination. Absolutely committed to the cause, resolute and unshaken in the face of difficulty and abandonment but not making everything about you and being willing to sacrifice and suffer and be an unknown so that Jesus would be known—these are the characteristics that separate great leaders from good leaders. Good leaders will have all kinds of great qualities and they might even have either hunger or humility. But great leaders will have both.

A person who is humble with little hunger will have a great foundation but will have little determination to do anything. These people are easily discouraged and quit quickly. They don't always have the fierce commitment necessary to overcome problems. People with hunger but little or no humility like the spotlight and usually have a somewhat inflated ego. Without the proper measure of humility they can quickly become arrogant. Both of these kinds of people can still be good leaders, and you'll be glad they're on the team, but you want to see them grow and improve. What you're watching for is their trajectory. Are they becoming less humble and hungry or more humble and hungry? The trajectory is what's important, because if it's backwards they can unravel into despondency and despair or arrogance and self-promotion relatively easily. But when you see the rare combination of both humility and hunger in a person, watch them and invest in them.

These aren't just qualities to look for in recruiting others, however. You can, and should, develop these qualities in yourself as well. All of us need to be growing in humility and growing a deeper hunger and desperation for the mission of seeing the lost saved and the nations won for Jesus.

Humble and hungry. That's the combination to watch for and to develop.

See also

49. You can only drive as fast as the car in front

43
The five C's

Before you spend too much time working out what you're going to do with a ministry and where you're going to go, you need to first focus on the 'who'. Who is on your team is more important than what your team is going to do or how they're going to do it. Getting the who right will always enhance what you do. But if you make a mistake with the who, those poor choices will always undermine what you try to do.

When Jim Collins was researching his magisterial study comparing companies that went from good to great with those that remained mediocre, he expected to find that a compelling new vision and strategy was what catalyzed the transformation of the great companies. The people, he reasoned, would then commit themselves to that vision. What he found was quite the opposite:

> The executives who ignited the transformations from good to great did not first figure out where to drive the bus and then get people to take it there. No, they *first* got the right people on the bus (and the wrong people off the bus) and *then* figured out where to drive it.[42]

The question is: How do you find great people?

Finding great people may be one of the most important tasks you undertake. You know it's important, but it's even more important than you think. You will be constantly recruiting. The recruitment treadmill will never stop. So how can you make sure you recruit the right people

42 Collins, *Good to Great*, p. 41 (emphasis mine).

and calibrate your internal instruments to detect a destructive person early, before they do damage?

There are many ways in which you can assess people to make sure that you recruit well, and each method has its strengths and weaknesses—whether you're looking for FAT people (Faithful, Available, Teachable) or using a Myers-Briggs type personality assessment or a more sophisticated screening process.

One commonly used, and very helpful, set of criteria is often referred to as the three C's. Each C stands for a different lens that you'd use to look at someone: character, convictions and competencies. The order of the criteria reflects their order of importance: character and convictions are most important, and each flows out of the other. What you believe is deeply connected to what you do. A person may be of good character but not believe some fundamental Christian doctrines—there are many highly moral people in the world who wouldn't claim to be Christian. Equally, there are many highly intelligent, scholarly people who are profoundly orthodox—and yet their life and conduct don't match up with what they know. Paul reminds us in 1 Timothy 4:16 to watch our life and doctrine closely, and so we need to ask ourselves whether our character is shaped by the gospel we believe. Both character and convictions are equally supreme. Following these two is the important, though not as critical, category of competencies. That is, how competent is the person in the skills required for this particular task?

I would like to insert two more often-overlooked C's: chemistry and capacity. Again, the order is important: character and convictions, chemistry, competencies, and capacity.

Each C is less important than the one before it. Character and convictions are, together, the most important criterion, and capacity is the least important. So if someone has a strong character and is honest, reliable, and so on, but has a low capacity, we shouldn't automatically disqualify that person. Low capacity in that case would just be an orange light and we'd need to think carefully about where and how we might deploy this person. Or, in the case of a staff position, we'd have to determine whether they would be the best person for the job. On the other hand, if someone has a high capacity but also has large character deficiencies, that person is much more likely to be disqualified—since character is the most important factor.

How rigorous you should be in applying these criteria will be a discussion worth having with your key team. Which roles require how much rigor for which criteria? For example, for a paid staff position or a member of my key leadership team who's a volunteer, I'd want a fair degree of rigor in all five of the C's. I wouldn't be ruthless and require perfection, but I would have high standards in each area. For a general member of a team I might find a lower level of chemistry, competence, or capacity acceptable. For some roles there may even be room for flexibility in the C's. This would be a good conversation to have and clarify with your key leaders.

Briefly, then, each C breaks down as follows.

Character

Character is the collection of a person's values, personal virtues, and motivations. It's not so much *what* a person does as it is *how* a person does those things. Examples would be things like honesty, reliability, faithfulness, servanthood, humility, and so on. These are qualities that are very hard to teach a person and that take a long time to develop or change—though they can be, and often are, taught, developed, and changed.

The reason character is so important is because it will colour how a person does everything else. It's also important because character takes a long time to grow, and some people never change their character at all. One person may work hard out of servanthood, humility, and faithfulness while another will work hard out of a mercenary spirit, pride, and competitiveness. Both will work hard, and on the surface they'll look very similar, but underneath they'll be poles apart. Both will get the job done, and both will probably do it well, but for very different reasons and blooming out of very different underlying traits. But while in the short term they might appear very similar, over the long term you will notice significant differences because in critical moments they'll make very different decisions. The principle is that you always build around character rather than talent.

Convictions

Convictions are what people believe deep down about who we are, where we are, what matters in life, what's wrong with the world, and what the solution is. In Christian contexts, the question of convictions becomes more specific as Christian convictions revolve around what you think of Jesus, his death, his resurrection, his Bible, his Spirit, his Father, his exclusivity, and so on. What are you willing to stand for? What are you not willing to compromise on and what are you willing to be flexible on? These core convictions shape who you are, what you do, and how you make decisions—which is why convictions and character belong together. They mutually reinforce one another. Your character grows and flows from your gospel convictions. And your convictions are dead unless they're expressed in your character.

Chemistry

Chemistry has to do with how a person gels with the rest of the people on your team. Chemistry is not at all on the same level as character. People can score high on character, align completely with the values you value, and share the same convictions you do, but just not be enjoyable to be around. This isn't a failure on anyone's part—you just don't click. They don't share your sense of humour, or they don't relate to people the way the rest of the team relates to people, or something else is out of synch. The chemistry isn't right.

There was a time when I thought that chemistry wasn't as important as competencies and should come fourth or even fifth on the list. But I've since changed my mind. Chemistry is a more important factor than we often think.

In some circumstances you might choose to get along with someone who you don't enjoy being around as much as other people. You can learn to get along with people, and often it's a way to grow in the disciplines of patience, bearing with one another, and longsuffering. In some circumstances you might not have much of a choice. Sometimes this person you wouldn't choose to be around is the only person available and you may make the call that their character and convictions and competencies are great and the role is too important. But, as a general rule, keep an eye on the chemistry. If you need to work closely with a person you might as well get on well with them on a personal level—otherwise every interaction will be much harder and require more energy than it needs to, and the tasks in ministry are hard enough as it is. Over the years I've begun to trust my intuition for chemistry more and I've seen my teams gel and be more cohesive with less friction and fewer personality clashes.

Chemistry is sometimes hard to identify before you've actually worked alongside a person, but other times it's clear and obvious. Again, it's not a failure on anyone's part.

The danger of overemphasizing chemistry is that you create a monochrome team of clones, a homogenous unit that doesn't reflect the breadth of personality within the created order and that excludes people who don't fit *my* mold. This is a corruption of chemistry. Chemistry doesn't mean lack of diversity, and enjoying people's company doesn't mean only being with people who are exactly like me. I enjoy being with people who have all sorts of different personality types and backgrounds. It's worth being aware of the danger, but don't let it stop you from considering the chemistry of your team.

Competencies

Competencies are the skills a person possesses to do the job and fulfil the responsibilities. A certain degree of competency is required for most jobs, but usually you can work with a person with lower competencies who has a willingness to learn. Competencies can be learned and perfected with time, practice, and helpful feedback. Don't focus on what people can currently do—instead try to imagine what they have the potential to do. What they have done in the past or can do in the present isn't as important as what they will do in the future.

Be leery of the star player with all the skills who doesn't fit with the team, either because of chemistry issues or—more likely—because of character issues. A star player who doesn't work well with others is not a good person to have on a team. Someone with amazing competencies who rubs the rest of the team the wrong way will often, in fact, be less effective overall than a person with a lower competency level who doesn't suck the will to live from the rest of the team. A cohesive team will, more often than not, outperform the team with the star player who everyone hates being around. There's no wisdom in starving the workhorses to feed the show pony.

Competencies can be taught and improved. If a person wants to learn and grow, is willing to put in the time to practise, is receptive to feedback, and is willing to persevere, that person will always improve and become highly skilled. Anyone with enough drive, time, and coaching can learn anything.

Capacity

Capacity refers to how much work a person can get done at once, how many different tasks they can manage concurrently, or how much pressure they can withstand. Some people seem to be able to do a lot more with the time they have than other people. It's not necessarily that they work longer hours; these people are just more productive in the hours they have. They're more focused and are mindful of the task before them.

I think of it in terms of plate sizes. Each person has a certain plate size, and they can only fit so much food on their plate at once. It doesn't matter how much you want to put on your plate, or how much you're asked to put on your plate. At a certain point, your plate fills up and you can't put any more on it without taking something off (usually a bread roll). The bigger the plate you have, the more food you can put on it. In the same way, each person has a certain capacity to do a certain amount of work at once. It might be the number of tasks, it might be the breadth of those tasks, or it might be the amount of responsibility the tasks entail, but there's only so much a person can handle. Some can handle more, others less. It depends on your plate size.

Some people have high capacity and others have low capacity. Sometimes people's capacities change at different stages of life. When people have babies and the amount of sleep they get dramatically decreases, their plate size will change. Or when other demands in life become heavier to carry and more burdensome their plate size will change. If a family member becomes very sick, or a parent far away is dying, for example, people will have less space for work.

Plate sizes change. They get smaller and they can also get bigger. Spending time with people who have bigger plate sizes than you do will help you grow your plate size. If you want to become a high-capacity person, start spending more time with high-capacity people.

The positions of capacity and competency are a bit more fluid than the other three. Sometimes a person with a higher capacity but a lower competency level will actually achieve more overall than a highly skilled person with a smaller plate. But that's not always the case. So these last two C's depend more on the person, the situation, and the responsibilities involved.

Obviously, if you can find a person who's at a high level in all five areas they'll be a MVP and you need to keep them around, keep them interested and excited, and let them score goals. When you stumble across them, thank God for his bountiful provision. Most of the time recruitment will be a series of trade-offs and compromises. Good character but low competencies, or great convictions but the chemistry isn't perfect. This is normal; life is full of tensions. But the five C's are a powerful conceptual tool to help make those trade-offs clearer in your mind. They will help you clarify which trade-offs you're willing to make and which ones you never will.

The point of the five C's is not, of course, that we can categorize people and paint over them with a broad brush. God created each person with dignity and complexity and our job is to love, not to label. Yet it's because of that very complexity that we sometimes need tools to help us make decisions about the people we want to put in various positions without becoming overwhelmed or lost in the details.

See also

18. If you're not a good follower then you're not a good leader
44. Choose your lieutenants

44
Choose your lieutenants

Since leaders have to make a lot of important decisions, leadership books often spend a lot of time talking about decision-making. But one of the most neglected topics in this area is the importance of the decisions you make about who will be your inner circle.

Choosing your key leaders—your lieutenants—is one of the most important, if not *the* most important, set of decisions you make as a leader. Steven Sample, former president of the University of California, writes:

> To a large degree, leaders live and die through the actions of their chief lieutenants. Choosing these people, motivating them, supporting them, helping them grow and achieve, inspiring them, evaluating them and firing them are among the most important things a leader does. When he carries out these duties well, his cause or organization has a good chance of flourishing. But if he fails at these essential (and unglamorous) tasks, he and his followers are almost certainly doomed to failure in the long run.[43]

When we're talking about lieutenants, or an inner circle, we're not necessarily talking about the leaders who lead the biggest groups—although your lieutenants may also lead large teams. Your lieutenants make up the circle of leaders closest to you. They're the ones you rely upon the most, the people who help you the most to implement the plans you have, the ones you listen to the most, and they're the ones you share with and confide in most often. Your lieutenants are the people in your key leadership team.

43 Steven B Sample, *The Contrarian's Guide to Leadership,* Jossey-Bass, San Francisco, 2002, p. 139.

You might be thinking, "I don't have an inner circle. I don't want one. It sounds exclusive. I love everyone." And of course you love everyone and don't want to exclude anyone. An inner circle of lieutenants isn't a clique of popular people and insiders. The reality is that you already have an inner circle and you already have lieutenants. There are people you spend more time with than others, people you share with and confide in more than others, and people you go to first for advice. Having lieutenants is a factor of being finite—you can't spend deep time with everyone or listen equally to everyone. Jesus himself had an inner circle. There were the crowds and there were the twelve, and within the twelve there were the three. Even within the three, Peter was the rock upon which Jesus would build his church and John was the disciple Jesus loved.

Your inner circle already exists. The question is whether those people are part of that circle on purpose or by accident. The decisions you make about who's in your inner circle will have huge implications for your leadership. Your lieutenants will either multiply or minimize your effectiveness as a leader—which is why choosing them is one of the most important sets of decisions that you will make as a leader.

Lieutenants impact your leadership in five key ways.

1. They filter you

You can't talk to everybody about everything. No matter how much you might like to do that, it's just not possible—and the bigger the group of people you lead the more impossible that will be. You'll make decisions and choose directions, and even though you'll communicate them to big groups as well as through various other channels, you won't be able to have a conversation with every person or every group about every detail.

Instead, the message will be filtered through the leaders closest to you. This is something you can't avoid, but if you have the right people around you this filtering will be a positive thing because they can do a great job communicating the information. They can rephrase it, clarify it, and tailor it to specific groups in ways that you simply might not have the time to do.

If you have the wrong people in your inner circle, however, they can corrupt the message by changing it as they pass it on. They may communicate it poorly or unenthusiastically. They can undermine and even covertly oppose the message as they talk with other people.

2. They represent you

If filtering you is about the message, then representing you is about the manner. If it's not already explicit, people will soon figure out who your inner circle is. Because of their relationship to you, the way your lieutenants treat people will reflect back on you.

In a lot of ways this is unfair and doesn't make a lot of sense, but it happens nonetheless. Because your lieutenants have your stamp of approval and tacit endorsement, people will make connections, even unconsciously, between you and your lieutenants. Even if people in your inner circle are conducting themselves in ways you do not approve of, or haven't authorized, people will assume that you approve.

People may confront you to question you about something one of your leaders has said or done. They may ask whether you agree or approve. When this happens, you'll be able to explain and clarify where you stand. The problem is that a lot of people will never come and ask you—they'll just assume.

Because of these kinds of connections people make, your lieutenants can engender a lot of trust and goodwill towards you and your leadership by the way they behave and treat people. But they can also engender a lot of distrust and hostility if they act poorly.

3. They counsel you

Another significant way that your lieutenants impact your leadership is through their counsel. You'll often seek their wisdom on difficult issues or problems. You'll want to know what they think. You'll allow them to question and challenge you, maybe even to rebuke you. They'll be in positions of great influence.

If you have lieutenants who are wise and who provide good counsel, they'll help you avoid mistakes and maximize opportunities. Counsel, however, isn't the same as opinion. Proverbs 11:14 puts it like this:

"Where there is no guidance, a people falls, but in an abundance of counselors there is safety". Everybody has an opinion, to which they're entitled, but a lot of people also think that their opinions are worth sharing. People will be happy to give you advice whether you ask for it or not.

The more people you lead, and the wider your influence, the more criticism and opinions you'll receive. All of this can be difficult to interpret, as some of it will be good advice and some of it will be bad and some will be good but communicated in a bad way. Some of it will baffle you. A storm of criticism quickly becomes very confusing, and you can easily lose your way. Your lieutenants will be the people whose counsel you can trust.

This doesn't mean that your lieutenants will be 'yes-men' or 'yes-women'. People who only ever agree with you and flatter you will do you a lot of damage. Good lieutenants will make you better through wise counsel, and they will also make you better as they rebuke you. Good lieutenants will tell you when you've made a mistake or stepped out of line. They'll warn you when you're veering off course or when they see signs of something unhealthy developing in your life or in your heart. Good lieutenants will speak up about these things—not because they're looking for a chance to criticize you but because they love you and they want to see you flourish.

Your effectiveness is in large part determined by whose advice you heed. If you listen to the wrong people you'll end up in the wrong place. If you have an unwise inner circle, or an inner circle full of people who tell you what they think you want to hear, you'll make a lot of poor decisions and your leadership will be undermined.

4. They focus you

A great inner circle will free you to focus on the things that only you can do. Good lieutenants will help you to attend to the most pressing issues by doing for you whatever they can on your behalf. They'll enable you to rise above the details so that you can get out front and lead. Good lieutenants will always be trying to find ways to help you play to your strengths and ways for you to be able to focus on what you do best so that everyone moves forward more quickly.

Poor lieutenants, instead of freeing you to think above the details and forge ahead, will keep dragging you back down into those details with issues that they should be able to deal with themselves. They'll make your life harder, not easier.

5. They support you

A good lieutenant will love you. They'll want to honour you appropriately. A good lieutenant will be for you and want what's best for you. They'll love your family and want what's best for them. They'll be an encouragement and a bright spot in your life.

It's not that they won't look you in the eye and tell you the hard truths. If they love you, then that's exactly what they'll do. If they don't tell you when they see things in you that are hurting you, hurting other people, or making you less effective, then they don't really love you.

You'll need encouragement and support and people who can disagree with you and love you at the same time. Your inner circle must be made up of people who strengthen and energize you to keep going and not give up. They'll be people who love you, who are loyal to you, and who will be there to support you.

Multipliers

Who you choose and allow into your inner circle will determine how effective your leadership is. These people will either multiply or minimize your effectiveness. Choosing lieutenants unwisely can cripple your ministry. Poor lieutenants can undermine a leader in so many different ways it's almost staggering. But the value of a great inner circle is hard to quantify. A great group of lieutenants makes everything better.

Beware boss-haters

The most common mistake I see leaders make when choosing lieutenants is selecting boss-haters to be in their inner circles. Jack Welch, former CEO of General Electric, describes boss-haters this way:

> Boss haters are a real breed. It doesn't matter where they work—big corporations, small family firms, partnerships, nonprofits, newspapers, or government agencies. Boss haters enter into any authority relationship with barely repressed cynicism and ingrained negativity toward 'the system'. And even though the reasons behind their attitude may be varied, from upbringing to personality to political bent, boss haters are unified in their inability to see the value in any person above them in a hierarchy.[44]

Boss-haters are often very competent people who are highly skilled and highly intelligent—which is why they often seem to end up in people's inner circles. They tick so many of the boxes for what makes a great lieutenant. They give you great counsel, they allow you to focus, and you don't need to micromanage them. All of those things make them attractive choices to be lieutenants. It's easy to imagine them helping you to get a lot of things done and multiplying the ministry. And they might do that in the short term, but in the long term they will cause you nothing but grief and trouble. They don't love you, they won't support you, they won't filter you well, and they'll end up undermining you.

Boss-haters have something of a sixth sense and are able to locate other boss-haters. They'll gather together, and soon you'll have a whole flock of boss-haters—or maybe it's a pride or a murder of boss-haters. They'll find strength in numbers, and the low-level negativity they secrete will increase as they begin to turn the atmosphere toxic. If there are one or two boss-haters in your inner circle, they can do fierce damage. If you realize that there's a boss-hater in your inner circle already, you need to get them out as quickly as possible. They cannot stay.

Beware of boss-haters in your team generally, and whatever you do don't allow or invite them into your inner circle. Your lieutenants have a huge impact on the effectiveness of your leadership and on the ministry. Choose them wisely.

44 Jack and Suzy Welch, *Winning: The Answers: Confronting 74 of the toughest questions in business today*, HarperCollins, New York, 2006, pp. 217-18.

See also

14. Play to your strengths
30. Faithfulness buys responsibility
39. Public fans and private critics
43. The five C's
50. There's no point having a dog and then barking yourself

45

Understand the life cycle of a team

Simply gathering a group of people, giving them a common purpose, and calling them a team doesn't automatically make them a team. As we've seen, a team behaves differently from a group of people. Once a group begins to form into a team, though, they won't function in only one way as a team. The way the team behaves will change and evolve over time. Teams have a clear and predictable life cycle. Generally speaking, teams will function in a certain way at the beginning and then their behaviour will continue to change in broadly predictable ways. This life cycle of behaviour corresponds with a life cycle in individual members of the team. That is, both the team as a whole and the individuals who make up the team will progress through broadly similar phases of behaviour.

Four stages

Every team progresses through four distinct stages. All teams will go through these four stages. Though some teams and individuals will pass through certain stages more quickly than others, no team will shortcut or skip over any of these stages.

It's important to know these stages, because once you determine which phase your team is in you will know better how to lead them. Understanding the different stages will help you to understand what's normal and what's not. You'll know how much you should worry about a certain behaviour and what markers you should look for when your team is moving into a new stage.

Various observers have noted these cycles, and everyone gives them different titles.[45] The titles don't mean much—it's what's actually happening in these distinct stages that's most important.

Stage 1: forming

Teams come together as a collection of individuals who are trying to achieve a specific task. Roles are either assigned or simply taken on unofficially, and ad hoc rules are set up regarding how the team will work and what is expected. These rules and expectations aren't so much verbal and stated but are rather predictable patterns as to how things are actually done. The team has a degree of excitement and enthusiasm.

Stage 2: fighting

The team begins to lose motivation and enthusiasm and can become somewhat disillusioned and jaded. People start arriving a bit later for meetings than they used to and they're slower to get on top of problems or solve issues. As their leader, you shouldn't panic or get angry—this is normal. These behaviours can't be tolerated, though, and so as the leader you will to address them and care appropriately for the individuals involved. This loss of enthusiasm and struggle for motivation is an issue that can't be fixed with reprimands and rebukes, because in this fighting stage the issue isn't knowledge or willpower. The loss of enthusiasm is caused by things like a lack of clarity, an awareness that their skills aren't yet sufficient, or the fact that they've forgotten the vision and why they started in the first place. As the leader you'll need to deal with these behaviours head-on, but your method should focus on reminding, not reprimanding.

If you deal with issues head-on, provide clarity where needed, help people understand where they're dropping the ball, provide training and feedback in areas where people need to improve their skills, encourage people, and remind them of the vision, you should be able to move through this stage in due course with the team intact and stronger for the experience.

More conflict than normal is to be expected at this stage, and team members will be confused or unsure of their roles and purpose.

45 A good example would be the One Minute Manager series by Ken Blanchard, especially *The One Minute Manager Builds High Performing Teams,* rev. edn, William Morrow and Co., New York, 2000.

Frustrations will mount. In some cases this will be due to the fact that team members are still unclear about their roles. There might also be frustration because the honeymoon period is over and problems that had been suppressed for a period of time will begin to surface. If team members put up with another team member not doing what they said they'd do for a certain period of time, for example, they might now reach the limits of their grace and self-control.

If, however, you ignore issues, don't deal with things quickly, fail to provide clarity, avoid difficult conversations, and expect people to remind themselves of why they're there and what they're trying to do, you can expect this stage to be a drawn-out affair and your team may even see some people hit the eject button.

Stage 3: figuring

If you're able to stay focused and active in confronting issues through stage two, individual team members will start to settle into their roles and the team will begin to own and understand their responsibilities. The different personalities involved will begin to gel and the team will get into a groove where teamwork becomes more natural and trust will grow quickly.

The team will be able to achieve more and move faster at this stage than they have before. They'll be able to handle change and unexpected circumstances with less disruption. Individuals will begin to see what the team as a whole is achieving and how it's functioning—rather than simply focusing on their own individual contributions.

Motivation and enthusiasm may still fluctuate in this stage, and you'll need to continue to help people remember why they signed up in the first place. Keep pointing out the good things the team is achieving and keep encouraging individuals to see their own personal growth and development.

All of this happens as the team begins figuring itself out.

Stage 4: flourishing

In this final stage, the team begins firing on all cylinders. People really catch and own the vision and understand their place and role within the team. Processes will happen with minimal fuss or blockages and deep trust will form between team members. The team will be able to identify problems and find solutions quickly without blaming others or taking it personally. More is achieved with less effort and confidence is high as people perform roles naturally without having to consciously think through steps. Motivation and enthusiasm are high as people are confident in their skills and see why what they do is valuable. Team members love being a part of this team with these people.

Leading through the stages

Different leadership styles will fit each stage of a team's life. You cannot lead a team in stage two in exactly the same way you'd lead a team in stage four. In stage four, problems are raised and dealt with quickly and without much heartache. In stage two, problems fester under the surface and sometimes are only raised once they blow up. In stage two you need to actively ferret out problems by digging beneath the surface. In stage two people require specific training and coaching, whereas in stage four that same style of training would feel condescending and might communicate lack of trust in the team. Different stages demand different styles of leadership from you as the team leader.

Leadership of a team is further complicated by the fact that individuals go through a similar cycle. This means you might have a team that, as a whole, is in stage three while some individuals on that team are in stage two and others are in stage four. So sometimes teams as a whole need a different leadership style than do the individuals within that team.

Being aware of the broad life cycle of teams and the complexities involved in leading a team will enable you to be sensitive to, and aware of, what's happening and will help you to lead in a more sophisticated manner.

See also

15. Change your default style
46. People deserve to know the truth
47. Find the awesome
48. Treat them like children

46
People deserve to know the truth

We know we should tell the truth. The Bible says we should, we've been taught since we were little to do it, and we're Christians. Of course we tell the truth, right?

Although we don't want to lie or communicate less than the truth, we probably don't speak the truth as much as we think we do. You're probably aware of how many times you don't say what you're really thinking or feeling so you can be 'kind'—to a boss, a co-worker, or a person you lead. Whether it's one-on-one or in a meeting, we often don't say what we're thinking because we don't want to be cruel or to publicly embarrass or upset someone. No-one wants to do that.

We want to be gracious and self-controlled. We don't want to hurt anybody's feelings and so we don't say what we think. We don't speak up or disagree—at least to the person's face.

And yet we know, as Paul reminds us in Ephesians 4:15, that we need to speak the truth in love. But we're often much more comfortable speaking the truth in love *about* a person instead of *to* the person.

Kind but cruel

It's right for us to not want to berate a person or beat them down with our honesty. That's a good instinct. But there are many options besides hurtful, brutal truth and silence. There's a way to speak the truth in love, to be full of grace *and* truth, and to make a point without making an enemy. It's not easy, but it is possible and we should at least try.

The people you lead, the people on your team, deserve to know the truth. If you're leading them, then they deserve to know what you think about how they're going. You don't need to tell them everything about everything. There are some things people don't need to know, and other things aren't appropriate for everyone to know. But when it comes to feedback, they need to hear it from you. It's not just that it's preferred, if you get around to it. No, they need it from you and they deserve it from you.

Not telling a person how they're going, whether good or bad, not telling them whether they're improving or not, isn't kind. It feels kind, and it's much easier, but it's actually cruel.

Jack Welch, former CEO of General Electric and *Fortune Magazine*'s 'Manager of the Century',[46] describes lack of candour as a huge problem. He says:

> Now, when I say 'lack of candor' here, I'm not talking about malevolent dishonesty. I am talking about how too many people—too often—instinctively don't express themselves with frankness. They don't communicate straightforwardly or put forth ideas looking to stimulate real debate. They just don't open up. Instead they withhold comments or criticism. They keep their mouths shut in order to make people feel better or to avoid conflict, and they sugarcoat bad news in order to maintain appearances... That's all lack of candor, and it's absolutely damaging... forget outside competition when your own worst enemy is the way you communicate with one another internally![47]

Elsewhere he says:

> No matter where we travel, we hear about organizations that are slowed down and gummed up by the very human tendency to soften hard, urgent messages with false kindness or phony optimism. This tendency is particularly prevalent when it comes to communicating about poor performance. Very

46 Time Warner, '*Fortune* selects Henry Ford Businessman of the Century', 1 November 1999, Time Warner, New York (viewed 11 September 2014): http://www.timewarner.com/newsroom/press-releases/1999/11/01/fortune-selects-henry-ford-businessman-of-the-century

47 Welch, *Winning*, pp. 25-7.

> often, bosses don't come right out and tell underperformers how badly they are doing until, in a burst of frustration, they fire them. That's terribly unfair to the person on the receiving end.[48]

Imagine if you were in hospital and the doctor wouldn't tell you whether you're getting better or not because she didn't want to make you sad. There's nothing kind about that. You need to know. Imagine if you were training to be an Olympic swimmer and your coach wouldn't tell you how fast you swam and whether it was faster than last time or not. Although there's something kind and noble about not wanting to hurt your feelings or make you upset, it's not actually kind, is it? Not telling you that you're not swimming faster or better or withholding your diagnosis isn't kind—it's cruel.

People deserve to know the truth—especially about their own results and progress.

At some level we all know this. It's just very hard to do, it's rarely fun, and it takes a lot of courage.

Giving feedback

So how can you start giving honest feedback and doing it better?

The number-one thing to do is to start immediately. It will feel strange and maybe even awkward—and especially if your team has a history of never receiving feedback. But waiting won't change this in any way. The only way to change it is to change it.

So start immediately. Explain to the team that you want to start giving them feedback, so that they know what they're doing well and where they can improve. Apologize that it hasn't happened until now and explain that they're not in trouble. Make sure they understand that you want to help them get better and enjoy their roles more. And then start. It won't be as awkward as you think it will be, and that discomfort will disappear more quickly than you think it will.

The key to giving good feedback is to do it constantly. Most places that acknowledge its value and actually give feedback save it all up for

48 Welch, *Winning*, p. 99.

an official review once or twice a year. Performance reviews can be quite helpful, but if you only give feedback in sit-down formal reviews one or two times a year, you're missing many opportunities to develop and encourage your team.

Feedback needs to become part of what you do, part of the fibre and weave of your team. The more you do it, the more people will accept it and get used to it. The more you give feedback, the more confident the people in your team will be because they'll know where they stand. They'll know what they do well and where they can improve. The more you give feedback, the faster the people in your team will develop.

Let's say you want to start right away and give feedback constantly and consistently. What exactly should you do? What kind of things should you be saying? When you give feedback you need to be doing two things. First, you need to be showing gratitude and praise. Second, you need to be telling people how they can improve.

Praise like a whale

Praising people is very important, but for some leaders this is the hardest part of giving feedback. Observations on how people can improve are easy and obvious for some of us, whereas observations on what people have been doing well are usually harder to produce. I'm sure there's a profound reason for this imbalance—I just don't know what it is. What it means, though, is that we need to work particularly hard at observing what can be praised.

Praise needs to be specific. It will not be helpful to rush past this bit by saying, "Great job. Here are some things to work on." Slow down and be as specific in your praise as you will be in your criticism. In fact, if possible, be even more specific with your praise.

Giving praise isn't just the hand-holding, touchy-feely entrée to the main course of constructive criticism that some people imagine it to be. In general, we tend to underestimate the power of positive feedback. Praise isn't the necessary sugar to help the medicine go down or the introduction that loosens us up so we can get to the actual information that will shape us. Praise itself is a very powerful tool we can use to help people develop.

If you've ever been to a water park where they train killer whales to jump out of the water, launch their trainers through the water, and all kinds of other amazing feats, you might have wondered how they train them to do those things. Well, they train killer whales by praising them and rewarding them. That's it.

Putting aside whatever your views might be on training animals in captivity and keeping animals designed for the open ocean in relatively small and shallow enclosures, this is still an amazing thing to contemplate.

They never reprimand or punish the killer whales. From one perspective, this makes a lot of sense. Imagine that Fred the killer whale trainer has just reprimanded the killer whale with some kind of physical deterrent for not doing what he asked. And now it's time for Fred to get back in the enclosure with the giant animal he just physically reprimanded.

"Off you go, Fred. Back in the water."

Killer whales earned their name—it's not an ironic name. Killer whales are some of the most fearsome predators in the ocean. They can and will eat almost anything. They can grow to weigh more than 6000 kilograms.

You don't just intimidate a killer whale, put him in the naughty corner, punish him for not doing as you asked, and expect to live to see your daughter's wedding day. That's not how it works. Miraculously, however, humans still manage to train these enormous creatures to do amazing feats on command.

And they do it through only praise and reinforcement.[49]

As leaders of ministry teams we're not, of course, dealing with temperamental killing machines with relatively low intelligence—at least not all the time—and so constructive feedback still has its place. God himself gives us negative reinforcement as well as positive. He praises and rebukes, rewards and punishes. So we know that negative reinforcement isn't wrong in itself, and we're wise to include it in our feedback.

What the whale training teaches us, though, is the power of positive feedback. It's a formidable mechanism for change in a person, just as negative feedback is a formidable mechanism for change. Because

49 For more on this see Ken Blanchard, Thad Lacinak, Chuck Tompkins and Jim Ballard, *Whale Done! The power of positive relationships*, Free Press, New York, 2002.

positive feedback is so powerful, we need to think it through carefully and be specific.

In general, people want to do a good job and do the right thing. And so when you tell someone that a specific thing they did was a right and good thing to do, that it worked, they'll want to do it again. They'll understand a bit more clearly what it is they're supposed to be doing because you pointed out an example of what the target looks like. With that knowledge, they'll be that much better at spotting it for themselves, aiming for it, and hitting it. People will do more of the things that you praise.

Noticing what people do well takes conscious effort and discipline. You'll generally notice bad things whether you're looking for them or not. But you'll need to consciously look to see good things.

The only time you notice the person pushing the button for the data projector is when they mess it up. If your church is anything like mine, when that happens everyone in the building turns around and looks at them—as though everyone looking at them will help in some way. But if they don't make any mistakes we tend to forget there's a person back there at all.

Take the time and make the effort to notice the good things. There's always something that you can honour in what a person does, even in the most dismal of circumstances. It's your responsibility to find it, to see what no-one else notices, and to point it out.

When you feel thankful or grateful for something someone did, you need to find a way to express it—whether it's by telling them, texting them, writing a note, or finding some other way to communicate your appreciation. Gratitude that's felt and never expressed is like a gift that's wrapped but never given.

Criticism that's actually heard

In addition to giving people praise, you also need to point out where and how they can improve. No-one will do everything perfectly—there's always room for improvement. So we need to tell people a few ways they can improve. People will find it hard to hear and it's not a fun experience. But they'll improve and get better as a result of this feedback.

The best way to ensure that the feedback you give is actually heard is to do everything you can to make the circumstances not feel threatening. You need to strip any adversarial overtones from the conversation. It's not you against this person, and you're not accusing him or her. You're coming alongside this person and working with them to help them improve.

This is not about being soft and fluffy; it matters, because it's about making sure people actually hear and process what you're saying. Neuroscientists talk about the brain in various ways, but one way is to look at the upper brain and the lower brain. The upper brain is where all the higher-functioning activities happen—like thinking, analysing, logic, creativity, forward-planning, prioritization, and all those other good things you want people on your team to do. This is the brain you want them to use when they make their decisions. The lower brain is all about one thing: survival. This is the part of the brain that kicks in under stress and threat. The lower brain works in the areas of 'fight or flight'. Technically, that should be 'freeze, flight or fight'. Not much of what we would call thinking happens in this part of the brain—it's all instinct. There are only three options: we freeze, we run away, or we stand and fight.

Henry Cloud explains why all of this matters for giving feedback:

> In the fight-or-flight syndrome, a collection of stress hormones are released into the brain, which essentially shuts down all of the functions that make us smart and, instead, activates another part of the brain designed just to respond to danger. Its mission is to stop thinking, and act... That should explain a lot of behavior you have seen when someone feels threatened, no matter whether the danger is real or perceived. No doubt you've even experienced it yourself. People get defensive, they push back, or they avoid the conflict and move away. And, even worse, they may do impulsive things—speaking before thinking or acting out in anger.[50]

If the way you give feedback makes people feel threatened, then what you're doing is shutting down their brains so that they will not and cannot process what you're saying. Obviously there's no benefit to this, but we

50 Cloud, *Boundaries*, p. 54.

tend to give feedback in this way because we want people to understand the seriousness of their mistakes or to feel the appropriate levels of remorse. But it often backfires because people end up hearing less and feeling less because we've shut down their brains.

What we need to do instead is to be hard on the issue and soft on the person. We need to be against the issue, the problem, the behaviour—but not against the person. We need to stand shoulder to shoulder with the person, on the same team, and tackle the common enemy together.

How you do this is very important. You don't want to browbeat someone and make them feel small. But you want to be clear that you want them to stop doing this, or to keep working on that. People deserve to know exactly where they stand. What are they doing that you want to see less of? What are they doing that they haven't quite mastered yet? What do they need to do to improve what they're doing in this area?

It's almost always a mistake to give feedback in real-time. It's tempting to give feedback immediately after someone has finished doing something—whether it's preaching or leading a meeting or something else. You want to give the feedback straight away while it's fresh in your mind and fresh in theirs. If it's of utmost importance—if someone's safety is involved or the person spoke heresy, for example—right away is a good time. But that's not normally the case, and you should allow a bit of time to pass before you give the person feedback. Some distance will help them to separate themselves, and who they are, from what they did. It also helps them to gain some perspective on what they did, so they can see it a bit more clearly and perhaps even provide their own reflections on what was good and how they could improve. It's almost always a discussion rather than a top-down relay of information.

Don't labour the point when you give people negative feedback.[51] If there's something you need them to stop doing, say it as clearly as you can and provide an example if you need to. Tell them why you want to see it change. And then move on. If it's something they need to improve, then

51 I'd like to challenge the idea that giving negative feedback undermines people's self-esteem. The problem is a fixed mindset versus a growth mindset. The fixed mindset believes talent is innate, and if you're good at something it should be easy for you to do it. With a growth mindset, by contrast, people believe that they get better at things because they try hard and practise and fail. It's this fixed mindset that causes anxiety and self-confidence issues.

again say it as clearly as you can, tell them why, and then perhaps give them some ideas of concrete things they can do to improve.

I try to give people at least three specific things I've noticed that they're doing really well and that I want them to keep doing. I also try to give them up to three areas to keep working on. Whatever you do, don't give them more negative points than positive points. If possible, have more positive than negative. When people receive feedback, negative comments weigh at least twice as much as positive comments. They land heavier and are more memorable. An equal number of positive and negative points is okay. But giving more positive comments is better because people will more easily hear all of them and won't be overly weighted towards the negative.

The people you lead deserve to hear the truth about what they're doing. They deserve to be clear on what you think they're doing well and what you think they need to improve. Not wanting to be mean or cruel is a great instinct, but it doesn't mean you shouldn't tell the truth. It just means you need to do the hard work of mixing grace with your truth.

Truthful meetings

You can tell a lot about a church by observing their meetings—either staff meetings or key lay leader meetings. You can tell a lot about their culture, whether or not they raise problems, how they raise problems, whether they trust each other, what's important to the team, and so much more. People deserve to know the truth, and giving feedback is a key way to implement this principle. But it's not just people in one-on-one situations who deserve to know the truth. People in meetings also deserve to know the truth.

One of the most destructive ways that a lack of truth shows itself in a team is the meeting after the meeting. This happens when we don't say what we really think during the meeting, we hold back our thoughts, and then once the meeting is over a smaller number of us have a smaller meeting. Sometimes this happens around the table once others have left, sometimes it happens out in the car park in hushed voices, and other times it happens in the hallways days after the meeting took place. The meeting after the meeting is where we discuss what 'they' just decided and how it will never work and what a bad idea it is.

These meetings after the meetings are destructive for a number of reasons.

First, when there are meetings after the meeting it means that your main meeting is a waste of time. When it's meeting time you want everyone's head in the game and you want to harness everyone's collective wisdom. If people have input, thoughts, perspectives, questions, objections, and wisdom that they keep to themselves and that we're not hearing then, as a team, we're not as smart as we could be. Our plans won't be as sharp as they could be. Even if we don't end up using those particular ideas to modify the plan, that plan is still stronger for having worked through some objections. We'll know what some of the downsides and potential objections will be and we'll have taken them into consideration. But if people hold back in meetings, then the plans that are made won't be as strong and the whole point of the meeting is undermined.

Second, when there are meetings after the meeting where we discuss what 'they' just decided it means that people don't realize that 'they' is 'us'. The team that just made that decision is the team of which the dissenting person is a member. If people are complaining or dissatisfied with the decisions that 'those people' just made in the meeting, they're signalling that 'we' are not 'those people'. This means there's a team within a team. If there's disunity in the leadership, then there will be problems in the ministry before long. Meetings after the meeting are extremely unhealthy and a sign that deeper problems exist.

Third, meetings after the meeting destroy relationships. It can all start so innocently. We don't verbalize our disagreement with a person's idea because we don't want to hurt anyone's feelings. But imagine this scenario, which might sound familiar. You're in a meeting. Someone puts forward an idea that's stupid. Bob says that we should raise money for the kids' ministry by importing spice from the Dutch East Indies. No-one questions Bob's idea, you all say thanks and move on. You don't want to disagree with him and risk hurting his feelings. After the meeting, you and some others have a laugh about the renewed interest in the spice trade before jumping into your cars.

At the next meeting Bob puts forward some more stupid ideas, and you sneak a smirk at some of the others in the room but don't say anything.

Every meeting it's the same, and as the meetings roll on your eyes roll more. But you still don't say anything. Your conversations afterwards become more pointed about the stupidity of Bob's ideas.

You begin to resent Bob's stupid ideas more and more, and word begins to spread. One Sunday over morning tea someone lets Bob know that everyone's talking about how stupid he is. And now you've absolutely crushed his spirit.

But at least you didn't disagree with his ideas.

The cause and solution

Patrick Lencioni observes:

> Most leaders have learned the art of passive agreement: going to a meeting, smiling and nodding their heads when a decision is made that they don't agree with. They then go back to their offices and do as little as possible to support that idea. They don't promote it on their own team, and they certainly aren't willing to run out onto the tracks waving their arms to prevent a train wreck. Instead, they sit back and watch problems develop, quietly looking forward to the day when things go badly and they can say, "Well, I never really liked that idea in the first place".[52]

Does that, unfortunately, describe you or your team? It's absolutely essential that the truth is told in meetings in your church. But that requires a certain kind of trust.

For a team to function well, to be cohesive and effective, the members of the team need to trust one another. It seems almost stupid to state this obvious fact, but it's shocking to me how few teams actually do this. As we've discussed, teams need the type of trust where they can be transparent with each other, where they can admit and show weakness, where they can openly and honestly disagree with each other.

When a team trusts each other like this and its members are able to be vulnerable with each other, they won't waste energy trying to appear better

52 Lencioni, *The Advantage*, p. 49.

than they are or more together than they are or pretending to be more in control than they are. They'll instead begin to speak more freely with each other and they'll be more willing to share their thoughts or concerns about an idea without fear of looking silly or offending others. On the flip side of that equation, people will also be able to handle it better when others question or disagree with their ideas. In this kind of environment, the meetings after the meetings will soon wither and die for lack of fuel.

If your team is characterized by meetings after the meeting, the cause will be one of three things: it might be because of something you're doing; it might be something to do with the people in your team; or it might be some mutually reinforcing combination of the two.

Are you doing anything to shut down deep discussion in your meetings? Are you yourself uncomfortable with vulnerability and conflict? Do you view discussion as a waste of time or do you end up making it a waste of time by guiding the discussion such that it exists purely to give people an opportunity to agree with the decision you made before the meeting started? Do you punish people, consciously or unconsciously, for voicing dissenting opinions?

Is there a lack of clarity within the team? Are people more committed to their ministry fiefdoms than they are to the combined mission of the team? Are people in your meetings representing their constituencies rather than considering what's best for the whole? Do members of the team have unresolved baggage that's stopping them from being transparent? Are there members of your team who will not sacrifice their ego for the sake of the team? Are there people on your team who believe that the part they play is bigger than what they're a part of?

You need to make it a top priority to kill the meetings after the meetings. You need people to tell the truth while they're still in the meeting, instead of waiting until it's over to say what they think. You want people to say what they believe is the best way forward in the meeting. Meetings after the meetings are cancerous, and you need to cut them out with great urgency.

Figure out what's stopping people from bringing the truth to light in your meetings—whether it's a problem with you or with them or both. And, once you figure out what the blockage is, do everything you can to overcome it.

Your meetings, with individuals as well as with groups, should be held together with both grace and truth. Giving clear feedback so people know exactly where they stand—what they're doing that you like and what you want them to work on—will be a huge help in encouraging your people to grow and develop. Decide to commit to speaking the truth in love, both in formal appraisals and also as the texture of all your interactions. People deserve the truth, and deep down they want the truth. As the leader, you're responsible for making sure the truth is spoken in your team.

See also

27. You're just the leader
37. Phrases to learn
39. Public fans and private critics
41. Two foundations of team-building
63. Meetings are where real work is done
77. Bad news is good news

47

Find the awesome

A lot of people say that the role of a great leader is to attract and recruit great people. And there is some truth in that. But I think that attracting and recruiting great people is what *good* leaders do. What *great* leaders do is to take ordinary people and help them to become great.

When you're running a church ministry you don't always have the luxury of being able to canvas the market to recruit a great person. You might be able to do that when you're looking to hire a staff member, or a well-discipled and well-trained person might arrive at your church from another church, but generally speaking the people who are available to you are those who are currently in your church. Thinking ahead, of course, you want to look forward to that pool widening as those who are currently outside your church are converted in the coming years. It's your responsibility to take the people that God has given you, and whom he has gifted, and find what makes them awesome and develop them to see them become great.

God uses ordinary people and he gifts ordinary people. It's your job to help them figure out how he has gifted them and how he might use them in the spread of the gospel. Everyone is gifted, everyone has awesome within them, and everyone has a role to play in building God's church. It's your job as the leader "to equip the saints for the work of ministry" (Eph 4:12). This means that, in the end, if there are people in your church who haven't found the awesome within them and who aren't contributing to the ministry of the church, that's somewhat your responsibility. You are, at least partially, at fault. It's your job to help them find the awesome and deploy the awesome for the glory of God.

How do you do that?

Be convinced everyone is gifted

It can be harder than it sounds sometimes to find someone's gift. Some people's awesome sits closer to the surface. But others have an awesome hidden under layers of awkwardness, ineptitude, nonchalance, or ingrained mediocrity. Are you convinced that everyone is gifted and that there is awesome within everyone? Theologically you might know this to be true, but do you believe it in a way that affects how you act and talk and develop people?

Certainly some people are more gifted than others. And some are more self-motivated to improve and develop than others. Some people's life experiences have advantaged or disadvantaged them. But none of that overrides the fact that God has gifted every person. Every person can be great at something and can contribute and play a part.

Most people don't know what they can be awesome at doing. Some people may know about one area—like being able to sing, for example. But they may be awesome in some other areas as well that they haven't yet discovered or developed. Either way, whether people are aware of where they're awesome or not, it's your job as the leader to help them figure it out.

Focus on what people could potentially do

When there's a role to fill or a new opportunity to tackle, the questions we often ask are: Who's the best person to lead this? Who can take this on and do it well?

These aren't bad questions, and sometimes they're simply the necessary questions we need to ask. But they're not the best questions to ask. A better set of questions would be: Who has the potential to lead this? Who might have it in them to grow into this role?

The strength of looking for people who have already identified and developed their awesome is that you can have confidence that they'll be able and equipped to perform well in whatever the role is. You can be reasonably sure of a certain level of competence and quality. That confidence is a powerful thing, and there may be circumstances or responsibilities that will require that level of confidence.

But is that level of quality and confidence always necessary? Are there times and occasions where you could allow someone to grow into certain competencies?

The problem with only recruiting people who have already identified and developed their awesome is relatively obvious: you won't be expanding that circle of people and you'll be leaning on those same people for more and more ministries. How much better would it be if, every year, that circle of awesome people could expand—maybe by one person, maybe by five people?

That circle can expand either by awesome people transferring from some other church into your church or by you intentionally developing someone who is not-yet awesome so that they become awesome. And in order for that to happen you need to begin looking into the future. You need to develop that kind of intentional imagination. Could this person become the kind of person who could lead in this area at a high level of competence? Do they have the determination and drive to learn how to lead at this level? Can I imagine them leading at a higher level in a year or in 18 months?

If you only focus on what people can currently do, you will only ever have people who do what they currently do. You break out of this by focusing on people's potential. Who has the potential to be great at this, with some training, help, feedback, and support? Who can I sow into and develop to become more than they currently are? In order to expand this circle of people you're going to need a way to get to know the people you're serving. Perhaps you'll get to know each person individually or perhaps you'll have others, whom you trust, getting to know each person and how God has uniquely gifted them. Helping a person discover and develop their awesome requires close, personal work. In order to find people you'll need to know people.

Expect failure

People aren't generally good at things the first time they do them—even when they're learning things they'll be awesome at one day!

A crucial but counterintuitive part of helping people find their awesome is to instil in them an expectation of failure. Sometimes people just touch on an area where they can be awesome and they're instantly and blindingly brilliant. But this is rare. Really, really rare. Even people who have an inclination and aptitude in a certain area still need to develop a skill set and learn how to reallocate their time. The learning curve is almost always steep.

If the expectation is that when you find your awesome you're going to be instantly great at whatever it is and better than most others, people will quit way too early. Finding your awesome takes hard work and perseverance.

When people join our teams we ask them to mentally commit for a tentative two years. It's not a rigid commitment—circumstances change, life is in flux, and no-one knows what next year will look like. But we ask them to plan to be around for at least two years because in the first year they won't be that good and they'll make a lot of mistakes, but then in the second year they'll start getting really good. And we tell them that upfront and set that up as an expectation: in that first year they'll make lots of mistakes and they won't be great. But finding their awesome takes time, practice, trial and error, and exposure to different tasks and environments.

Expecting failure gives people the freedom and permission—and also allows them to give themselves the freedom and permission—to try and to experiment and to be patient. We don't want people to walk away prematurely from a path that leads to awesomeness.

Intentionally develop people

People don't just become awesome. People find their awesome when other people believe in them, invest in them, give them opportunities, and let them know how they're going. And none of that happens by accident—it requires intentionality. What can you do to help develop people?

Entrust some responsibility to them. It doesn't have to be a big thing—it could be a smaller part of something big. But you need to actually give the responsibility to them. You've noticed that Mary is always one of the first people to greet newcomers after your church service and you suspect that she may be a person who could not just organize but also improve your whole welcoming ministry. So you explain the welcoming ministry and why it matters on a Sunday morning and ask her if she'd be willing to join that team. Mary says that she'd love to. Then you watch and see what happens. This observation is a critical step. You can't just give her the responsibility and then look away. What does Mary do with that responsibility? How does she react to it? Does she arrive late, on time, or early? What happens when she's entrusted? All of this tells you something.

If she comes to you with questions, resist the temptation to tell her what she should do. Instead, ask her what she thinks. Let her know that this is an important decision and that you're giving her the authority to make it. And, again, watch her. Did she make a good decision? Tell her; praise her. If she makes a good decision you need to give her the confidence to make another decision. And another. And another. Bigger decisions. Decisions with more significant consequences.

Let's say Mary does well with this role. What next? You might give her some more responsibility. What if you invited Mary to be part of the small team planning the Christmas services? This might be way above where Mary is currently at, but you want to introduce her to thinking at that higher level about what we do at church and why we do certain things. And you might want her interacting with other people who shoulder that kind of responsibility.

Believe in the people to whom you give these kinds of responsibilities. Imagine what they might be like or could become and tell them what you see. It's not a prophecy, a word from the Lord, or a vision of the future. It's imagination. It's what might be, could be, what potentially may happen. Not everyone thinks that there's awesome within themselves. So sometimes you'll need to believe it for them.

Developing someone doesn't mean, primarily, sitting down and talking through a training paper. There's nothing wrong with that when it's appropriate and what's needed, but it's not the main way to develop someone and help them find the awesome. You want to be intentional about finding opportunities for people to take on, and be a part of, bigger and bigger responsibilities. You want to give people the chance to develop new skill sets in a relatively progressive way so that they can be stretched without being overwhelmed.

If they don't thrive in a particular role or ministry, that's not the end of the road. You have a conversation about what's going well and what's not working and you try and find a role that maximizes the good and minimizes the bad.

You might be able to think of examples of people who became awesome without you doing any of those things—people who just developed without any intentional input on your part, who found their awesome and become high-level leaders. I can think of examples of those kinds of people too. So if people can become awesome without intentionality, why am I saying we need it?

Just because someone became awesome without you being intentional doesn't mean that no-one was being intentional. Most people find their awesome by way of a group of people intentionally developing them. And the people in that group may not even be aware of anyone else's involvement. Parents may be involved, perhaps sporting coaches or a spouse, maybe a boss at work, and the person him or herself might have sought out training or mentors—it's often a multi-facetted process. But the point is that just because you weren't intentionally involved in the process of a certain leader's development doesn't mean that there wasn't intentionality or a process. It's just that you weren't involved.

All of this intentionality can sound overwhelming, but it doesn't need to be. One way of doing this is to invite one or two new people along whenever you have a planning meeting for something—an event, a special church service, or training night, for example—along with a team of people who you already know are great at that kind of thing. Then have these new people be involved in the discussion and give them some tasks for which they're responsible. And just see how they go. See how they go contributing and interacting in that group and see how they go with their assigned responsibilities. If they seem to enjoy it and are faithful, then find more opportunities for them. If they don't engage much or cancel at the last minute or flake out on their responsibilities then ease off and look for some other people who might step up if given an opportunity.

Including a sliver of intentional development in things you already do will keep the responsibility of finding the awesome in people from becoming overwhelming or too difficult to even contemplate.

There's a ministry at my church that, from the outside, looks as though it attracts the best and brightest from our church. It has a disproportionate amount of greatness. People sometimes complain that this ministry takes the best people and leaves the rest for every other ministry.

But when you stop and look more closely you notice that that's not the case. What you notice is that the blue chip, can't-miss, currently great prospects are just as likely, if not more likely, to join other ministries. And this particular ministry recruits ordinary people who are just keen to join and serve. And then these ordinary people *become* great. This ministry helps them find their awesome.

As a leader it's your responsibility to help those you lead grow and get better. It's your job to help them find the awesome that everybody has within them. We know it's true theologically, and it's our job to help people know and discover it experientially. And you'll be able to look back and see the paths people have taken from feeling ordinary to finding the place where God has brought them to find and develop their awesome—and you'll know you're the kind of leader God wants you to be, equipping the saints for works of ministry.

See also

30. Faithfulness buys responsibility
34. Fail forwards
48. Treat them like children
64. Learn relaxed concern
70. Ignore the org-chart
76. Seek raw beauty

48
Treat them like children

I've learned a lot about leadership from observing the way I treat my children. For instance, the way we treat our children when we teach them new skills is very effective. No-one teaches us to act like parents; we do it instinctively. And I think it would be wise for us to treat the people we lead more like children. I don't mean that we should talk down to them or downgrade their responsibilities or anything like that. But there's a lot of wisdom that can be gleaned from the methods we use to help kids move forward.

When I'm leading people I'm constantly helping them to learn new skills, use existing skills in new contexts, or behave in some new way. There are three principles I've noticed in how I help my children to behave in new ways, and these same three principles have also proven incredibly clarifying as I've led adults and helped them to develop.

1. Close enough is good enough

One of the things I've noticed is that kids don't really know how to do much of anything. Some things come instinctively, but there are lots of things kids need to learn. Like learning to talk. When my daughter was a year old and learning to talk she didn't seem to know much about it. She was pretty good at making noises, but it was very hard to work out what she was trying to communicate. And in a lot of ways, at least as far as I could tell, she had almost no idea what she was doing. And this is often the case with adults who are tackling a new task. Most of the time—more often than we perhaps care to admit—we have no idea what we're doing. So we're in a very similar position to a one-year-old learning to talk. How do we teach children to talk?

When I was teaching my kids how to say words, the principle I went with was 'close enough is good enough'. If I was teaching my daughter to say 'dog' and she pronounced that short 'oh' sound and pointed to the dog, I praised her like she'd just solved the mystery of perpetual motion. She got close to the general ballpark. Hurray!

As saying 'oh' became the usual, I slowly scaled my praise down over time. Then I tried to teach her to make the 'g' sound. When she finally said 'og' and pointed to the dog, I again ramped up the praise and made her into the house hero. She was getting closer and she was doing a good job.

And then I again slowly scaled down my praise as she became confident with 'og' and I again pushed her forward to get that 'd' sound. When she finally said the word 'dog', I ratcheted up the praise again like she'd just saved Ghandi's kitten from a horrible death.

Close enough is good enough. Until it's not. And then when someone moves forward, close enough is good enough again. Until it's not.

2. Praise progress

The second principle, then, is that with children we don't wait until they nail something perfectly before we praise them. We don't praise perfection; we praise progress. We'd still praise them, of course, if they did hit perfection, but the point is that's not the only time we praise them. We don't wait for that. When my kids are learning some new skill or activity I don't wait until they've mastered it before I praise them.

Imagine if a child who was learning to speak didn't receive any praise until they had learned to speak in grammatically correct sentences. Or just imagine that you didn't praise a child until they spoke a new word perfectly correctly.

"No. Wrong again. It's not 'og'. It's '*d*og'. D-O-G." That's crazy.

Or imagine that you didn't praise a child until they coloured completely inside the lines with no mistakes. Until they did that perfectly, you just critiqued and pointed out their mistakes.

As parents we don't wait to praise perfection. We don't even wait until competence to praise.

We praise progress. We look for even subtle displays of progress—

sometimes for those that are imperceptible to all but the most ardent observer. And when we see a sign of progress, no matter how infinitesimally small, we praise the child for it. "You're getting much better at that." "I can see that's getting much easier for you." "Great work on putting your shoes on all by yourself! That's such a grown-up thing to do. Let me help you get them on the right feet."

When you're seeking to praise your children, noticing their progress doesn't just happen. You need to be actively looking for something you can praise. Sometimes those somethings can be very hard to find. And it's the same with the people we lead.

If you're not concentrating and actively looking for progress, you only notice big strides or big changes. But those big changes are often made up of hundreds of small, gradual improvements. The trick is to be aware and alert for those hundreds of small steps. The job of a leader, as a parent, is to see things that others don't.

Don't wait for perfection. Don't even wait for competence.

Praise progress.

3. Create milestones

The last principle I noticed when teaching my kids new skills was that I almost never gave them the end-goal task to achieve without breaking it down into steps. And we also celebrated the mastery of each step along the way to that goal.

From talking to eating real food to riding a bike to reading books, I broke each new skill into a series of milestones. I didn't hand my four-year-old *Lord of the Rings* and say, "Hey, let me know what you think of the ending". We started with picture books. Then books with one word on each page. Then we moved on to books with one sentence per page that they 'read' because they'd memorized them. Then longer books. And now short chapter books.

In addition to helping people learn through the principles of close enough is good enough and praising progress along the way, we also need to think about breaking the tasks and skills we want people to learn into manageable chunks and milestones. And then, as they hit each milestone, we need to celebrate in some way with them. Most of the time that celebration will simply be praise. The difference here is that you're not just praising progress ("I can see you're getting better at sounding out those hard words"), but reaching a concrete milestone ("You just finished that whole chapter book"). But every now and then you might do something else, something small, to mark a milestone and show your appreciation. Perhaps someone who's been helping design some flyers for you has just designed the entire flyer for your Christmas services, and it's the first time he's been responsible for the whole project from concept to the final product. You might put that flyer inside a small frame with the words 'Designed from start to finish by John Smith' to celebrate and show your appreciation for that milestone.

People are much more likely to stick with a challenging task if they know that they're not wasting their time and can see that they're making progress. And it's your job as their leader to help them see what they perhaps can't see. You need to help them see the progress that they're making, even if it's small—and especially if it's small. It's your job to find it, notice it, and point it out.

If we treated the people we lead more like children, we'd develop better people.

See also

15. Change your default style
29. Praise publicly
34. Fail forwards
47. Find the awesome
64. Learn relaxed concern
76. Seek raw beauty

49

You can only drive as fast as the car in front

Eighty kilometres (50 miles) per hour is fast. If you could run at 80 km/h you'd be moving very quickly indeed. When you're on a road with a speed limit of 100 km/h and you're stuck behind a car travelling 80 km/h, however, 80 km/h feels excruciatingly slow. It takes a lot of patience and self-control not to bubble over with frustration. You have somewhere to go. You could go faster. But you're trapped and it's taking longer than it should.

This feeling of frustration is similar to the frustrations felt by the leader below you who can lead at a higher level than you can. They'll feel trapped behind you. Things will be moving more slowly than they're able to move them and will take longer than they should. You will be a bottleneck, and the people you lead will struggle to be led by you.

They won't be struggling because they don't like you or because they aren't committed to the people they're leading or to the team or the vision. They'll struggle precisely because they do like you and they're committed.

They will be behind you

Because you're the leader, people will do what you say and do as you do. Being a leader means being followed.

When people follow you they will, to a large extent, take their cues from you. When they're not sure how to behave they'll check how you behave. When they're not sure what to do they'll check what you do. They'll push forward as fast as you do. You can only drive as fast as the car in front. If you're truly leading your team, then they'll be following you. They'll be lining up behind you. And just like when you're driving on a one-lane road you can only go as fast as the car in front, so a team will only be able to go as fast as the leader in front.

As Bill Hybels puts it:

> Leaders must never expect from others anything more than they're willing to deliver themselves. They should never expect higher levels of commitment, creativity, persistence, or patience than what they themselves manifest on a regular basis. If you cannot say, 'Follow me,' to your followers—and mean it—then you've got a problem. A big one. Speed of the leader, speed of the team.[53]

It's not that people are sheep who can't think for themselves and so they'll fit unquestioningly into a prevailing culture or system. Of course people are responsible for themselves. They can and will make their own decisions. But, at the same time, they'll make decisions based on the parameters and boundaries you set for them.

When the leader sets the tone in terms of energy, joy, gratitude, or hours worked, it won't take long for members of the team to align their efforts with those of the leader and the leader's expectations. If the leader always turns up late the team will soon turn up late. If the leader is always complaining about having to stay late, the rest of the team will eventually start doing the same thing.

Individual team members may work faster or harder on their own projects when they have relative autonomy, but the leader sets the pace for reaching the objectives of the team as a whole. It's very difficult to move faster than the leader—it's not impossible, but it does take more effort and people will rarely do it for long.

Options for deceleration

If the team wants to move forward with a decision or a program and the leader agrees that it's good and needs to be done but, for whatever

53 Bill Hybels, *Axiom: Powerful leadership proverbs*, Zondervan, Grand Rapids, 2008, p. 94.

reason, is not comfortable with the speed of the team, that leader has multiple options for slowing them down. The leader can say "not now" or use other methods to put the handbrake on—like waiting to see how it plays out, thinking about it more, or putting it on next week's agenda. The leader may say yes and then have a change of mind and say no and even go back and forth multiple times. Or the leader may control how quickly the various items move through the organizational system. Regardless of the tactic he or she chooses, the leader can very easily slow down or undermine the strength and speed of the team.

Feeling as though you're stuck behind a slower leader quickly becomes frustrating. If this is happening in a team you lead you'll find that, over time, your best leaders will leave. This is not what you want! But they won't be leaving because they don't love you or the people you're serving or because they aren't Christlike or don't care about the kingdom. They will leave because the kingdom is more important to them than being in your team and doing this specific ministry. They'll want to maximize what they can do for the kingdom and serve Jesus as best they can. If they can serve Jesus better outside of your leadership, then they probably should—for the sake of the lost and the growth of the kingdom.

The importance of getting better

If your team members in this situation are Christlike and kingdom-minded, the decision to leave will be tough and they'll struggle with it for a long time. Eventually, though, they will leave to go do more elsewhere because they felt like cars itching to go faster.

Prolific leadership author John Maxwell makes this same observation:

> The less skilled follow the more highly skilled and gifted. Occasionally, a strong leader may choose to follow someone weaker than himself. But when that happens it's for a reason. For example, the stronger leader may do it out of respect for the person's office or past achievements. Or he may be following the chain of command. In general, though,

> followers are attracted to people who are better leaders than themselves.[54]

So if you want to attract a higher calibre of leader it's of utmost importance that *you* keep growing as a leader. Great leaders like to be around other great leaders. And as you model the virtue of personal leadership development your team will also continue to grow and improve.

When they see you putting in effort and growing, those leaders under you who can go further and faster than you can just might stay. All is not lost because you're not yet a great leader. You can get better. And the better you get, the better the people around you will be.

The faster you drive, the faster those behind you will drive, and the quicker you will all get to where you need to go.

See also

12. Lead yourself
18. If you're not a good follower then you're not a good leader

54 John C Maxwell, *The 21 Irrefutable Laws of Leadership: Follow them and people will follow you*, 10th anniversary edn, Thomas Nelson, Nashville, 2007, p. 76.

50

There's no point having a dog and then barking yourself

Let's imagine that your neighbour just purchased a Rottweiler as a guard dog. They found the best, most well-trained dog they could afford and brought him home and set him up in the front yard with a good view out the front fence and a nice bowl of water. But then you noticed the owner himself sitting next to the dog. And whenever someone walked past, your neighbour would start barking at them.

What would you think of that person sitting next to their dog in the front yard, barking at passers-by? That's right. You'd think they were off their meds.

And yet a lot of leaders make this same mistake with the people and teams they lead. Instead of being the leader of the team and doing team leader's work, they do the work of the team members—which means that they end up competing with their own teams.

There will of course be things that you as a leader can, and probably should, do. There may even be things that you can do better than anyone else you lead. And when you give responsibility for a task to another person and—heaven forbid—they don't perform that task exactly the way you would have done it, or even as well as you would have, you will be tempted to sit outside and bark yourself.

As a leader, however, it's your job to mobilize and multiply the people for whom you're responsible. And you can't do this when you're doing all the work yourself. You'll need to hand things off to other people on your team and let them take those things and run with them. And it will be your job to coach and develop them so that they perform those tasks as well as you can—or better.

Five reasons it's so hard

This kind of delegation makes perfect sense—so why is it so difficult for leaders to focus on leading their teams rather than competing with them? Five reasons:

1. You got to be a leader by being really good at particular tasks in a particular area—whether it's running Bible study groups, preaching, or meeting one-on-one with people. And as your growth in those skills increased, someone noticed and asked you to move into a leadership role where you'd be responsible for leading a group of people who in turn would be responsible for those tasks.

   It can be difficult, emotionally and even psychologically, to give up the very things that got you to this position in the first place. But if you're going to lead a team you need to be able to let that go.

2. You also probably really enjoy doing these things that you got into ministry to do in the first place. These might be the things you used to do in your spare time, and perhaps now you even get paid. And though it's difficult to give up and give over things we love to do, again, that's exactly what you need to do if you're leading a team.

3. You will often, at least at first, watch people performing these tasks who are not doing them as well as they could be done, or as well as you could do them yourself. Maybe your bark really is louder, or quicker, or clearer, or more eloquent than theirs at this point in time. And when this is the case you're more tempted than ever to sit down with them and bark more loudly, quickly, clearly, or eloquently.

   The temptation to take back the tasks can be so subtle that you might not even notice it—or it might even seem to you like the responsible thing to do. "This ministry matters," you might say. "These people should have the highest level of care. The preaching needs to be outstanding. This group needs to be run in a first-rate manner. So I should step back in and take over."

The main problem with this kind of thinking is that there's some truth to it. Excellence is a virtue, quality does matter, greatness is important, and you probably are better at doing these things right at this moment. But it's almost always the wrong call. Your new responsibility is to help, coach, and encourage the members of your team to become as proficient as you are, if not better.[55]

4. At first it will be quicker and easier to do things yourself. It takes a lot more time to meet with the people beforehand to explain the responsibility and then debrief with them afterward. Then meet and debrief. Then meet and debrief. Over and over. So you're right—it is quicker to do it yourself.

But just because it's quicker and easier doesn't make it better. And it isn't quicker and easier in the long term. Doing it yourself won't be quicker and easier six months down the road when the time you've invested begins paying dividends and you have a team of people equal to, or better than, you doing far more than you alone could ever dream of doing.

5. Lastly, it might be difficult to let others take over these tasks because your ego struggles when others get more praise than you do for the things that you can do better than they can. People noticed you doing these things well, which is why you were asked to take on this leadership role in the first place. It's nice when people notice that you did something well and it can be painful when that praise and recognition stops and is transferred to someone else. And it can be even more upsetting when you're the one standing behind that person being praised—helping, training, and coaching them to be great. So you're tempted to jump back in so you can have some of that affirmation you used to get. But if you're going to lead a team you need to deal with your ego.

55 Sometimes, though, stepping in and taking over a task may be the right call. But that's rare. The cost to the team and to the individual person will be so high that you have to make sure it's worth it. It should be the exception. See the next section for more on this.

Six reasons it matters

Since it is difficult to delegate and let go of tasks you enjoy, it's important to know why barking yourself is so bad. As long as the job gets done, why does it matter who does it? A leader's job isn't just to get things done, but to get things done *through people*. Here are six reasons it's important to refrain from barking yourself:

1. It restricts the amount of ministry that can be done to what a single person can do. If you keep taking tasks back from people and doing them yourself, less will get done. Fewer people will be cared for and discipled, fewer preachers will teach God's word. One of the purposes of a team is that it multiplies the ministry. Doing everything yourself restricts the ministry that can be done.

2. It severely limits the amount and quality of on-the-job training that can happen. Coaching and feedback are the best methods for developing people as leaders. As we've seen, people need to be taught how to do something, then they need to do it under observation and receive honest feedback and coaching on how to do it better next time. Then they need a next time, another opportunity, so the process can be repeated. If this process is short-circuited, or taken away completely because you're barking yourself, then the people you're developing will have very little real-time training.

3. It will undermine the enthusiasm of the leaders in your care. When you delegate a responsibility to a leader and then step in and take it back, that's a powerfully demoralizing experience. If this becomes the standard procedure—you give a responsibility, things start not to go well, you take back the responsibility—then what you're teaching the team is not to try and not to invest in the task because it will be taken away. You'll also be communicating to your team that you don't think they're capable of the task. This will lead to you taking tasks back more and more quickly because the team will be putting in less and less effort. Eventually people will stop saying yes at all when you ask for their help. It's a vicious cycle that will eventually destroy your leadership and severely restrict how much ministry will get done.

4. Beyond demotivation, barking yourself may also cause bitterness amongst your team members. If it happens regularly, or on projects that people are particularly excited about or that are very important or high profile, then it's a short, unbroken line from disappointment, embarrassment, and demotivation to bitterness and anger.

   Imagine that you've given a leader responsibility for a new, exciting, and important initiative. This person is very excited and invested, but things don't go as brilliantly right out of the gate as you were hoping they would. The leader has overlooked some key decisions and hasn't done some things that should have been done. Instead of meeting with them, asking questions, reflecting with them, and redirecting them, you take back the responsibility and begin overseeing the project yourself. After all, you tell yourself, it's a very important initiative. Now imagine what that leader is experiencing. They were so excited and invested in this new role that's been taken away. Imagine the disappointment—this was a high-profile task. Imagine the embarrassment they'd feel as they talk to their peers and as their peers talk to each other. Imagine the demotivation they'd feel. *Why should I even bother trying? Why should I bother taking on any further extra tasks when I'm asked? Why bother even trying in my regular responsibilities? Why would I even think about doing more than the bare minimum?* Imagine the bitterness and anger that would well up within them. No help. No feedback. No coaching. No warning. There's a very short step from being severely disappointed and embarrassed in front of peers to becoming frustrated and bitter.

5. It will hinder the creativity of the team. If the team knows that you'll take back responsibility if it's not done *your* way, then what you're doing is training them to never innovate or try and improve. You're training them to do it the same way at all costs, rather than training them to try and do it a better way.

6. It will rupture the trust between you and the rest of your team. Long term, this is probably the most damaging effect of barking yourself. If you give people responsibilities and then step back

in to do things yourself you will erode the trust your team has in you. Once you lose the trust of those you lead, you've lost any legitimate influence that you had—and so, effectively, at that point you've lost your leadership. You may still have a position and a title, and people may still do what you tell them to do, but you won't be leading them. The trust of your team is one of the most precious commodities that you have as a leader, and you need to be vigilant to never do anything that would erode or break that trust.

If you've given people authority and responsibility for a task then make sure you allow them to own the task and see it through. Give them clear instructions and guidelines. Give them honest coaching and feedback along the way and watch them improve. That's a leader's job.

Having a dog and then doing the barking yourself is a horrible idea. It restricts the amount of ministry that can be done, it stunts the growth of your leaders, and it inhibits new ideas and innovation. It erodes trust, demotivates people, and may even lead to anger and bitterness. It's not just that there's no point having a dog and barking yourself—it's also a recipe for failure.

See also

28. Anything worth doing is worth doing badly
44. Choose your lieutenants
47. Find the awesome
51. Get out of the way of good people
64. Learn relaxed concern
76. Seek raw beauty

51

Get out of the way of good people

We all want to work with good people and we're all trying to fill our teams with good people. Sometimes the people who join us on our teams or staff are already brilliant and ready to go, but more often they're pretty good but not yet great. Or they're keen and faithful but not yet that good at performing the tasks we need them to do. Most of the time, people need to be trained and developed. They need opportunities and feedback. They start out decent and available and we develop them to become good, and sometimes even great, at what they do.

The trouble comes once people have become good at what they do, because as leaders we can sometimes be the last to notice. So we keep treating them as if they're still just decent but available. Instead of helping them continue to develop and get better, we end up getting in their way and slowing things down.

If you're leading your people well—being attentive to their progress and giving them clear feedback—this shouldn't be a problem. But sometimes things don't go the way we'd like and sometimes we drop the ball. In the hustle and bustle of ministry it's easy to focus on the squeaky wheels, and so as leaders we can overlook all the progress and competence developing in the people around us.

If people are good at what they do, we need to let them do their thing. Treating competent people as though they aren't yet competent will have three results: it will waste your time, it will waste their time, and it will frustrate them.

1. Wasting your time

It's a waste of time to tell people who are good at what they do exactly what to do. These people no longer need such counsel from us. They don't need us there as a safety net in their normal operational tasks. They know what they're doing and will be able to call their own plays to achieve the goal. Scripting the moves for a good person who already knows them is a waste of time that we could be spending doing other tasks and investing in other people.

When I talk to other leaders, one of the main complaints I hear is that they have too much work to do and not enough time to do it. This will probably always be the case, as there's always more ministry to be done and people to be helped. But when I dig a little deeper I often find that this isn't what is causing their work overload. The problem is that many leaders are doing the work of those below them, and sometimes even the work of the people below those people. They're doing two jobs, or even three. They're spending so much time doing the same work as their teams that it's difficult for them to find time to do their own work. When you start doing the work of the team rather than the work of the team leader you end up competing with your teams and wasting your time. You end up doing work not just that other people *can* do, but also that other people are *responsible* to do.

Sometimes we need to get out of people's way and let them do their jobs while we do ours.

2. Wasting their time

In addition to wasting our time, this kind of duplication of effort also wastes the time of those to whom we've given responsibility for the tasks. They already know how to do it. They don't need our help. Our insistence on helping them and formally approving all of their decisions only wastes their time and slows them down. If the decisions they make are always good, then let them make the decisions without your approval. If the decision they need to make is a decision they can make, then let them make it. Otherwise you set yourself up as a bottleneck and everyone beneath you has to line up to have their decisions approved before they can continue. They can't move forward while they wait for your approval so you end up wasting a lot of their time.

3. Frustrating them

The final reason it's important to let good people do their thing is that there's almost no more efficient way to demotivate someone than to micromanage them. Micromanagement is fine when a person is new to a role or specific task and they're still learning. But once that person knows what to do and how to do it, the only thing micromanagement achieves is to frustrate a good person.

If you give a competent person a task to be responsible for but then you also involve yourself in achieving that task, the person will feel as though you don't trust them or that you're competing with them for some reason. It's a good way to lose someone. Good people don't need to be motivated; they just need you not to demotivate them. So let them do their thing and support and encourage them along the way. Find a way to get them whatever resources they need to do a good job and then get out of their way.

Getting out of a person's way doesn't mean leaving them alone to do whatever they want. It doesn't mean never checking in with them or letting them make *every* decision. Of course you'll still meet with them regularly for progress updates. You'll still want to be consulted when they face difficult decisions and make sure they know they can come to you for help with problems and roadblocks as they face them. You'll want to be clear about which decisions are theirs to make, which ones you need to be consulted about, which ones you need to approve, and which ones you'll need to make as the boss. Getting out of their way doesn't mean giving them free reign, but it does mean letting them be responsible for the tasks you've given them.

If someone is good at what they do, then trust them to do a good job. If you trust them, then get out of their way and let them run. And then be there to dust them off and pick them up when they fall.

See also

27. You're just the leader
43. The five C's
47. Find the awesome
50. There's no point having a dog and then barking yourself

52
Give credit and take blame

Imagine that you're at the supermarket buying groceries and you begin to notice, off in the distance, the sound of screaming, crying children. As you continue shopping the noise grows louder and you seem to be moving closer to the locus of this maelstrom. When you turn down the cereal aisle you see that you've reached ground zero. There's a mother surrounded by three small children, all of whom are bawling their eyes out. In exasperation the mother turns to the crying children and screams at them to stop crying before she turns back to storming around the supermarket, grabbing nappies and frozen meals and shoving them in her trolley.

You think to yourself, "What a horrible mother. Who could possibly yell at such obviously distraught children? All they needed was a hug from their mother."

But when you're the one who goes shopping with a swarm of whinging, crying children constantly poking each other and incessantly badgering you and making the shopping trip twice as long as it needs to be, and when you lose your patience after 45 minutes of constant battle and yell at them, it's obviously because your children are possessed by Beelzebub and can't be controlled by any human being.

This is what psychologists have called the fundamental attribution error.[56]

The basic idea is this: when I succeed it's because of my own innate qualities, whereas when other people succeed it's the result of favourable circumstances because they were in the right place at the right time. Or,

56 See *You Are Not So Smart: Why you have too many friends on Facebook, why your memory is mostly fiction, and 46 other ways you're deluding yourself* by David McRaney (Penguin, New York, 2011), pp. 264-74.

negatively, when I fail it's because of extenuating circumstances, things beyond my control, whereas when others fail it's because of some innate flaw in who they are. That is, we *attribute* their problems to something *fundamental* about who they are, yet we do everything we can to excuse ourselves. My faults are the result of circumstances, whereas the faults of others are due to flaws in who they are. This is the fundamental attribution error.

The fundamental leadership attribution error

When you're a part of a team, whatever you achieve belongs to the entire team. Every member plays a role in the success of the team. For example, even if Mary's idea is discarded and John's idea is used, Mary was still a part of the process of getting from where we started to where we ended up. Perhaps Mary's idea sparked John to come up with an idea that wouldn't otherwise have occurred to him. We know, too, that whether or not a visitor ends up coming back next week isn't all up to those who welcome them at the door. The way people are welcomed is important, but there are other factors as well. The preaching, the music, how clean or messy the church is, whether they're ignored by people at morning tea, and lots of other things all combine and play a role in whether they'll return or not. Things that are both obvious and not so obvious all come together, and any success belongs to everyone as everyone plays their part.

Even though we know this is true, it can still sometimes be a struggle when it comes to assigning credit and blame. What happens by default, when leaders aren't consciously aware of this principle, is that leaders take credit for the team's successes and assign blame when things go wrong. When the team succeeds, we think, it's obviously because of our leadership. But when things fall in a heap it's clearly in spite of our brilliant leadership—the people on the team simply dropped the ball.

The fundamental attribution error causes leaders to attribute their team's successes to their leadership and their team's failures to the team members not being up to the task. This is the exact opposite of how leaders should operate.

Instead of taking credit yourself and assigning blame to the team, as the leader you should give the credit to the team and take the blame yourself.

When the team achieves something, make sure you give the team the credit—both privately and publicly. When a part of the team runs something, organizes something, or goes beyond the job description to get something done, give them the credit. People will assume you were involved because you're the leader and you'll still get credit anyway. Leaders always do. And even if people don't give you any credit, who cares? Humility is a virtue that most of us struggle with and we should welcome opportunities to cultivate it. What does it matter if, every now and then, no-one gives you the kudos you deserve? God sees all things and he is the one who rewards. Give the credit away to your team members.

Responsibility and fault

And when things fall apart and everything crashes and burns, you as the leader should take the blame. The team leader's job is to make something happen, so when it doesn't happen the responsibility sits on your shoulders.

Responsibility is different from fault. When something goes wrong it might not be your fault—someone else might have been at fault in that direct sense—but as the leader you're responsible. You're responsible for the activity, for the person, and for the team. Even if something isn't directly your fault, it's still your responsibility. When something happens on your watch, you take the blame.

This doesn't mean that the person who was at fault has no responsibility or shouldn't expect consequences or reprimands. Accountability is important and responsibility honours people. It's okay to point out, "John, we really needed you to come through on that and it didn't happen. What happened and what did you learn?" But as the team leader you also need to be quick to show that, in the end, you're responsible and are willing to accept the blame.

Give credit and take blame—not the other way around. Taking credit and giving blame destroys teams and undermines people's confidence in you as the leader. A leader who takes all the credit for a success and then leaves the team out to dry to absorb the blame for a misfire erodes the team's trust. People will soon figure out that you're a mercenary leader, that you're not committed to the cause or to the team, and they'll eventually stop following you. You still might be the 'team leader', but it will just be an empty title.

Give credit and take blame. Your team will feel appreciated and will have increased respect for you and trust in you as their leader.

See also

27. You're just the leader
29. Praise publicly
37. Phrases to learn
41. Two foundations of team-building

53
Free volunteers aren't cheap

Most of the people that most of us lead are not paid staff. Most of us lead volunteers most of the time.[57]

Apples with apples

Volunteers are different from staff in a lot of ways. They're working for slightly different reasons with slightly different motivations, and the influence you as a leader have over volunteers is slightly different—that is, it's often less institutional and structural. Yet, because of that, it can also be more powerful. The difference between paid church staff and those who aren't paid isn't about the quality of effort expected. The difference has more to do with time available, the amount that can be done and, in some cases, level of ability. Because staff and volunteers are different, we treat them in different ways.

One obvious way we treat them differently is that we pay staff and we don't pay volunteers. We pay staff so that they can afford to live without having to get another job so they can devote that time instead to ministry in and around the church.

When you ask a staff member to do something, there's an expectation that it will be done faster than when you ask a volunteer to do something.

57 I don't mean to imply that the church is a volunteer organization, because it's not. It's a community. It's a body. It's a family. So we don't really have volunteers, technically speaking. We have people engaged in various forms of formal and informal ministry. Some are paid and others aren't. But, just for ease of communication, let's use the word volunteers. You know what I mean.

This isn't because staff are faster and better at things than volunteers are, but because volunteers have all kinds of other things they need to do during the day—like work a job or look after their children—whereas a staff person has been released from those demands in order to have more time to do those ministry-related things we're asking them to do.

But just because volunteers work for free that doesn't mean that they're cheap. The fact that they don't get paid can sometimes trick us into thinking that they don't cost any money. But that is, at best, a half-truth.

It is true that you can have a team of volunteers and spend absolutely nothing. But, as a general rule, if a team of volunteers costs you nothing then they will never develop to their full capacity. This free team will be a team of volunteers you *use* to achieve your purpose or to fulfil your ministry. But using people is always a dangerous strategy, and while it may be effective in the short term it's guaranteed to be disastrous in the long term.

If you want to grow your volunteers so that they will mine every gift God has given them and lead at a high level, you'll need to pour resources into them. Free volunteers aren't cheap.

Volunteers require time

Developing your volunteers will take time, and time is a precious resource. As we saw earlier in our discussion on being on time, theological giant Karl Barth said:

> ...to have time for another, although in the abstract this says little, is in reality to manifest in essence all the benefits which one man can show to another. When I really give anyone my time, I thereby give him the last and most personal thing that I have to give at all, namely myself.[58]

Someone will need to invest time in your volunteers to genuinely care for them and catch up with how they're going as a person and in shouldering this particular responsibility. They'll need time invested in them to train

58 Barth, *Church Dogmatics I.2*, p. 55.

them how to be more effective in their area of ministry and in the use of their gifts. They'll need someone to take the time to encourage and inspire them, and remind them that what they're doing is worthwhile.

Volunteers require resources

Developing volunteers to be the best that they can be will often, though not always, require material resources. Here are three ways that you can resource your volunteers to help them develop. These aren't the only ways, but they're three good places to start investing in your volunteers if you don't already. All of them cost money.

1. You might buy books and read them together. If you want your team to learn and be challenged on an issue, reading a book together is a good way to go. Read one a year, maybe two. Not everyone is a reader and not everyone loves reading. So you might not want to burden people with a book every two weeks. But one book every six months seems like it would be doable for most people.

   You might have only your key leaders read a book. Maybe you invite any leader who's interested to join you.

   But the ministry pays for at least a portion of the books. Maybe the ministry covers the entire cost, maybe the ministry pays half and the leader pays half. For most books that means they pay about $10. That's not a burden. Half and half is my preferred option, because the leader has the extra incentive since they have an investment in it. But you could go either way.

   It doesn't need to be a leadership book. You might want your key leaders to read a book on a particular doctrine or topic because you want to help them sharpen theologically. Great idea! Maybe each year you read one theology book and one leadership book. The point is that you intentionally invest in your team.

2. You might help your volunteers to get to training and conferences that will equip and inspire them. There are so many conferences that could help develop your people. Pick one. This can get expensive quickly, but free volunteers aren't cheap.

Deep down you might wish you could pay for every leader to attend the conference, but this gets very expensive very quickly. So you might do for one leader what you wish you could do for all of them. You might put out a general invitation to all of your leaders to come to the conference and then have a private word with one person that you particularly want to invest in and you pay for their ticket. Then the next year you invite everyone again but pick another up-and-coming leader that you particularly want to be there and you pay for that person's ticket. Another way forward is to ask some other people to provide scholarships (privately) so that younger leaders who couldn't afford the cost can go to conferences they wouldn't otherwise be able to attend.

3. You might throw parties to celebrate milestones or the completion of big events or the achievement of success of some description. Celebrating is a terrific way to thank and honour volunteers. It helps them to see and remember the great things God has done in and through them. It helps them to know and feel that their contributions and sacrifices were worth it and were also in some way noticed.

   But parties cost money. Having to pay an entry fee for a party that's thrown for you takes some of the fun out of it. Which means that celebrating will cost you money.

As the leader, your responsibility is to be constantly thinking about how you can grow the people in your team, and some of those ideas will cost money.

When you invest time and money in your people it communicates that you value them, that you believe in what they're doing, and that you want to see them develop. It's not the only way that you communicate those things, but it is one way. And it will be the main way that some people on your team feel those things from you.

The cost of volunteering

The cost of volunteers will also help you remember the other side of volunteering. You might be reading this as a volunteer or you might be a paid staff member who was once a volunteer. The other side of free volunteers not being cheap is to remember that, for the volunteers themselves, volunteering isn't cheap. There's the cost *of* volunteers and there's the cost *to* volunteers.

Volunteering costs people time—time that they might have spent instead with friends or family, or refreshing and recouping—especially if they use time off work to volunteer. Volunteering may cost them money in missed opportunities for work or time away from work. When someone volunteers, there's always a cost.

Being involved in ministry is, of course, about service and sacrifice. And the Christian life is about denying oneself in order to gain something better. It is more blessed to give than to receive, and the joys of ministry are great. All of that is true. But it's also true that it's good to notice and recognize people's commitment, faithfulness, and sacrifice—to thank them for it and encourage them in it.

Volunteering may very likely be costly to the volunteer him or herself, and if you're committed to equipping and developing your volunteers and to investing in them as people, it will be costly to you also.

Free volunteers aren't cheap.

See also

29. Praise publicly
47. Find the awesome
78. Celebrate

54
Don't be afraid of off-ramps

You work hard to build a great team. Lots of recruiting, observing, and feedback. Lots of time and money invested in developing people. Lots of unrepeatable experiences and lessons learned. Lots of costly failures.

And then they leave the team.

They join another church or another ministry and you have to start over again. You lose momentum and you lose expertise. Sometimes they've become friends and you miss not seeing them as much anymore. So you do everything you can to keep people—at least the good ones. You want to keep people because you care about them and enjoy having them around, but also because of all you've invested in them and because of the costs that you'll inevitably incur as you train up replacements.

Methods for retaining people

There are lots of ways to keep people on your team. The quality of your leadership is important, as are the quality and culture of the team you create. Most of the important and effective ways to keep good people are hard to do and take a lot of time. But there's an easier option that shortcuts all of that effort and time: you block up all the off-ramps.

By off-ramps I mean natural moments that occur in the rhythm of a church or organization at which people might want to transition out of one of your teams. For me in my ministries that means the period from the end of the school year, mid-December, to the beginning of the next school year, late January. This is the natural time for someone to leave my team and join another.

Some leaders will make these transitions as difficult and awkward as possible for their team members so as to discourage them from leaving.

Often it's not that explicit or even something they do consciously. Leaders might simply assume that a person wishes to continue and talk to them as though they're staying without ever checking. Or leaders might try to hide the off-ramp by not ever mentioning it so that people might forget it exists. Or when someone from another team is looking for good people to join their team, or to be promoted, a leader might hide his or her people—saying, for example, that there's no-one who's any good in their team so they won't lose anyone. Leaders might use language that implies that leaving the team would be a personal betrayal, or a betrayal of the team, and they might subtly blackmail good people into staying out of guilt. They might use that language of betrayal as a joke but use it just often enough to create some doubt about how much of it is a joke.

And, in the end, these tactics are both cruel and counterproductive.

Hiding off-ramps is a bad idea

Such tactics are cruel because they don't treat the person with respect. Hiding off-ramps or discouraging people from using them treats people like they're equipment being used to create a desired outcome. One of the most effective ways to disrespect a person is to take away their choice.

It's also counterproductive behaviour, because people can tell when they're being used and not cared for. They also know when they're being guilted, shamed, or slightly blackmailed into staying and they'll begin resenting it. People don't like being manipulated or tricked, even if it's for a worthy cause. And you want people on your team who want to be on your team. If someone deep down, desperately wishes they were somewhere else and isn't committed to the cause, it's probably best—for them, for you, and for the rest of the team—for them to find a place where they can serve wholeheartedly. Nobody wins when there's someone on your team who doesn't want to be there. The rest of the team doesn't win, the person him or herself doesn't win, and the people you're seeking to serve don't win either.

So don't be afraid of off-ramps. Give people regular and systematic opportunities to leave gracefully. And when they do leave thank them, honour them, and let them leave without guilt, shame, or embarrassment.

The benefit of providing off-ramps yourself is that you can place them where they'll best suit you and the team. If people are going to leave at some point anyway, it might as well be at a time that's minimally disruptive. One of the questions in our end-of-year self-evaluation is: Would you like to stay and continue in your current team, or would you like to change teams, or would you like to leave this ministry altogether and join another ministry, or would you like to start something completely new that no-one's thought of yet? It's an explicit, systematic off-ramp where, every year, we give each leader the chance to exit if they want to.

Don't be afraid of off-ramps. The healthier your team is, and the clearer the off-ramps are, the less people will use them. But you have to have them. Everybody leaves eventually; no-one stays forever. You might as well accept that and help people to leave with as little disruption and as much grace as you can—for their sake and for the sake of the people you're serving.

See also

26. Leading is loving
53. Free volunteers aren't cheap

Section four

Leading the ministry

55

The point is clarity, not labels

It doesn't matter what you call them

One of the words most often heard in leadership circles today is vision. Everyone's talking about vision. If you're reading a Christian leadership book they'll be so excited about vision that they'll probably misquote the Bible. And I happen to think vision is important too—really important. But it's worth stopping to think about what we mean when we talk about vision.

It's the same with mission statements. Everyone says you should have one. But what exactly is a mission statement? Some people say it's the same as a vision, or a vision statement. Other people say it's different.

What about strategy? What does that mean? Or tactics? What's the difference?

Some people say you need a vision, a mission, and a strategy. Others say you need a vision, a strategy, and tactics. Others say you just need a vision. People very rarely, if ever, differentiate or clearly define these terms. And they almost never argue for their particular idiosyncratic collection of 'things you need'. It can be very frustrating and confusing.

But here's the inside tip: as far as I can tell, all the different books and experts basically think the same thing. They just use different labels and either put everything under a catch-all term or tease out the various aspects of it.

All of those things that they talk about are helpful and important. But it doesn't matter what you call them. The point is that you need to think about what you're doing.

The reason vision, mission, and strategy matter is because they help you provide clarity. And clarity is what everyone wants and needs. People want to know what they're supposed to be doing and how they're supposed to be doing it. If you're the leader, then it's your job to clarify those things for them.

An idea of the future

Leadership is about having an idea of what you think the future should look like and then trying to move people from where they are presently to where you think they should be.

You should have an idea of a preferred future—of where you want to go. Some people call it a vision while others call it a mission. In the end it doesn't matter what you call it so long as you know what it is and you know that you have one. I call it a vision, but if you want to call it something different that's absolutely okay with me—so long as we both know what we're talking about.

For more detail on vision, why it's so important to have one, and what to do with it once you have it, skip ahead to chapter 69, 'Your people should be able to do a good impression of you'.

You probably have an idea of where you're trying to go and what it might look like when you get there. It might be very specific or it might be vague. You might be able to zoom right up to it in your mind and see the details, or perhaps when you try to zoom in it gets pixelated very quickly. Either way, you already have an idea of a preferred future. The clearer you can see it the more useful it will be, both to you and the people around you.

Regardless of what you call this preferred future towards which you're leading people, you want to do your best to communicate it to people as often as you can so they know where they're going.

Clarity is the key.

What is strategy?

What about strategy? Business books, seminars and courses all talk about strategy. It's a term that pops up everywhere but is rarely well defined. I think sometimes people who use it don't actually know what they mean by it.

Some people say the way to differentiate strategy is to compare it to tactics. And then they say that strategy is the 'what' and tactics is the 'how'. But this isn't particularly helpful, because the what and how can be interchangeable, depending on how you ask the question.

Say, for example, that our goal is to evangelize the whole suburb. "What then will we do?" We'll go door-to-door to every house (strategy). "How exactly will we do it?" We'll use a questionnaire and then *Two Ways to Live* (tactics).

That seems straightforward. We have a goal. The strategy is the what and tactics is the how.

But consider the following example. Our goal is to evangelize the whole suburb. How are we going to do that? We'll go door-to-door to every house (strategy). What exactly will we do at each house? We'll use a questionnaire and then *Two Ways to Live* (tactics).

Strategy is the how and tactics is the what. When you can ask different questions but give the same answers, that's a sign that your questions aren't powerful enough.

What and how don't help you get clarity.

The best definition I've ever found for what strategy is comes from Patrick Lencioni. He says:

> An organization's strategy is simply its plan for success. It's nothing more than the collection of intentional decisions a company makes to give itself the best chance to thrive and differentiate from competitors. That means every single decision, if it is made intentionally and consistently, will be a part of the overall strategy.[59]

It's not very practical or useful, but it's realistic. Your strategy is what you do to achieve your goal. You can have a good strategy or a bad strategy; a clear strategy or a jumbled strategy.

Your strategy is your plan. What are you going to do to get to the

59 Lencioni, *The Advantage*, pp. 107-8.

future? How will you get from where you are to where you want to be?

But this take on strategy isn't that useful by itself when it comes to planning. The way to make this idea of strategy useful and actionable is to think in terms of what Lencioni calls strategic anchors. These strategic anchors are three (or perhaps four, but definitely no more than that) poles that will determine the boundaries of your strategy. These anchors will inform every decision and provide the clarity that people need to make decisions that will best help you get to your idea of the future. They help to protect you from mere pragmatism and from making inconsistent decisions that will take you all over the place. These anchors act like a filter to keep your decision-making on target.

Retro-engineer it

The idea of strategic anchors sounds like it could be helpful, but it also sounds like it could be difficult to implement. Where do you start? How do you decide on your strategic anchors?

The best way to do this is to reverse engineer it. You'll start by writing down everything you're already doing and work backwards from there.

What you need is a blank sheet of paper. Write down everything you currently do. You can do this for your whole church or you can do this for one segment of it, say the children's ministry. You can involve your whole leadership team, just the key leaders, or you can do it by yourself.

As you write everything down, try not to make a list—just write them all in a big bunch, like a cloud of items. It's easier to see patterns and relationships that way, which will become important in the next step. Write down absolutely everything that comes to mind. Don't worry if there are things that are similar or even the same. Just keep writing. Maybe leave it for a day or two and then go back to it and add anything that you overlooked the first time.

Once you have that page full of stuff, start to clump them together into common themes or ideas. Are there any patterns that you can see? Keep collapsing things down into summaries until you get down to three, or a maximum of four. If you have more than that, keep going until you can get it to three. The fewer there are, the easier it will be for people to use them as anchors to help guide decision-making. This can be a difficult process, and it's unscientific and a bit intuitive and messy. But it really works.

What you end up with are the strategic anchors that you currently have and use. You might like them, or you might want to change them. Your summarized categories will be the strategies you're re-employing and the original big bunch of things will be the tactics you're employing. Sometimes what this process will show you is that you might not be doing what you think you need to be doing and that a change might be in order.

Here's an example of the process (and if you flip forward a page, you'll get an idea of the messy blog/cloud we ended up with). At our church we wanted to work out the strategy for the youth ministry. Here's a list of everything we do (it's a bit summarized already just to save space so as not to bore you):

- preach the gospel
- help students deal with whatever problems they have
- create environments where students feel safe exploring Jesus
- build genuine relationships with students
- create a recognizable brand
- website
- encourage and invite to church
- leaders being actively discipled
- personal Bible-reading and prayer
- leaders being friends with each other
- annual leader camp
- train preachers
- Explore groups (our 4-week evangelistic small groups)
- leaders read books together to grow
- leadership training for senior high students
- students inviting their friends and leading them to Jesus
- meetings to train/inspire/encourage leaders
- Scripture in Year 6 classes
- Scripture in high schools
- annual youth camp
- equipping students for ministry
- discipleship in small groups

- Instagram
- train apprentices
- leaders recruit leaders
- create communities of love
- sweet-looking brochures
- going to external conferences and training

After working through all of those things we saw these four patterns:

1. Bring, build, send with the gospel of Jesus
2. Investing in people is a priority
3. Transformation happens in small teams through real relationships
4. Beauty is valuable (before you send that angry email, please note that this is referring to art and visuals—not perpetuating unhealthy body image)

These are our strategic anchors. Clarifying them has helped us make any number of decisions from budgeting all the way through to programming. This is our plan for how we're going to make disciples of all nations through our local high schoolers. This is the grid through which all of our decisions must pass if they are to be strategic for us.

Three-layer clarity

Don't get too caught up on names and labels. The point of it all is clarity—clarity for you and clarity for the people who work with and around you.

Vision, mission, strategy, tactics, logistics. They're all just ways to think about and break down the overall objective. What are we trying to do? What do we need to do to make this happen? What do we need to do to make that happen? And what will we then need to do to make that happen? And so on and so on.

I've found that it's most helpful to break things down into three layers of time. The first layer is the end goal. The future you're working towards. It might be "seeing all the nations bow the knee to Jesus" or it might be a more immediate future, such as "we're going to raise the money to extend our current building".

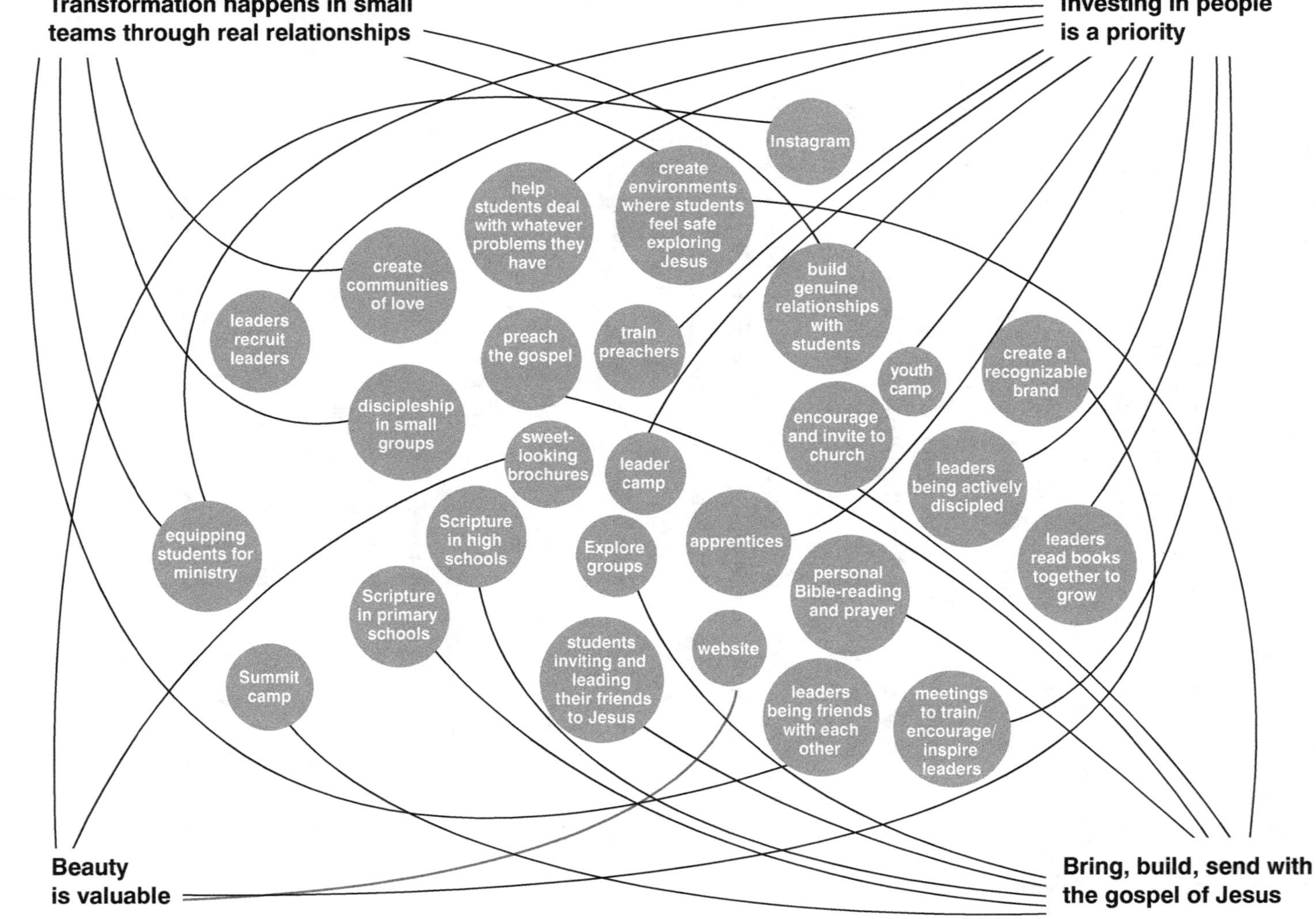

Transformation happens in small teams through real relationships
Investing in people is a priority
Instagram
help students deal with whatever problems they have
create environments where students feel safe exploring Jesus
create communities of love
build genuine relationships with students
leaders recruit leaders
preach the gospel
train preachers
youth camp
create a recognizable brand
discipleship in small groups
encourage and invite to church
sweet-looking brochures
leader camp
leaders being actively discipled
Scripture in high schools
Explore groups
apprentices
equipping students for ministry
leaders read books together to grow
personal Bible-reading and prayer
Scripture in primary schools
website
students inviting and leading their friends to Jesus
Summit camp
leaders being friends with each other
meetings to train/ encourage/ inspire leaders
Beauty is valuable
Bring, build, send with the gospel of Jesus

The next layer is closer to the present and describes what kinds of things we'll do to get us to that future. It's more specific than the end goal but it doesn't involve any specific decision.

For example, if our end goal is going to the beach, then this next layer is the broad plan of how we're going to get there: We're carpooling and heading along the freeway and stopping at Maccas (that's McDonald's to the rest of the world) on the way.

In the final layer, then, are the specific decisions and practicalities. It's the 'what will we do on Monday' type thoughts. This layer is more immediate and even more concrete: We're taking Matt's car, I'll meet him at his place by 8 am, and we'll stop at this specific Maccas.

Thinking in terms of these three layers will help both you and your team work out what you want to do, how you're going to do it, and what you need to start working on now.

Whether you call it vision, strategy, and tactics or vision, mission, and strategy or something else entirely doesn't really matter. Call it whatever you want so long as you all know what you're talking about. The point is knowing where you want to get to, how you're generally planning on getting there, and what specifically you're going to be doing—right now and then next after that and so on.

The three questions you need to be able to answer, for yourself and for your team, are:

1. Where are we going?
2. How are we getting there?
3. What do I need to do right now?

See also

33. Communicate from the inside out
58. Think in steps
69. Your people should be able to do a good impression of you

56

What are you trying to achieve?

One of the key attributes of leaders is that they're good at getting things done. Working hard. Doing stuff. It's often a lot more difficult to be clear on exactly what we're trying to achieve. Getting things done is one thing, and it's a very important thing, but the more important question is whether the things we're getting done are actually the things we should be doing. Are they even worth doing in the first place? Although we often forget to ask them, we should ask these kinds of questions early and often. And our answers should be razor sharp. We need to ask: What are we actually trying to achieve? Because if we don't know what we want to see happen, we can end up doing all kinds of good things without doing the things that we really need to be doing. Even more than that, we can be doing all kinds of good things that actually achieve very different results than what we were hoping for. As Andy Stanley puts it:

> Most churches do not have a reliable system for defining and measuring what success looks like at every level of the organization. Instead they post some general statistics that give them a vague sense of progress or failure as a church, and they go through the motions of continuing to do ministry the way they always have, productive or not. *Thus it is possible for a church to become very efficient at doing ministry ineffectively.*[60]

60 Andy Stanley, Reggie Joiner and Lane Jones, *7 Practices of Effective Ministry*, Multnomah, Sisters, OR, 2004, pp. 70-1 (emphasis mine).

A clear endgame

In my experience, it's very rare for people to have no idea—literally no idea—what they're trying to achieve. Every now and then you do come across people like that, and they're relatively easy to spot. They're the ones wandering around looking constantly bewildered and despondent. But, most of the time, people have a vague or general sense of where they're heading or what they're supposed to be doing, it's just that nothing is crystallized. I'm not suggesting that you need to have the endgame cross-stitched and framed on the wall to be a good leader. But at every step and stage you do need to be crystal clear about what this flurry of activity is supposed to be achieving. And you need to be able to articulate it in full HD so that everyone on the team knows exactly and specifically where you're trying to get to.

We live in a big world, and there's an infinite array of things you could possibly do. But there's a much smaller collection of things that you probably should do and an even smaller collection of things that you absolutely must do. Working out which activity fits into which of those categories can be next to impossible when you're not clear on what it is you're trying to achieve. Having a clear picture of the endgame helps you to be intentional about what you do, where you spend your time, what you say no to, and what opportunities you take. And the clearer that picture of what you're trying to accomplish is, the easier it is to decide quickly whether an opportunity is a must do, a should do, or a could do. Otherwise, you and your team are always guessing what to do and what the point is.

Knowing how you're going

When the team isn't clear on what they're trying to achieve, evaluation is very difficult. "So how do you think it went?" someone might ask. And people will say, "Good. It went well." Sometimes they may add some reasons why they thought it was good, relative to their own criteria. "Lots of people came." "People seemed to have a good time." "The night ran smoothly." All of these are good things, but unless the goal was to have lots of people in a building or to give people a good time or to run something smoothly, these observations don't tell you whether or not you achieved your aim.

Unless you have a clear idea of what exactly you're trying to achieve it's nearly impossible to work out whether you're doing well or not. Without a clear goal, how can you look back and evaluate what's happened or run post-mortems on events or programs or put together end-of-year reflections? How will you determine whether you're achieving your goal or whether you're on the right track or moving closer to or further away from where you want to be? How will you know if you're doing a good job?

When no-one really knows what they're trying to achieve, each person will have their own idea about what the goal is, and each person's image of success will be different. And so this kind of evaluative discussion will take place with the assumption that everyone's on the same page, but what will actually be happening is that everyone will be using the same words to describe a very different reality. This is the worst kind of miscommunication—everyone thinks they're being understood and everyone's agreeing with one another but no-one's even speaking the same language.

When we all know

When you know what you're trying to achieve and the goal is so clear that everyone on your team can articulate it with a reasonable amount of precision and uniformity, you're much more likely to run events, ministries, and programs that help you achieve what you want to achieve.

The key question for every event, program, and ministry is this: What is it trying to achieve? And is an ongoing program or event still achieving that original goal or is there a better way to get there? If you've been running a group to reach new mums, for example, you should ask if any new mums are coming. Or do all the same mums keep coming? If the group's supposed to reach out to new mums, is it still doing that or is there a better way? These are the questions to ask early and often. The reason you run events, programs, and ministries is because they help you achieve what you need to achieve.

You should be able to describe exactly what each program and event, and each element of each event, is seeking to achieve. More than that, you should take the time and effort to describe and articulate what all of these elements should accomplish because people forget. Keep saying it over and over. If something you're doing doesn't have a goal or point, let alone a good goal or point, then you need to ask why you're doing it in the first place.

But asking what we're trying to achieve is the first step in arriving at that clarity. Everything achieves something. The question is whether what you're doing achieves what you want it to achieve. Some programs seem to exist purely so that those who run them feel good. Now maybe that's okay, and maybe you wouldn't necessarily cancel it, but it's good to know that that's the reason this particular program exists.

You should know why every program exists. Every meeting. Every event. Every element that makes up an event. They should all have a purpose and a point. They should all be trying to achieve something. And you should be able to articulate exactly what you want each thing to achieve.

See also

31. Energy is more efficient than efficiency
46. People deserve to know the truth
58. Think in steps
59. Hold hands with your programs
63. Meetings are where real work is done

57

Where is here?

Leaders spend a lot of their time in two places: 'back then' and 'when we get there'. Those places can be good or bad.

'Back then' is a helpful place to be when you're evaluating what's happened and trying to understand why things were successful or not. 'Back then' has a lot to teach us so we can learn and get better. Learning organizations and learning leaders spend time 'back then'. But 'back then' can be a dangerous place if it becomes a glorious temple to past achievements and to highs we will never reach again. When 'back then' becomes a museum to the glory days of an era we wish we could go back to, spending time there is a dangerous distraction. At that point, more time needs to be spent in 'when we get there'.

'When we get there' is the place in the future that you're working towards. It's where you want to be and where you're taking people and where you want your efforts and energies to lead you. Leaders spend a lot of time talking about 'when we get there'. One of the main currencies that a leader deals in is the future. Leaders talk about it, paint pictures of it, describe it, and work out how to get there and what it will cost. But leaders can end up spending too much time in the future and so forfeit time they should spend learning from the past. Leaders need to learn from their own recent past—gleaning what they can from the mistakes and successes there—and they also need to learn from the mistakes and successes of others in the more distant past.

Most leaders will tend towards one or the other, spending more time learning from 'back then' or spending more time envisioning 'when we get there'. While leaders need to spend time in both places, they need to be careful not to spend too much time in either one—and they also need to be aware of a third place they need to spend time.

Questions between 'here' and 'there'

Between 'back then' and 'when we get there' is a third place—'here'. Unfortunately, 'here' is an often-neglected place. When you neglect 'here', 'back then' becomes much less useful and 'when we get there' becomes much harder to get to.

You need to work out where you are currently before you can begin evaluating 'back then' or planning for 'when we get there'.

"What's the best way to get to the Sydney Opera House?" a tourist once asked a local. "Well," the local replied, "the best way is to not start from here". In the same way, you need to know where you are before you can work out where you need to go to get where you want to be.

Working out where 'here' is can be harder than it sounds. The following questions will help you gain some clarity.

1. Who can help us work it out?

Gather a group of others around a table, literal or proverbial, to help you clarify where you are and the lay of the land. You'll want people who have a wide perspective, a unique perspective, a particular power of insight or influence. You'll probably have some feel for where 'here' is because you're the leader and overseeing the whole. But, because you're finite, fallible, and possibly blinded because you are the point person as the leader, you'll want to invite others to the table to share their wisdom so you have a more accurate picture of 'here'.

2. Where are we deficient or weak?

You'll want to ask this question at the table. It requires honesty, and depending on the people at the table, the culture of your church, and how well you've done welcoming bad news previously, this may be the toughest question to find the genuine answer to. But you need to confront the reality of the situation in all its savagery, and not just the situation as you wish it to be. Keep searching and searching and digging and digging to unearth everything you can. If there's an elephant in the room, you need to make sure you bump into it.

3. What are our strengths?

Depending on your church, this might be an easy question to answer or it might be a very difficult one. As with the question about weakness, you want to keep digging until you uncover as many strengths as you can. Sometimes things that are strengths don't at first sight seem like strengths. Try not to overlook anything. There are often mountains of overlooked and unidentified strengths. It's always better to build from strength than to try to shore up a weakness.

4. What resources do we have?

Don't just think money in the bank, although you'll want to include that as well. Think about potential money in the bank from reinvigorated generosity. Think about hours people have to give, skills and talents, contacts in the community, geographical position, and historical goodwill. All of these are resources that you have, and if they're not being leveraged they're probably lying dormant and overlooked.

5. What are we assuming? Are these assumptions true?

This can be a very difficult question to answer because an assumption is, by its very nature, something that we assume. But sometimes we can see them or hear them in others better than we can in ourselves. Listen carefully for the assumptions you hear behind things that others around the table are saying. When you hear someone say that the church can't add any more ministries because there isn't space in your current building, you might ask whether the assumption that all of your events need to be held on your premises is a valid assumption. Sometimes challenging circumstances will cause us to be aware of assumptions we've held ourselves. What are these assumptions? And are you sure they're true?

6. Who holds the power?

It's not only the people who have official titles who hold power in an organization. Sometimes the people with titles actually wield the least power. There's a difference between positional power—that is, power that comes with the position and title you hold, power *ex officio*—and power that is organic and earned. In every church there are people—sometimes just one person but often times many people—who may not have an official title but who are respected opinion leaders. Who's the patriarch or matriarch of this particular church? Who is that person who's been there as long as anyone and to whom people look naturally for leadership? It's often not the senior minister. If this person likes an idea and supports it, then the idea will become a reality. If they don't like it, you have no hope. These people are gatekeepers. Perhaps there's a nasty gossip in your church who has influence over a large group of people. Maybe there's a powerful warden or treasurer who has a very itchy veto finger. But who really holds the power? Don't just think org-charts, hierarchies, and titles. Think relationally and socially and in terms of influence. Who do people respect or fear?

Answering these six questions will help you begin to get a handle on where exactly you are.

Although it's always worth knowing where you are, it's especially important to slow down and take the time to get clear on where 'here' is before you plan anything and before you change anything.

Before you plan anything

When I talk about planning, I mean thinking about the future and working out what we'll do before we rocket into it. The temptation is always to jump straight into thinking about the future. What do we want to see happen? Where do we want to be this time next year? In five years? That's the exciting bit, where the action is—that's where we dream and make decisions. So of course we want to jump in and get started on doing some 'real work'.

Imagine there are three people giving directions to a person who wants to know how to get to the local shops. You're one of the three people, and you're giving directions over the phone. The problem is, all three of you think the person is starting from a different place. So you might tell her to turn right while someone else tells her to turn left, and so on. In the same way, if you want to plan something for the future and all of the people involved in the planning are imagining a different starting point, your directions on how to get there will end up being very different and even at odds with each other.

So it's important to slow down and be disciplined to do the work of clarifying where 'here' is before you start. Otherwise the location of 'here' is just assumed and people will begin with false information or end up with conflicting plans and directions.

It's important to clarify and agree on where 'here' is so that your plans actually impact and solve real problems, but also so that everyone agrees what problem you're trying to solve in the first place. When you skip this step in your planning people waste a lot of time later bickering and arguing about what problem they're actually dealing with. So to avoid unnecessary conflict and wasting time later, pinpoint where it is on the map that you're beginning your journey into the future.

Before you do any strategic planning, tactical planning, or vision casting, you need to know where 'here' is.

Before you change anything

It's also important to know where 'here' is before you change anything. Planning is thinking about what you'll do in the future, and changing things is a subset of that. In particular, I'm thinking of those things that you're considering stopping in the future.

Perhaps you're doing some things that you've realized aren't achieving what you hoped they would or that aren't worth the effort it takes to make them happen. These might be individual events, whole programs, or even structures that enable other things to happen. Or perhaps you're newly arrived in a position or at a church and there are some things that seem to serve little or no purpose that you think should probably be stopped.

In these instances it's important to clarify where 'here' is to make sure your assumptions are actually true. Is that program actually doing nothing or is there more going on than meets the eye? Is that event really a weakness and a resource drain? Is that system for one-on-one meetings genuinely ineffective or does it just appear to be? How sure are you that something you'd like to change isn't a beloved project of the unofficial powerbroker and gatekeeper of the church? (Even if it were the pet project of the church gatekeeper you still might close it down—you'd just perhaps do it differently and with an awareness of the potential danger and political fallout such a decision could create.)

Knowing where 'here' is, and not just assuming we know, is important before we change anything so that we don't end up changing something that was actually a vital component of the overall ministry. Before you tear down the fence it's a good idea to make sure you know why it was put up in the first place. Just because I don't know the point of something doesn't necessarily mean there's no point.

Spending time 'back then' is a good idea, and so is spending time thinking about 'when we get there'. Just remember to also take the time and make the effort to deeply understand where 'here' is. It's harder than it looks and is more helpful than it seems.

See also

58. Think in steps
69. Your people should be able to do a good impression of you
73. Red Queen syndrome: a nine-step process for implementing change

58
Think in steps

Regardless of what kind of leadership you exercise or what kind of ministry you're involved in, life is constant and busy and it's easy to focus exclusively on organizing and executing the next task. This is especially true if you have a regular, consecutive program like a church service every Sunday that you need to organize. Sundays really do keep coming, but unfortunately sometimes our focus narrows to simply getting the next event in the program accomplished.

When you have such a relentless schedule, and the main goal is always executing the next event in the program, what you tend to want from your people is that they would be faithfully committed to attend your program and ensure that their body is inside the building for the next event.

From programs to steps

There's nothing wrong with wanting people to be faithfully committed to attending our programs, but when we shift to thinking exclusively or primarily in terms of programs, we should be wary. When our highest aim is that people attend the program, our aim is too low. We need to love people better than that. Simply attending the program or event isn't the point of the event, is it?

Rather than thinking programs, we need to be thinking in terms of steps. Andy Stanley says it this way:

> When you 'think steps' there is a fundamental difference in your perspective. Now the primary goal is not to meet someone's need, but rather to help someone get where they need to go.[61]

61 Stanley, Joiner and Jones, *7 Practices*, p. 89.

Jesus' desire for people is not ultimately that they attend our program. And the job Jesus gave me is not to get people to attend my program. Attendance might be a good means to an end, but it's not the ultimate aim. And sometimes it might be the case that my program isn't even a good means to an end.

Begin with the end in mind

When Alice is lost and afraid in Wonderland she asks the Cheshire Cat, "Would you tell me, please, which way I ought to go from here?"

"That depends a good deal on where you want to get to," the Cheshire Cat replies.

Alice answers that it doesn't really matter. The Cheshire Cat smiles and says, "Then it doesn't matter which way you go".[62]

Steps only matter if you have a destination in mind. If there's no end goal then the steps, as steps, don't matter. The two questions to ask in order to move to thinking in terms of steps are these: Where do we want people to be? And then how can we help them get there? Asking these questions will help you turn your thinking towards pathways—that is, breaking down your goal/s of where you want people to go into steps that people can take to get from where they are to where they need to be.

In Christian ministry and leadership, the place we want to help people get to is, in the broadest sense, to be disciples who are totally devoted to Jesus and totally competent to go make more disciples. That's the endgame that we're working towards. So the next question is: What steps might be required to get people there? Notice that this is a very different question from the usual question, which is: What event should we put on or what program do we not yet have?

Now I don't want to imply that events and programs are bad, because they're not. The point is to zoom outward and to think about events and programs within the larger framework of steps and pathways rather than as discreet units that exist on their own. In fact, a better way to ask this

62 Lewis Carroll, *Alice's Adventures in Wonderland & Through the Looking-Glass*, reissue edn, Bantam Classics, New York, 2006, p. 49.

second question would be: to help someone take this next step along the path, is a program the best way? And, if so, what would the program look like? It's all about thinking in terms of a pathway leading people to where people need to be and helping them to takes steps along that pathway.

Pathway analysis

Once you've begun to think in terms of steps along a pathway, the next phase is to begin to analyse the pathway as a whole and the space between each step. Sometimes there are unnecessary steps along our pathways that don't move people forward. Sometimes there are lots of good steps along our pathways but there are one or two important steps missing. You'll begin to ask questions such as the following: Is the distance between step A and step B too big? Is it a big jump for people to go from here to there? Is it too big for most people? Do we need to put another step in there? If so, is a program the best way to help people?

What if, for example, our goal is to integrate new members into the life of the church and have them join a Bible study or home group. The step from coming for the first time on a Sunday to joining a group might be too big for people. So perhaps you host a new member lunch and talk about small groups and their importance in your church and present the different groups people might join. But some people still might find it too intimidating to join an existing group. What if you created a small group especially for newcomers that ran for four weeks to help them dip their toes in the water and then helped transition these people into existing groups?

Another way to analyse your pathway is to make sure that every step, program, and event includes a 'What next?' component. Where do we want people to go next? After someone comes to this event, where do they need to go next? What step do they need to take? How will we help them take it? How will they know what to do next? What do we need to tell them? Without a clear 'What next?', people who come to the event or program will probably be confused and might have a hard time getting traction and direction to keep moving forward. But if you plan in terms of a pathway then you'll know what comes next and you'll be able to direct people clearly.

People who think mainly in terms of programs focus on accomplishing and finishing the event as best as they can. And of course this is a good thing. We want our events and programs to be run well. Part of running an event or a program well, however, is understanding how it fits within the context of the pathway that's helping people get where they need to go. Running an event or program well means thinking primarily in terms of steps and focusing on what needs to happen next to help people keep moving forward.

Think primarily in terms of steps and pathways rather than programs and events.

See also

59. Hold hands with your programs
61. Why systems matter

59

Hold hands with your programs

You know what you're trying to do and what you want to achieve. You've clarified your mission and you have a clear vision of where you want to get to in the future. Now it's time for you to actually do something. Most likely you won't have just one thing to do—you'll have multiple things to do and you'll need to do those things more than once. That is, you'll create some sort of program. It might be meeting one on one with someone once a month to read the Bible or it might be running a weekly event with a team of leaders and lights and food and microphones and preaching. Both are programs—one is just more complicated than the other.

The mission is forever

Your programs exist to help you achieve your aims. Your biblical aims and biblical strategies don't change—unless, of course, you refine them to get closer to what God says in his word. But, broadly speaking, they don't change because God doesn't change and God's word doesn't change and God's methods don't change. God is still in the business of making disciples of all nations through the work of his Spirit coming alongside the loving proclamation of his word, the gospel of the Lord Jesus, by his disciples as they seek to live faithfully obedient lives for his glory. The mission is to make disciples who trust Jesus, love Jesus, love people, and want to see others saved and enjoying what we enjoy. That doesn't change and it's always relevant. This is the mission.

You marry your mission. You're committed to it and you vow to love it and pursue it for the rest of your life and you promise to never cheat on it or leave it for another. For better or for worse. For richer or for poorer. In sickness and in health, till death do you part. You marry the mission.

The program is for now

The programs you run exist to help you achieve that biblical and unchanging mission. As culture shifts, moods change, demographics evolve, and technology develops, you'll need to assess and maybe change your programs so that they continue to best engage and serve those you're trying to reach. The message and the goals and the basic methods won't change. But the programs and packaging will. While you marry your mission, you hold hands with your programs. Programs aren't forever. Love them, care about them, enjoy them, but don't make promises to them. Just hold hands.

The temptation is to get attached to programs and systems—especially if you had a hand in developing them. It's easy to feel as though they are, or should be, much more permanent and that they will always deserve to exist. If a program has been successful and blessed by God with growth, you may be tempted to tie that success to the program itself and so be reluctant to change it.

But programs are temporary. You marry the mission and hold hands with your program. One day you'll need to say goodbye to your program. No matter how successful it once was.

What will you use to bring them?

When you first set up your program, or when you evaluate a program that already exists, the main thing to consider is what you'll use to bring people to your program. People will come to events for all kinds of reasons. And we don't really have much, or any, control over why people come to the things we offer. But we do control our own plans and purposes. The first question to ask of any program is: What will you use to bring them?

If you use the power of your own magnetic personality, then what happens when you leave or die? If the whole thing is built on your charisma, then you're setting it up to fail. If you set up your program to run based on the closeness and intimacy people have with you as the leader, then you're setting it up to be small and to reach only a few people—because the intimacy and closeness that are the attractions will quickly deteriorate as more and more people become involved.

If your plan is to draw people in with free ice cream, and if people come because you hand out free ice cream, what happens when the ice cream stops? The people coming for free ice cream will stop coming.

If the plan is to draw people in with an awesome band, and if people come to see that awesome band, what will happen next time when the band isn't there? The people coming for the awesome band won't come back.

If the plan is to draw people in by having an outing to go tenpin bowling, and people come to go bowling, what will happen next time when you're not going bowling? Those who came to go bowling won't come back. Or if the plan is to have heaps of meat to cut up and BBQ, what happens next time when there's no meat and no BBQs?

What you use to bring them is what you'll need to use to keep them.[63]

If you're planning to have free ice cream every week, or if the band will be there every week, then people will keep coming back. Whatever you're using to bring them you'll need to use to keep them. If the people who are already coming are genuinely loving and you talk about Jesus and that's what you use to bring new people, so long as those things are there next week the people will keep coming back. So long as whatever you're actively using to bring people in is going to be there each time, then you're on track to keep the people coming back. Of course it's not guaranteed that they'll keep coming back—nothing in life is guaranteed and people will come and go for all kinds of reasons—but if what you're planning on using to keep them is what you're also using to bring them then your program is set up to work along with your best intentions and not against them. So as you set up a program and decide what you will use to bring them, you also need to ask: Is what we're using to bring them something we can and want to continue using to keep them?

63 I'm forever indebted to Tim Hawkins for this insight. *Fruit That Will Last: How to develop a youth ministry with lasting impact* (10th anniversary edn, Good Book Company, New Malden, 2010) is a must-read for anyone in ministry. Although the examples involve high-schoolers, it's an invaluable book about doing ministry.

Programs exist to help you

The other key question you need to ask of any current and planned program is this: does this program actually help us achieve what we want to achieve? The program might be well run and fun. Lots of people might attend and enjoy it and give you only good feedback. Maybe it's been running for ages and the children of people who participated when they were kids are now participating and the program has become a much-loved institution. It's humbling to realize that all those things can be true of a program that might not actually be achieving anything eternal. That fun, successful, well-loved program might not be making an ounce of difference for the kingdom. You wouldn't have any programs like that, would you? It might be worth checking and asking the question. Does this program actually help us achieve what we want to achieve?

It takes courage to ask these two questions about your programs:

1. Is what we're using to bring them something we can and want to continue using to keep them?
2. Does this program actually help us achieve what we want to achieve?

But if you answer these questions honestly, no matter how big and well-loved those programs are, and if you're disciplined and courageous to act on what you discover, you will go a long way to creating ministries that actually make a difference to the kingdom and don't just keep people happy and distracted.

Programs shouldn't exist for their own sake; they need to help you achieve your aims. And no matter how great they are, or were, and regardless of how long they've existed and how much emotional attachment people have to them, at some point they will stop being effective in achieving the aims they were first created to achieve. When that day comes, the program will need to be reassessed and tweaked, transformed, or terminated. As painful as it might be, the day will come when you will need to let them go.

Biblical aims stay the same and biblical methods stay the same and the biblical mission stays the same. But programs are always temporary. Marry your mission, but hold hands with your programs.

See also

55. The point is clarity, not labels
56. What are you trying to achieve?
58. Think in steps

60
Creativity is a lost art

Most of us realize that, as the rate of change in the world increases, our need for innovation and new problem-solving techniques increases at the same rate. New problems require new solutions. Yesterday's solutions won't work for tomorrow's problems. And if you want innovation and new ideas and a culture of problem-solving and finding solutions, then you need to foster a culture of creativity. But how do you do that? That's the magical question.

As children grow up they learn a number of processes and ways of thinking that serve them extraordinarily well in navigating life as adults with responsibilities. They learn to be sensible and follow the rules. They learn to be serious and find the right answer. The problem is that those ways of behaving easily and swiftly become blockages for creativity.

Deep down, I believe that everyone is creative. How do I know that? Every child draws.

If children have pencils or crayons and paper, they draw. Even children who rarely have access to these things will draw and colour when they get the opportunity. You don't need to teach them. You might teach them how to draw better or how to colour inside the lines, but you don't need to teach them to want to express themselves this way.

Every child sings. Every child dances.

But as children grow they often slowly stop doing those things. They stop drawing, dancing, and being creative. Maybe they're told that it's not productive. Maybe they use the time for 'more important' tasks. Maybe they simply start to forget how to do them. Sometimes life just beats the creativity out of them.

And I'm not talking about people who take dance lessons and learn to sing. When little children sing they aren't concentrating on notes and pitch and technique. When they dance they aren't rehearsing moves and choreography. They just sing. They just dance. And I don't do that—not anymore. It makes me sad to think that the best I may ever be able to do is to learn to make noise that equates to a note or learn some dance steps. Learning to sing and dance are both amazing and noble in themselves and to be appreciated. But these activities are not the same as a child freely singing or dancing. There's something different. There's something missing.

Sometimes I wish I would dance when I'm happy. Or dance when I'm sad. Or dance to remember. Or dance to forget.

But the point is that everyone is creative. We're born that way. It's just that most of us have forgotten how.

Developing and sustaining a creative culture takes work. Developing it in the first place is hard work, and then you need to be vigilant in order to maintain the creative culture you've developed. Building any culture requires intentionality and focus. How do you start?

Because creativity isn't a mechanical process there's no step-by-step guide, but there are certain behaviours and environments that encourage creativity and others that will restrict creativity.[64]

Here are ten principles to get you started.

1. Be the culture

Whatever the culture you want to create, it always starts with you, the leader. If it's not who you are, or who you want to be, it will never be the culture.

If you want to build a culture of creativity, you need to be that culture. Your team will take their cues from you, so you'll need to model what you want to see. You'll need to set the agenda and insist on creativity. You'll need to champion and applaud those who go out on a limb. You'll need to call a foul when others try to impose the old culture. You'll need to explain and re-explain how you want things to be.

If you want the culture to change in your church, or in your team, it needs to change within you first. You'll need to be the change you want to see.

64 For more insights on mental blocks to creativity, see *A Whack on the Side of the Head: How you can be more creative* by Roger von Oech (3rd edn, Warner Books, New York, 1998). I first encountered some of the insights in this chapter in that book.

2. Put it in the calendar

When something goes in the calendar it automatically gains importance, whether it's in your personal calendar or in the church-wide calendar. If you want to give something that level of importance, you set a date and mark it down.

If you're planning an event, maybe a camp or a special service like Christmas or Easter, put a date in the calendar for a creative planning meeting. Invite people who already are, or who you suspect might be, creative thinkers. By setting aside the time and putting it in the calendar, you signal to everyone that this is important.

Putting it in the calendar also forces you to make it happen. When you gather for the meeting explain that you want to see creativity burst open and that this is where it starts. Then lead a discussion about what you might do that you've never done before. Give people the permission and the space to be creative. See what comes out of it. You might get one great idea out of the whole exercise. That's great! Keep doing it. Year after year. Event after event.

And you can schedule these kinds of creative thinking sessions for anything—not just events. You might be up against a problem. The car park is full. No-one seems to be reading the Bible in personal devotions. Gather a team to think creatively about the problem. Sure we could make announcements, but what else could we do?

3. The 'right answer' is a mirage

There are right answers for a lot of things. At school we're taught to find the right answer. And there's nothing wrong with that. Maths, for example, has right answers. Lots of things do. But the problem comes when this quest for right answers gets drilled into us so deeply that we think everything has a right answer. We look for that one right answer to every problem so that, once we've found it, we can stop looking.

For most questions in life, though, there isn't one right answer. For example, what's the right way to get to my house? Well, there isn't one. First, it depends where you are, where you start. And it depends whether you want the fastest route, or the most scenic route, or the route that takes you past a KFC. There's no right answer—there are multiple right answers.

We often get stuck in this trap of looking for the right answer to everything. And it blocks our creative thinking because we self-censor each idea that's not 'the right answer'. We think that if we don't say the right answer we will, by definition, be saying the wrong answer and that people will laugh at us. Since we don't want to be laughed at, we keep our ideas to ourselves.

The right answer is very often a mirage. Of course there are times when there's only one right answer. But most of the time that's not the case. If you find one right answer, keep looking until you find another one. You'll often find that there are many right answers. And you'll help people become more creative as you encourage them to keep looking for more right answers.

4. Play is productive

There's work and there's play. When you're working you're not playing, and when you're playing you're not working. That's right, isn't it? Or is it? Sure, maybe you can play while you're supposed to be working. But it's not productive, is it?

The idea that play isn't work and that work isn't play is also a misconception. Play is productive. It's for children and for adults. If you want to be creative, have fun. Allow your team to have fun.

There are lots of ways to do this. Here are a few to try out:

1. Ask "What if...?" Make up a scenario that's ridiculous and then have people think about what would happen. For example: What if we had church under water? What if when you became a Christian you instantly grew a sixth finger on each hand? What if, at random intervals during church, gravity just stopped? What if Batman ran the church? What if men weren't allowed to come to church anymore? What if people never needed to sleep? What if every four years everyone had to move churches? What if church ministers were only allowed to meet with ten people per week?

   Playing around with ideas for a crazy 'what if' forces people to start thinking outside their normal, often unconscious, constraints.

2. Ask people to come up with as many similes for church, or whatever your ministry is, as they can. Sunday morning church is like...

   ...running with the bulls.

   ...mining for gold.

   ...climbing Everest.

   ...having a baby.

   ...riding a roller-coaster.

   ...peeling a mandarin.

3. Challenge people to come up with as many funny or irreverent mottos or slogans for your church as they can—with no consequences. 'St. Generic's Church...

   ...where the Big Boss really does know everything.'

   ...where innovation is acceptable so long as it's been done before.'

   ...where brand loyalty really matters.'

   ...where action-oriented people meet, and meet... and meet.'

   ...close-minded since 33 AD.'

4. If you're stuck solving a problem think about how another person would solve it. What would Genghis Khan do? How would he solve it? What would Picasso do? What would Mickey Mouse do?

5. Sometimes reversing the problem can help you find a solution. If your problem is not having enough money then spend some time thinking what you would do if you had too much money. What would you do if the car park were too big? What would you do if people were reading their Bibles too much?

Just play around. See what happens. It's not a waste of time. Play is productive.

5. Constraints, not freedom, produce creativity

People often think that creativity comes from throwing off the constraints—that opening every option is what really allows you to be creative. While there's some truth to this, constraints can also be incredibly freeing.

Yes, there are many mental constraints that hold back creativity—mental blockages like trying to find the one right answer and not wanting to look like an idiot.

Here's a quick exercise: Get out your phone and time yourself for 15 seconds. Grab a scrap piece of paper and write down as many things as you can think of that are white. Go.

Reset your timer, and this time write down as many things as you can think of that are white and that you might find inside a refrigerator. Go.

Most people find it easier to think of white things inside a fridge than they do to think of any white things imaginable. The constraint of the fridge actually helps you to be more creative.

Our brains don't work as well when everything is an option. We quickly become overwhelmed. But when you add in some boundaries the creativity begins to flow.

The lesson is that when you're trying to solve a problem or come up with a creative way forward you might want to place some artificial constraints on your thinking. Try this two or three times and see what you come up with each time.

Constraints aid creativity while too much freedom will muffle it.

6. Forget about 'being reasonable'

Fear is one of the biggest barriers to creativity. People are afraid that they'll look silly, say the wrong thing, have a bad idea, or be ridiculed so they self-censor. People often assume that all kinds of rules exist and then act within them. They make sure their ideas sound 'reasonable'—whatever that means. Or they make sure they follow the rules, even if there aren't any rules.

Of course following the rules is a good thing—especially if the rules are a good idea. But in order to be creative, every now and then at least, we need permission to ignore the rules. Sometimes this means making an explicit statement that you want people to brainstorm and say what they think and dream big and wild without any thought to what's possible or within reach. Other times it means protecting crazy ideas from being shot down too early with comments about being reasonable. You need to think reasonably at some point if an idea's going to become a reality, but this kind of thinking shouldn't come in too early and definitely not during the creative brainstorming time. When it's time to be creative people need the space and safety to think thoughts without too much self-censoring.

7. Creativity is cumulative

Not every idea will be a great idea. Most ideas won't even be that good. You need to be aware of that and be okay with that. Help your team to grasp the fact that not every idea they throw out needs to be a polished diamond—or even a diamond in the rough. Some of them can just be rocks and pieces of charcoal.

Some ideas exist to be stepping-stones. That is, one idea might not be that good at all but something in it will spark someone else to think of a much better idea. This much better idea sparks someone else to come up with a different, though related, idea. Then a fourth person combines what's great about these two good ideas and puts forward a brilliant idea.

While it was the fourth person who articulated the brilliant idea, they would never have come up with it without the other two good ideas and the first mediocre one. The mediocre idea was necessary, even though it wasn't used.

Regardless of who actually put forth the final idea, that idea was still the product of the whole team and process. The creativity snowballed and ideas bounced, played, and sparked off each other to create the final piece. This is how creativity often works. It's cumulative, and great ideas are often sparked by lesser ideas and sometimes even by largely unrelated ideas.

8. Run on 2 x 4s

One of the absolute essentials for all of our creative enterprises, whether we're trying to come up with a slogan, a piece of advertising, or a piece for social media, is what we call a 2 x 4. We didn't invent this, but we use it a lot.

The idea is simple: before you decide on any idea, take a sheet of paper and divide it into eight squares made up of two rows of four. It should look something like this:

Now fill in each square with a different idea. You can't finish and make a choice until you've filled every square. So if you're trying to come up with an advertising campaign slogan for your Christmas events, for example, you'll come up with eight different slogans.

The point of this exercise is to force you to be creative and to come up with the second 'right answer', as well as the third, fourth, and fifth right answers, and so on. It also gives you options to choose from. Your first idea won't always be your best. The discipline of the eight empty squares will force you to keep thinking and scratching for creativity—especially when you think you have nothing left. It's a tool that forces you to get creative. We love it, and the best part is that the 2 x 4 is a tool that anyone can use and all you need is paper and a pen or pencil.

9. Cross-pollinate

Great ideas can come from anywhere, and often they come when two seemingly opposite arenas crash into each other. Christian ministry is a unique activity. There's nothing quite like it. But there are some things that are similar, and there are some aspects of ministry that are similar to other activities.

Who else has solved the problem you're facing? Has someone outside the arena of Christian ministry solved the same or a similar problem? Is there some wisdom from another field that you could take and tweak to help you solve your problem?

Preaching isn't the same as stand-up comedy, but they're both forms of monologue. Is there anything we can learn about preaching from stand-up comedians?

Lots of industries take disparate yet talented individuals and seek to turn them into highly functioning teams. Is there anything we can learn about building teams from professional sporting coaches?

Planting a church isn't at all the same as opening a McDonald's fast food restaurant, but is there anything we could learn about choosing a location from how they do it?

Obviously there will be things that all of these groups do that we will never do and that would compromise fundamental aspects of who we are and what we're seeking to do. But might there be a kernel of wisdom in some of the things they do that you could appropriate. Or something they do to solve a problem might spark an idea in your head that ends up solving your problem.

Why not, once a year, read a book about another industry that interests you or that you think might have some crossover? Why not, once a year, organize a meeting with someone who does something that's similar to what you do or are trying to do, and ask them questions about how they think, what problems they face, and how they solve those problems?

10. Good ideas happen in the margins

It's very rare to hear people say that their best and most creative ideas came to them when they were overloaded, stressed, and stretched thin. In my personal experience, this has never happened. People more often have their best ideas when they're on holidays, or doing something totally unrelated, or even in the shower.

Creativity doesn't seem to happen when you're overloaded and doing a whole pile of stuff. Creativity seems to happen once you stop and allow your brain to process the issue and let it percolate. Ideas seem to bubble up as the thoughts sift, meld, and mix together.

This means that you need to create space for creativity. A half-hour block of creative thinking time squeezed between two other meetings probably won't bring about the best results. You need to somehow create some margin in your life, some space where you can breathe and slow down and allow your thoughts to mingle and fuse into ideas. That margin might be a retreat, an off-site meeting, a short break away, or just a week where you clear your calendar of commitments and allow yourself to follow whatever trail grabs your attention.

The point is that creativity often requires space.

Everyone is creative. These ten suggestions are a starting point to help you and others rediscover your creativity and start to cultivate a culture of creativity in your team.

See also

32. Ideas are born ugly
49. You can only drive as fast as the car in front

61 Why systems matter

Whether you're aware of it or not, your church is full of systems. There are big systems and small systems. There are systems within systems. There might be some that you created on purpose and there will most probably be a number of systems that you've created unintentionally.

A system is any ongoing and interconnected process made up of more than one step or activity that achieves a certain outcome. You might call it a method, routine, or a procedure depending on the goal it's designed to achieve. Another way to say it is that it's the collection of activities you do to get things done.

Perhaps the most familiar systems are those within the human body—the nervous system, the respiratory system, the digestive system, and the cardiovascular system, for example. Everybody has them and they function without much, if any, conscious thought. They just happen automatically so that you can focus your energy on other more important concerns, like making a sandwich. You don't need to think much, if at all, about your cardiovascular system while you're sitting in a meeting. It's just doing its thing pumping blood around while you concentrate on what's being said and what you think about it.

But if at one point during the meeting you started to experience massive chest pains and began to black out, you'd suddenly be very aware of your cardiovascular system because something was wrong with it. You'd then spend a lot of time and a lot of the insurance company's money to figure out what was wrong and how to fix it.

When it's working fine, you don't notice it. But when something goes wrong, all of a sudden you become very aware of that system.

In a similar way, most of the systems in your church are working away and you don't even notice them. You'll have systems for collecting money, systems for spending money, systems for what happens when a new person first comes to your church, systems for how people get into small groups, and loads more. And it's likely that you don't think about them very much. They're just constantly working. But every now and then one of these systems will break down and you'll suddenly be aware of it because you'll need to put in time and energy to discover what went wrong and how to fix it.

It's important to be aware that systems exist and to appreciate their value so that, when we find ourselves in the position of having to fix or update one, we understand why they're worth our time and focus. Here are five reasons why systems matter.

1. Systems already exist whether you realize it or not

Systems matter because they already exist in your church. The question is not whether you want systems but whether the systems you have are the systems you want. The question is whether your systems exist intentionally or by accident.

You may be the type of person who loves systems and processes, and thinking about systems might make you happy. Or you may be the type of person who can think of nothing worse than studying systems. You want to get back to doing ministry, talking to people, sharing the gospel. And I totally understand that. But the reality is that, if you're the leader, you're responsible for the systems in your organization and so it's part of your job to think about them.

The systems already exist so you might as well make them good.

2. Systems are about people

Even though systems are usually a few steps removed from people, they do impact people a lot. The reason you have systems at all is so that you can help people. If you've ever called a business and been put on hold in a priority queue because your call is important to them you'll know what I mean. You're a part of their system. From the voice recording to the music that's playing, from the very idea of being in a queue on the phone to the software that keeps everyone in their proper order, and finally to the staff member who eventually—hopefully—answers your call, it's a system. Someone designed the whole thing. Perhaps they carefully crafted every detail with purpose or perhaps they just threw it together without thinking. Someone chose the music that is slowly sucking your will to live. Someone was responsible for training that person with whom you finally speak for two seconds before they push the wrong button and end your call, meaning that you have to call back, start all over again in the queue, and waste even more of your time being blindingly angry.

That's a system. And it impacts real people. So if you're a people person who cares about people then you'll be a systems person. Real people are impacted by, and sometimes have to endure, your systems. And those systems already exist in your church, so it's worth doing an audit to make sure that what's happening in those systems is happening because you want it to.

If there are one or two hundred people in your church your systems are probably fairly simple and straightforward. But it's still worth working through them to make sure they cover every step and to make sure all the systems you want to exist actually do exist.

But if your church is much larger than that your systems will probably need to be a bit more complex, which is even more reason to audit them, and to audit them regularly, to make sure they're still achieving what you designed them to achieve.

3. Good systems deliver good results with minimal supervision

Unless you're on something like a ventilator, your respiratory system will work whether you think about it or not. Whether you're awake or asleep, breathing will keep happening. And only when you're doing more work than you'd normally do and so putting that system under stress—when you're running, for example—will you perhaps need to focus your conscious energy on taking a few deep breaths to restabilize that system. In other words, it will deliver results without your conscious supervision.

And it's the same with your church systems. Once you've designed a good system it will achieve the outcomes you set it up to achieve without you having to focus on making each and every step in the process happen.

Once a year we send a big mailout to hundreds of people that includes a number of different items: a letter, a flyer, a sticker, an address label for the front of the envelope, and a stamp. One way of doing it is for me to block out a whole day and sit down and do each envelope myself. The end goal would be achieved—every envelope would contain the right items and be sent to the person we want to contact.

But that's not how we do it. We organize a big team of people, we all eat KFC and hang out, and then we set up a production line. Some people fold letters, others compile all the items and put them in envelopes, others seal the envelopes and affix the address labels and stamps. In other words, we create a system. And the job usually gets done in less than an hour and doesn't require my focused supervision. I go because I like hanging out with people and I take one of those roles on the production line. But I don't need to be there and I don't need to supervise each step in the process. The system delivers good results with minimal supervision. You've probably done something similar at some point in your life. You'll know how this works. The challenge is to intentionally implement more permanent systems in your church.

While good systems produce good results with minimal supervision, minimal supervision isn't the same as no supervision. Like everything else in the universe, your systems will decay, fall apart, and generally tend toward chaos. You can't just think that once you've set up a system it will work perfectly forever. You will need to maintain it. You might want to set up regular times, once a year perhaps, to look over all your systems and see if you can improve what you do to get more of what you're hoping to achieve. Good systems still require some supervision but it doesn't need to be constant.

4. Systems create behaviours (most of the time)

Whatever your system is currently giving you is exactly what you've created it to give you. It's only a system so it does only what you, the brains behind its design, tell it to do.

If I forgot to include the stamps as part of the process in our production line, then none of those letters would make it through the mail to the houses of those people. And that wouldn't be the fault of the system. That would be my fault. I created the system.

Or if some people didn't receive their letters because they had moved house and we hadn't updated the details in our database, that wouldn't be the system's fault. It's a system's *problem,* but it wouldn't be the system's *fault.* The system gives me exactly what I've designed it to give me—nothing more and nothing less. And so if it isn't giving me the outcomes I want it's because I've designed it poorly.

"But what about human error?" I hear you ask. Great point. If my system involves people, then I should include some checks and balances and safeguards as part of that system in case of human error. And if I don't do that, then again it's not the system's fault that I've created a system that allows for human error. And if human errors occur and make it through unchecked that's because I've created a system that will allow that. The system will give me exactly what I've designed it to give me.

But, I can hear you thinking, these systems haven't created any behaviours yet. Good point. But systems do. Or at least they make certain behaviours easier and other behaviours more difficult.

In our youth ministry a few years ago, for example, we were having real trouble getting our leaders to talk with the high-schoolers who were coming along about Jesus. So we spoke about the importance of it at meetings, we clarified the doctrine of hell, and we made sure we were all on the same page about how valuable these high-schoolers were as people; but nothing seemed to make any difference. But then one week we made two changes to our system:

1. We told the leaders that we wanted them to ask the students this exact question: "So what do you think about all this Jesus stuff?"
2. In our meeting after youth group each week, the first question we asked was: "So who did you talk to about Jesus tonight?"

That's it—we only changed those two things. The first week no-one said anything. No-one said anything the second week either. But the third week two people shared conversations they'd had. We were so excited. After about six months, more than half our team were sharing stories every week about conversations they were having with both Christian and not-yet-Christian students about Jesus. All because we tweaked the system.

Do you know one of the best ways to begin losing weight? It's not to join a gym or to go for a walk—it has nothing to do with exercise. The best way to start losing weight is to buy smaller plates and bowls. Smaller plates will encourage you to eat smaller portions. Eating smaller portions will help you lose weight. In other words, you tweak the system.

Do you know one of the best ways for a business to create return customers? Those frequent-sipper cards at coffee shops. You know the ones they stamp each time you buy a coffee and then the tenth one is free? You probably have heaps of them in your wallet or purse with only one stamp. Do you know the best way to get people to use them regularly? Give them two stamps the first time you stamp it. People are much more likely to come back if they're already 20% of the way there as opposed to only 10%. That's a system that creates a behaviour.

Systems create behaviours by acknowledging and rewarding the behaviours that you want—which make those behaviours more attractive to people—and by building in consequences for the behaviours you don't want.

People are their own masters, of course. They're not robots and they're often unpredictable. That's why systems create behaviours most of the time but not all the time. There will always be those people who continue to do what they want no matter what. The sooner you just accept that fact, the happier you'll be. But on the whole, most of the time, systems create behaviours.

5. Poor systems create frustration in good people

If you only pay attention to systems when they break down, then you might not have ever had to pay attention to systems. That might be because you have really good unintentional systems, but it's more likely that you have good people who pick up the slack and step in when there's a hole in the system. They cover for your system when it's missing a key step.

That's great, right? What's the problem?

The problem is that the cost of this is frustration in your best people. And if I had a choice about whom I would frustrate, my best people wouldn't be my top pick. I want to support my best people. I want to care for my best people. I want them to work within systems that release them and make it easy for them to do great things. I don't want them to have to work within systems that frustrate them, block them, or restrict them.

Creating good systems is about loving people—loving both the people who are helped by the system and also the people who have to work within the system.

You can still have good outcomes if you have great people working within poor systems. But it's much better if you have great people working within great systems.

A warning

The temptation is to keep poking and fiddling with systems and overhauling them every year. Systems take time to set up and time to gain momentum. Changing a system every year is, in general, a bad idea. You need to give most systems time to get set up and start functioning. A good rule of thumb is to allow at least 18 months before you totally overhaul a system. Tweak it along the way with small course corrections but don't totally change it until around the two-year mark. Only then will you be able to tell if you have a system problem or a people problem.

The question isn't whether or not your church has systems. Your church definitely already has them. They exist under the surface and behind the scenes. The question is whether or not your systems are good and whether or not they're the ones you want. A system is just how your church gets something done.

Systems matter. So create them intentionally.

See also

26. Leading is loving
58. Think in steps

62

Know the reason for the season

When we plan out our lives we often start by thinking in terms of years. We naturally begin with January 1 and then it all winds down on December 31. This creates a kind of calendar rhythm. Within that rhythm different people will break the year down into smaller units. If they have children or work in education or are pursuing a further degree themselves then they'll probably break their year down into terms like a school year. Others will break their year down into seasons: summer, autumn, winter, spring. These smaller units also contribute to the calendar rhythm.

Different rhythms

Different churches will plan their years around different rhythms. If your church is made up of a lot of families, for example, you might organize your ministries around school terms because most people will organize their lives that way already. There's nothing wrong with organizing yourself that way and there's nothing wrong with organizing according to the seasons of the year, say, in a more rural church.

These social rhythms aren't the only ones at work within your church, however. The school calendar and relative temperatures and seasons are only a few of the possible ways of conceptualizing the times and rhythms of a year. Your church itself also has rhythms and seasons.

Easter and Christmas, for example, are big moments in the church calendar and each requires a lot of thought and energy—more than a lot of other moments in the year. Different churches will have different key events and seasons depending on any number of factors. Some will celebrate Lent. Some will run a big holiday program for kids. Some will take the whole church away to a camp or a conference. All of these things will contribute to the rhythm of your church.

It's worth taking the time to work out what the rhythm of your particular church or ministry is. You might find that you don't like those seasons and want to change them, you might like them and want to keep them, and you might find that you're not able to change them whether you like them or not. Regardless, being aware of them will help you to be more intentional and work along with those seasons.

As Easter approaches you know there will be a big push and you'll want your teams to invest a lot of energy, so you might want to take things a bit easier during the month leading up to Easter so they can invest their energy during Easter well. Or maybe you want to take it a bit easier the month after Easter and not plan any big events to give people a chance to catch their breath. Either of those would be good options, and there are probably lots of other ways you could sync up with the rhythm here as well. But the point is to be aware that these seasons exist and then to be intentional about how you lead up to them, through them, and out the other side.

In the same way, if you're planning a big evangelistic initiative which will involve doing everything you can to present who Jesus is and what he's done and why people need to put their trust in him, you'll want to have also planned what happens next. Will you have small groups for people to plug into to find out more about Jesus and Christianity? Will you run a follow-up course so people can find out more? Will you preach a series on the foundations of discipleship or on a section of one of the four Gospels so people can see Jesus in action? Again, it's important to know what season you're in and what specifically you'll be doing in that season.

Evaluating the reasons for the seasons

The first step in evaluating the rhythm of your church calendar is to work out what it is. What are the seasons? You probably have Easter and Christmas, but what else? Where are the peaks, the times where you make a bigger effort and invest more time and energy?

What are the seasonal rhythms of individual ministries in your church? The rhythm of the kids' ministry is probably not the same as the rhythm of the ministry to older people. What's the rhythm of your small group ministry?

Once you understand the rhythm of your calendar, the second step is to decide whether you like this rhythm or not. Someone created it—it might have been you, but that doesn't mean you have to like it or accept it. Maybe you never noticed what kind of seasonal life you were creating. It might have happened by accident as you developed different events and ministries. It might be that many of the big peaks where you need to expend a lot of energy are all clumped together and this rhythm exhausts people and burns them out so it gets harder every year to drum up people to help out because they've seen how draining it is. Maybe your church doesn't have much of a rhythm and even Easter and Christmas are pretty low-key with not much additional energy or enthusiasm put into them. Maybe the church rhythm is more about going through the motions and chugging along. And perhaps you want to change this.

The third step, once you've discovered and decided to keep or adjust the seasons of your church, is to begin to think and make decisions with this seasonal rhythm in mind. How does this rhythm impact your teaching and preaching program? How does it impact when you encourage people to join small groups? What about when you put the call out to get people engaged in serving? In your church's rhythm, when is the best time for an evangelistic push? When is it best to talk about giving and generosity? When is the best time for the staff to take holidays? When is the worst time? Is January the best time for all the staff to go on holidays? You'll be able to consider the best answers to these questions and others as you keep the seasons and rhythms of your church in mind.

Knowing the seasons is the first step

As you look into this concept still further you'll notice that the dates and programs of your church calendar create a unique rhythm in your specific church. This date-and-program rhythm will interact with the rhythms of the lives of the people in your church, which will help create the overall seasonal rhythm of your church.

The year will have peaks and troughs. A time to sow and a time to reap. Everything is beautiful in its time. Part of the leader's task is to know and understand these seasons and to find ways to maximize the strengths of each season, to find what makes each season beautiful.

Knowing the reasons for the seasons enables you to ask more intelligent questions. For example: What are the advantages of the rhythm that can be accentuated? If lots of visitors come at Christmas, how can you maximize this and help those people engage further with the claims of Jesus on their lives? If lots of fringe-Christians or maybe-Christians or sleepy-Christians or loosely Christian people come along at Easter, how can you maximize this and help those people move forward and take the claims of Jesus more seriously? If people are particularly tired at a certain point in the year, say after Easter for example, how can you best use this time to re-energize the troops? When you're aware of the seasons these are the kinds of questions you'll be able to ask and answer.

It's important for a leader to know the seasons. Knowing what makes those seasons beautiful and thereby maximizing their potential impact is critical. Knowing the season is good. Knowing the *reason* for the season is even better.

See also

57. Where is here?
65. Everything has an upside and a downside
75. Waiting is doing something

63

Meetings are where real work is done

Meetings can often be awful. We all know that. They're boring. They're frustrating. They're a waste of time. They exist to be endured and to remind us that life could be worse. They often feel like the payment we have to make so that we can all go back to our desks and get on with some real work.

But it doesn't have to be this way. This isn't the necessary DNA of a meeting. Meetings aren't supposed to be like that.

Meetings are a big investment

Meetings are, in fact, one of the most important things that your church does. Whether they're staff meetings or meetings with teams of volunteers, these meetings will tell you a lot about your church or your ministry and how it's going. Patrick Lencioni says:

> No action, activity, or process is more central to a healthy organization than the meeting. As dreaded as the 'm' word is, as maligned as it has become, there is no better way to have a fundamental impact on an organization than by changing the way it does meetings. In fact, if someone were to offer me one single piece of evidence to evaluate the health of an organization, I would not ask to see its financial statements, review its product line, or even talk to its employees or customers; I would want to observe the leadership team during a meeting. This is where values are established, discussed, and lived and where decisions

> around strategy and tactics are vetted, made, and reviewed. Bad meetings are the birthplace of unhealthy organizations, and good meetings are the origin of cohesion, clarity, and communication.[65]

So why do we dislike meetings so much? It's probably because they are often terrible and boring.

But meetings don't have to be boring. They can be interesting. They might not be the absolute most interesting things in the world, but they should be kind of interesting. Meetings don't have to be frustrating. They can be times where enthusiasm grows and commitment is strengthened. Meetings don't have to be a waste of time. They can be useful and things can actually be decided and achieved at meetings.

Meetings can actually be places where real work is done. It's not just that they *can* be such places, but they *should* be such places. Say you're gathering six people for a meeting that lasts two hours. That's 12 hours of time that you're cumulatively investing in that meeting. That's a lot of hours. If you're going to invest 12 hours of people's time in something you'd better do everything you can to make sure you accomplish something worthwhile, right?

What sometimes happens—and this is crazy and probably never happens in your meetings—is that people come to meetings planning to not engage. They sit there not contributing, counting down until they can get back to their real work. Once the meeting wraps up they go back to their desks and make phone calls and write emails clarifying things that should have been discussed, decided upon, and written down *in the meeting they were just in*—things that would have been discussed, decided upon, and written down had they chosen to participate. Lencioni writes:

> The thesis behind all of this is worth repeating: a great deal of the time that leaders spend every day is a result of having to address issues that come about because they aren't being resolved during meetings in the first place. That's why it's really hard for executives to make a credible case for

65 Lencioni, *The Advantage*, pp. 173-4.

> spending less time in meetings, assuming those meetings are good ones.[66]

But what if our meetings aren't good ones? How can we make them better? Why is it that we often feel like we're not doing any real work when we come to meetings? Why is it that the moment the team gathers in a room is the moment when we stop moving forward and getting things done instead of being the time where we're energized and surge forward? How can we change meetings so that they become at least kind of interesting, places where decisions are made and things actually get done?

Here are six tips on how to transform your meetings from punishments to be endured to key gatherings where real work gets done.

1. Know why the meeting is important and tell me as well

Just because you say it's important doesn't make it important. Not really. And just because the meeting has a lot of people in it doesn't make it important. And just because it will consume 12 people hours and so is quite expensive doesn't make it important. That just makes it expensive.

Why exactly is this specific meeting important? This is a very important question for you to answer in your own mind. And if you can't think of a persuasive answer then maybe you should rethink whether you should have the meeting in the first place.

The other week we had a planning meeting for a camp that was coming up. The reason that meeting was important was because what we discussed and decided in that meeting would shape the substance and basic skeleton of that weekend. So if we made bad decisions or didn't think through them properly that would affect the rest of the planning and execution of this camp. The camp might still be good and worthwhile, but it would have to struggle through and around our poor decisions. So the meeting was important. And as we started I explained that to the people who were there.

You need to clarify for yourself why every meeting is important and you need to let the people who are at each meeting know as well—perhaps before the meeting, but always by the time you start.

66 Lencioni, *The Advantage*, p. 186.

2. Don't be random

Plan the meeting and prepare both what you'll talk about and also the order. This step is often overlooked. It would be rare for someone to call a meeting and then have no idea what they'll do in that meeting. Although I'd be surprised if that has never happened, most people do have an idea or a list of items to be discussed.

The problem comes when you just discuss this list of items in the order that you thought of them, or in the order that you remembered them and wrote them down. Lencioni calls this "meeting stew". He writes:

> Imagine a clueless cook taking all of the ingredients out of the pantry and the refrigerator and throwing them into one big pot, and then wondering why his concoction doesn't taste very good. Leaders do the same thing when they put all of their issues into one big discussion, usually called a 'staff meeting'. All too often they combine administrative issues and tactical decisions and creative brainstorming and strategic analysis and personnel discussions into one exhausting meeting. And like that cook, somehow they're surprised when the result doesn't turn out so well.[67]

But there's a better way to do it.

First, you should split the items to be covered into three main categories: FYIs, tactical topics, and strategic topics. Not every meeting will always have all of these types of items, but these are the broad categories.

FYIs are those things that don't really require discussion but are more information sharing or updates on progress—whether personal or on behalf of a project or event—or generally administrative matters.

Tactical topics are those specific items that have to do with the details and nuts and bolts of what you're doing—double-checking the run sheet, deciding the Bible readings for this Sunday, who's on the roster, that kind of thing.

Strategic topics are those wider discussions that are not so much about the specifics of doing something but that consider instead the broader view

67 Lencioni, *The Advantage*, p. 174.

of how you do something or whether or not you should do something. So, for example, a strategic topic would be 'should we do evangelistic events in the first place', not 'who should speak at the evangelistic event'.

So as you plan your meeting you split the topics to be discussed into these wider categories. Talking about a strategic issue requires a different way of thinking than discussing tactical nuts and bolts. And shifting your thoughts from one type of thinking to another can often be quite hard. Constantly switching back and forth can be mentally exhausting. You want people to use their mental energy to tackle the problems rather than wasting it by constantly changing mental gears. So to minimize these shifts you want to group the different types of issues together. If at all possible, you'll want to have separate meetings for tactical issues and strategic issues. The temptation is to put them back into the same meeting, but if it's at all physically possible don't do that. Hold two separate meetings—one strictly for tactical issues and the other strictly for strategic issues. You'll then do them both justice and your people will be far less exhausted by the end of each meeting.

If you absolutely cannot have a separate strategic meeting and you have to discuss both kinds of issues in the same meeting, then block the issues together. So you talk about all the tactical issues together and all the strategic issues together—preferably with a break between the two—rather than switching back and forth from tactical to FYIs then back to tactical again and then strategic and so on. Lencioni calls this separation of tactical and strategic issues "the single most important piece of advice for [leadership teams] when it comes to meetings".[68]

Once you've grouped them into categories, you can order the items within those categories in whatever way seems best. And you can order those broader categories in whichever order seems best as well. You might start with FYIs, then move on to discuss tactical issues, and finish with a strategic topic. Or equally you might start with a strategic issue, then talk FYIs, and finish with tactical concerns. What matters is that you have a reason for the order you choose.

You'll also need to make sure that you signal to the people in your

68 Lencioni, *The Advantage*, p. 184.

meeting that you're moving from one broad category to another so they can switch gears. You might do this by letting people take a few minutes to stretch or grab a drink before you move on.

3. Clarify the decision

Discussing an issue is a great part of any meeting. People get to say what they think, ask questions of others, and clarify their own thoughts and position. But the discussion needs to go somewhere. We need to make a decision—or at least clearly move closer to a decision.

Once you think you've made a decision, as the meeting leader you need to state what the decision is so that everyone can agree that, yes, that's the decision. Then make sure you write it down right away.

The lesson I've learned is that no matter how clear I think the decision was, just because it was clear to me doesn't mean it was clear to everyone. Once I was running a meeting with 12 other people. We had discussed a topic for 30 minutes and come to a decision: we would do A and not B and we would do it on day C.

So I clarified that decision and someone said: "What? I though we were doing B." So I restated that we would be doing A and not B on day C. Someone else said, "Wait, I thought we were doing it on day D". I clarified again. "Wait", another person said. "Are we doing A? I thought we were doing B." I clarified again that we had decided to do A, not B, on day C. We did this literally three more times because three more people were confused about what we were doing. I thought it was a prank they were playing. But unfortunately it wasn't a joke. Their confusion was genuine.

No matter how clear you think you've been, make sure you explicitly clarify the decision and write it down.

4. Clarify who and when

In addition to clarifying the decision, you also need to clarify who will own each action item. Who will be responsible for making it happen and when?

So if we're going to find four people to help set up the chairs for the special service next month, who here is going to own that and when are they going to make sure it's done by? Before the next meeting? Report back in two weeks?

Unless a specific person is assigned to own the action item there's a good chance it won't get done and we'll come back to the next meeting and we'll all say we thought it was someone else's job.

5. End the conversation

One of the responsibilities of the leader is not just to facilitate discussion but also to end conversations that are off-topic or that are not worth everyone's time to discuss in the meeting.

One of the worst moments in a meeting is when the discussion either devolves into, or never was anything but, two people having a conversation while the other four or five of us sit there bored or start checking Facebook on our phones or iPads.

If all this item was ever going to be was a conversation between two people, then save it for after the meeting or for a phone call later. But don't waste my time by making me listen to you two decide when the best time is for you to meet up for your one-on-one meeting.

If the discussion does unravel into a conversation between two people, that's a good time for the meeting leader to step in and end the conversation. These two can follow it up outside the meeting and come back next time with a proposal or a solution. Once we've identified the problem and assigned a person to own it, we can most likely move on to the next item.

6. Recap

Before the meeting ends, read back one more time the decisions that were made and who is responsible for what and when, in case someone forgot to write it down or wasn't paying attention. It's worth double-checking that everyone agrees on who is doing what and by when.

This recap will also remind people, right at the end of the meeting—no matter what else happened in the meeting and no matter how sloppy or messy or poorly run it was—of the actual work that got done and what the next steps are. It will reinforce that the meeting was worth being at because of all the things that got done and decided.

Meetings don't have to be a waste of time and a distraction from real work. These six tweaks aren't huge game changers, but they're tweaks that will radically alter the usefulness and productivity of your meetings. A big door opens and closes on small hinges. These six tweaks are six small hinges, but if you implement them thoughtfully and consistently you'll open the door for meetings that actually get things done and that people perhaps even look forward to attending.

See also

26. Leading is loving
33. Communicate from the inside out
37. Phrases to learn
40. Team communication is exponential
41. Two foundations of team-building
46. People deserve to know the truth
56. What are you trying to achieve?
72. Hellos and goodbyes matter

64

Learn relaxed concern

When you're a leader there's lots to be stressed and worry about. You often have multiple things to prepare simultaneously, and there are usually many things happening all at once—deadlines, problems, setbacks. The job frequently feels like a heady concoction of pressure and preparation.

A lot of leaders spend a lot of time being stressed or worried, even though we know that being in a constant state of stress is unhealthy. And knowing about the negative effects of stress and worry gives us one more thing to stress and worry about. And the cycle continues.

Furthermore, both stress and worry can be contagious to your team. If you're always stressed and worried, dashing around frantically, this flows over to those you lead. The leader has a lot of power when it comes to creating the emotional climate and setting the tone for the team. Your constant state of stress creates a stressed team environment. And it's hard to enjoy being part of a team that's constantly stressed and on edge.

But the fact that stress and worry are a waste of time makes it still worse. They're sideways energy, they don't move you forward. Worry is unproductive thoughts spiralling around a centre of fear. And it's the same with stress. All of these unproductive thoughts clutter your mind and keep you from thinking about the things you need to think about in the ways you need to think about them.

Yet you wouldn't want to be so laid back that you don't care what happens—that would be equally unhelpful. What you're doing matters, and so of course you care how it turns out. Being overly casual communicates to your team that what they're doing isn't that important. There's a danger in being so relaxed that you treat things that are urgent and significant as though they're not priorities. The opposite of worry and stress isn't laziness and apathy.

Being overly nonchalant is unhelpful. Being quasi-neurotic is unhelpful too. There needs to be a middle road.

The art of both/and

Being concerned is a good thing; what you're involved in is important and you're responsible and it needs to get done. Being *overly* concerned is the problem. Being relaxed is a good thing; you think more clearly, you treat people as they deserve to be treated, you don't blow out your adrenal glands. Being *overly* relaxed is the problem.

Instead, we need to cultivate the art of relaxed concern—being relaxed and concerned at the same time. We need to be concerned about deadlines, problems, and setbacks without losing our cool, panicking, or becoming paralysed and so accomplishing nothing in a froth of unproductive activity. We need to be relaxed about deadlines, problems, and setbacks without becoming lazy, disinterested, or procrastinating so that we wallow in a swamp of unproductive apathy. The art of relaxed concern combines the two and holds them together in tension.

There's a time for worry and stress and pushing for things to be done quickly. But we shouldn't live at this altitude. Relaxing and taking it easy is a good thing, and there's definitely a time for that. But it shouldn't be the default gear in which we work.

The misunderstanding of both/and

People sometimes find it hard to understand relaxed concern and, depending on who they are, they may criticize you for being too much one way or the other. Highly stressed people might say that you're too relaxed, and totally chilled people might think you're too concerned. When different people are voicing both criticisms, that's a good sign that you're on the right track.

When I was at theological college, each year all the students were placed in different groups to do an evangelistic project together. Each group partnered with a local church to share the gospel with people for a week. In one of our preparation meetings, my group was sharing what we were stressed or worried about and praying for each other. We shared around the circle, and after each person shared someone volunteered to pray for that person. It was all going well until it was my turn to share.

The problem is that I don't really get stressed or worried or anxious. My wife thinks I have some kind of brain damage. She's probably right. So I found it very hard to think of something that I was worried or stressed about. I told the group that I don't get stressed much, and that I wasn't particularly worried about anything, but I asked people to pray that I'd prepare my gospel talks well and that as I had opportunities to share the gospel with people I would be bold and clear and that God would give me the right words to say in each situation.

As far as prayer points go, I thought that was pretty good. A volunteer was asked for, and a guy put his hand up to pray—we'll call him Derrick. Derrick was one of the most highly strung people I'd ever met. He was so tightly wound that coiled springs often followed him around and took notes on how to do better. Derrick was from another country, and so I assume he was always struggling to acclimatize to the culture. I'll never forget his prayer because it was the first—and so far the only—time I've ever had someone pray for me as a veiled form of public rebuke. It still makes me giggle when I think about it. Derrick prayed, "Dear God. We pray for Craig and we ask that you'd help him understand the importance of what we're doing. Help him to care about the gospel and whether or not people are saved. We ask that he would see this time as serious and that he would prepare for it properly. Amen." The whole group said "Amen" in agreement—and so did I, just out of reflex, but I don't think I meant it.

People on the outer extremes will misunderstand your relaxed concern and you'll need to help them understand. But instead of living at one of those extremes ourselves, or swinging like a pendulum from one to the other, we need to find a third way that takes the best from both of them.

It can be very difficult to develop this way of life. Being aware that it is possible in the first place is a good start. Jesus himself was a model of this relaxed concern. He cared deeply for people and sought to meet their needs at every opportunity. But he always prioritized time alone with his heavenly Father and didn't allow the stressed-out worry of the disciples or of people like Martha or the crowds to override that priority. Even in the most stressful moment of his life, as he faced the grim future of the cross in the garden of Gethsemane, Jesus again sought to calm and resolve himself by time in prayer with his Father. As Christians we know that because of Jesus' work for us on the cross all things are at work for our good. And we too have a heavenly Father who has taken care of absolutely everything we need. So, when we begin to feel anxious or stressed, a good place for us to start is to follow Jesus' example and turn to God in prayer, trusting him to work in any and every situation for our good and for the good of everyone involved in the potentially stressful situation at hand. And then it's worth double-checking that we're not taking ourselves too seriously and that things really are as catastrophic as we think they are; it's worth making sure that our worry isn't the result of our out-of-control perfectionism. We can aim for relaxed concern as our default position—for our own sakes and for the teams we lead.

See also

28. Anything worth doing is worth doing badly
49. You can only drive as fast as the car in front

65

Everything has an upside and a downside

Strengths are a good thing and we should be grateful for them, whether they're personal strengths—things we're good at or enjoy doing—or strengths of our church or ministry, like being welcoming or teaching the Bible well. We should praise God for these things and do all we can to develop and improve on them.

Strengths are sometimes weaknesses

When we think about strengths and weaknesses we're usually thinking of two different sets of things. A strength for our church, for example, might be that there are a lot of people involved in ministry—and a weakness might be that we don't have much off-street parking. No-one is good at everything, and we know that every person and organization has both strengths and weaknesses. What we don't often realize is that every strength has the potential to become a weakness. I'm not talking about something that was a strength suddenly changing course and taking a nosedive into weakness. No, sometimes strengths become weaknesses by continuing on their upward trajectories as strengths. This seems counterintuitive. While it's easy to imagine a strength beginning to decay and transforming into a weakness, it's more difficult to imagine how a strength, continuing to improve, can transform into a weakness. But in fact every strength has, built into it, the possibility to become a weakness *precisely by being* a strength.

Humans need a cluster of ingredients in order to survive—water, food, sun, shelter, clothing, and so on. I'm not sure that's an exhaustive list, but you get the idea. Water is good. Food is good. Sunlight and shelter are good. We need these things. Try to imagine each of them as a strength necessary for survival. Now imagine that you have each of these in abundance. Each one of them keeps growing from strength to strength in your life. The good things that you need to live soon become the things that kill you.

You need water to survive, but if you drink too much water it's called water intoxication and can be fatal. And if you're surrounded and enveloped by water you could drown.

You need food to live, but eating too much is dangerous. It's the same with being in the sun too long or being indoors, in the shelter that protects you, for too long. Too much of a good thing can become a bad thing. Moderation, moderation, moderation. But don't overdo it.

How it works

The same principle applies to strengths. Imagine that one of your strengths is strategic planning. You see opportunities around the corner and you put thoughtful and careful plans in place in order to make the most of those opportunities. This is a very valuable characteristic to possess. But if you're so strategic that you begin to see, or at least treat, people as commodities to be moved around like pieces on a chessboard, this strength becomes a weakness. You may make people feel as though you're using them but not actually caring about them. The quality of being strategic has an upside and a downside.

Or imagine that one of your strengths is your focus on people. Relationships are highly valued by you and your church. What a brilliant and important strength to have. This strength could become a weakness, though, if in your passion for people you begin to focus on what you can do to be liked and approved of instead of doing what's right. This strength can also turn into a weakness if you spend all your time with people and neglect the tasks of planning or organizing and so miss a whole boatload of opportunities that would have helped you love and help even more people. Or if your drive to focus on people leads you to set yourself up as a spiritual guru and cultivate relationships in which people depend on your opinion for making life decisions, this strength has become a dangerous weakness.

The sad thing is that these are some real-life examples. Strengths can be dangerous things and can lead people to end up in bad places. Everything has an upside and a downside. Being aware of the risks can help you avoid the dangers inherent in any strength or opportunity.

My point is not that you shouldn't get too good at anything and instead embrace safe mediocrity. Mediocrity has its own problems, and of course we should pursue our strengths and build on them. The point is simply to be aware that a strength can become twisted and transform into a weakness.

Be strategic, but avoid being clinical with people. Be relational, but avoid people-pleasing. Be aware of the dark side of every strength you have. Know where it can turn bad if you allow it to and be vigilant. Constantly check your motivations. Key questions to ask yourself honestly are: Am I using my strength to bring glory and recognition to myself or to God? Am I using this strength to help and serve others or is it only helping me? Everything has an upside and a downside. Find the upside and avoid the downside.

See also

14. Play to your strengths
47. Find the awesome

66 Numbers don't matter… except when they do

It's extraordinarily difficult to determine whether or not you're successful in ministry. For one thing, it's hard to figure out what to measure. How do you measure people's faith? How do you measure patience? How do you measure kindness? Even generosity, which you'd think might be easier to measure, is actually not as straightforward as it seems. Increase in giving per person doesn't actually indicate generosity, does it? A measure for generosity would have to take lots of other things into account as well, such as people's income and expenses, how generous a person is with their time, or how generous they are with discretionary income. What they give towards the ministry of the church would be a part of that generosity but it's not the whole picture.

The quest for affirmation

The old faithful measurement of success in ministry seems to be the number of people who attended. When ministers meet together, the first question they often ask is, "How many people are at your church?" Or "How many people come to your [insert ministry here]?" And even when it's not the first question, there's a sense that the other minister is, deep down, thinking about it and merely assessing the social landscape for the most appropriate time to ask. "Too early and I'll seem too eager. Too late and it'll be awkward."

When other ministers ask me this question I often wonder if they're asking so they can try to work out whether they're doing a good job or not. If my answer is a lower number than theirs they seem to be energized and can't wait to tell me their number. If my number is higher they seem to almost visibly deflate and they sheepishly tell me their number, as though it's some shameful sin they're confessing.

Numbers aren't great communicators

But here's the thing: the numbers don't tell you anything! They don't mean anything. So you have about 20 people who come to your youth group? That number doesn't tell you anything about whether you're doing a good job or not. Having 50 women come to your weekend away doesn't tell me anything about whether it was a success or not.

What if all 30 guys who came to your men's ministry came because you offered free beer? Does that tell you anything about whether or not you were successful? What if all 20 high-schoolers came to your youth group because you offered free beer?

What if 80 people showed up to your event but you probably should have had more like 400 come? The numbers themselves don't tell you anything. They don't tell you if you're doing a good job and they don't tell you that you're doing a bad job.

Imagine a ministry to 100 men. They run amazing events, everyone has a great time and raves about it, people write articles about the ministry, and they have really well-produced videos that they made themselves. And imagine that none of these men are Christians and, after four years of ministry, there is still not one Christian among these 100 men. Now imagine another ministry. There are four men. They meet to read the Bible and pray together. They laugh, they talk about life and family, they hold each other accountable for loving their wives and spending time with their kids, and they've been trained to minister to their friends and share the gospel. At the end of four years of ministry there were still only four men in the group. They had all led one person to Christ and all of them moved to different churches and are continuing to have a ministry to their unsaved friends. Which ministry would you prefer to be a part of? I know which one I want to be involved with.

The point isn't that big ministries are bad and small ones are good. The numbers could easily have been reversed and we could have talked about an effective big ministry and an ineffective small ministry. The point is that the numbers don't matter. They don't tell you whether or not you're being successful.

What's the point of comparison?

I understand why people always ask and want to talk about numbers. What other common metric can you use to give people a snapshot of what happened? And what other metric can you use to compare what you're doing with what someone else is doing?

There's nothing necessarily wrong with comparison. Too much can be stifling. Not enough can be myopic. In our world of social media we have comparison overload, and this overload can be paralysing. And yet comparison itself is healthy and proper. Comparison helps us to learn new things, find better ways, isolate problems more quickly, and identify solutions. But when you compare numbers all you're doing is comparing numbers. This ministry has more people in it than that one. My ministry has fewer people in it than his does. It doesn't tell you whose is better; it just compares the number of people in the room.

The point of comparison is not to try to figure out who's doing a better job, or to rank each other on a scale, or to find our value in being better than other people. The point of comparison is to learn better ways of doing things from others—to learn and to teach and to share. If I compare our two methods of training people in small groups and find that your way is better—more biblical and with better results in terms of what people learn—then great! I've learned a better way and I'll be more helpful in training people.

But comparing numbers doesn't lead you to learn or teach or share. Because numbers don't help you do any of those things.

And yet numbers do still matter. Just because they don't matter when it comes to judging success or the worth of the ministry or minister doesn't mean that they don't matter at all. The book of Acts is very deliberate about letting us know how many people joined the church early on in Jerusalem. Plus there's a whole book in the Bible about Numbers so they can't be all bad. Numbers matter because they represent people and because knowing the size of a group helps us to lead more effectively.

1. Numbers equal people

When you count attendance, every number that you count represents a person. And people matter. And the number matters because that number is a person. So if you're a church of 50 people, that matters because you're a church of 50 *people*, and those people matter and there are 50 of them. If you're a church of 1000 people, that matters because there are 1000 *people*. And when six people are converted, that's important not because it's six but because it's *people*.

2. Size matters

Over the years the church has been influenced and helped significantly by insights from secular research about the way small groups function. We've taken a lot of this wisdom onboard as we run small group Bible studies. This kind of thinking is common knowledge for most people in most churches. In a small group you have the joker, the know-it-all, the quiet person who says nothing, and so on. We know that sitting in a circle is best for group dynamics. Getting people to talk early in the meeting, through an icebreaker or something similar, better increases the likelihood that people will talk throughout the rest of the meeting. People are more likely to remember the things that they said than what other people said. So it's important to encourage everyone in the group to say something good and helpful by the end of the meeting so they'll remember at least one good thing from the group. None of these insights are in the Bible as far as I know, but they seem to be true of how small groups work—not just small groups studying the Bible, but any small group doing anything. And this wisdom has been helpfully incorporated into church small groups with great success and has become a kind of accepted and assumed knowledge.

The church has not been so quick and enthusiastic to incorporate insights from research about the way that large groups function. What we've often done instead is to try to apply these generally accepted principles about small groups to large groups. This has been far less successful, because large groups don't function the same way as small groups do. They actually function quite differently. And methods that work well for leading small groups are very often counterproductive for leading large groups.

For example, arranging the seats for a small group so that every person can easily make eye contact with every other person is a very important component of the planning for that group—and so a circle is the best option for the chairs. But imagine a Sunday morning service of 200 adults with the chairs set up in a huge circle. Intuitively you feel that would be a bad idea before you even try to articulate why it's a bad idea. People wouldn't be able to hear each other. People would disengage from the conversation. Part of the reason it's a bad idea is because in a large group the relationships of each person with every other person aren't a primary reason for meeting in the way they are in a small group. Those relationships still exist and are still important, but what's happening up at the front is the weightier reason for the large group's gathering. And so we arrange the seats to reflect that focus, hence rows facing the front. And this isn't a church-only insight. There's nothing in the Bible about this. This is drawn from sociology. This is how, people have observed, large groups of people generally behave.

So numbers matter because groups of different sizes function in different ways. And churches of different sizes function in very different ways too. These insights have been researched, described, and verified most thoroughly by Lyle Schaller, who has been a church consultant since the 1970s.[69]

Imagine that you have two churches, each with about 60 people in attendance on a Sunday. One is Anglican and the other Baptist. Putting aside theology for a moment, which may or may not make a big difference, let's focus on how these churches function. Those two churches will have more in common, and will function more similarly, than a 60-person Anglican church and a 600-person Anglican church. The leadership of these two Anglican churches will function in a completely different way, as will their decision-making processes, their welcome and integration of newcomers, how each church handles staffing issues, how they

69 Schaller discusses these issues in almost every book he writes, but he discusses them most fully in *Effective Church Planning* (Abingdon Press, Nashville, 1979), pp. 17-63. My favourite book of his is *The Multiple Staff and the Larger Church* (Abingdon Press, Nashville, 1980). Most of his books are out of print, but they are well worth tracking down. Find one that sounds interesting and fits your church size or the issues you're currently facing and give it a go. It'll be worth your time.

communicate internally, and a whole host of other factors. By contrast, the staff and members of the two 60-member churches from different denominations will have a lot in common and face similar issues and decisions.

Numbers matter not because bigger is better or smaller is better but because bigger and smaller are very different. Bigger isn't just smaller with more people. A big church is a totally different kind of thing—it's not like a smaller church is a pony, a medium-sized church is a racehorse, and a large church is like a draughthorse, basically the same but each one taking up more physical space than the last. They're actually three very different types of things.

When it comes to judging success or evaluating ourselves, numbers don't matter because they don't tell us anything. But numbers do matter because people matter and because every number represents a person who's valuable to God. Numbers also matter because groups of different sizes function quite differently. And so you need to make sure you're using the appropriate research and wisdom for the size group you're leading.

See also

26. Leading is loving
40. Team communication is exponential

67 Never waste a crisis

Life doesn't always go to plan. Regardless of what that plan is, of how carefully we make it, or of how well we think through our projections, life throws us curveballs. Sometimes they're minor and require only small course corrections. Sometimes, though, the difficulties are huge and we find the path we were travelling down completely blocked off so we need to find a completely new way to go. The plan we worked out so carefully simply will not work in these new circumstances and we find that we're in the midst of a crisis.

Maybe a key leader is stepping down or moving on, or the resources you'd counted on for a major project aren't available anymore, the facility you've planned on using for a major event is, at the last minute, unavailable, or someone on your team is facing some serious legal allegations. The list is endless, but the kind of ministry planning crisis we're talking about here is not a small annoyance or setback. A crisis is a big impediment in your way that you didn't, or couldn't, plan for. Maybe you brought on the crisis yourself, maybe it was caused by someone else, or maybe it's just one of those things that no-one really caused. What do you do?

In a crisis you have options

People's reactions in the face of crises differ widely—from indifference to frustration to despair. These are all natural reactions to a crisis and to carefully laid plans being rendered functionally useless. But the important thing to note is that they're not the only possible reactions. There are many ways you can choose to respond to a crisis. Crises present opportunities for you to step in and lead so long as you're willing to step up.

While crises often create frustration and blame, they also offer opportunities to think new thoughts and teach your team.

A crisis is a good time to remind people of what your goals are and what you are, deep down, trying to achieve. It's a good time to remind people of the vision. It's a good time to remind everyone that the plans and programs are the tools you're using to achieve your goals but that they aren't the goals themselves. A crisis is a good time to remind people that we trust in a sovereign God who always has things under control—even when we don't.

Crises can create creativity

A crisis creates constraints. Suddenly you have less time, or fewer people, or less money, or less of whatever it is that the crisis has taken away. Because the usual, obvious options are no longer available you can't just do what you always do and execute plan A. You might not even be able to execute plan B or plan C. This creates a certain amount of stress and pressure. But stress and pressure aren't necessarily bad. Though consistent and constant stress is damaging and tiring, small doses of stress and pressure created by constraints mixed with a dash of enforced creativity can be an extraordinarily energizing blend—as long as you harness it rather than allowing it to paralyse you.

While people often assume that creativity is maximized when we can think without constraints and entertain every option, we've seen that the opposite is often true. Contrary to popular opinion, constraints don't stifle creativity—they often enhance it.

Just as necessity is the mother of invention, so also constraints promote creativity. If all the obvious ways forward have been blocked off, it's going to take more creativity to find the less obvious, less intuitive ways forward. And sometimes, when a crisis means you can't choose the easy and obvious solution, you end up finding a better and unique option.

The question is not: How much has this crisis wrecked our plans? Instead, we should ask these kinds of questions in a crisis: How can we leverage this moment to move us towards our goal? What new opportunities does this situation create that didn't exist previously? What options that were always available to us, but were eclipsed by the obvious, can we now see? How can we use this as a time to help people?

Not all crises are created equal

I've been using the word crisis here as a way of talking about roadblocks to our plans. These are plans that, in the grand scheme of things, may not be that important. But what about a real crisis? A death? A disaster? A diagnosis? What about a real crisis? The principle still stands: don't waste a crisis.

The temptations in a real-life crisis are the same: to be frustrated, to despair, to blame, or to do nothing and not mention it and to move on, business as usual, as if nothing had happened. But crises present opportunities to step up and lead. Since crises are, hopefully, rare occurrences, they provide rare opportunities to love and lead people at unique moments in their lives.

In a life-threatening crisis people can be frustrated or despairing, and we want to be as helpful as possible and use the crisis as an opportunity to love them more, talk about deeper issues, and help them grapple and process and move forward.

The question in a real-life crisis is the same as the one we ask in a ministry planning crisis: How can we leverage this event to help people and retrieve as much good from this as we can and find unique opportunities?

Never waste a crisis.

See also

24. The way you view a problem often is the problem
25. Hopetimism
60. Creativity is a lost art
64. Learn relaxed concern
77. Bad news is good news

68 Opportunity does not equal obligation

Opportunities are deceptive. They often feel so urgent, so important. And because they're usually unique we often feel pressure to say yes to them. We don't want to waste or squander them. We want to capitalize on them. When we talk about a wasted opportunity we're generally referring to an opportunity that we didn't take. But that's not always the best way to look at it.

Though it is true that sometimes a wasted opportunity is one that we *didn't* take that would have helped us move forward with what we're trying to achieve, it can equally be true that a wasted opportunity is one that we *did* take that took us away from, or distracted us from, what we're really trying to achieve. A wasted opportunity might be one that siphoned resources away from an initiative that would have used those resources more effectively.

Opportunity does not equal obligation. Just because an opportunity comes up doesn't mean we must take it.

It's all about focusing on what you're trying to achieve. Will this opportunity help us go where we want to go or should we use those resources in our existing projects? If the opportunity helps us do what we want to do and go where we want to go, then we should think about taking it. If the answer to that question is no, then we should ignore the opportunity and get on with what we're trying to do.

Opportunities create artificial pressure

Opportunities are often only available for a limited time. And this countdown produces extra pressure—that feeling that we're going to miss out if we don't take this. But the fact that it's a once-in-a-lifetime opportunity is actually totally irrelevant. It may be a once-in-a-lifetime opportunity to jump forward towards our goal in a big way. Or it may be a once-in-a-lifetime opportunity to squander a whole lot of time and money on something that will take us sideways, away from the goal. But being once-in-a-lifetime is neutral. The opportunity itself is what matters and what we need to focus on. The idea that we may miss out on something makes us feel like we need to take it, and psychologically it plays in our heads like that. But the only thing that's relevant is moving forward with the mission.

The question is: Will the opportunity take us where we need to go, or will it be a fun and interesting waste of time that takes us away from where we believe God is taking us?

Opportunities do inflict a certain amount of psychological pressure—or perhaps it's pressure that we inflict on ourselves. We hear the ticking clock, feel the pressure of the once-in-a-lifetime factor, fear a wasted or missed opportunity. And we get so wrapped up in the decision that it's hard to be objective. And yet having a bit more objectivity is exactly what we need. Here are three tools to help you when the opportunity pressure is on.

1. Alternatives release opportunity pressure

In the early 1990s Shane Frederick was in the market for a new home stereo. He was agonizing over the choice between a $1000 Pioneer stereo and a $700 Sony. He stood in the store paralysed with indecision for over an hour, vacillating between both options, until a salesperson approached him with a question. The salesperson simply asked, "Well, think of it this way: would you rather have the Pioneer or the Sony and $300 worth of albums?" That question cut the Gordian knot in Frederick's mind. The extra features and the look of the Pioneer were enticing, but not nearly as enticing as $300 worth of new music.

They call this process an opportunity-cost analysis, and it's the first tool to help you evaluate the opportunities you encounter. It's about pinpointing what you will need to give up in order to make your decision. If you take this opportunity, what will the cost be? Hence the name 'opportunity-cost analysis'.

What stunned Frederick was that the question was so obvious but it hadn't even occurred to him to ask it. And it most likely never would have occurred to him had the salesperson not asked him. This intrigued him so much that he withdrew from his Masters program in environmental studies and switched to a PhD program in decision sciences.

He and his colleagues designed the following study to see if consumers instinctively made opportunity-cost analyses or not:

> Imagine that you have been saving some extra money on the side to make some purchases, and on your most recent visit to the video store you come across a special sale on a new video.[70] This video is one with your favorite actor or actress, and your favorite type of movie (such as a comedy, drama, thriller, etc.). This particular video that you're considering is one you have been thinking about buying for a long time. It is available for a special sale price of $14.99.
>
> What would you do in this situation? Please circle one of the options below:
>
> a) Buy this entertaining video
>
> b) Not buy this entertaining video[71]

The results of this survey were that 75% of people bought the video and only 25% passed on the opportunity. You'd probably make the same decision.

Later on the researchers gave a different group of people the same scenario, except this time they made a slight modification (printed in bold below):

> a) Buy this entertaining video
>
> b) Not buy this entertaining video. **Keep the $14.99 for other purchases.**[72]

70 For the sake of younger readers, a video is kind of like a DVD but lower quality. And we had whole stores that you actually had to go to in order to rent a video overnight that you then had to physically take back to the store the next day. Once you finished watching it you had to *rewind it* before you could watch it again. It was a savage world.

71 Heath and Heath, *Decisive*, p. 43.

72 Heath and Heath, *Decisive*, p. 43.

Surely that addition in bold is obvious and doesn't need to be said. It's even perhaps a bit condescending. Do people really need to be reminded that if they don't use their money to buy this they can use that money to buy something else?

Apparently the answer is yes. When that simple, almost stupid, addition was made to the question, 45% of responders decided *not* to buy the video. That one sentence almost *doubled* the number of people who passed on the opportunity to buy the video.[73]

I'm not saying that buying the video is necessarily a bad idea and that not buying it is the right thing to do. But the point is that most people didn't even register that the money could be used for other things unless it was specifically pointed out to them.

What this shows is that even considering the faintest hint of an alternative—*should we take this opportunity or should we do something else with the time, energy, money, and people*—can help us improve our decision-making when we feel the pressure of opportunities.

2. Get some distance

Another big problem with opportunities is the emotional attachment we develop. We really want this to work and for it to be true that this is the best way forward. So we begin to seek out information subconsciously that confirms this emotional bias. What we really need is a way to look again at the opportunity with fresh eyes.

Intel faced this same problem back in 1985. The then president of Intel, Andy Groves, talks about those days in his memoir *Only the Paranoid Survive*. Intel had been known for their production of memory chips, and for a long time they were the world's only memory chip manufacturer. But over time others entered the market and so there was more and more competition and the Japanese were beginning to produce memory chips that were being recognized as far superior to Intel's own.

In the late 1970s a small team at Intel had developed another product, the microprocessor. And so at this point in 1985 Intel was a company

73 The Shane Frederick story is retold from *Decisive* by Chip Heath and Dan Heath, pp. 42-4.

with two products—memory chips and microprocessors. They had built their company and their name on memory, but the memory business was beginning to haemorrhage both money and market share while the microprocessor side of the business was rapidly making gains.

Debate raged within Intel over how to respond to the Japanese competition. And, after many months, the executive team was exhausted and no closer to a decision.

Groves recalls sitting in his office one day with the then CEO Gordon Moore as they discussed what to do about the memory problem. Groves writes:

> I looked out the window at the Ferris wheel of the Great America amusement park revolving in the distance, then I turned back to Gordon and I asked, "If we got kicked out and the board brought in a new CEO, what do you think he would do?" Gordon answered without hesitation, "He would get us out of memories".
>
> I stared at him, numb, then said, "Why shouldn't you and I walk out the door, come back in, and do it ourselves?"[74]

What would our successors do? Why don't we just do that? It was the burst of perspective and clarity that they needed to break the weight of history and the emotional paralysis and the political pressure. Walk out and come back in.

Another researcher who has sought to understand why people irrationally intensify their commitment to pursuing losing courses of action is Barry M Staw. He says a good way to distinguish reasonable pursuit of an opportunity from overcommitment is to ask this question: "If I took over this job for the first time today and found this project going on, would I support it or get rid of it?"[75]

Groves and Staw give two different ways of asking the same thing. Both questions help you to gain distance and perspective on your decision.

74 Andrew S Grove, *Only the Paranoid Survive: How to exploit the crisis points that challenge every company*, Doubleday, New York, 1999, p. 89.

75 Barry M Staw and Jerry Ross, 'Knowing when to pull the plug', *Harvard Business Review*, March-April 1987, pp. 1-7.

3. Forget who is right and find what is right

Sometimes when opportunities present themselves the people on our teams are not going to be in agreement about how to respond. In these cases we need to allow people to be wrong without feeling that they're wrong. Often disagreements simply lead to people digging in with their position and defending it against all comers. The discussion becomes like trench warfare. Defending their position becomes tied up with defending themselves; who they are gets intertwined with taking this opportunity. This is extremely counterproductive. Business author and thinker Roger Martin observed this same recipe for disaster, where disagreements would "descend into adversarial position-taking"[76] which, in his opinion, is the single biggest obstacle for effective decision-making and strategy creation.

Read that last sentence again. The single biggest obstacle. If he's right, then that means this is one of the most important blockages that you need to overcome. But how do you do it?

Martin suggests that the way forward is to stop arguing about who's right and to instead take each option individually and ask: What would have to be true for this option to be the best choice? Surely, since we're all reasonable human beings, it's possible that there is a set of evidence that would convince us to change our minds. What would that set of evidence need to be?

This question changes the tone of the discussion. Instead of arguing, we're analysing. Instead of being adversaries, we're back to being on the same team trying to solve a problem together. It allows us to disagree without becoming disagreeable. It enables us to imagine a set of circumstances where we would change our minds about this opportunity without losing face or having to be 'wrong' or feeling as though we'd lost an argument.

Martin says, "This subtle shift gives people a way to back away from their beliefs and allow exploration by which they give themselves the opportunity to learn something new".[77]

Opportunities require discipline. It takes discipline to stay on task and let opportunities that look fun, exciting, and interesting pass you by

76 Roger Martin, 'My eureka moment with strategy', *Harvard Business Review: HBR Blog Network*, Watertown, 3 May 2010 (viewed 27 January 2015): http://blogs.hbr.org/martin/2010/05/the-day-i-discovered-the-most.html

77 Martin, 'Eureka moment'.

because they don't help you achieve your purposes. That kind of focus is difficult to maintain but is essential to long-term success. There are so many opportunities that come along—whether they're ministry opportunities or opportunities to partner with others or conferences to go to or promote—that we need to ignore the vast majority of them. We don't ignore them because they're bad, necessarily, but because even though they're good they don't help us do the things we're trying to do. The key is to be crystal clear on what it is you're trying to achieve and what your mission is, and then to pursue those things with rigorous focus.

Opportunity does not equal obligation.

See also

56. What are you trying to achieve?
58. Think in steps
71. Decide how decisions are made

69

Your people should be able to do a good impression of you

Suspicion of vision

Here's an honesty moment: sometimes I get sick of hearing about 'vision'. A vision for this. A vision for that. Do we have a vision? What's the vision? We need a vision.

And the more the word vision is used, the less interested I am. And you want to know the real tragedy?

I'm often the one who's doing the talking about vision.

But I often hear other people talking as if vision (whatever that is, exactly) is the secret key to everything and if you don't have an incredibly tightly crafted, yet impenetrable, sentence that encapsulates it then you'll never succeed. If you don't have a statement that sounds like you've used a thesaurus to replace every word then you'll never achieve anything good. Because heaven forbid your vision statement should sound like something a normal person would say.

Here are three vision statements. One is from a relatively well-known company and an online mission statement generator created the other two.[78] Can you spot which is the real one?

- Respect, integrity, communication, and excellence.
- Our job is to enthusiastically disseminate high-quality products in order to assertively facilitate cost-effective technology.

78 Try it yourself! It's both fun and sad at the same time: https://cmorse.org/missiongen/

- Our customers can count on us to professionally restore low-risk high-yield solutions while endeavouring to interactively revolutionize error-free services while promoting personal employee growth.

So many vision statements devolve into a stew of corporate buzzwords and empty aspirational phrases that don't inspire anyone and don't communicate what the organization does or is trying to do. The main thing most vision statements do, it seems to me, is produce opportunities for copious amounts of ridicule and cynicism.

But now that I've offended all the lovers and crafters of vision statements, let me go to the other side and offend the visceral vision statement despisers by saying that I actually like vision and the idea of vision statements. When they're done well, vision statements can be powerful tools to clarify what we're doing and rally people to the cause.

I think that the critical necessity of vision statements gets overplayed and that most vision statements are silly. I often wonder if maybe well-meaning people have been convinced to have a vision statement without really understanding what vision statements are for and what they're supposed to do.

By the way, the first out of the three vision statements above was the real one. It was the vision statement for Enron, one of the greatest examples of corporate fraud and corruption in history. It's a great example of how stupid and out of touch a vision statement can be and why they so often produce cynicism rather than enthusiasm.

The normalcy of vision

Having a vision is a very normal thing. Not a vision as in a vision from the Lord, like "The word of the Lord came to me at K-Mart..." but a vision of what you think you want to do next. It's just a fancy way of talking about where you're going or what you want the future to be like. You don't know the future—only God knows the future. But you have an idea of what you'd like the future to be like. You have an idea or a goal of what you think should happen. Though most people would call that a vision, some wouldn't. It doesn't matter what you call it.

It can be a specific idea, a vague idea, or a mundane idea. You might have a vision for what you'll make for dinner tonight. Mashed potatoes. That might not be a particularly inspiring vision, but it's a picture of the future that you're planning to arrive at. And it gives you some idea of the things you might need to do in order to get there: buy potatoes, for example.

You might have a vision for where you'll go on holidays: Next year we're going to Disneyland. That's a vision. It's what you want to see happen, where you're planning on going, what you think the future should look like.

So having a vision is normal and not a spooky, esoteric, big deal. Most people have some kind of vision for their lives. You probably have all kinds of visions for different facets of what you do and who you are. Sometimes it'll be big: When I grow up I want to be a marine biologist. Other times it's small: I need some new socks.

It doesn't need to be highly crafted and polished: I will intrepidly acquire high-quality low-cost manufactured woollen footwear in order to enable pain-free and blister preventing movement between multiple locations while ensuring maximum fashion-and-utility consciousness.

Sometimes buying new socks is just buying new socks.

The importance of vision

When it's just you by yourself, you don't really need to articulate your vision for new socks to anyone else. You just know you want new socks and then you work towards getting them. But when that vision has an impact on someone else, like a spouse, you may need to articulate it to them: "After work today I'm going to drop in to the shops and pick up some new socks". Your vision for the future might affect them because, for example, you might arrive home ten minutes later than usual. Your spouse might have a vision for the future that will dovetail with yours and will be mutually beneficial, for example: "While you're there, can you pick up some milk?"

It's the same when you're leading a team or a church. When you're leading a group of five or ten or 50 or hundreds or thousands, you need to articulate your vision for what you're doing and where you're going so that everyone knows what's going on and what they're supposed to be doing.

This is the real point of vision and vision statements. Clarity.

The point of articulating the vision is so that the people you're leading know where you're trying to go together. If they understand the vision they will know, in all of the details of the things they do, what the one thing is that they're ultimately doing. That's a vision.

Another reason it's good to have a vision is so that you can use it as criteria for how you should act in the present. Let's say your vision is that you want to arrive at the movie theatre on time to see the trailers. That's an idea of a preferred future, a vision. This is something we're probably all familiar with—going to the movies—but the difference is that we usually do it unconsciously and it feels foreign when we start thinking consciously about it.

Since you want to get there on time to see the trailers, you shouldn't swing past your parents' house on the way. That's crazy. They live an hour away and you'll never make it back in time. The movie starts at 8:00, so if you get there by 7:30 you'll probably have time to go to the shops to buy a drink. If you get there at 7:50 you'll probably have to buy a super-expensive drink from the candy bar. If the line's too long you'll have to either skip the drink or get someone else to buy it for you so that you don't miss the trailers.

And so on.

Your idea of what the future should look like helps you to make all kinds of decisions along the way about what you can and can't do. When you start getting distracted by the TV at home, the plan to see the trailers snaps you back into action and motivates you to turn off the TV and find your keys.

That's the power of a vision—or whatever you want to call your idea or goal for the future. That's why it's a good idea to have one.

You can have enduring visions that will always be there, something like: make disciples of all nations. That one's enduring. It won't change until Jesus comes back. But you might also have time-bound, or temporary, ones, like: start a new congregation, plant a church, or raise money to hire a new staff member. Those are all temporary ideas of a preferred future.

The reason people talk in such elevated terms about visions in organizations and churches is because clarity is so difficult to achieve. If you were to ask people in your team or your church "What is this church/ ministry trying to do?", how many answers do you think you'd get? It might be fun to ask some people and see what happens.

If you have a staff team, it might be interesting to ask them that question and have each person write down their answer. How many different answers do you think you'd get?

The point of vision, and the point of carefully articulating it and even writing it down, is to help everyone to be crystal clear about exactly what you're all doing and what you're trying to achieve and where you're all going and what the future you prefer looks like. A vision helps people get on the same page and stay on the same page. The more people there are, the more important it is to carefully articulate and even write down the vision.

This isn't a new idea. In 1986, an influential church leader named Lyle Schaller wrote this:

> Effective leaders rarely allow themselves to become captives of what others claim is the most urgent immediate issue. Many will argue that the two most crucial qualities in a leader are vision and the ability to inspire others to want to turn that vision into reality.[79]

Later, in 1992, he wrote that the number-one reason so many churches have become large churches...

> ...is not location or favorable demographics or seven-day-a-week programming or a particular theological stance. The number-one factor... is transformational leadership by a visionary pastor who knows how to rally people in support of a cause... In addition, these transformational leaders (1) can conceptualize a vision of a new tomorrow, (2) can articulate that vision so persuasively that people rally in support of it, and (3) know how to turn that vision into reality.[80]

79 Lyle E Schaller, *Getting Things Done: Concepts and skills for leaders,* Abingdon Press, Nashville, 1986, p. 261.

80 Lyle E Schaller, *The Seven-Day-a-Week Church*, Abingdon Press, Nashville, 1992, p. 58.

The point isn't to have a sentence full of buzzwords with way too many clauses and semicolons that you can hang up on a tapestry somewhere. The point is to articulate as clearly and simply as you can what you're doing and where you're trying to get to.

The repetition of vision

Bill Hybels has famously been saying for decades that "vision leaks".[81] And he's exactly right. One of the main problems people have with vision, apart from the fact that vision statements are often confusing and obtuse, is that they think once they've said it once and written it down everyone gets it and we can move on. But that's just not the case.

If the vision is my vision—I thought it up, I crafted it—I think about it every day. It lives in my head, it's almost always close to the front of my mind, and my job is to see it become a reality. So I think about it a lot.

But other people don't. The rest of the leaders on my team and the people at church don't wake up thinking about the vision and how to implement it. They wake up and go to work and live their lives and try to pay their bills and plan their holidays and worry about their kids, and the odds are good that my vision doesn't turn up on their radar at all during the week. It leaks out.

And different people have different-sized holes in their buckets where they keep my vision. Some people's buckets have lots of big holes, others have smaller holes, and some people's buckets feel like they're open cylinders so everything that goes in goes straight out again. My own bucket has holes in it as well. Sometimes even I forget the vision that was my idea! Even when we think about this picture of the future a lot, multiple times a week for long periods of time, it still leaks out of our heads. Most people that we lead aren't thinking about it that much and so they forget very quickly. Vision leaks.

It's like when you forget that you need to get going if you're going to make the movie on time. You sit on the edge of the chair to put your

81 "Most leaders think that if they fill people with vision once, they'll stay full forever. But that's just not true. Vision leaks, even out of our best people" (Bill Hybels, *Courageous Leadership*, p. 44).

shoes on and start watching a news story on TV. You get distracted, you forget, you lose your urgency. Vision leaks. Your idea of the future that you're trying to head towards fades from view and you focus on some other immediate concern.

This is why it's so helpful to be as clear as we can about our idea of the future. Vague is easy to forget and hard to communicate. So our ideas need to be as clear as they can be and we need to talk about them often so that we don't sit down and get distracted.

We need to keep talking about the vision over and over again. And over again. And when I'm starting to be bored by it that's probably when people are starting to vaguely remember it. Because I'm thinking about it a lot and I'm thinking a lot about how to communicate. Which means I'm going to get bored and familiar with it much faster than people who only hear it in short bursts and bites every couple of months.

You need to talk about your vision all the time. As often as you can. You need to be creative in how you do this. The time for talking about the vision isn't just in vision-casting sermons once or twice a year. It's not just in vision meetings. It's whenever you can—in conversations, in emails, in a sentence or two in sermons where it's appropriate, in announcements—everywhere you can as constantly as you can.

You need to articulate the vision often enough so that your people are able to do a good impression of you articulating the vision. They should be able to quote a key phrase, or a number of key phrases. When people can do a good impression of you, that's when you know you're doing well in communicating the vision. People are beginning to remember the sound bites.

This whole idea of vision becomes an art form when you're able to talk constantly and consistently about the vision without boring people. The challenge is to carefully craft sound bites that people can grab on to and remember without simply repeating the whole vision verbatim each time. You need to be able to speak about the vision so that it becomes familiar, repeating key ideas without being repetitive. You do that by talking about the exact same thing without always using the exact same words.

To repeat without being repetitive you'll have your cluster of key phrases that you do want to repeat and that you do want people to eventually memorize so they can do an impression of you. Then keep coming up with new ways to explain those sound bites. Keep harvesting stories that illustrate and illuminate those phrases from everywhere you can—books, TV, movies, history, other fields like science or psychology, stories from within your own church that embody the vision. Gather quotes from books and sermons from other preachers that reinforce the vision.

You keep repeating the vision sound bites and constantly find new ways to explain and fill out what they mean.

Vision is normal, and the point of it is to provide clarity for everyone on what exactly you're seeking to accomplish. You probably already have some ideas about where you think the people you lead need to get to in the future. You're already taking them somewhere. You might just need to spend some time clarifying and articulating what you've been doing by instinct. And because vision leaks you'll need to talk about it over and over and over again. Your people need to be able to do a good impression of you. When you start to see that happening you know you're on the right track. That impression is not the sign to stop or slow down—you haven't reached the destination. That impression is a guidepost that tells you you're on the right track. Repetition without being repetitive.

See also

33. Communicate from the inside out
55. The point is clarity, not labels
56. What are you trying to achieve?
59. Hold hands with your programs

70
Ignore the org-chart

As you start this chapter you might be thinking, "Hey, great! Ignoring the org-chart will be easy. I don't have one. I don't even know what one is!" Well, let's go back a step.

Everyone has an org-chart

An org-chart is a visual representation of the people in your organization and how they're grouped and who is responsible for whom. So if there's more than one of you in your organization you have an org-chart. It might not be written down on a piece of paper, but it exists.

Typically an on-paper org-chart will have the key leader or the point leader at the top of the page. Under him or her will be all the people who report directly to that person and for whom that person has a primary responsibility to care. Under their names, the chart will show all of those for whom those people are responsible. And then, depending on how many people are in your organization, the layers will continue downwards.

Your org-chart might not exist as a physical piece of paper or even as a document on a computer, although maybe it does. Whether it exists in one of those forms or not, the point is that your church will have some set layers of responsibility. People who answer to other people. Teams of teams led by leaders of leaders. And you'll have this whether you want it or not and regardless of whether you designed it on purpose or it happened by accident.

For example, you might have a person who's responsible for music during the Sunday service. You and this person pick songs, talk music, and debrief about how it's going at church. Then that person runs the Sunday morning music team. That's a three-layer org-chart right there: you, the music person, the music team.

You might have a group of key staff members who report to you, and each of them might have paid staff members who report to them, and those staff members might have a mix of paid staff and unpaid volunteers who report to them and who each lead teams of volunteers. In other words, you might have a deep and complex org-chart. If that's the case, it's more likely that yours exists visually and physically.

Every organization will organize its people in some way. Every organization will have an org-chart. They're a very good thing and they will help you run with clear roles and responsibilities and will help your people know who they need to take orders from and who has the final say on different decisions.

Org-charts don't make the decisions

But org-charts are a tool. Org-charts don't set the agenda. Like lots of things, they're good tools but terrible masters.

When you call meetings you should ignore that org-chart.

Sometimes we feel that our meetings should include everyone in the layer below us. They're our direct reports and they should be in the meeting. But this kind of thinking is letting the org-chart dictate the terms. The org-chart doesn't make the decisions, you do. So before you call a meeting, stop and consider the purpose of the meeting.

Is the purpose of the meeting to update everyone on what the team is doing? Or is the point of the meeting to plan some specific piece of the ministry, perhaps an event? Or is the point to solve a problem or make a decision, perhaps to do with finances?

Find the best brains

Once you've clarified the purpose of the meeting you can start thinking about who would be best to have present at this meeting. What kinds of expertise would be helpful? What kinds of experience would be helpful? What kind of thinkers would be helpful—a creative thinker or a strategic thinker? A visionary or a details person? A risk-taker or a more risk-averse person? All of the above?

You need to give yourself the freedom to invite the best people for the purposes of that particular meeting, regardless of where they are in the organization. If you're at the head of the org-chart you will have the most freedom here. If you're further down towards the middle of the org-chart you probably have some more constraints as to the people you're free to include in your meetings, but you should still think about the entire group of people you have in your circle.

The best people to have at the meeting might not be the people who report directly to you. Or maybe some of them are and some of them aren't. You need to create a culture where, when you invite some and not others, the people who aren't invited don't interpret that as an insult or as a lack of confidence. If all of your direct reports are brilliantly pastoral, caring, and people-focused but struggle or get easily bored by numbers and spreadsheets, then why would you invite them to the budget-planning meeting? And if your direct reports are details people, why would you invite them to the strategic-vision-five-year-plan meeting?

If some of your direct reports are the best people for the meeting then invite them. And if others aren't, then don't invite them to this meeting. And if some people two or three layers below you are best for the meeting, then you need to feel comfortable to reach down into the organization and invite them.

The point is to have the best brains for the purposes of each specific meeting.

Leadership development

The other reason to ignore the org-chart and to be free to invite all the people you think should be at the meeting is so that you can introduce junior leaders to higher-level leadership discussions.

There will often be leaders lower down in the organization who you think may one day be a good choice to lead other leaders or teams of leaders. People who have potential but who aren't ready yet for that responsibility. It's a good idea to begin inviting them to some appropriate meetings where they can learn. This way you can expose them to bigger or wider discussions. You introduce them to other leaders. They can start getting a feel for whether or not they enjoy leading at that level and it gives you a chance to watch them and see how they interact and think and contribute to those meetings.

Ignoring the org-chart means you can turn your meetings into a training opportunity for lower-level leaders. You wouldn't want to have everyone in the meeting be training from a lower level, but if you have a few they will be able to learn without compromising the quality of decisions.

Who and how to invite

The general principle is to only invite people below you and connected to you in the org-chart. So you shouldn't invite someone from across the org-chart. That is, people who belong to a team run by a peer, someone on the same org-level as you, should be left alone unless you really, really want them in your meeting. If this is the case, you should speak to their leader first and ask permission. Down from where you are is fine. Across requires express permission and should be done sparingly.

Here's what it would look like to invite down the org-chart instead of across. This principle means that the children's minister can invite anyone *down* within children's ministry to his or her meeting. But the children's minister shouldn't reach *across* to the youth ministry and invite people from there to the meeting. This should only be done if it's absolutely necessary and only after asking that person's leader. Down is good, across is bad.

This means that if you're the leader at the top of the org-chart—if you're the senior minister or equivalent point leader of your organization—then you should be free to invite anyone in the organization to any meeting you hold and you should also be free to not involve anyone you like in any meeting you run.

If you are the senior minister, it's also your responsibility to create this culture in your church. You set the tone and the agenda and you model to the entire church how meetings are run and whether or not it's acceptable to invite people to meetings because of their titles alone or because of what they contribute.

Handle with care

What if other leaders in the org-chart are hurt or offended by this process? What if they feel hurt that they weren't included? Or what if they're offended because you invited one of their team members to a meeting with your team?

If they're hurt that you didn't invite them, the way forward is to have a conversation with them and to check what's going on. Check with them in case you did say or do something that was hurtful—and if you did, apologize immediately. Perhaps they *should* have been involved in that meeting, and if that's true then assure them that it was a mistake and that you'll make sure they're included next time. However if they're upset because they believe they should have been at the meeting since they report directly to you, you'll need to carefully and gently explain that that's simply not how it works—or at least not anymore. Explain that no-one has a right to be at a meeting and that you, as the leader, need to have the freedom to have all the people you think best at your meetings. Explain that there's nothing personal, assure them of your respect and trust, remind them that you value them, reassure them that this isn't the first sign that you're preparing to remove them (unless you are, of course), and let them know that there will be other meetings where their insight and experience will be needed, but that this wasn't that meeting. You could also explain that not inviting them to this meeting wasn't because you don't value them but because you *do* value them and their time, and because their focus is not in the area of this particular meeting you knew that wasn't going to be the best use of their time.

If this culture doesn't exist within your whole church and you aren't the senior leader you can still create this culture in the patch for which you're responsible. Where you have authority you have the potential for creating culture. Just begin reaching down from where you are and involving the right people in the meetings that you lead. One of the best ways to influence those above you is to take what you think should be done across the church and to scale it down and create it in your area of responsibility. And then when the women's ministry begins flourishing and you're getting the best minds around the table to tackle your problems and decisions and you start making good decisions and creating a rumble, others will ask what it is you're doing. And then you'll have some capital to influence how others run their meetings.

But just because it doesn't happen above you doesn't mean it can't start with you and so happen below you. And while it's true that culture normally and most easily flows downstream, from the senior leaders down to the frontlines, this isn't always the case. Normal doesn't mean always. Culture creation can flow upstream. It takes longer and is less certain because there are lots of factors working against it, but it can happen. You can change the culture of your church from the middle of the org-chart.

Org-charts are good things. But when you plan your meetings you should invite the best people for the meeting, not the people with the titles or who happen to be at a certain level. When it comes to meetings, ignore the org-chart.

See also

47. Find the awesome
56. What are you trying to achieve?
63. Meetings are where real work is done
74. Be an agent of disorganization

71
Decide how decisions are made

A lot of leadership is about making decisions. When we talk about being a leader this is often simply another way of saying that you're willing to make decisions. People will look to the leader to make the decision, and conversely if you put yourself forward as one who's willing to make decisions people will begin looking to you as a leader. Whether or not you're a good leader or make good decisions is another question. But making decisions is what a leader does, and being willing to make decisions means you're willing to be a leader.

Unfortunately, leaders sometimes begin to think that leadership means making decisions on his or her own. They decide that leadership is unilateral decision-making and that real leaders make decisions without advice or consultation.

This is a mistake—a tempting mistake, but a mistake nonetheless. When you see a problem that needs to be solved, it might seem obvious to you how to fix it and you might be tempted to make the decision and then announce to your team what you're going to do about it. It seems a very efficient way to solve a problem. But when you're working in a team, efficiency isn't your number-one aim.

There will be lots of decisions that you will need to make on your own, either because they need to be made very quickly or because they're simple and mundane decisions. But when the problem is complex or vague, when there are people who are closer to the problem than you are, when a solution will affect a group of people, or when a decision will mean changing something that was already discussed and decided upon, you should bring others into the decision-making process.

Involve others in the process

Whenever possible, as long as the problem isn't a crisis that requires an immediate decision, involve your team in solving the problem and making the decisions. Get their input on the problem, identifying and clarifying exactly what the problem is. Get their input on options for how to solve it. Use the brains, experiences, and expertise of the people around you. Whenever possible, involve other people in the decision-making process.

There are plenty of benefits to doing this. First, your team will provide insight on the issue at hand. They might know some information that you don't. They may have experienced something similar before and have some wisdom on actions to avoid. They might understand the contributing factors at a deeper level than you do. They may think up a solution that would never have occurred to you.

Second, if your team is involved in the process of creating the solution to the problem then they will be onboard and much more inclined to help implement that solution than they would have been had you simply dropped the solution on them from on high. This sense of ownership then functions as internal motivation for the team members as they move forward to make it work.

Third, when you show your team that you value their insight and input in a real-time problem with real consequences they will know in a tangible way that you appreciate them. For team members who might be feeling a bit useless or demotivated, simply being involved in the discussion may provide that kick of enthusiasm they need as they see that their time and contributions to the team are valued and useful.

Involving others in problem-solving and decision-making will help you not only to make better decisions but also to make better team members.

It would be very unusual, however, for you to make *every* decision in this way. Sometimes this kind of process is simply not realistic because of the situation you're in or because your team members might not have the kind of expertise necessary to help solve this particular problem. If the issue is a financial one, for instance, and this specific team doesn't have the financial acumen to be of any real assistance, you might ask them to be involved in part of the process but not all of it. Other times there may not be time for this kind of process. Not every problem can be solved in this way. Some decisions require more speed or a restricted circle of input based on expertise or experience. You may instead pull in an ad hoc team whose members will add value to the decision-making process in this instance. But, where possible, problem solve as a team as often as you can.

When you include a team in the decision-making process it will be important to clarify how the decision will be made. They have come and you want their opinions, experience, and expertise. But how exactly will they be involved in making the decision? People will come to the meeting with varying assumptions and it will help if you clarify the process so that there are no surprises later on.

There are three main ways a decision can get made: you can have a majority vote; the leader can decide; or you can go with a consensus. Different situations and dynamics will call for different processes. Whichever process you plan to use, the most important part is that you make it clear so that people know the rules and what to expect.

Let's look briefly at each of these three major ways of reaching a decision and the benefits and downsides of each one.

Majority vote

In a majority vote you propose two or three options—or any number of options, but realistically two or three genuine options will be enough—and then every person votes for the option they think is best. Whichever option gets the most votes is the decision that is made.

The benefit of this process is its clarity, because it makes space for multiple options and alternatives. It also gives each person equal weight in the decision-making process. This levelling dynamic can be very helpful if you have a team where one person holds a great deal of power but perhaps doesn't always use it to do what is best for others. Or maybe one or two people have a lot of power and often use that power to make decisions that go against the wisdom of the room. And maybe their decisions more often than not turn out badly. In order to counteract this scenario you might use a majority vote to level the playing field by redistributing power somewhat.

While it does give everyone an equal say at the table, the downside is that with this process you will be least likely to get full support from the team for the final decision. This is because a vote will necessarily split the team into winners and losers—those who voted for the winning option and those who didn't.

In some circumstances, though, in some teams and for some decisions, there are others factors in play so that agreement isn't the top priority.

Leader decides

The second broad option is that the leader decides. In this scenario the team leader makes the final decision after input from the team. This can work very well as long as everyone in the team has a chance to put forward their case and there's enough time allowed for a sufficient discussion to take place so that people feel they're heard. Each option is weighed and considered. Then, once alternatives have been canvassed and outliers have been discarded, the leader chooses one of the remaining options as the final decision.

The strength of this option is that you can dream up and discuss multiple options without anyone needing to pin their flag to the mast only to have that idea later 'rejected'. Instead people can love all the ideas or see the flaws in each without needing to commit their ego to one option over against others.

The other strength of this approach is that politics and personality are minimized. In a majority vote people can be tempted to ally themselves to a powerful person rather than rallying to the best idea. This can often happen unconsciously and, while it can still happen in a situation where the leader decides, it is rarer and less powerful an influence because people aren't forced to choose a side.

This process requires that the team have a fair degree of trust in the leader so that when that leader makes the call the team can unite around that decision. There are two common danger points with this process, and if either of them is present there's strong potential for negative consequences. This process will be dangerous if the team has a low level of trust in the leader and/or if the leader wants or needs to decide against the wisdom of the team. If either of these danger points exists and isn't addressed there will probably be dissatisfaction and resentment amongst the team.

The leader doesn't necessarily need to do what the group collectively thinks should be done—it depends on what rules you set up at the start. As the leader you can always decide against the wisdom of the team, but it requires careful thought on your part. The key is to be conscious and careful when you set up the decision-making rules to begin with and then you need to make sure you honour those rules. If you set up a majority vote decision-making process but then veto the decision, the rest of the team will not, understandably, take this well because you've broken the rules and cheated. If, however, it was always set up as a decision the leader would make then there's no breach of trust when the leader makes the final call.

The other version of this option is when the leader makes the decision with little or no input from the team. As we discussed earlier, there are times when this is necessary and legitimate—such as when there's a crisis and therefore little time for discussion. But making decisions this way also requires a high level of trust from your team, and even then you wouldn't want to use it too often if you didn't absolutely need to.

Consensus

The last broad option for decision-making is consensus. This option is often misunderstood. Consensus doesn't mean unanimity, and although it can mean this it doesn't only mean this. Consensus means that, as the discussion has taken place, the vast majority of the room has become sufficiently convinced that one of the options is the best way forward. In a consensus decision, everyone in the room is convinced that this option is at least as good as any other and is happy to get 100% behind it as the way forward and do everything they can to make it work, even though they may prefer a different option. The leader then acknowledges the consensus and declares the decision official.

The difference between consensus and leader decides, as defined here, is that when the leader decides, the final call is expressly in the hands of the leader. In consensus, by contrast, the best option is allowed to rise to the surface as discussion progresses and then it's officially recognized by the leader as the decision.

The obvious downside of consensus is that you leave the team extremely vulnerable to 'groupthink', which we'll speak about in a moment.

In the real world of decision-making the discussion doesn't always work out as neatly as it's described here. It may be more likely that you begin by aiming for consensus, and then when it becomes clear that consensus isn't going to be achieved you settle for leader decides. This isn't a horrible outcome or a sign of a poorly run meeting or poorly reached decision. It's just how things go sometimes, and in that case you should make the decision, thank people for their input and energy, and move on.

The dangers of yes

No matter which approach you plan to use, your job as the leader is to make sure the best decision gets made. The challenge is that including more people doesn't guarantee that a better decision will be made. The majority isn't always right, the status quo is a powerful force against new and innovative ideas, and decisions made by committees can sometimes be less sharp and bold due to people and leaders wanting to please every constituency represented rather than doing what is right or best.

As a general rule, people are most likely to be motivated and enthusiastic about ideas with which they agree. Which means that the more you can get people to agree on a decision the more likely those people are to own it and put effort into accomplishing it. It's difficult to get people to dedicate the same level of energy to a decision they disagree with as they would towards a decision they passionately agree with.

The other side to this equation is that healthy conflict and disagreement make ideas better. An idea gets sharpened and shaped as the room bats it around and knocks off weak or poorly conceived facets and refines the idea as a team. The idea improves in the back and forth. Unanimous agreement can actually be a sign that a bad decision is about to be made. This phenomenon is known as 'groupthink'.

Psychologist Irving L Janis first scientifically mapped out the idea in 1972. Janis was trying to understand why a group can make a great decision on one occasion and then make a horrible decision the next. What he found was that a lack of disagreement and discussion of opposing ideas or points of view led teams to make bad decisions because alternative proposals were being ignored or sidelined. The sinking of the Titanic and the US Bay of Pigs fiasco are examples of groupthink leading smart people to make disastrous decisions.

Groupthink is a bad thing that happens for good reasons. People are striving for group cohesion and for consensus, not wanting to be negative contributors or to disagree with someone they like and make that person look inferior in front of their boss or peers. These are good and kind impulses. But they override other good desires such as finding the best solution for the problem people are facing or providing solid alternatives or critiquing a less-than-perfect option.[82]

If a leader gets the sense that groupthink is beginning to creep in, that people are just agreeing so as to not be disagreeable, or that people aren't thinking about alternatives, it's a good idea to postpone the decision and name the groupthink problem.

It may also be the case, however, that as the idea is batted around by the group it gets worse—less focused and more sloppy—instead of getting better and more refined. New facets that perhaps don't really belong on the decision get bolted on to its sides and the idea just gets more unwieldy in the process.

Including your team is no guarantee that a good decision will be made. Whichever process you use, your job as the leader is to make sure that the best decision is made, so you need to play an active role in ensuring this happens.

Regardless of which of the three decision-making options you use, the final factor you need to clearly establish is what happens once the decision is made. People have to agree that, once the decision is made, discussion and dissenting are over. The team must agree to do everything they can to make the decision work, contributing the same level of energy they would have if it had been their own idea. They must also agree to publicly defend the decision against critics. Every team member doesn't

82 McRaney, *You Are Not So Smart*, pp. 127-30.

need to agree that the decision is the best decision, but they need to agree to implement the decision with everything they've got once the decision has been made. Discussion and disagreement are fine as the decision is being made. In fact, they're necessary in order for the final decision to be the best it can be. But once the decision is made the team needs to agree to cease discussion and disagreement and begin enthusiastic deployment.

Leadership isn't about always having all the answers and making all the decisions. Initiating the discussion, clarifying the issues, and then activating the implementation of the plan—even if others who know better than you developed the plan—is all the work of leadership.

See also

27. You're just the leader
41. Two foundations of team-building
44. Choose your lieutenants

72
Hellos and goodbyes matter

Meetings are some of the most important gatherings that happen in a church. And I don't mean Sunday church services. I mean meetings like parish council meetings, staff meetings, or other meetings of ministry leaders. Running good meetings is a key skill for a leader because good meetings are a key part of any ministry that functions well. Two of the most often overlooked aspects of running a good meeting are what happens at the very start of the meeting and what happens at the very end.[83]

It's easy to overlook the obvious

It's often noted that you need to think carefully about how you'll open a meeting, in the same way you work hard to craft the opening of a speech or talk or sermon. You need to capture people's attention and engage them in the first 30 seconds. You need to explain why the meeting is valuable and why what you're going to talk about or decide upon is worth the time you're all about to spend on it. And this is true—it's important to set the right tone and engage people at the official start of the meeting.

It's also often noted that how you end the meeting is important. You need to recap what you've discussed and decided. You need to make sure that each task has been assigned and that each person knows what their responsibilities are, when their tasks are due, who they're responsible to, and so on. And all that is true as well.

83 I first read this insight in Bill Hybels, *Axiom*, pp. 96-7.

But those aren't actually the first or the last things you do at the meeting. The first thing you do is greet people as they arrive. And the last thing you do is say goodbye to people as they leave. Both of these activities are very important and both are easy to overlook because they seem so obvious. But hellos and goodbyes are critical and they can be done well or badly.

Necessary pieces

It's simple to make the most of these key meeting bookends, and even though they might seem obvious it's worth pointing out three key points.

1. In order to greet everyone as they arrive you'll need to be there early enough so that you can actually do that. This communicates to people that the meeting is important, that you honour their commitment to being on time, and that you value their time enough not to waste it by being late.

2. Capitalizing on the beginning means that you need to personally greet every person as they arrive, at least saying their name and perhaps shaking their hand. You want to acknowledge them and show them that you're genuinely glad that they're there. It helps if you've already set up and photocopied everything you need for the meeting because you got there early enough to make sure it happened. But even if that part hasn't worked out as well as you'd planned, you can still greet everyone as they arrive while you set up. It just takes a little more focus and attention to look out for new arrivals as you're setting up.

   As more and more people arrive, greeting new arrivals becomes more difficult because you'll strike up conversations with those who are already there. People may have some items to discuss with you before the meeting officially begins. So you need to either keep watching the door in your peripheral vision or be conscious to face the door during conversations so that you can continue to greet people as they arrive while still maintaining the conversation.

3. Similarly, at the end of the meeting, making the effort to say goodbye to each person as they leave will again communicate that

you appreciate them, their time, and their contributions to the meeting. This is especially important if the meeting was tense or heated, or if there was some 'healthy and robust discussion' during which people publicly disagreed with each other or with you. After these kinds of meetings people will sometimes fear that the disagreement has harmed their relationship with you, or that disagreement over ideas means a more profound disagreement between people as people. By personally saying goodbye, thanking people for their input, and smiling you signal to them that the relationship is still okay and that you value them and their input. You'll be able to put them at ease, at least somewhat, as they leave.

Saying hello and goodbye properly is incredibly important. While it's fairly easy and obvious, it does take an extra level of concentration and effort to make it happen.

See also

41. Two foundations of team-building
46. People deserve to know the truth
53. Free volunteers aren't cheap
63. Meetings are where real work is done

73

Red Queen syndrome: a nine-step process for implementing change

Of all people on the planet, Christians should be able to cope with change better than anyone. We've been transferred from the kingdom of darkness into the kingdom of the Son. We're being transformed from one degree of glory to another. We're being conformed into the likeness of the Son in and through all things. The Christian life is all about change; it starts with a huge change of allegiance and keeps going from there. And as Christian leaders we're in the business of change. We're about seeing people's status and relationship before God change through the power of the gospel and the work of the Spirit. We're about seeing people's lives changed as they begin to live out the implications of their faith in greater depth and in more areas of their lives. And we're about seeing the way we organize what we do change in order to be more effective in reaching people with the love and message of Jesus. Change is what we do and who we are. And yet churches often seem to find it harder to accept change than almost any other group or organization—whether it's changing the colour of the carpet or the style of music or the clothes worn by the minister or the programs being run. People don't always like change, sometimes they fear it, and churches are no different.

It's not just those 'other people', though—whoever they are. It's us too. It's leaders as well. We can sometimes find it very difficult to change. Admittedly it's easier when the change is our idea. But how do you react when someone above you forces change on you? We don't always process it that well. And yet change is often a good, and even necessary, thing.

The Red Queen and the white post

In Lewis Carroll's *Through the Looking-Glass,* Alice and the Red Queen are running hand in hand, very fast, and still the Queen keeps yelling, "Faster!" In this strange scenario, no matter how fast they run they never manage to pass any of the trees or other parts of the landscape. It's as if they're running to stand still. When they finally stop, Alice protests:

> "Well, in our country... you'd generally get to somewhere else —if you ran very fast for a long time as we've been doing."
>
> "A slow sort of country!" said the Queen. "Now, here, you see, it takes all the running you can do, to keep in the same place. If you want to get somewhere else, you must run at least twice as fast as that!"[84]

This is why change is necessary. We need to be changing all the time just to stay where we are. We need constant change, constant improvement, and constant innovation just to maintain. We need to run as fast as we can just to stay where we are. This is the Red Queen syndrome.

When you first create something, say a program or an event, it often takes a lot of time and effort to craft it so it's exactly the way you want it. So by the time it's the way you want it you're probably a bit exhausted from the thinking and planning and are just happy to let it run while you take a break or concentrate on something else. But the Red Queen syndrome suggests that once you resign yourself to keeping your program like it is, it has already begun the slide into decline.

There are at least two reasons for this. The first reason is that every ordered system tends towards chaos. It wants to fall apart; it wants to stop working. Every system needs constant attention in order to keep functioning properly. Just like a car needs constant servicing so it will continue to work well and not break down, so ministries and churches also need constant attention so they will continue to work well and not break down.

The second reason our programs and ministries need to be constantly changing is because the world around us is also constantly changing—

84 Carroll, *Alice's Adventures in Wonderland & Through the Looking-Glass*, p. 135.

and at a rapid pace. This means that what worked yesterday may not work as well today. And what is relevant today may not be as relevant tomorrow. Think of the technology industry and how quickly items become obsolete. Our programs will quickly become obsolete as well without constant and thoughtful attention and change.

This doesn't mean, of course, that we should change our message in order to be relevant—although maybe that assumption isn't always as 'of course' as I think it is. Constant change doesn't mean we change the message. But what it does mean is that as our world changes around us we need to constantly change *how we deliver* that message. Whether it's using electric lights instead of candles or indoor plumbing or off-street parking or a data projector, we're constantly changing the processes and tools we use. We constantly change how we communicate the unchanging message.

The great GK Chesterton put it memorably when he said:

> Conservatism is based upon the idea that if you leave things alone you leave them as they are. But you do not. If you leave a thing alone you leave it to a torrent of change. If you leave a white post alone it will soon be a black post. If you particularly want it to be white you must be always painting it again; that is, you must be always having a revolution. Briefly, if you want the old white post you must have a new white post.[85]

When people argue so strongly for keeping things the way they are what they're actually arguing for is the illusion of continuity—because if you keep things the same they won't stay as they are. Change will happen whether you want it to or not so you might as well plan for it.

The difficulty of bringing change

Knowing that change is a good and necessary thing isn't the same as being able to introduce change well. Just acknowledging that change needs to happen—sometimes the changes needed will be big and sweeping and other times small and incremental—doesn't make it any easier. It's hard

85 GK Chesterton, *Orthodoxy*, Waterbrook Press, Colorado Springs, 2011, p. 171.

enough to convince yourself that change is necessary; being able to do something about it is even harder. This is partly because everyone finds change hard and will resist it to some degree. But it's also because, as leaders, we often don't know how to introduce change and so we do it clumsily and make it more painful than it needs to be—which only makes it even more difficult to introduce change the next time, and the time after that, and so on.

Bringing about change is always difficult and is never without pain. And the process for introducing change is more complicated than we think it is. From what I've observed, it seems leaders often think introducing change is basically a three-step process:

1. Decide change needs to happen.
2. Tell people it's happening.[86]
3. Do it.

This process may work when the changes in question are miniscule and unnoticeable. But when the changes are significant and people are heavily invested in the program or ministry that will be changing, the above process is clumsy and naive. Helping people successfully navigate change is much more complicated than this three-step process. Introducing and successfully implementing change is difficult, and the bigger and more wide-ranging the change the more difficult it is.

But Christian leadership is often about change. Whether we're helping individuals change, changing programs, or even changing the mindsets of a whole group of people, Christian leaders are always at work changing things. If change is so constant and such a central part of our work, it makes sense to try to figure out how to maximize the success of our plans while also minimizing the pain.

Nine steps for better change

The following nine-step process for change is based on the work of a number of different authors. I have integrated, adapted and modified this

86 Optional.

material through my own experience in navigating change initiatives—sometimes successfully and other times unsuccessfully. Even when I did an absolutely horrible job at times I learned valuable lessons and share the wisdom gleaned from those experiences here.[87]

These nine steps don't guarantee success, and following them won't ensure a painless process. But what they will do is make the change initiative far more likely to succeed and less painful along the way.

Before we dive into the specific details of navigating a change process here are some broader, overall rules for the change game:

1. You need patience and discipline. When you know things need to change you'll want to move quickly—and you should move quickly. But moving quickly should never mean skipping one of the steps or starting the next step before you've nailed the previous one. Make sure you follow every step and move through them in order.
2. Work hard early on when it feels like nothing is happening. The stronger your foundation, the easier the later stages will be. Things don't actually start changing until you get to step five. This means that for almost half the steps in the process you won't actually be changing anything and it will feel like nothing is really happening. The temptation will be to skip through these steps quickly so that you can start doing something and seeing results. But resist this temptation because a lot *is* happening and what's happening is important. If you burn through the first four stages because you're impatient to get to the bit where you're actually changing things it will make every subsequent stage both harder and less likely to stick. If you don't have many allies, or they're the wrong people, or you don't have them at all levels, everything else will be more difficult and less likely to be accepted. Build a strong foundation in the first steps of the process.

87 John P Kotter, *Leading Change*, Harvard Business Review Press, Boston, 2012; Chip Heath and Dan Heath, *Switch: How to change things when change is hard*, Broadway Books, New York, 2010; Heath and Heath, *Decisive*; and Joseph Grenny et al., *Influencer: The new science of leading change,* 2nd edn, McGraw-Hill, New York, 2013.

3. Everyone experiences change as a loss in some way. For some people change will be a bigger loss than for others. The change will impact some people very close to their core concerns. For some it will just be a minor inconvenience while for others it will fundamentally transform how their world works. The difference will be in degree, not in kind. Everyone involved will experience any change as a loss to some degree. You need to know this and be prepared for it.

With these ground rules in mind, here's the nine-step process for giving any change you want to make the best shot of succeeding.

1. Create urgency

If you want to see something change you most likely have a good reason for it. You think it will be worth the effort to make it happen. But just because you know it and feel it doesn't mean that anyone else knows it or feels it. If all change is hard, and at least a bit painful, then people will need a good reason to come with you. You need to help people see and understand why this change is critically important and how the pain of maintaining the status quo will be worse than the pain of change. People need to be convinced that it's urgent.

Why change now? What are the threats if we don't change? What problems do we avoid if we change? What are the future scenarios you're envisaging that this change will help us avoid? What opportunities are there that we need to exploit? What are the opportunities that we need to grab hold of but that we will lose if we don't change now?

Begin having some honest conversations with people about these questions. Make sure they're honest and make sure they're conversations. Do your best to help people see what you see. People need to see the point and understand what you understand.

Leaders often skip or rush through this step. Most other people aren't thinking about what's happening at church all the time. They're thinking about their jobs and paying bills and what's happening with the kids and getting the car serviced and planning the holiday and when the homework is due. Just because you've spent all day every day for the past six months thinking about this issue that needs to be changed doesn't mean everyone else has too—especially if this is the first time you've mentioned it.

You'll need to give people time to sit with the idea and become convinced. People very rarely change their minds instantly. It usually takes time. The more familiar someone is with an idea or an experience the more they like it, so give them time to become familiar with the urgency of the situation before you make them commit one way or the other.

Don't be threatened by people pushing back and, whatever you do, don't be antagonistic. If you become antagonistic and turn the conversation into an argument then you force the other person to become entrenched in their position in order to argue. The more entrenched they are, the harder it will be for them to change their mind later on because changing their mind will mean admitting they were wrong and losing face. If you force them to commit to a position early, they'll commit to the status quo. It's safe, easy, and familiar. Expect people to disagree and be sceptical at first because the idea is new. But if your reasons for change are good reasons, then the more familiar they become with them, and the more time they have to mull them over before they officially commit, the more likely it is that they will come to see what you see. But for this to happen at all you need to help people see and feel the urgency that you feel.

2. Gather allies

It's tempting to overlook or rush this step as well. But you can't introduce lasting change all by yourself. You need allies. You need a coalition. You need people who are convinced that change is necessary, who will talk about it with others, and who will promote and defend the idea to other people.

This is important because you simply can't always talk to everybody—or maybe you could, but it would take a long time. People have networks, often deep networks. Others will be able to talk to people that you might not be able to talk to. They'll be involved in conversations that people might not have when you're around. People who are often reluctant to disagree with the leader when the leader is present, but who for whatever reason are much more comfortable voicing their disagreement and honest concerns when the leader isn't around, will discuss concerns openly with others. Your allies can talk about the change with these people when you're not there.

Once you've begun talking to people about the urgency of the situation and the necessity of change, there will be people who will begin to see what you see and feel what you feel. These people are the first recruits for your group of allies. Spend some more time with them talking about the change and listening to their perspectives and insights.

In your group of allies you want both 'influencers' and also those who are more faithful followers. The non-influencers are just as valuable as the influencers, so make sure you guard yourself from showing favouritism. Ignoring the non-influencers would be a huge mistake—because God is serious about us not showing favouritism but also because it's not that strategic. If you deliberately ignore and leave out a big chunk of people, they will notice and be hurt. How likely do you think it is that they'll embrace your proposed change when they know you didn't care about them or their opinions? You also need to remember that just because people aren't influential doesn't mean they aren't insightful. Good ideas and insights can come from anywhere. If you overlook people simply because you don't deem them influential then you're poisoning your own well.

Yet you'll also want to gather people who are true leaders and influencers of others. It's equally a mistake to overlook these people. The best-case scenario is there will be some true leaders in this first group of allies. True leaders are people who other people respect and listen to. They may be staff, or elected leaders like wardens or elders. They may have official titles or they may simply be people who have been at the church for a long time.

The other reason it's important to gather allies is because when the rest of the people become convinced and begin following you they won't actually be following you. They'll be following this first group of allies. This is the group everyone else will become like. These early adopters are very important to find and to embrace. They're the ones, if everything goes to plan, everyone else will end up following.

The reason gathering allies is so important has to do with the power structure in a church, so let's take a quick detour to talk about power.

Detour: the power landscape in the local church

Power feels like a dirty word when you first say it—especially in the context of church and ministry. But power isn't inherently a bad or compromised fixture of reality. God himself is an all-powerful being. And he's good. So power itself can't be inherently bad. It's neutral. It just exists. The problem comes when people pursue power for their own gains or use it for evil purposes. And it's true that people have often used it for evil ends to exploit or oppress others. This happens both in the world and also, tragically, in the church. So I understand people's reluctance to talk about power.

As leaders, though, we need to deal with both vision and reality. We need to deal with both how we'd like the world to be and also with how it actually is. And the reality is that power exists. And you can't accomplish anything unless you have power. Either you have the power to open the new jar of jam or you don't. But if you want the jam then either you need the power yourself or you need to enlist an ally who has the power you need. Either way, without power nothing happens. Nobody will have any jam.

Broadly speaking, there are two kinds of power: executive and persuasive. Executive power is that kind of positional power where the boss says, "Jump!" and you say, "How high?" It's the power someone has to tell you what to do and to fire you if you don't do it. This is the power that comes with a title. It's a power that's given to a person by someone else or by an organization, and it's what most people think of when they think of power.

Persuasive power is a power that you earn. It's the power that comes from helping people see what you see. It's the power of common goals, of gained trust and willing cooperation. Persuasive power is harder to get and harder to wield, but it's much more powerful than executive power.

Both types of power are often in play in every organization, although different organizations will lean more one way than the other. Church leadership is far more about persuasive power. Executive power still exists in churches, but the dynamics often don't work as well because of the landscape and distribution of power in the local church.

The power structure in a business is often very rigid and clearly defined. The CEO is at the top and has the most power over the most people. In the church, the power structure is more complex and diffuse. Everyone has a little bit of power, and some people have more than others, but it's rare that anyone in a church has enough power to lead with the kind of full executive power we see in the business world.

Jim Collins tells the story of a lady named Frances Hesselbein who became CEO of the Girl Scouts of the USA. She began leading a very complex structure of hundreds of local Girl Scout councils and over 650,000 volunteers. She didn't have full executive power to make decisions that would then be immediately and dutifully implemented by all those people. Each council had its own independent governing board and they had considerable latitude to either do or not do what they were told. And yet Frances Hesselbein managed to implement huge and sweeping changes. Collins writes:

> When asked how she got so much done without concentrated executive power, she said, "Oh, you always have power, if you just know where to find it. There is the power of inclusion, and the power of language, and the power of shared interests, and the power of coalition. Power is all around you to draw upon, but it is rarely raw, rarely visible."[88]

It's similar with church leadership. In order to be able to do what needs to be done you need to gather enough packets of power into one place. The power is there; it simply needs to be rallied. Everyone has a small packet of power. True leaders have a larger packet than others. But that power needs to be aggregated.

By yourself you don't have enough power to get done what needs to be done. When you have allies, you have access to and can draw upon their power. This is the importance of allies.

Back to step two: the ally matrix

You can view your allies through the true leaders lens, and you can also view them through the lens of the stakeholder. Stakeholders are those who will be most deeply affected by the changes you're proposing or who have direct power to approve those changes. These could be people like the senior minister, the senior minister's wife, wardens and elders, the treasurer, or other staff members as well as the people most affected by

88 Jim Collins, *Good to Great and the Social Sectors: Why business thinking is not the answer*, HarperCollins, New York, 2005, p. 10.

the changes. It's important to recognize and be aware that stakeholders could be anyone, depending on what it is you're looking to change.

Keeping track of all your allies and stakeholders can be a tough job. Who have you spoken to? Who do you still need to speak to? Who's onboard? Who's still resisting? Here's a method for making it easier to keep track of where you are.

Make a list of all the stakeholders, influencers, and potential allies with whom you're planning to speak. I find it helpful to think in terms of a matrix like this one, with power on the vertical axis and how interested they are in the proposed change on the horizontal axis:

High Power Low Interest	High Power High Interest
Low Power Low Interest	Low Power High Interest

Where do you think each of your potential allies and stakeholders belongs based on their power in the church and their level of interest in this particular change initiative? People in different quadrants will need different levels of persuasion from you. The idea isn't to box people in or demean them or treat them as though they're resources. The exercise is simply to help you think through how best to use the limited time and energy you have.

You'll want to put in minimal time and effort trying to persuade those who are low power and low interest. They don't care and can't do anything one way or the other. Why are these people even on the list? It's not that these people aren't important or valuable just because they can't help you when it comes to your change initiative. It's just that, when it comes to implementing change at your church, there's not much point investing huge amounts of time persuading the cashier at the local burger shop, who doesn't even go to any church let alone your church, that your plan has merit.

You'll want to keep those with high power but low interest informed. They don't really care that much, so don't annoy them, but make sure they're in the loop. Be careful of overfeeding these people with information and discussion about the change. If they start getting annoyed by the whole thing they might just want it to go away—and the quickest way to do that is to put a stop to it entirely. Give them enough time and information to keep them on your side without wasting their time or annoying them.

Spend as much time as you need to with those who have low power but high interest. They're valuable allies. Don't overlook them just because they don't have much power. This isn't a political, manipulative exercise. It's an exercise to help you use limited resources and not waste your time. If these people are interested then invest in them. Talk with them. Ask them for their opinions and insights. Low power doesn't mean low importance or low usefulness or low value. It just means low power.

You'll need to do everything you can to help those who have high power and high interest see what you see. They're an obviously strategic group of people to spend time with. As much as you can, you want to have these people onboard with your changes rather than working against them or vetoing them.

Again, it's important to remember the unique power map you're dealing with in a church setting. Just because someone isn't on staff or isn't a recognized leader doesn't mean that they have no power. The church grapevine, for example, is an unfortunate but real factor you need to consider. Gossips have much more influence and power than we like to admit. The problem isn't that the grapevine exists. The problem is that it's used for gossip, stories of moral failure, half-truths, and negativity. When good news and accurate information spread through the grapevine, that's a great thing. When rumours and complaining spread, that's damaging.

But what if you could harness the grapevine for something productive? What if the grapevine could be full of reports of why things need to change and why it's urgent? What if people could be talking about how important the change will be? If you can have some key members of that grapevine spreading positive news about your change, then they will be powerful allies. It's much better to have the grapevine working for you rather than against you. So why not try and have these people alongside you as allies?

Lastly, as you build your allies make sure you have allies at every level of the church—from those in authority to those who are faithful attendees. Faithful attendees will often have helpful insights about why your plan won't work or who is a stakeholder that you have overlooked, and so on. Everybody deserves the chance to be involved. Don't just try to persuade the powerful as though they're the only ones who are important. God has a lot to say about showing favouritism towards the rich and powerful, including the relationally rich and powerful, and none of it is positive. Remember that the point of all this isn't to label or pigeonhole people or to treat them as fuel for your schemes. The point is to help you make decisions about how to use your finite time and energy to talk about this particular proposal for change with the people who care about it and who will either help to bring it about or oppose it.

3. Develop the vision for change

Once you've raised the sense of urgency and gathered a coalition of allies from all levels and areas of the church, it's time to develop your specific vision for change.

The first question you might ask here is: Wait, if we're only now developing our vision for change, what have we been talking to people about for the past two stages?

Good question. The distinction at this point is between raising the problem and convincing people it exists (step one), gathering people who agree that there's a problem and who think that we should definitely do something about it and who might have some ideas (step two), and now identifying and clarifying exactly what you're going to do and how you're going to communicate it. You might have had some pretty clear ideas all along about what should be done, but if that's the case then it's very important to be disciplined and keep them largely to yourself until you get to this third step. If you do speak about your ideas before this stage, make sure you present them as possible ideas without the force of conviction that communicates that "this is definitely and exactly what we're doing".

After having talked to a lot of people about the problem and after discussing in broad detail how you might go about solving it, you will no doubt have a lot more ideas and tweaks from all the conversations and input you've received. At this point it's time to crystallize exactly what you're going to do.

Developing your vision for change is itself a three-step process. Before you get too far into planning the change you want to see happen you'll need to ensure that the decision you're planning to present is between at least two options—and not a decision about whether or not to do option A. Making it a decision between option A or option B is a critically important step. Adding one more real, genuinely possible option will dramatically increase the likelihood that you will make a good decision. Read that sentence again. Doesn't it sound absurd? How could adding one extra option make the decision that much better?

In the past 40 years there's been a flurry of research into decision-making and the psychology behind it. One study investigated how teenagers make decisions. It's often been observed that teenagers aren't always leading the way in competent and careful decision-making. A professor named Baruch Fischoff wanted to understand why this was the case. He found that the majority of decisions that teenagers make fall into one of two categories. They make either "statements of resolve" decisions or "whether or not" decisions. A statement of resolve would be something like, "I'm going to be more encouraging". A whether or not decision would be something like, "Should I get dinner from McDonald's or not?"

Fischoff found that these two categories account for 65% of the decisions that teenagers make. This means that most of the time when a teenager is making a decision they're not making a choice at all. They're simply deciding between only one option. In Fischoff's study, only 30% of teenagers' decisions involved considering more than one option—which explains in part why so many decisions made by teenagers aren't very good ones.[89]

And as it turns out, somewhat depressingly, most organizations use the same decision-making process as hormone-charged teenagers.

Paul Nutt is another researcher in decision-making who focuses on how organizations make decisions. He spent his 30-year career collecting and collating information on how businesses, non-profits, and government agencies make decisions. His research is rigorous and laborious. After

89 Heath and Heath, *Decisive*, pp. 33-4.

studying all of these decisions, he found that only 29% of decisions made by these organizations were between more than one alternative. 71% of these decisions by organizations were whether or not decisions—which is the same percentage as the decisions made by teenagers!

More than that, Nutt also found that 52% of the whether or not decisions that organizations made failed over the long term. That is, half of the whether or not decisions ended up being bad decisions. Decisions that were made between two or more options, on the other hand, failed only 32% of the time.[90] Whether or not decisions are a recipe for failure. By adding just one genuine alternative you dramatically increase the likelihood of making a good decision and are about twice as likely to make a successful decision. When you hear people say "whether or not" you should hear alarm bells—that phrase is a sign that a bad decision is about to be made.

It's important also to note that the option needs to be a real one. It can't just be: "Should we start a night service or should we poke our eyes out with pencils? Jerry, what's your opinion?" It has to be a real, genuine, you-might-actually-choose-it option.

Once you've developed some options and the decision has been made about which one you're going with, the next step in developing the vision for change is to *find the feeling*. People don't change because they know they should; people change because of their feelings. Smokers don't quit because they discover that smoking is bad for them. They already know that, and knowing that doesn't help them stop. They quit because of their feelings. They quit because they feel that being addicted means they've lost control of themselves and their lives or because they want to be able to run and play with their kids one day or because they see a smoker die a horrible death and they're afraid that that's a glimpse of their future. Feelings change people. So you need to figure out what the feeling is that people need to find so that they'll change.

Is it being part of something that matters? Is it being a certain type of person? Is it wanting to please God and hear him say, "Well done, good and faithful servant"? Is it the joy of seeing lives radically transformed? Is it feeling like they used their life well and didn't waste it? Is it the thrill of

90 Heath and Heath, *Decisive*, pp. 36-7.

being a pioneer? What's the feeling that will drive people to embrace and implement this change? The feeling might be being part of something bigger than yourself, or belonging to something, or the joy of making a positive impact in someone's life, or the satisfaction of knowing you're doing what God wants. Once you've figured out what the feeling is, the next step is to figure out how you can help people discover that feeling for themselves.

Detour: thinking about feeling

It's worth pausing here to consider the dangers of manipulating people. Because we never want to manipulate people, we need to be careful when we appeal to their emotions. Manufacturing feelings to make someone do something you want them to do sounds manipulative and borderline abusive. But that's not what we're talking about here. Setting out to help people feel something so that they'll be onboard with your idea might, to some, sound manipulative, but what we want to do is to help them catch a vision of what's possible in the church, to motivate them. Wanting people to feel a certain way, and then doing certain things to make it happen, is something that we do all the time. When we want people to feel happy we open the curtains and put fresh flowers in the room. There are many times in our lives where we know the right thing to do but don't feel like doing it. Motivation is made up of both right thinking *and* right feeling. A logical argument often isn't enough to move someone to action. If we want to motivate people we need to tap into their feelings as well as their thinking.

In his book *The Heart of Change Field Guide: Tools and Tactics for Leading Change in Your Organization*, Dan Cohen says that most people think change happens like this: *analysis-think-change*. If people are struggling to change it's because they're struggling to *understand*. But that's rarely the problem, and analytical arguments almost never overcome people's hesitancy. If a friend is having second thoughts about whether or not to marry his fiancée you probably aren't going to try and persuade him by talking about tax advantages and superannuation benefits. Cohen saw that in the vast majority of successful change initiatives, the process that led to that change wasn't *analysis-think-change* but *see-feel-change*.[91] You present the evidence—and that's important because your goal isn't to manipulate—and that evidence causes people to feel something. What they feel might be shock at the depth of the problem or excitement at the possibility of a healthier process, but either way the evidence hits people at an emotional level. If you appeal only to logic, you will have direction but no motivation.

In their book *The Heart of Change: Real-Life Stories of How People Change Their Organizations* John Kotter and Dan Cohen tell the story of Jon Stegner. Stegner was convinced that the company he worked for was wasting millions of dollars a year. He knew that they could save upwards of a billion dollars over the next five years, but for this to happen there would need to be a huge shift in the company's processes and procedures. Stegner knew it would be difficult to convince his bosses that changes on this scale were worth the effort.

So he set out to find a compelling example of the company's poor purchasing system. He roped in one of the company's interns and focused his investigation on one item: work gloves. These gloves were used in most factories in the company. The intern's job was to find all the different brands of gloves that were being used and track back how much the company was paying for each.

He found that the company purchased 424 different kinds of gloves! What's more, they purchased them from different suppliers. Some factories were paying $5 for a pair of gloves and others were paying $17 a pair for the exact same gloves!

Most of us might crunch the numbers and put together a blistering multi-tabbed Excel spreadsheet and perhaps accompany it with some PowerPoint slides. Stegner did something different. He had the intern collect all the different gloves the company purchased and tag them with the prices the company had paid for them. He then piled them up on the conference table and invited the company executives to a meeting. It's worth quoting what happened:

91 Dan S Cohen, *The Heart of Change Field Guide: Tools and tactics for leading change in your organization*, Harvard Business Review Press, Boston, 2005, p. 7.

> What they saw was a large expensive table, normally clean or with a few papers, now stacked high with gloves. Each of our executives stared at this display for a minute. Then each said something like, 'We buy all these different kinds of gloves?' Well, as a matter of fact, yes we do. 'Really?' Yes, really. Then they walked around the table... They could see the prices. They looked at two gloves that seemed exactly alike, yet one was marked $3.22 and the other $10.55. It's a rare event when these people don't have anything to say. But that day, they just stood with their mouths gaping.[92]

Stegner didn't make an analytical appeal. If he'd done that, perhaps some would have agreed and the issue would have made it onto next year's agenda of possible things to do. But instead he broke through to the executives' feelings. He didn't manipulate them, but he shocked them into moving. They thought to themselves, "This is crazy. We're crazy!" And then they fixed the problem.

When we're talking about 'finding the feeling' we're not talking about manipulating people but about motivating people. While logical arguments appealing to the analytical parts of our brains might work for small tweaks, they won't be effective in motivating people when it comes to massive overhauls or grand and uncertain change. It's about finding a way for the logic and facts to affect and motivate people. *See-feel-change.*

Step three: continued

You've developed some options and chosen one, you've found the feeling, and now you're ready for the final step of developing your vision: crafting an elevator pitch. The idea of an elevator pitch is to imagine that you're in an elevator with a person who's getting out at the next floor. As the doors close, they ask you what you think needs to be done to turn this place around. The elevator starts moving, and you have maybe two sentences to give your answer. How would you do it? What would you say? How would you communicate your vision for change in one short elevator ride

92 John P Kotter and Dan S Cohen, *The Heart of Change: Real-life stories of how people change their organizations*, Harvard Business Review Press, Boston, 2012, pp. 29-30.

so that the person understands and is maybe even a bit keen to join you or at least hear more? Crafting this short pitch is like hammering out a Haddon Robinson-esque "big idea" for a sermon.[93] It's like digging for gold. It will demand time and effort. A lot of time and a lot of effort. You might feel like it's not worth it, but once you've struck that gold it will be worth more than everything you've done so far.

What we're trying to cut through here is the fact that people generally don't care. Whatever it is we're talking about, they basically don't care—or, if they do care, they don't care for very long. You often have only a short window and you need to make the most of it. That's the point of the elevator pitch. Make them care as quickly as you can.

An elevator pitch for changing meetings, for example, might be: If we tweak our current meeting structure, and separate tactical issues from strategic issues, not only will our meetings run more smoothly, but we'll have more engagement, we'll come up with better ideas, and we'll achieve more things.

Once you have your elevator-pitch version of the vision you can expand it and think about how you'd explain it in about five minutes or less. That's still not very long, but it's long enough to communicate well in a conversation or with a brief opportunity and a microphone. Having the elevator pitch will give you that laser-focused clarity you need to stay on topic with more time. Is there a way you can articulate your vision as, or including, a story? People love stories and connect with them easily. If you can include a story, do it. If you can make your entire explanation a story, even better.

Once you've developed your vision for change, you're ready to think about putting it into action.

4. Plan

Now it's time to turn that vision into a plan of action. What will you actually do? In order to craft a plan that will work well you should think in terms of three distinct but related spheres: people's knowledge and thinking, people's feelings and emotions, and physical space and systems.

93 Haddon W Robinson, *Biblical Preaching: The development and delivery of expository messages*, 3rd edn, Baker Academic, Grand Rapids, 2014, especially chapter 2.

Sometimes people need to learn some new things before they're ready for change. Perhaps there are some biblical truths they need to understand. You might plan a sermon series or a series of small group studies or both. People might need some training to know what you want them to do differently. They might need some checklists to help them remember all the new things you want them to know. They might need some clarity on what exactly they're supposed to achieve.

In addition to helping people change their thinking you'll also want to help them change how they feel. If you've done your preparation well you'll have already found the feeling by this point. But there's still more you can do. What else will you do to help motivate people to do this new thing? How will you help them feel included and part of the group when they act in this new way? How will you reinforce these feelings? How will you help them to focus not on *analysis-think-change* but rather to *see-feel-change*? Think of Stegner and the table covered in gloves. How can you do something similar to show people why the change matters?

Doing anything new takes a lot of energy. People will be constantly drifting back to the old way because it was automatic, familiar, and easy. If people feel like they're all alone this drift will happen more quickly and more often. But feeling like they're part of a group doing this together will help them to keep going.

One thing you might do is to interview people who are adopting this change and have them talk about how brilliant it is and how glad they are they did it.

You'll want to do everything you can to help people see that they're making progress. When people feel like they're moving forward, they're more motivated to keep going. There's almost nothing more frustrating and demotivating than putting in a mountain of effort and discovering that you haven't gone anywhere and nothing has changed. But if you can help people see for themselves how far they've come, they'll be more likely to keep going and keep changing.

Leaders often overlook physical space and systems when making plans to implement change initiatives. Consider what changes will need to be made to the physical space or to the systems and structures that people need to work with and within. What you will do in this area to help the change happen? How can you change the space to make it easier for people to do what you want them to and harder for them to do what you don't want? What can you do visually? Could you make posters or signs to communicate the new initiative in a powerful way? Can you rearrange the physical space to facilitate and encourage the change?

How can you tweak your current systems to help reinforce the changes? Is there a way to change the rostering process or what you hand out on the way in to church? How can you recognize the people who are behaving in the new way and how might you reward them? Rewards don't always need to be a tangible gift of some sort. A reward can be as simple as specific private praise from you or some kind of public recognition. The idea is to make it easier for people to act in the new way and harder to continue in the old way. Making sure the systems reinforce the change and run smoothly rather than work against it is a crucial part of the process planning for change that requires careful thought and planning.

As you plan your change initiative, make sure you include items in each of these areas: thinking, feeling, and space and structures.

5. Go public and implement

Once you've raised the urgency, gathered allies and stakeholders at all levels, crafted your vision, and planned action steps in all three spheres, you're ready to go public and implement the plan. At this point you'll put into action all the thinking and preparation of the first four stages.

Not everything will go smoothly or exactly to plan. It's important not to try to spin these problems or minimize them. Admit these obstacles and complications, own them, and address people's concerns and anxieties head-on, immediately and openly. It's important to do this early on, once you've officially announced the changes, and to continue to do this throughout the process. Be honest about what's not working and what you're planning to do about it. This isn't the time to hide things or be political. People need to trust you from the outset—and you need to give them every reason to trust you.

Once you've announced the plans and begun to bring them into being the temptation will be to stop talking with people and get on with doing. This is a mistake. You'll need to keep talking about the vision. In as many contexts and groups as you can, big groups and small groups, you need to be constantly selling the vision for change. Don't confine this kind of talk to official 'vision meetings' or 'vision sermons' or 'vision announcements'. Talk about it whenever you can in as many different ways as you can. If anything happens that connects to the change, or flows from the change, point it out and mention it. Tie everything you legitimately can back to the vision of change that you're working towards.

6. Ensure easy wins

Here at step six you might feel like you're a long way into the change program, and this is true for you. You've been thinking about this and working on this for a long time. But remember that, from everyone else's perspective, you only recently launched it. It's early days. So while you might be feeling tired and perhaps bored with the whole thing, everyone else is just at the beginning. So you'll need to be on your game when it comes to energy and enthusiasm if you want to help people come with you. They're still processing what's happening.

Change is a difficult process and normally takes a long time and a lot of energy. Your vision for the future probably isn't a picture of next week. It's probably further away than that—maybe six months or a year away or even further into the future than that. It will be a long time until you get there. You need to keep people motivated along the way. There are two key points in particular where you'll need to be sure to keep people motivated: early on in the change program and also at the midpoint. And in order to keep them motivated you're going to need to ensure some easy, early wins.

The midpoint is important because it will have been a long time since you started and there will still be a long way to go until you finish. The light at the end of the tunnel is a long way away and the light from the beginning will have all but faded. It's always darkest in the middle.

And the beginning of a change initiative is challenging because it requires a lot of energy. The old way always feels so comfortable—even if it's not actually that good or helpful, it still feels right and normal. So people often fall back into doing something the old way without thinking. The new way, by contrast, requires conscious effort and thought and feels strange and sometimes a bit awkward. At the beginning people will need regular encouragement, help, and reminders to keep going with the change precisely because it is so new and different.

Everybody wants to be on a team that's winning. Everybody wants to know that they picked the right train and that they're moving forward. But change is often a long process. Sometimes it's months before things start turning around or visibly shifting and people will need to see some progress before that. So you need to give them some signs that things really are changing.

These early wins need to be highly visible and relatively easy to achieve. Perhaps you make a visual change—a new logo, a new slogan, a new brochure, or you could rearrange the furniture or change the lighting—something that signals things are different, things are changing, and we're making progress. Because you know you really are even though it's probably not measurable yet. So, very early on, you'll need to think of as many easy and visible wins as you can.

They'll need to be genuine wins—you can't make them up. They have to be real, but they should also be easy. You need to plan for them and make it a priority to make them happen—and you'll need to point them out. In the early stages of a change initiative you need to be neurotic about finding early wins and making sure everyone notices them.

Easy wins create hope. And hope is fuel for change.

7. Remove obstacles

It won't all go to plan. It just won't. There will be setbacks and obstacles. These might be people—critics and naysayers—but they could equally be systems that aren't built for this new role or procedures that don't quite fit the new landscape. These are normal and to be expected, though they're also hard to predict.

Your job is to be relentless in tracking these obstacles down and removing them as quickly as possible. When the obstacle happens to be a person, removing that obstacle doesn't mean somehow removing the person via nefarious means. It means figuring out what the problem is—what is this person seeing or feeling that has turned them into an obstacle? Have they noticed something you haven't? Once you've found the problem you need to work out a way forward so that everybody wins or at least so that the right thing is done. But it's your job to make it a priority to remove the obstacle. At this point the change process is still fragile and needs all the momentum it can get.

Obstacle removal has to become your obsession. Obstacles are annoying and frustrating for those in the middle of a change initiative, especially if they're structural or systems problems. These kinds of problems make people pine for the good old days when at least they knew what they were doing and things seemed to work. You don't want to give them any reason to long for the good old days or to undermine the urgency of the change. You don't want to make the change any harder or more frustrating than it absolutely needs to be. This is why you need to be obsessed with finding obstacles and blowing them up.

Sniff those obstacles out like you're a starving Beagle so you can minimize people's frustration with the changes.

8. Build on the change

By the time the change has been implemented and has been in process for a while you're definitely on your way. People will have begun to accept the new status quo, the new way of doing things, and since you've been removing the obstacles as they materialize the changes will be rolling on. Though it might feel like the time to move on and focus on something else, it's not. It's a common mistake for the person running the change initiative to take their eye off the ball and move on to something else at this point. But it's not over yet.

You need to keep building on the change. This is the time to start tweaking and adding to what you've already done. Keep refining it. Change is to be constant, which means you need to constantly be changing.

The changes you make at this point won't be massive changes of direction; they'll be tweaks and refinements. There will be a myriad of mid-flight course corrections that you'll need to make due to unforeseen circumstances or new changes to the landscape or even just due to mistakes and oversights on your part. This is normal and to be expected. So long as the destination is still clear, the tweaks along the way won't be a problem. You're *building* on the change, not starting again. So keep finding ways to make what you've done and where you are even better.

9. Embed the change into the culture

You want your change initiative to move from 'that thing that's different to how it used to be' to 'this is how we do it here'. And that transition takes time and intentionality. The goal is for the change to move from being primarily attached to you, as the person who's driving it, to being a part of the way the church runs.

This will mean making sure it's embedded in the language and terminology that your church uses. It needs to be embedded in the systems of rewards that your church distributes, whether that's personal praise, public praise, interviews from the front, or written thank-you notes. You'll need to make sure the changes are encoded in whatever documents and training manuals you have. The goal is for the change to be planted deep into the church's culture. This process can take years and will be done in parallel with other changes you'll introduce over that time.

Once the change has become part of the automatic way things happen in the church and you sense that this is the case, that's when your change initiative is officially over and successful. This might take a couple of years or even longer or it might happen much more quickly, depending on the change itself and how open and responsive people are. But because of the nature of this process you may end up having multiple change initiatives of various sizes and scopes occurring at once, with each being at a different step in the process. This will require a huge amount of your effort and concentration so you can lead each one with the focus and creativity it will need to succeed. Be careful of attempting to do too much at once.

Leading a successful change initiative requires an enormous amount of energy and planning. Great change leaders understand that, in order for a widescale change to successfully take root, they will need to over plan the process and overlap multiple methods of influence. Successful change is often far more multifaceted than we think.

Christian leaders are in the business of change. We're about seeing people's status and relationship before God change through the power of the gospel and the work of the Spirit. We're about seeing people's lives changed as they begin to live out the implications of their faith in greater depth and in more areas of their lives. And we're about seeing the way we organize what we do change in order to be more effective in reaching people with the love and message of Jesus. Change is what we do and who we are.

All change takes planning, patience, creativity, concentration, and a whole lot of energy. It takes all the running you can do just to stay in the same place. If you want the old white post you must have a new white post. That's the Red Queen syndrome.

See also

20. People who praise you are probably just as mistaken as those who criticize you
21. If you're planning on not being hurt then you're planning on not being a leader
27. You're just the leader
32. Ideas are born ugly
33. Communicate from the inside out
40. Team communication is exponential
42. Humble and hungry
56. What are you trying to achieve?
57. Where is here?
59. Hold hands with your programs
61. Why systems matter
69. Your people should be able to do a good impression of you
70. Ignore the org-chart
71. Decide how decisions are made
74. Be an agent of disorganization
75. Waiting is doing something

74

Be an agent of disorganization

Organization is a good thing. A necessary thing. Your ministry or your team can be disorganized and still function, and maybe even thrive, for a period of time. But at some point it has to get organized. You'll need to start organizing things like when you'll meet, what you'll do, and who will do it. Organization is necessary for everyone to be able to do their best. Disorganized groups don't function well for long. When people are confused and unclear, the quality of what they're doing atrophies and they either give up or start doing their own thing.

Organization is the first step to disaster

The danger of organizing, however, is what happens next. Once a group is organized, the danger becomes complacency. Complacency is a virus in a ministry or in any organization. Complacency is that idea that says, "We've finally worked this out and now we have it all sorted. It's all under control." But new problems will continue to materialize and complacency will keep them hidden. This love for the status quo is the first step towards becoming a museum of how a once-useful church did things.

Complacency is bad enough, but the complacency virus can quickly evolve into worse strains—namely, delusion and arrogance. It's a small step from "We're finally getting organized" to "We've worked it all out. Every last thing." This is delusion. The world is constantly changing. The people you're serving are constantly changing. Individuals grow and change and people leave and new people enter the picture. Your carefully organized systems and practices will all slowly stop working. People will get tired, they'll lose focus, they'll forget why they started and what they're trying to achieve. The system will begin to decay. Unless you're constantly putting energy into something it will begin to unravel—no matter how well organized it once was.

Once an organization has crossed from complacency into delusion it's another small step to arrogance: "How we do it is the best way to do it in every possible detail". And once you hit delusion and arrogance—that you do all things the best possible way—you're only a few steps away from complete organizational collapse.

Obsessive destabilization

Avoiding this disaster is the leader's responsibility. Once things are running smoothly, the leader's job is not to be the chief organizer. The leader's job is to be the chief disorganizer.[94] The leader's job is to question everything—to be constantly sceptical, almost fanatically sceptical, about whether the way we do something really is the best way to get it done. The leader also needs to be sceptical about whether what once was the best way is still the best way. The leader's job is to be vigilant and to notice how the organization operates and what rules and laws, both explicit and implied, are followed and believed. The leader needs to consistently doubt the developed habits of the organization and to constantly doubt conventional wisdom.

An agent of disorganization keeps picking at and harassing the systems, assumptions, and routines in the organization. An agent of disorganization asks the hard questions and is not satisfied with pre-packaged answers. An agent of disorganization has an almost paranoid approach to uncovering the actual facts of situations and is never convinced by, or satisfied with, the vague anecdotes people relate with confidence and certainty.

As the leader it's your job to be constantly asking questions such as: How do we know that's true? Is that really the case? If it weren't the case, how would we know? What would be different? Do we have any facts or

94 I first discovered this idea in Oren Harari's book *The Powell Principles: 24 lessons from Colin Powell, battle-proven leader*, McGraw-Hill, New York, 2004, pp. 15-17.

is it all just anecdotal and subjective? When you say 'lots of people are saying...' who exactly are these people? Exactly how many is 'lots'?

As an agent of disorganization your job is to check under the bed, open the cupboards, wipe a finger along the tops of the bookshelves. Your job is to search obsessively for any hint of mediocrity or complacency or untested assumptions, to keep digging and probing and rattling and shaking, and so to constantly refine the organization. You need to know what problems are coming long before they ever bubble to the surface.

Contentment and complacency lead an organization to drift towards immobilization and decline. Complacency will always keep you from uncovering what cannot be seen because you will believe it cannot, and will not, be there. The answer to complacency isn't more organization. The answer is controlled destabilization leading to reorganization. And then you do it all again and again. You never stop.

Your responsibility as a leader isn't to organize everything. Your responsibility is to be an agent of disorganization.

See also

31. Energy is more efficient than efficiency
57. Where is here?
70. Ignore the org-chart
73. Red Queen syndrome: a nine-step process for implementing change

75
Waiting is doing something

> For everything there is a season, and a time for every matter under heaven... He has made everything beautiful in its time. (Eccl 3:1, 11)

The confusion of action-bias

As you read this or that leadership book—this one included—you might feel frustrated by the persistent bias towards action. If you're wired that way, then that will be a happy reality and you'll appreciate the emphasis. But if you're still learning how to function as a leader this emphasis can be wearying, somewhat confusing, and often less than helpful.

The value of a leader who takes the initiative, who is proactive and seeks to uncover problems before they become problems, cannot be overstated. But leaders who are more reactive, who tend more towards maintaining the status quo and who are far more comfortable enabling initiatives that others bring rather than initiating such things themselves, can sometimes feel devalued and as though they're second-class leaders.

This simply isn't the case. Churches need leaders at all levels—not just one leader at the top surrounded by a number of 'helpers'. A church with leaders from the top all the way down to the bottom is much healthier and is able to get more done than the 'genius-with-a-thousand-helpers' type of set-up. And these enabling leaders are extraordinarily valuable up and down the layers of the church.

But it is also true that when an enabling leader, rather than an initiating leader, is the leader with the most authority, the church will not be lead as well as it could be.

This is why so much leadership input focuses on doing, action, decisions, taking risks, moving forward, recruiting around a vision, and so on. These resources are designed to help enabling leaders edge more towards fulfilling the role of initiating leader.

But all of this emphasis on action is rarely accompanied by more concrete instruction about which actions to take, which decisions to make, and which risks to rally behind. Surely not all risks are equal? And is moving forward always a positive thing? Which vision should we rally around? Even though the answers to those questions will be specific to every church and context, we still feel as though it would be good if there were at least some help to light the path.

The emphasis on action can also seem somewhat unhelpful because it feels so unrealistic. But there's a good reason for that. It *is* unrealistic. We're not always doing something. Being labelled hyperactive is rarely a compliment, in my experience.

Timing is everything

One of the things that makes leading people so difficult, and yet so enjoyable, is that it's not just a purely scientific exercise. There is a science to leadership, but what makes good leadership such an art form is that it's also about doing the right things *at the right time*.

And sometimes you can make the right decision and do the right thing with the right people—but not at the right time. The bias in leaders towards action can mask the fact that doing something, even the right thing, isn't always a good idea. And the fact that it's the right thing and that you're actually doing it can cloud your view as to whether or not the timing is right.

True leadership is often counterintuitive. And the bias that so many leaders and books have towards action and moving forward and taking the next hill creates the false image that you're only doing something if you're doing something.

But that's just not true.

Doing nothing is sometimes a very important thing to do. Waiting is not doing nothing. People sometimes ask me why we're not doing anything about issue A or person B. My reply is usually, "Oh, but I am doing something. I'm waiting." When I say waiting I mean all kinds of things—I mean praying, seeking counsel, weighing options, and things like that. But I also mean just waiting. Allowing the minutes to tick by. Waiting to make the decision. And for those of you who are more naturally inclined towards an initiating style of leadership, who are more activists, this concept of waiting might sound crazy. I put myself in that activist category. Waiting and not making a decision sounds absolutely bananas at first. But it's counterintuitive. Not making a decision isn't not doing anything.

Waiting is doing something. And it's often a very important something. Making the right decision is not always the only thing that matters. Timing is crucial. It's about making the right decision at the right time.

People usually want quick decisions, and especially when they're the ones who come to you with the request. The reason for this is fairly obvious: the faster you make your decision, the faster they can get on with their job. We shouldn't downplay the importance of this consideration. A leader who always waits and drags out every decision ends up being a bottleneck and unnecessarily slows down the church or organization. This is a good way to frustrate the people you lead for no good reason and to ensure you repel the best leaders you have. This is a good example of how leadership is more art than science. Making quick decisions and avoiding bottlenecks and frustration is a good skill to have and a good thing to do; yet someone's desire for you to make a quick decision shouldn't be the most important factor when it comes to the timing of any decision.

Here's how you can strike a balance and be swift and action-oriented while also valuing the necessity of waiting: never make a decision today that can be reasonably put off until tomorrow.[95]

At first read this might not strike you as a great principle for leadership. It sounds like the average slogan of a professional procrastinator. Isn't this giving institutional space to a lack of courage? It might be, depending on who you are. But it doesn't *have* to be. The idea sounds so counterproductive to most people when they first hear it that they immediately decide it's

95 I first came across this idea in Steven Sample's book *The Contrarian's Guide to Leadership*, pp. 81-3.

pure nonsense. But it's actually one of the hidden keys to leadership and good decision-making. Read it one more time: never make a decision today that can be reasonably put off until tomorrow.

The key word here, the word that changes everything, is 'reasonably'. That's what distinguishes this idea from procrastination or decision-paralysis cowardice. The word reasonably transforms this concept into what you might at least call artful procrastination. Working out the 'reasonably' part of a decision is where the art of leadership really comes into play.

When you're a leader people will come to you constantly, wanting decisions from you. They will always want you to make these decisions quickly so they can go and get on with their work. And so they may, sometimes deliberately and other times inadvertently, inflate the urgency of the decision. They may also want you to make the decision quickly so you won't have time to consult with others—and will therefore be more likely to make the decision they want you to make.

But as the leader you need to make sure that you set the agenda rather than allowing others to force their agendas on you. The question to ask is: How much time do I have to make this decision? And then you keep asking that question until you're satisfied that you have the truth, not just the timeframe that suits the person asking you.

Waiting for options

The other advantage of putting off a decision is that it creates the space in time for more options to open up than might have been available at first. New resources may present themselves, new people may step forward and put their hands up, new training conferences may be announced, events that had been planned may be cancelled, new technology may become available, and so on. And if you've made the decision already, before you needed to, then all of these options are either off the table for you or you need to reassess your decided-upon decision in light of whatever the new context is. But if you put off the decision until it actually needs to be made you won't have these regrets or waste your time or anyone else's time in revisiting the decision.

Sometimes you simply cannot reasonably put off a decision until tomorrow. "The church is on fire. Who should we call?" Putting that decision off until tomorrow is not a reasonable option. Some decisions have to be made quickly. Some decisions even have to be made now. If that's the case, then make the decision. It would be unreasonable not to. It's worth double-checking, though: is this decision as urgent as I think it is? Or is this decision as urgent as this person is trying to tell me it is? It's part of your job as a leader to assess the true urgency of the situation and to act, or wait, accordingly.

Don't abdicate decision-making

There will also be times when there's no reason to put off making the decision but we're scared and would rather not have to make it. While it's usually easy enough to convince yourself that's a reasonable reason, it's not. Fear is never a good reason for indecision, whether it's fear of being wrong or fear of criticism or consequences. In those instances the way forward is to pray for wisdom, seek counsel, find your courage, and make a call. And in those instances the more quickly you make the decision the better—because the sooner you decide, the sooner you can find out you were wrong, and the more time you'll have to fix it and find the right way forward.

The obvious danger of putting a decision off until tomorrow is that you might wait too long and, instead of having options open up, you'll find your options beginning to narrow. If you wait too long to make a decision in some cases it won't be just individual options that close to you. Sometimes all the options can close off in very quick succession, or even all at once, and the entire decision can be made for you.

I heard a story once of a minister who wasn't sure whether he wanted the youth to be allowed to go on an overseas mission trip that a group of adults from the church was planning. By the time he decided that yes, the youth should go, there wasn't enough time for anyone to get visas so the whole trip had to be cancelled. And the people in both countries who had put a lot of time and effort into planning the mission were disappointed.

As a leader, the last thing you want is to allow other people, adversaries, or outsiders to make your decisions on your behalf. Yet when we delay a decision too long, so that it's made for us, it ends up being the same as allowing those other groups and factors to come into our church or organization and set the agenda and make our decisions for us.

It's one thing to consciously delegate a decision to a trusted team member or team leader. It's quite another thing to relinquish a decision to outside forces or even to people who are against you. Having a decision taken away from us or made by default because of paralysis or fear or laziness or cowardice is unacceptable and unreasonable. If the decision will be taken out of our hands or if our options will be significantly pruned after a certain date, then we need to act with courage and make a call. It would be unreasonable to let it happen any other way. As the leader it's your responsibility to be aware of the timeframe you're working in, to be conscious of when in that timeframe various options will collapse, what the ramifications will be, what trade-offs you're making, and what today's date is.

But putting off a decision that can reasonably wait until tomorrow allows the opportunity for new options to make themselves known.

When you're doing something isn't the only time you're doing something. Sometimes doing nothing is doing something. Leadership is more than just doing the right things with the right people. It's also about *when* you do the right things. Timing is often an under-appreciated factor in effective leadership. Everything is beautiful in its time. Waiting for and recognizing a beautiful time to make the right decision, and so making a beautiful decision, is part of what makes leadership an art.

See also

71. Decide how decisions are made

76
Seek raw beauty

One of the tensions that we deal with in ministry is the tension between a commitment to doing ministry through and with unpaid volunteers—equipping the saints for works of service—and a commitment to seeing things done with quality and excellence. Add to that the further tension of not wanting the quality to be such that it takes away from the heart of what we're doing. We don't want people to be so blown away by the beauty of the morning tea table that no-one dares to actually touch the cookies, let alone eat one. In addition, the size of the group has a bearing on the level of quality that people expect.

The challenge of quality

God has gifted all of his people with gifts, talents, and abilities that they're to leverage and use for the growth of the kingdom. The priesthood of all believers and every-member ministry are central biblical ideas but they bring with them the challenge of quality. It's not that you can't have a quality ministry staffed by volunteers or that volunteers are necessarily less skilled than paid staff. The issue isn't one of skill but of time and focus. A volunteer has only so much time he or she can allocate to serving in ministry in church. Volunteers also have many more outside commitments that compete or clash with ministry. They have jobs that they need to turn up to, for instance, in order to earn money to pay their bills and feed their families. And that's a legitimate commitment that needs to be honoured, but the result is that he or she doesn't have as much time or freedom to serve. If they had that time and freedom, of course, they could accomplish much more or achieve higher quality results. Thus quality can be a challenge.

We want to do things well. We want our ministries to be helpful and we want people to see that the things we do are valuable and worth being a part of. There's no reason to deliberately run something badly or awkwardly or to do something that's poorly planned or not well thought through. Most of us have been involved in running something that was poorly done or badly thought through, but most of us wouldn't do that intentionally. Though it sometimes happens, it's not our ministry philosophy.

An equal but opposite mistake is to want to do things so well, to such a high standard, that they come off as superficial and inauthentic, all sizzle no steak, super-slick hype-fest performances. These types of productions often seem more damaging than helpful because, in addition to giving off this vibe of style without substance, they can also discourage people from getting involved in ministry because the skill-level bar is set so high. These productions can communicate to people—sometimes intentionally but often unintentionally—that participation is exclusive to the super-elite.

I'm all for having a high bar for people in terms of moral character and commitment. More often than not, a high bar in those areas encourages more people to jump over it in the long run. But a high standard for the level of skill required just to join and start out in a ministry will usually end up turning more people away than it encourages.

I'm not against having a bar at all when it comes to skills for a ministry. That would be foolish. I'm still after excellence. I still want things to be done well. I'm still seeking beauty. But it's unhelpful if the skill bar is set as high as the character or commitment bar. The skill bar needs to be lower.

Doing something well and putting in effort and showing people that what we do matters doesn't necessarily mean that we need to be slick and polished. We just need to seek to do things well. And 'well' doesn't have to mean polished or perfect.

Consider the size factor

The other factor that influences this question of quality is the size of the group. Large groups function and behave differently than small groups. As a group gets larger, or in our case as ministries get bigger, a higher degree of quality and professionalism is expected. The expectations that a group of five people brings regarding quality are far more modest than the expectations of a group of 500 people. But professionalism doesn't mean professional. Professionalism means more planning, more intentionality, more structure. Yes, we're seeking quality and a certain kind of beauty; and yes, beauty takes effort and intentionality.

A certain type of excellence

I describe the certain kind of beauty we're after as 'raw beauty'. There's a type of beauty that's slick and polished and unblemished. That beauty is created through make-up and Photoshop. And it can be quite beautiful in its own way, but it's a fake beauty. An unrealistic beauty. It's the beauty of a show home. Yes, it's clean and tidy and beautiful, but it's also fake and empty and without real life and love. Raw beauty is different. Raw beauty is a lived-in beauty, an imperfect beauty. It's a beauty despite, or even because of, its imperfections. Raw beauty is a concept that's almost impossible to describe and define, in the same way that beauty is an impossible concept to define. Different people will define it differently and different times and cultures will define it differently. But you know it when you see it, and you know when it's not there.

So raw beauty will look different in different churches, in different places, and in different cultures. But with raw beauty there will be a genuineness, a real sense of real people, a relationality, reflecting people's personalities rather than displaying a polished, fabricated, airbrushed, manufactured beauty.

Another way of saying it is that raw beauty is a certain type of excellence. It's an excellence that's not distracting. At a certain level of excellence and quality, this perfection distracts people from what you're actually doing. People begin to focus on the excellence itself rather than on what the excellence is itself pointing to and helping to facilitate. Distracting excellence is a problem in the same, but opposite, way that mediocrity can be distracting. Raw beauty is an excellence that's not distracting.

We're not aiming to look professional. We're aiming for an appropriate degree of professionalism. The sweet spot that we're shooting for is excellence that's not distracting and that doesn't call attention to itself. It's a raw beauty.

See also

28. Anything worth doing is worth doing badly
47. Find the awesome
48. Treat them like children
64. Learn relaxed concern

77
Bad news is good news

Everybody loves good news. As Christians we have a particularly strong love for Good News. I don't know anyone who likes bad news more than good news. And because we all love good news so much it's tempting to seek it out and reward those who deliver it because it signals success and accomplishment while making you, as the leader, feel good and feel like you're making a difference. It's also tempting to hate bad news and to avoid it, minimize it, and get upset when people deliver it. This isn't a modern phenomenon either—the clichéd image is of medieval kings and rulers flying into a rage when bad news was delivered and beheading the bearer of such news. No-one wants to be the bearer of bad news. We love and reward good news and we despise and discourage bad news.

This imbalance is foolish and very likely destructive.

As your team begins to learn that good news makes you happy and bad news makes you angry—and especially if you have a habit of shooting the messenger—they will soon learn either to keep bad news from you or to colour the bad news when they present it so as to make it not seem quite so bad. As you respond to each type of news you receive from the people you lead, you're training them as to what kind of news you want from them and, most important, what kind of news they should try to suppress.

If you react negatively to bad news, you will increasingly receive either less accurate information or less important information. You'll be training your team to keep information—either in part or in full—from you. Even if you say you want accurate information and you want to know everything, the people you lead will act based on how you react and what you reward rather than what you say with your lips that you want. You can say it all you want, but they will take their cues from how you act.

Face reality

The tragedy of all this is that bad news is always very helpful. Read that sentence again. Do you agree? Bad news is helpful because you need to know what's happening—what's *really* happening. You need to know what isn't working. You need to be crystal clear on what the problems and issues are so you can take steps to address them. Bad news, though sometimes painful, is good news—because it helps you see reality that much more clearly. And seeing reality clearly is always a good thing, no matter how painful or disappointing. Nothing good comes from avoiding reality. Avoiding reality is a sickness that needs to be treated, not a virtue that needs to be cultivated. Bad news gives you a better picture of what's actually happening. And knowing what's actually happening is always a good thing.

This is why bad news is good news and why you need to take special care with how you respond when people give it to you. This will probably be a long-term project for you and your team, as you try to create a culture where bad news is encouraged. It will be hard work for people to relearn the value and importance of bad news, and it will be hard work for you to relearn how to value and appreciate the pain of receiving bad news.

But it's worth the effort and energy required to create a team dynamic like this, because your team will be able to navigate and make decisions about what's happening in your ministry rather than making decisions that have no connection to reality.

No last-minute surprises

In order to create this culture of bad news being good news you'll also need to create another culture at the same time—one where last-minute bad news is discouraged. You need to create both cultures at once because the two cultures will create a feedback loop in which they will feed off each other and mutually reinforce each other.

Bad news is always a surprise. Even if you're a pessimist or a realist and you're expecting bad news, the bad news that actually comes is often not the bad news you were expecting. Sometimes it's horribly worse and other times, delightfully, it's not as bad as you thought it would be. But it's almost always surprising.

When someone says that they'll do something we expect that they'll do it. When we say we'll do something we all want to get it done. No-one likes disappointing people or letting someone down or being the one who drops the ball.

But the reality is that we will all do it. At some point we'll say too many yes's and not enough no's and we'll get swamped, an unforeseen complication will spring up, and we'll have to back out of something. It happens to everyone. Not one of us is perfect. At some point it will happen to someone involved in one of the things you're running, to someone who has promised to do something for you. What happens then?

When that happens, as it inevitably will, you'll need to have built a culture where there are no last-minute surprises. Or, if you're in the process of building that culture, you'll need to carefully distinguish between the bad news, for which you're grateful, and the last-minute-ness, which is a problem.

If someone's not going to come through on his or her responsibility I want to know as soon as possible. I want to know in enough time to execute a plan B or a plan C. I don't want to find out five minutes beforehand. I want time. I want to know as early as humanly possible. As soon as it's clear they're not going to be able to fulfil their responsibility, I want to know.

I don't like surprises, and people we're leading need to know that we don't like surprises.

But if people are going to tell you the bad news as soon as they're aware of it, not only do you need people who will tell you bad news, but you also need to have worked hard to create a culture where they're confident that they won't be yelled at and destroyed for letting you know. This is a culture where bad news is good news, and where people who give early warning of failure get rewarded rather than punished. In this culture you've clearly communicated that you want to know early if things aren't working out. It's a culture where it's okay to fail and it's okay to ask for help because it's not a sign of weakness. In this culture people know that, if they think there's a 50/50 chance something won't happen, you want to know and have time to get a backup ready. And they'll be willing to tell you because they know they won't suffer any negative consequences for telling you. Only in that kind of culture will people come to you early with bad news.

The two cultures reinforce each other. No last-minute surprises means bad news needs to be communicated straight away. And bad news being good news means that bad news should be communicated early and not at the eleventh hour.

Developing these two cultures will result in the creation of a third culture.

Bad news will be fast news

If there's some bad news coming your way, news that will require last-minute changes or critical decisions to be made under the pressure of time constraints and potentially unexpected fallout, you want that news to come to you as quickly as possible. And you want that news to be as accurate as possible so you can make the best decisions you can. If bad news is good news, then bad news also needs to be fast and accurate news.

This will never happen if you think bad news is bad news, if you treat bad news as bad news, or if you treat messengers of bad news badly. If you do, then bad news probably won't be fast or accurate—or, over time, bad news will get slower and more ambiguous.

Here's how this might happen. Let's imagine a leader comes to me and says, "In two weeks I'm not going to be able to make it to our meeting". How should I respond? I could say, "*What?!* We've had this meeting booked for ages! You know it's really important. I can't believe you'd do this. What could be so important that you blah blah blah..." And then, whenever I see him during the following two weeks, I could mention that he's not coming or remind him how disappointed I am.

What am I doing when I react this way? I'm training my leaders to say instead, "I might not be able to make it tomorrow". What I'm teaching them is that the more notice you give Craig, the worse it will be. It will turn out better for you if you wait until the last possible moment and then make it as vague as you can so that you don't have to deal with his disappointment for an extended period.

But I don't want to know the day before that they may, or may not, be there. I want to know for certain whether or not they'll be there and I want to know as early as possible.

If that's what I really want, then I need to communicate to my team that I want fast and accurate information. And I need to communicate that both by saying it clearly to them so they know and by responding to them in the moment in a way that reinforces that message.

So what should I say in response to the news that they'll be missing the meeting in two weeks? What if I said, "Thanks for letting me know. Is everything okay?" They'll tell me whatever it is they're going to instead of the meeting; it might be a concert, but it might also be a funeral. Maybe they're going okay and maybe they're not going okay. But this response opens a conversation and gives me a chance to find out. It also gives me a chance to show the person that I care about them and about what's happening in their lives. If they have a totally legitimate reason, like their mum is dying and they want to spend as much time with her as they can before she goes, then I'd respond in a certain way. But if I don't think their reason for missing the meeting is that legitimate, whatever that reason is, the fact is that for them it's more important than my meeting. And that's just the reality. A good question for me to ask myself in that moment might be, "What am I doing, or who am I being, that this meeting doesn't seem as important to them as I know it is?"

But then I still need to reinforce bad news is good news and to discourage last-minute surprises, so I might say something like, "Well thanks again for letting me know in plenty of time. I know you know how important this meeting is, so this other thing must be really important to you, so if you have to go then you have to go. We'll catch up next time."

Now that's probably not the best response possible, but it's better than the first one.

Raising anxiety levels

The other problem with hating bad news and shooting those who deliver it is that you increase the level of anxiety in your team. It makes you unpredictable. You cause them to wonder, "Is this news bad enough that I'm gonna get roasted? How much do I need to sweeten it so it's palatable? Even if I do sweeten it will I get roasted anyway?" If people are asking themselves these kinds of questions they will be less inclined to tell you the truth.

But if your response to news, whether it's good or bad, is to thank the messenger for the important information without any reprisals, then your response becomes predictable and you lower the anxiety people will feel. When people feel they can approach you without anxiety, you will receive more and better information.

Bad news needs to be good news and it needs to be fast news. So you need to create an environment where people feel safe to bring you bad news. You need information, and especially bad news, to arrive early and be fast and accurate. And only you have the power to create the cultures that will make that happen.

See also

38. Shut up and listen
39. Public fans and private critics
54. Don't be afraid of off-ramps

78 Celebrate

Leaders are all about doing things. Moving forward. Getting things done. Achieving things. Accomplishing things. Planning ahead. Solving problems. The future. The next thing. And there's nothing wrong with that. But every now and then you need to pause, take a breath, and look around at what God has done. As you take stock of what God has done in, among, and through the team it's right to stop and thank him for showing up and being at work. That is, the right thing to do is to celebrate.

Looking forward is a good and necessary thing. But looking back is equally necessary. It's good to keep marching ahead and figure out which hill you're going to take next. But it's also good to stop and look around and enjoy the view.

The God of celebration

You might be surprised by how often God legislated for his Old Testament people to take time out to celebrate. Leviticus 23 outlines seven different feasts. The people celebrated Passover and the day after that they celebrated the Feast of Unleavened Bread. The Sunday after that was the Feast of First Fruits. Fifty days after Passover they celebrated Pentecost. In September they celebrated the Feast of Trumpets. Nine days later they celebrated the Day of Atonement and then five days after that was the Feast of Tabernacles. That's a lot of remembering and celebrating.

Not only did the people celebrate these different feasts throughout the year, but some of these celebrations also lasted for a long time. The Feast of Tabernacles, for example, went for seven whole days. All of these feasts in the Old Testament were God's legislated, intentional celebrations for his people. A time for them to stop, to remember, to notice, and to be grateful for what God had done for them and was doing among them. There's a good reason he went to such great lengths to describe and legislate all those festivals: both celebrating and gratitude are important to God.

Not only are they important to God, but celebration and gratitude are good for your team too.

In the New Testament Jesus tells us repeatedly that God is a celebrating God. He tells us that when one sinner repents, for example, there's a celebration in heaven. When the Prodigal Son returns, the father had to celebrate. And so should we. When your team scores a win, celebrate! Celebrate them in small ways as you go and then also schedule time for big, official, intentional celebration.

Celebrating says something

Celebrating communicates so much. It communicates that God is the giver of all good things and all growth. It communicates to your team that thankfulness and gratitude are important. It communicates that you're not just interested in squeezing as much productivity as you can out of your team but that you want to sow into them as well. It communicates clearly what it is you see as a win and what the vision looks like in practice, because those are the stories you'll be highlighting and celebrating. And celebrating communicates that this team is worth belonging to.

No matter how enthusiastic, godly and developed your team is, they will still lose momentum at times. The friction of ministry will push against them and the grind of the task will sap enthusiasm from them and slow them down. This is just part of life and to be expected.

But this is yet another reason you need to intentionally take time out to recognize what God has achieved among them and to make sure that they see why all their effort has been valuable. They need to know that what they're doing matters. They may not be able to see it for themselves and they may need you, and others, to point it out for them. And while it's probably true that God doesn't reveal to us most of the positive impact we have on people so that we don't get puffed up with pride, it's also true that he does reveal just enough to keep us in the game. And when you're working as a team sometimes there's only one person who's aware of the win, but it's a win the whole team had a hand in achieving—because you're a team! So the whole team needs to hear those stories and it's your job as the leader to be the collector and curator of those stories.

For some of us celebrating will come normally and naturally. But for most of us it won't. We'll be too busy moving on to the next thing and planning the next adventure. The lesson to learn from God's Old Testament feasts is the wisdom of scheduling celebrations into the calendar. Put them in the diary. Lock the dates down early on. Depending on the rhythm of your church, there will be natural and obvious places to plan celebrations. At the end of a big season of ministry is a good time. After Easter. After Christmas. After an intentional season of mission. Celebrate a job well done. Celebrate when you make progress towards your vision. Celebrate every conversion.

Celebrate as your heavenly Father celebrates!

See also

53. Free volunteers aren't cheap
56. What are you trying to achieve?
69. Your people should be able to do a good impression of you

matthiasmedia

Matthias Media is an evangelical publishing ministry that seeks to persuade all Christians of the truth of God's purposes in Jesus Christ as revealed in the Bible, and equip them with high-quality resources, so that by the work of the Holy Spirit they will:

- abandon their lives to the honour and service of Christ in daily holiness and decision-making
- pray constantly in Christ's name for the fruitfulness and growth of his gospel
- speak the Bible's life-changing word whenever and however they can—in the home, in the world and in the fellowship of his people.

Our wide range of resources includes Bible studies, books, training courses, tracts and children's material. To find out more, and to access samples and free downloads, visit our website:

www.matthiasmedia.com

How to buy our resources

1. Direct from us over the internet:
   – in the US: www.matthiasmedia.com
   – in Australia: www.matthiasmedia.com.au

2. Direct from us by phone: please visit our website for current phone contact information.

3. Through a range of outlets in various parts of the world. Visit **www.matthiasmedia.com/contact** for details about recommended retailers in your part of the world.

4. Trade enquiries can be addressed to:
   – in the US and Canada: sales@matthiasmedia.com
   – in Australia and the rest of the world: sales@matthiasmedia.com.au

Register at our website for our **free** regular email update to receive information about the latest new resources, **exclusive special offers**, and free articles to help you grow in your Christian life and ministry.

www.ingramcontent.com/pod-product-compliance
Lightning Source LLC
LaVergne TN
LVHW020052110826
845155LV00022B/74
* 9 7 8 1 9 2 2 2 0 6 7 1 8 *